Cautious Crusade

CAUTIOUS CRUSADE

FRANKLIN D. ROOSEVELT,
AMERICAN PUBLIC OPINION, AND THE
WAR AGAINST NAZI GERMANY

Steven Casey

OXFORD

UNIVERSITY PRESS

2001

OXFORD
UNIVERSITY PRESS

Oxford   New York

Athens   Auckland   Bangkok   Bogotá   Buenos Aires   Cape Town
Chennai   Dar es Salaam   Delhi   Florence   Hong Kong   Istanbul   Karachi
Kolkata   Kuala Lumpur   Madrid   Melbourne   Mexico City   Mumbai   Nairobi
Paris   São Paulo   Shanghai   Singapore   Taipei   Tokyo   Toronto   Warsaw

and associated companies in
Berlin   Ibadan

Published by Oxford University Press, Inc.
198 Madison Avenue, New York, New York 10016

Oxford is a registered trademark of Oxford University Press.

Library of Congress Cataloging-in-Publication Data
Casey, Steven.
Cautious crusade : Franklin D. Roosevelt, American public opinion, and the
war against Nazi Germany / Steven Casey.
p. cm.
Includes bibliographical references and index.
ISBN 0-19-513960-7
1. World War, 1939–1945—Propaganda.   2. World War, 1939–1945—United States.
3. World War, 1939–1945—Public opinion.   4. Public opinion—United States—
History—20th century.   5. Propaganda, American—History—20th century.
6. Roosevelt, Franklin D. (Franklin Delano), 1882–1945—Views on Germany.
7. United States—Foreign relations—1933–1945.   8. United States—Foreign relations—
Germany.   9. Germany—Foreign relations—United States.   I. Title.
D753.3 .C37 2002
940.53'73—dc21   2001016276

The photographs used in this book appear courtesy of the
Franklin D. Roosevelt Library, Hyde Park, New York.

1   3   5   7   9   8   6   4   2

Printed in the United States of America
on acid-free paper

FOR MY PARENTS

Terry and Margaret

ACKNOWLEDGMENTS

Since 1995, this project has evolved from a master's thesis into a doctoral thesis and now into a book. Along the way, I have incurred numerous debts. Louise Fawcett was an excellent supervisor, whose careful reading and incisive comments sharpened my thinking on every facet of this work. Richard Crockatt first sparked my interest in the Roosevelt era when I was an undergraduate at UEA, and has offered me much encouragement and advice ever since. In the past three years, Roberto Franzosi's boundless enthusiasm and energy have also been a constant source of inspiration.

At Oxford, I have greatly benefited from the ideas, suggestions, and support of many people. I would like to thank my D.Phil. examiner, Bob O'Neill, for his helpful criticisms, and Rosemary Foot, Andrew Hurrell, Yuen Foong Kong, Neil MacFarlane, and Jonathan Wright, who at various stages have commented on different aspects of this work. Raymond Cohen and Avi Shlaim have both been very supportive. This book has also been greatly improved as a result of the careful evaluation by Waldo H. Heinrichs and Nicholas J. Cull.

This project almost came to an abrupt halt in the summer of 1996. I am extremely grateful to Adam Roberts, whose support, advice, and encouragement proved invaluable during that difficult period, and to Jesus College, Oxford, which elected me to a graduate scholarship in September 1996. This provided me with the income, time, and a congenial environment in which to complete the bulk of the research and writing. Research in the United States was also made possible by a British Association of American Studies Marcus Cunliffe grant.

Since October 1998, I have been a Junior Research Fellow at Trinity College, Oxford. The friendly atmosphere at Trinity has made the task of completing the final draft of this book an enjoyable experience. I would also like to thank my students, and especially the class of 2000, whose enthusiasm for the subject helped to sustain my own interest during the period in which the bulk of this book was rewritten.

Many friends have helped in important ways. I first experienced America with Stephen Bromberg. Alex Kershaw first showed me how to write. Michael Fullilove tracked down a number of important documents. Wolfram

Latsch and Vicky Redwood both read portions of the manuscript with great care and offered countless suggestions.

At OUP, my editor, Susan Ferber, has been unfailingly efficient, helpful, and supportive. I would also like to thank Lisa Stallings for her help and expertise during the production stages and Jack Rummel for his careful copyediting.

In the course of my research, I have visited a number of libraries and archives. All the librarians have been extremely helpful, but I would particularly like to thank the staff at the FDR Library, especially Raymond Teichman, Lynn Bassanese, Robert Parks, Mark Renovitch, Nancy Snedeker, and Alycia Vivona. During the many months I have spent in Hyde Park, I have greatly appreciated the hospitality of Art and Pat Costello and the friendship of Bob Parks and Chris Price.

During these long absences, Gemma has been extremely patient and understanding. She has also been a very thorough proofreader of various versions of this work and has saved me from numerous errors. Finally, my debt to my parents is immeasurable. They first encouraged me to pursue an academic career and have always been on hand with support and advice. This book is dedicated to them.

Trinity College, Oxford   Steve Casey
October 2000

CONTENTS

ABBREVIATIONS

AAF   U.S. Army Air Force
AEF   American Expeditionary Force
AIPO   American Institute of Public Opinion (George Gallup's
         polling organization)
AP   Associated Press
BoI   Bureau of Intelligence (polling and surveys branch of
         OFF and OWI)
CPI   Committee of Public Information (World War I prop-
         aganda agency)
GOP   Common abbreviation for the Republican party
NORC   National Opinion Research Center (Elmo Roper's
         polling agency)
OGR   Office of Government Reports
OPOR   Office of Public Opinion Research (Hadley Cantril's
         polling agency
OFF   Office of Facts and Figures (propaganda agency until
         June 1942)
OSS   Office of Strategic Services
OWI   Office of War Information (propaganda agency from
         June 1942)
RAF   Royal Air Force

CAST OF CHARACTERS

Arnold, Henry "Hap"	*Chief of U.S. Air Staff*
Barth, Alan	*Public opinion analyst in Treasury Department, then OFF and OWI*
Berle, Adolf A.	*Assistant secretary of state, 1938–44*
Biddle, Francis	*Attorney general, 1941–45*
Brown, Cecil	*Columnist and commentator*
Bullitt, William C.	*Ambassador to the Soviet Union, 1933–36; ambassador to France, 1936–40; occasional adviser to the president, 1940–43*
Cantril, Hadley	*Opinion pollster*
Carter, John Franklin	*Journalist who headed special intelligence-gathering unit for FDR*
Chamberlain, Neville	*British prime minister, 1937–40*
Churchill, Winston S.	*British prime minister, 1940–45*
Coughlin, Father Charles	*Extreme isolationist spokesman*
Creel, George	*Journalist and head of U.S. propaganda agency in World War I*
Davis, Elmer	*Head of OWI, 1942–45*
Davis, Forrest	*Journalist*
Dewey, Thomas E.	*Republican presidential candidate, 1944*
Dodd, William E.	*American ambassador to Germany, 1933–37*
Donovan, William J.	*Head of OSS*
Early, Stephen T.	*President's press secretary*
Eden, Anthony	*British foreign secretary*
Eisenhower, Dwight D.	*Commander in chief, Allied forces, 1942–43; supreme commander, Allied Expeditionary Forces, 1944–45*
Ernst, Morris L.	*Lawyer who produced "tidbits" of information for FDR*
Fish, Hamilton	*Isolationist congressman*
Gallup, George	*Opinion pollster*

Grew, Joseph S.   *U.S. ambassador to Japan, 1932–41;*
                                   special assistant to secretary of
                                   state, 1942–44; undersecretary of
                                   state, 1944–45

Halifax, Lord   *British ambassador to the United*
                                   States

Hanfstaengl, Ernst   *Hitler's foreign press secretary,*
                                   1933–37; supplied information to
                                   the White House through the
                                   "S-Project," 1942–44

Harriman, Averell   *President's special envoy;*
                                   ambassador to the Soviet Union,
                                   1943–45

Hearst, William Randolph   *Isolationist publisher*
Hopkins, Harry L.   *Special assistant to the president*
Hull, Cordell   *Secretary of state, 1933–44*
Ickes, Harold L.   *Secretary of the interior*
King, Ernest J.   *Commander of U.S. Fleet, 1941–45*
Knox, Frank   *Secretary of the navy, 1940–44*
Krock, Arthur   *Columnist and commentator*
Lambert, Gerald C.   *Financier of Cantril's OPOR*
Leahy, William D.   *Chief of staff to the president*
Lindbergh, Charles   *Isolationist spokesman*
Lippmann, Walter   *Columnist and commentator*
Luce, Henry   *Publisher of* Time *magazine*
Ludwig, Emil   *German-born Swiss emigrant*
                                   historian

MacLeish, Archibald   *Head of OFF, 1941–42; assistant*
                                   secretary of state, 1944–45

Marshall, George C.   *Chief of staff of U.S. Army*
McCormick, Anne O'Hare   *Columnist and commentator*
McCormick, Colonel Robert R.   *Isolationist publisher of the* Chicago
                                   Tribune

Mellett, Lowell   *Aide to the president*
Meyer, Eugene   *Publisher of the* Washington Post
Morgenthau, Jr., Henry   *Secretary of the treasury*
Mowrer, Edgar Ansel   *Columnist and commentator*
Murrow, Edward R.   *Columnist and commentator*
Nye, Gerald P.   *Isolationist senator*
Patterson, Cissy   *Isolationist publisher*
Pearson, Drew   *Columnist and commentator*
Roper, Elmo   *Opinion pollster*
Rosenman, Samuel I.   *President's speechwriter*
Sherwood, Robert E.   *President's speechwriter*
Shirer, William L.   *Columnist and commentator*

Smith, Gerald L.K.	*Extreme isolationist spokesman*
Smith, Kingsbury	*Journalist*
Stettinius, Edward R.	*Undersecretary of state, 1943–44; secretary of state, 1944–45*
Stimson, Henry L.	*Secretary of war, 1940–45*
Stout, Rex	*Chairman of WWB; head of SPWW3*
Sulzberger, Arthur	*Publisher of the* New York Times
Swing, Raymond Gramm	*Columnist and commentator*
Taylor, Myron C.	*Presidential envoy*
Thompson, Dorothy	*Columnist and commentator*
Truman, Harry S.	*President of the United States, 1945–53*
Wallace, Henry	*Vice-president of the United States, 1941–45*
Welles, Sumner,	*Undersecretary of state, 1937–43*
Wheeler, Burton K.	*Isolationist senator*
White, William Allen	*Journalist, interventionist spokesman, and chairman of CDAAA*
Wickard, Claude	*Secretary of agriculture*
Willkie, Wendell	*Republican presidential candidate, 1940, and internationalist spokesman*
Winant, John G.	*U.S. ambassador to Britain, 1940–45*
Winchell, Walter	*Columnist and commentator*

INTRODUCTION:
FRANKLIN D. ROOSEVELT,
AMERICAN PUBLIC OPINION,
AND FOREIGN POLICY

> But if history teaches us anything, it is that we must resist aggression or it will destroy our freedoms. Appeasement does not work. As was the case in the 1930s, we see in Saddam Hussein an aggressive dictator threatening neighbors.
> —President George Bush, August 8, 1990

> What if someone had listened to Winston Churchill and stood up to Adolf Hitler earlier? How many peoples' lives might have been saved, and how many American lives might have been saved?
> —President Bill Clinton, March 23, 1999

More than fifty years after the collapse of the Third Reich, America's crusade against nazism still exerts a powerful hold over the popular imagination. Not only do books, films, and TV documentaries on the subject continue to proliferate, but politicians, recognizing the resonance that this era still possesses, remain quick to compare every threat to U.S. security in terms of the danger posed by nazism in the 1930s and 1940s. So in their time, Stalin, Ho Chi Minh, Saddam Hussein, and Slobodan Milosevic have all been depicted as the new Adolf Hitler, no doubt in the hope that if the public equated them with this archetype of evil then they would both understand the nature of the enemy and rally behind the administration's calls for an energetic response.[1]

Implicit in this harking back to World War II is the notion that America's crusade against nazism was a uniquely popular war—that, unlike the subsequent conflicts in Korea and Vietnam, on this occasion the populace was united behind the government, doggedly determined to eradicate an undeniably expansionist and barbarous foe. Such a conception is endorsed by historians in numerous works, both scholarly and popular. According to Richard Polenberg, for example, "nearly all Americans accepted the necessity of taking part in World War II after Pearl Harbor," largely because they felt "a common sense of danger and [a shared] hatred of the enemy." John Morton Blum concurs. In his view, "the president enjoyed the unquestioning support of his countrymen," who not only shared his diagnosis of the nature of the enemy but also fully endorsed his strategies for destroying this foe. Studs Terkel, meanwhile, has described World War II as "a different kind of war. . . . It was not fratricidal. It was not, most of us profoundly believed, 'imperialistic.' Our enemy was, patently, obscene: the Holocaust maker. It was one war that many who would have resisted 'your other wars' supported enthusiastically." Thus it was, in his pithy phrase, "the Good War."[2]

That World War II was a "good war" appears, in retrospect, to be an almost unassailable assertion. Clearly, there was a broad consensus within the United States that the country's involvement in the conflict was necessary and vital. Clearly, too, any popular discontent remained within distinct bounds—on this occasion, for instance, there was no vocal and influential peace movement. Moreover, World War II undoubtedly had a profound, even beneficial, impact on America, not least because of the extraordinary achievements of the domestic economy, as war orders swiftly pulled the nation out of a depression that had lingered for more than a decade. "War is hell," observes Mark H. Leff. "But for millions of Americans on the booming home front, World War II was also a hell of a war."[3]

Yet viewed from a different perspective, the notion that World War II was a widely popular crusade seems somewhat overdrawn. With hindsight it might appear obvious that this was a just war; it might even seem safe to assume that there was little scope for opposition, apathy, or doubt when the enemy was as perfidious and brutal as Adolf Hitler. But at the time, the U.S. president, Franklin D. Roosevelt (FDR), was not always so confident. Indeed, what frequently struck FDR was not the high levels of support for the war, but the constant mutterings of discontent, the lack of awareness of the true nature of the enemy, and the sometimes half-hearted support for his administration's policies.

This book explores exactly how Franklin Roosevelt perceived domestic public opinion during the war, especially the extent to which he felt the American people fully shared his conception of nazism. To do so, I draw on a wide array of original primary sources—not only the numerous letters, memoranda, and minutes of meetings that shed light on Roosevelt's private beliefs about the German problem, but also the wealth of opinion polls, media surveys, and newspapers he used to monitor the popular mood.

Chapter 1 sets the scene, by showing how in the years before 1941 FDR's growing concerns about the Nazi threat were rarely shared by an isolationist public. Moreover, as chapter 2 demonstrates, even the shock of Pearl Harbor failed to jolt Americans out of their basic ignorance of what nazism stood for, the danger it posed, and the brutal techniques it employed. In the early period of the war, morale also seemed exceedingly brittle, dependent largely on battlefield fortunes and likely to wane the minute things went badly.[4] And although these problems started to ease in 1943, as the United States took the offensive and news of Nazi atrocities began to filter out, other troubles soon emerged to take their place. In chapter 5, for example, I highlight the glaring division that emerged during 1943 and 1944 over how to treat Germany in the postwar period. Specifically, whereas FDR's thinking hardened considerably during this period, so that he increasingly advocated a harsh peace that would punish the entire German nation, even at this late stage the U.S. public generally retained a more moderate view, with a clear majority still content to blame only a few leading Nazis for all the aggression and brutality.

Constantly plagued by such difficulties, the president's perception of public opinion was thus a far cry from the cozy, consensual atmosphere often portrayed in popular histories. How did Roosevelt respond? What attempts did he make to paper over or repair these constant cracks in the facade of domestic unity? These questions quickly lead us away from the historian's task of tracing the president's and public's perceptions of the Third Reich, and into the more vexed and contested political science debate over the exact nature of the relationship between opinion and policy. At the heart of this literature is the central question: who influences whom? Is the government able to ignore popular discontent, partly because public opinion is essentially a disparate, ignorant, and amorphous mass, and partly because officials can easily use their control over the means of communication to eradicate dissent and foster consensus?[5] Or is the government in some way accountable to the public? In particular, does it bow to popular pressure, changing course whenever opinion polls and media surveys show that official thinking is out of step with mass attitudes?[6]

According to Walter Lippmann, during wars this relationship between opinion and policy follows a distinct pattern. In Lippmann's conception, when a foreign threat emerges most Americans initially lag behind their leaders in recognizing potential danger, since to them it appears too remote to warrant U.S. involvement. In order to shake the public from this torpor, the government has to engage in a vigorous crusade. This it does by depicting the enemy as "altogether evil" and thereby inciting the masses "to paroxysms of hatred." In adopting this course, American leaders are able to forge a popular consensus behind the war effort. But such rhetoric also serves to narrow their options at a later date, since a public convinced that the enemy is evil is hardly likely to support a negotiated agreement; only unconditional surrender, and the total eradication of the evil, will do.[7] Such propaganda also makes it extremely difficult for democracies to pursue a balance-of-power strategy, because this often requires the flexibility to turn yesterday's enemy into today's friend, while the public tends to be reluctant to sanction an alliance with a nation so recently depicted as the Devil incarnate.[8] Concurring with this analysis, the noted diplomat and scholar George F. Kennan has wondered whether the American democracy is

> not uncomfortably similar to one of those prehistoric monsters with a body as long as this room and the brain the size of a pin: he lies there in his comfortable primeval mud and pays little attention to his environment; he is slow to wrath—in fact, you practically have to whack his tail off to make him aware that his interests are being disturbed; but, once he grasps this, he lays about him with such blind determination that he not only destroys his adversary but largely wrecks his native habitat.[9]

This conception has exerted a powerful, if subtle and indirect, influence over the literature on America's involvement in World War II. To begin with, an isolationist America was clearly slow to recognize the danger posed by the Axis dictators. According to some historians, in order to arouse the public, the government increasingly depicted "the Japanese and Germans alike [as] stripped of [all] their humanity."[10] Consequently, Americans came to hate their enemies; by the war's end, many had a particularly vehement animus toward Germany. Most also started to demand harsh measures, from blanket bombing of Axis cities to unconditional surrender and complete deindustrialization.[11] Richard Overy, for instance, argues that the public's response to government rhetoric "invited support for unconditional surrender," the famous formula that FDR announced in January 1943. "Since most of the war had been spent presenting the enemy as an abomination," he writes, by 1943 there could be "no question of negotiation or compromise. Roosevelt's call for unconditional surrender, though made casually at the Casablanca Conference, without reference to anyone, was the logical outcome of the Allied view of the enemy. The moral chasm between them had been made too wide to bridge."[12]

How accurate are these claims? Did the Roosevelt administration really seek to whip up popular hatred against the enemy? Did the American people increasingly begin to loathe each and every German? And was it ultimately the case that public opinion distorted policy, forcing rational and even-headed statesmen into intemperate and excessive actions? To answer these questions requires exploring the complex relationship between opinion and policy—both the attempts made by the government to shape and mold mass attitudes, and the impact that the popular mood had on officials' actions. The remainder of this introduction therefore looks at the central methodological problems that crop up in any consideration of the interaction between public opinion and foreign policy.

In chapters 1, 2, and 5, the focus will be on the propaganda attempts the administration made to spark enthusiasm for the war, banish ignorance about the enemy, and generate support for its policies. Here, before analyzing the content of the message that Roosevelt sought to disseminate, I first seek to uncover the opinion-persuading channels that the president had at his disposal. A key aspect of the Lippmann/Kennan approach is that public opinion can only be aroused from its torpor and lethargy by a vigorous crusade, which exaggerates and oversells the danger. Put another way, rather than educating the public by "providing correct, helpful information," officials seek to manipulate it by providing "false, incorrect, biased, or selective information."[13] To discover whether this was the case, I compare the government's public rhetoric with its private view of the enemy. Was its information campaign a reiteration of true convictions, or was the danger somehow accentuated for public consumption? When assessing the content of the administration's message, two techniques are employed: a qualitative analysis to examine the central themes that were developed, and a quantitative analysis of key words to reveal the frequency and consistency with which they were employed.

Throughout these chapters I also look at the efforts made by the White House to coordinate its message with other departments and agencies in the federal bureaucracy. The emphasis in previous work on American domestic propaganda activities during World War II has been on the bureaucratic rivalries that developed between the newly formed Office of War Information (OWI), and the War, Navy, and State departments.[14] Given, too, the notoriously fractious nature of Roosevelt's "competitive" bureaucratic structure, I take care to focus on the information efforts of the entire government.[15] It is then possible to judge whether the entire administration "sang from the same tune sheet," or whether, as Donald Cameron Watt argues, the president's message was often drowned out by a "cacophony of discordant notes."[16]

By examining the Roosevelt administration's propaganda campaign toward Germany in this light, two novel and original themes emerge. The first is that, although the president never explicitly controlled the output of other executive departments and agencies, there was nevertheless an impressive degree of tacit cooperation in the government's output. The second is that Roosevelt deliberately (if sometimes reluctantly) eschewed a vigorous and exaggerated crusade aimed at whipping up a mass frenzy against the enemy. In fact, he continually focused only on the ideological threat posed by nazism and persistently refused to indict the entire German nation even after he became privately convinced that the mass of Germans were little better than their Nazi masters. As chapter 5 reveals, there were various reasons for this circumspection and timidity, including fears of alienating German-American voters, bureaucratic inertia, and the need to counter Nazi claims that the Allies intended to enslave Germany. But perhaps the most important factor was that in the later years of the war Roosevelt was increasingly a prisoner of his own rhetoric, unable after years of exonerating the German people suddenly to change course and start excoriating them for the crimes committed in Europe.

That the president's propaganda campaign was consistently cautious helps to explain why the public continued to lag behind the government in its attitudes toward Germany, reluctant in the early years to recognize the full extent of the Nazi threat, and opposed in the later period to a harsh peace directed at the entire German nation. It also leads us naturally to the final theme of this book: the extent to which the public's moderate thinking about Germany had an impact on FDR's actions. Of all the problems addressed in these pages, this is the one that raises the most difficult methodological problems. After all, it is no easy task to uncover a statesman's motivation for adopting a particular course, let alone to isolate the impact that one variable has on any individual's thinking. The following pages therefore look in some detail at the questions that need to be clarified and the sources that have to be consulted in any consideration of the impact of opinion on policy.

One obvious problem in this area is the difficulty of actually defining the concept of public opinion. The work of political scientists James N. Rosenau and Gabriel Almond is useful here, since it attempts to provide some structure to this amorphous mass. They begin by dividing public opinion into two sets. The smallest group, around 1 percent of the population, consists of the "opinion makers," those with access to society's channels of communications. The rest are then lumped together under the heading of "opinion holders," before being further subdivided into two groups: the "attentive public" "who are greatly concerned and well-informed" about foreign policy issues, and the "mass public" "who are totally unconcerned and uninformed about world affairs."[17] In this book, these distinctions will be used as a point of reference. However, since my principal goal is not to obtain an objective assessment of what actually constitutes public opinion, but rather to assess the impact it had on government thinking, my definition of public opinion is confined to whatever the Roosevelt administration deemed it to be.[18]

In chapter 1, I begin by uncovering the opinion-gauging channels FDR constructed in order to monitor the popular mood, that is, the opinion and media surveys he received, and the newspapers and letters he read.[19] However, because it is possible that Roosevelt consulted a wide array of opinion polls but then dismissed them as unreliable or irrelevant I also look at his sensitivity to this information. This entails uncovering the president's normative beliefs about public opinion. As two political scientists, Douglas Foyle and Philip Powlick, have both argued, if officials tend to view public opinion as an uninformed and amorphous mass, then they are more inclined to ignore it when making decisions, confident that it can be manipulated to support their preferences at a later date. Conversely, if they believe public opinion ought to play a role in the policy process, then they are more likely to try to monitor and take account of it.[20]

Next, it is necessary to find out the president's practical beliefs about public opinion. When he consulted the data he received, what did he deem most important? Was he more sensitive to polls, media surveys, newspapers, or the mailbag? If it was opinion polls, did he view all the polling agencies as equally reliable? Moreover, did he focus principally on current opinion, as recorded by these sources, or was he more concerned with past opinion, based on long-term learning of what Americans had traditionally been prepared to accept? Perhaps he focused on "anticipated future opinion," projections of how the public would be likely to respond to a particular initiative, which also tend to be based on assessments of how Americans have reacted in the past.[21] Finally, it is also important to bear in mind that the nature of a government's public opinion problems can fluctuate. On some issues, for instance, only a plurality will be opposed to the official line, whereas on others popular discontent might be overwhelming; at other times, too, it may be the case that the people generally support the government, but that their attitudes are perceived as superficial or transitory. If such differences occurred, did they matter? Was the president's sensitivity conditional on the level and intensity of opposition?[22]

Chapters 3 and 6 then seek to establish what impact this material had on policy. In chapter 3, I examine the extent to which the public wielded an influence over the key decisions of grand strategy, including the second-front problem and the Allied bombing campaign, while in chapter 6 I reveal how popular opinion played a role in the debates over how to treat postwar Germany. In both, I try to determine at what stage of the process opinion played a role.[23] At the most fundamental level, it could have determined all the president's beliefs. Indeed, when H.L. Mencken joked that if FDR "became convinced tomorrow that coming out for cannibalism would get him the votes he so sorely needs, he would begin fattening up a missionary in the White House backyard come Wednesday," or when James MacGregor Burns characterizes Roosevelt as a "pussyfooting politician," who in his first term "seemed to float almost helplessly on the flood tide of isolationism," both are implying that he had few convictions and would do whatever was popular.[24] Put another way, they both suggest that the structure of his belief system was open, that he was a situational politician who, whenever exposed to new data on American attitudes, would alter his assumptions and policy preferences accordingly.[25]

But how true was this with regard to Germany? Did Roosevelt really have no basic convictions about this enemy? Of course, even if he did have a clear set of clear assumptions about the Third Reich, which not only helped him define the problem but also shaped his personal proclivities for solving it, public opinion still could have entered the equation at a lower level. To start with, if FDR favored one policy option and the public preferred another, mass opinion might still have determined the actual choice he decided to adopt; in other words, it might have been the case, as Frederick W. Marks contends, that FDR's foreign policy choices merely "sprang from a political strategy geared almost exclusively to movement on the home front."[26] And even if irrelevant here, Roosevelt's decision about when to announce the policy and the arguments to be employed to garner support for it might have been heavily shaped by his reading of mass sentiment. Thomas Graham, for one, asserts that "public opinion influences presidential decisions primarily about tactics, timing, and political communications strategy, rather than determining the ultimate goals of an administration's foreign policy."[27]

To sum up, then, when examining the impact of opinion on policy, I seek to establish the stage at which it played a role: Did it determine all the president's thoughts? Did it simply play a role in his choice of option? Did it only govern the timing of policy implementation?

But how is it possible to demonstrate if there was any link between the president's perception of, and sensitivity to, public opinion on the one hand, and his beliefs, choices, and timing on the other? One way is to trace whether public opinion was on FDR's mind at these different stages.[28] By examining sources such as minutes of meetings, memoranda of conversations, letters, and diaries, and by closely assessing the context within which each reference to the popular mood was invoked, inferences can then be drawn as to the relative significance he accorded to this one variable.

Process tracing is not without its drawbacks, however. For a start, it is rare indeed that officials discuss a particular problem, then refer to the latest polling data, and finally mechanically change their minds so as to adopt the popular course. In fact, as the political scientist Ole Holsti points out, there are often few references to public opinion in the surviving documents, not because decision makers did not take it into account, but because "attention to public attitudes [was] so deeply ingrained . . . into working habits that it was unnecessary to make explicit references to it." Similarly, the historian Melvin Small asserts that officials who believe that opinion should not play a role are frequently reluctant to bring up the subject, even if it is determining their actions, because to do so "would be to abnegate their sworn responsibility to maintain national security, insulated from the vagaries of uninformed and emotional currents of opinion."[29] On the other hand, even when officials do refer directly to public attitudes during policy discussions, they may be using it instrumentally, to bolster their case, rather than invoking it in a representational manner. As one OWI official complained at the time, officials tended to use "social sciences the way a drunk uses a lamppost, for support rather than for illumination."[30] When references were made to public opinion, care must therefore be taken to assess if it was not simply being employed as a prop to support a particular viewpoint.

Because references to popular opinion might be absent from policy discussions, or conversely because even allusions to it must be treated with caution, this study supplements process tracing with the congruence procedure. The aim of this technique is to deduce whether or not the decision maker's beliefs about public preferences were consistent with his choices at each stage of the policy process.[31] So, for example, if the president's assumptions, decisions, and timing were all in diametric opposition to his reading of the popular mood, then public opinion can be written off as an irrelevant factor. But if his actions were in some way congruent, then we can conclude that popular opinion probably played some role. Determining exactly how important it was requires an analysis of other possible influential variables. Indeed, simply to suggest that because the public favored option "A" and the government chose option "A," then opinion must have determined policy would be to ascribe exaggerated causal weight to this one factor.[32]

To avoid this pitfall, I consider other factors that might also explain the outcome. In the literature on U.S. policy in World War II, three non-public-opinion variables are often emphasized. The first is Roosevelt's private beliefs. As we have already seen, one preliminary task is to look at the president's thoughts in order to see whether or not they were completely controlled by public opinion. If they were not, then what role did FDR's image of the enemy play in shaping policy? Did the chosen initiatives simply reflect his personal preferences? The second common explanation for policy outcomes in this period revolves around bureaucratic infighting. Numerous historians have not only focused on FDR's "competitive" bureaucratic organizational structure but have also argued that the ensuing chaos this created merely enabled each agency to pursue its own preferred course. So in this conception, U.S. policy simply emerged from the squabbles and feuds between various government agencies.[33] The third and final alternative interpretation centers on Big Three diplomacy. According to writers such as Robin Edmonds, Herbert Feis, and Steve Weiss, it was the struggles with Britain over when and where to strike at Germany, or with Stalin over the shape of postwar Europe, which essentially determined which initiatives were undertaken. In this view, American policy was thus simply a product of the give and take of alliance bargaining.[34]

Ultimately, then, an examination of alternative explanations allows us not only to avoid making exaggerated claims for the role of opinion in determining policy, but also to assess the extent of its impact, whether it was controlling, restraining, reinforcing, or irrelevant.

Chapters 3 and 6 employ these methods (see diagram) to explore the opinion-policy relationship and, by so doing, shed some new light on the mainsprings of U.S. policy toward Germany during World War II. Indeed, my emphasis is very different from previous studies, which have been so preoccupied with tracing the origins of the Cold War back to this period that they have viewed the German problem purely as an irritant responsible for the downward spiral of superpower relations. By directing the spotlight on the domestic context of decision making, I attempt to demonstrate when and to what extent the popular mood was an important variable conditioning and constraining key choices—how in 1941 mass opposition to a formal and full involvement in the conflict forced FDR to espouse a limited-war strategy; how after the winter of 1942–43 liberal

The Method Employed to Assess the Impact of Opinion on Policy

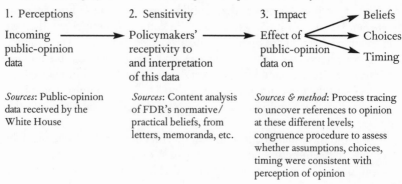

1. Perceptions	2. Sensitivity	3. Impact	Beliefs
Incoming public-opinion data	Policymakers' receptivity to and interpretation of this data	Effect of public-opinion data on	Choices Timing

Sources: Public-opinion data received by the White House

Sources: Content analysis of FDR's normative/ practical beliefs, from letters, memoranda, etc.

Sources & method: Process tracing to uncover references to opinion at these different levels; congruence procedure to assess whether assumptions, choices, timing were consistent with perception of opinion

criticism of the Darlan deal persuaded him to enunciate unconditional surrender; how during the course of 1943 concern that the U.S. public would fail to support an air strategy based on the slaughter of German civilians encouraged him to exaggerate the precision of Allied bombing; and how in the autumn of 1944 press criticism compelled him to back away from a punitive plan to pastoralize and dismember Germany in the midst of that year's presidential election campaign.

As the narrative unfolds, this book therefore has three central themes—the public's sometimes half-hearted support for the war, the government's cautious propaganda response, and the important influence opinion exerted over policy choices. Even on its own, each of these themes provides a fascinating story of American attitudes toward strategy and diplomacy at a watershed in U.S. history—the point at which the nation finally eschewed isolationism and emerged as a superpower.

But this is not the only contribution made in the following pages. This book also helps to show how the prisms through which Americans often tend to view their participation in World War II actually serve to distort, rather than illuminate, the reality. Indeed, rather than a universally popular war, or an excessive and overheated campaign, the pages that follow reveal that America's home front struggle against nazism is best viewed as a "cautious crusade."

Cautious Crusade

The Setting

My problem is to get the American people to think of conceivable consequences without scaring the American people into thinking that they are going to be dragged into this war.

—FDR, December 14, 1939

March 4, 1933, was a cold, gray day in Washington. As Americans contemplated a fourth year of economic depression, of bank panics, burgeoning unemployment, and plummeting incomes, Franklin D. Roosevelt took the presidential oath of office, carefully enunciating his determination to preserve, protect, and defend the Constitution. Then, turning to the large crowd that had assembled outside the Capitol, the new president began the task of trying to revive hope and confidence, famously assuring his audience that they had nothing to fear but fear itself before stressing his intention to act boldly and quickly. After announcing that he was calling a special session of Congress to deal with the economic situation, Roosevelt ended with a warning. If Congress refused to act, he declared, he would ask it "for the one remaining instrument to meet the crisis—broad executive power to wage war against the emergency, as great as the power that would be given to me if we were in fact invaded by a foreign foe."[1]

Unknown to Roosevelt at this stage, in Germany the prevailing economic chaos had just brought to power a foreign foe that would ultimately present an even greater challenge to America than the long depression, for

Adolf Hitler had recently been appointed the German chancellor. On March 5, the day after FDR's first inauguration, Hitler was able to consolidate his control over the German government when the Nazis gained a slim but sufficient victory at the polls. As the new American president set about valiantly trying to revive the ailing U.S. economy, confident that success in this task would consolidate America's democratic institutions and make a broad grant of executive power unnecessary, the new German chancellor had a very different set of priorities. Within weeks Hitler had secured passage of an enabling act permitting him to bypass the Reichstag. Within months he had moved to ban trade unions, eradicate rival political parties, and oppress the church. And within years he had not only constructed an efficient military machine but had also used this to terrorize Europe, sweeping away almost all his potential rivals and completely overturning the balance of power on the continent.

How did Americans respond to this new threat? In retrospect, of course, Hitler's assault on western civilization appears almost preordained, his actions once in office simply a fulfillment of the goals he had announced in *Mein Kampf*. Yet at the time, hardly anyone envisaged what was about to happen. After all, the Nazis had inherited a country that was also mired in depression, Hitler was anxious to mask his real aims until Germany became sufficiently strong, and in any case both the president and public were far more preoccupied with bread-and-butter issues closer to home. Small wonder, then, that FDR, like many Americans, was initially bewildered and bemused by what was going on in Europe, by the pace of change, the periodic crises, and the overall direction of events. "Things are moving so fast," Roosevelt complained at one stage in 1935, "that I feel my opinion of the situation today may be completely changed tomorrow."[2]

As the decade progressed, however, this uncertainty slowly started to evaporate. Over time, FDR gradually came to recognize the threat that Hitler posed. Many Americans, although remaining complacent about the proximity of the danger, also came to hate everything that the Nazis stood for. This chapter explores the learning process that occurred in the years leading up to Pearl Harbor. It begins by uncovering FDR's image of Germany—his unfolding assessment of Hitler's intentions and the Reich's capabilities. It then examines the president's sensitivity to, and perception of, public opinion: the opinion-gauging channels he developed, the credence he gave to them, and the information they conveyed on the German question. Throughout this period, Roosevelt constantly worried that much of the population did not truly understand the extent of the danger. The final section therefore looks at the impact that these mass attitudes had on presidential actions—the attempts FDR made to change the popular mood and the extent to which domestic opinion determined the choices Roosevelt actually took.

Fear Mixed with Hope: FDR's Image of Germany before Pearl Harbor

The man who entered the White House in March 1933 was supremely confident in his ability to handle the pressures and demands of the job. Roosevelt, as one political scientist points out, "had a love affair with power. . . . Almost alone among our presidents, [he] had no conception of the office to live up to; he was it. His image of the office was himself-in-office." FDR was also extremely optimistic and energetic by nature. Faced with a severe economic crisis, his immediate instinct was to search for creative solutions for the country's economic ills. "It is common sense," he once famously remarked, "to take a method and try it. If it fails, admit it frankly and try another. But above all, try something."[3]

FDR's confidence, optimism, and desire for action permeated his first months in office, the hectic one hundred days when fifteen major relief and recovery measures were hastily cobbled together and swiftly passed through a compliant Congress. This New Deal, although failing to spark a significant economic revival, was to remain one of Roosevelt's major political achievements, and he naturally expended much of his initial energy on formulating and implementing it. But even during these first frenetic months, the new president still found the odd moment to monitor what was going on in Hitler's new Reich. The image he gleaned was not at all comforting, because FDR soon realized that Hitler's domestic activities clashed with much of what he was trying to achieve in America.

A firm believer in the virtue and efficacy of democracy, Roosevelt was certainly troubled by the Nazi effort to stamp out dissent, bloodily suppress opponents, and establish a one-party state. An intermittent advocate of free trade, he was also somewhat uneasy about the new regime's attempt to detach and isolate the new Reich from the international economic system. And a proponent of using state power to improve the lot of the populace, he was increasingly disturbed by the Nazi persecution of the Jews, and tacitly (but not publicly) supported other politicians and diplomats when they openly criticized the boycott of Jewish shops in Germany.[4]

But Roosevelt also recognized that the Nazis initially had little power to do any real damage outside Germany's borders. They had, after all, only reached political prominence because the country was in complete chaos, the economy in tatters, and the social fabric in danger of unraveling. As FDR recalled later, "when this man Hitler came into control of the German Government, Germany [was] busted, . . . a complete and utter failure, a nation that owed everybody, disorganized, not worth considering as a force in the world."[5] The vital question, therefore, was whether the Führer would be able to effect a recovery. Could this erratic and unbalanced "madman" really revive the economy and increase German power sufficiently to start spreading his pernicious and violent influence beyond German borders? Until 1938 Roosevelt was not entirely sure, and this uncertainty was to pervade his response to the Third Reich during these first years.

On the surface, of course, Hitler soon appeared to be presiding over a rapid reversal in Germany's fortunes, at least in the military sphere. In October 1933 he brazenly walked out of the Geneva Disarmament Conference, following this up in March 1935 with the reintroduction of conscription and the creation of the Luftwaffe. A year later the Führer showed even less regard for Germany's treaty commitments when he sent in troops to remilitarize the Rhineland, while in 1936 and 1937 he was able to end Germany's diplomatic isolation by concluding pacts with two other revisionist powers, Italy and Japan.

Eyeing all these developments with a measure of unease and alarm, Roosevelt soon conceded that "from the point of view of the group which now controls the destinies of the German people, their policy is succeeding admirably."[6] For one thing, rearmament seemed to be giving a much-needed boost to the economy; as FDR put it in 1936, "there is no one unemployed in Germany, they are all working in war orders."[7] More ominously, the president also felt that Germany was accumulating the resources to expand in some shape or form. From time to time, he even worried that these moves implied that Hitler, together with the Italians and the Japanese, had aggressive and belligerent intentions.[8] Thus, in October 1933 and March 1935 he remarked that, while the vast bulk of the "people of the world really want peace and disarmament," the Nazis were part of a small minority who, "headed in the opposite direction, block our efforts."[9] By 1937, he believed that these "bandit nations" had reached "a secret agreement delimiting their spheres of influence." Whereas Japan would have a "free hand" in Asia, Germany would "be left to wreak her will against Austria, Hungary, Poland, Czechoslovakia, Lithuania etc."[10]

Rearmament and the emerging Axis alliance were clearly ominous developments, but at this stage Roosevelt was still optimistic that Hitler's early successes were based on very frail foundations. This was partly because FDR was not entirely convinced that the Nazis' eradication of democracy and Hitler's rearmament program were signs that the entire German nation was irredeemably authoritarian or aggressive. "I still believe," he wrote to a friend in April 1933, "that in every country the people themselves are more peaceably and liberally inclined than their governments."[11] Recent developments in Germany, he recognized, had "complicated" things a bit. But FDR nevertheless continued to maintain that the German people possessed a number of important virtues, including a regard for family life and a respect for property rights. Sometimes he even sympathized with this "unfortunate" nation for having to suffer the misfortune of living under the Nazi "type of government."[12]

Roosevelt's willingness to distinguish between Nazis and Germans was partly predicated on a good deal of hard empirical evidence from ambassadors and contacts in Europe. In his first years in the White House

FDR periodically prodded his officials to delve below the surface of the Nazi state, beneath the superficial propaganda picture of a "happy, prosperous people," in order to discover how ordinary Germans really felt about their government, because he was "convinced that all is not well at the bottom."[13] He then eagerly read those reports that pointed to the existence of a large, if disparate and mute, opposition to the Nazi regime. Thus, from 1933 to 1937 Ambassador William E. Dodd in Berlin—himself a firm believer that the German people were "by nature more democratic than any other great race in Europe"[14]—frequently referred to "a new and deep cleavage in German people," asserting that between 50 and 60 percent opposed the Nazi regime.[15] At the same time, other officials pointed the existence of "moderates" within the German government who favored accommodation and were opposed to Nazi excesses, while some sources stressed that the German home front was "beginning to seethe and creak under the surface."[16] Occasionally, Roosevelt did concede that this discontent was not readily apparent to the casual observer because true German sentiment was repressed by Hitler's security state and obscured by Josef Goebbels's propaganda machinery.[17] But he nevertheless felt that this control over the population was tenuous. And he was therefore convinced that, if only the peaceably inclined people were freed from the shackles of totalitarian repression and propaganda, then their voice might well play a role in restraining Hitler.

As the Nazis began to feverishly rearm, Roosevelt also hoped that this lack of internal political support would be exacerbated by economic difficulties. His optimism here stemmed largely from the belief that the enormous sums Hitler was spending on the military would ultimately backfire. Although deficit spending lay at the heart of many New Deal projects, FDR always felt that governments should not spend dramatically more than they could afford.[18] He was convinced, too, that an arms build-up was the most damaging way to waste a nation's resources; as he once told an aide, "don't forget what I discovered—that over ninety percent of all national deficits from 1921 to 1939 were caused by payments for past, present, and future wars."[19] It was hardly surprising, therefore, that Roosevelt felt that Hitler's costly rearmament program brought with it the high probability of bankruptcy, and that this could only briefly be staved off through the Nazis' "tricky" financial policies."[20]

In Roosevelt's opinion, the fragile nature of the Nazi economy offered both a threat and an opportunity. On the one hand, he was periodically concerned that these economic problems might encourage the Führer to lash out aggressively. As he noted on one occasion, "Hitler—bad shape—war as way out."[21] But on the other hand, Roosevelt's own experience of depression politics had left him with an acute awareness of the connection between economic health and political legitimacy. So as the German economy started to descend back into recession, perhaps even bankruptcy, he believed that the Nazis would find it extremely difficult to remain in power and that an internal implosion and revolution was highly likely. In January 1938, FDR enunciated such a view to the cabinet. "Since the first of the year," he asserted, "the economic situation in Germany has been getting very bad. Business is on the downgrade." The same was true in Italy and Japan. The president therefore had "the hope . . . that the type of government represented by these three countries is being severely tested from the inside, especially in Germany, and that there may be a break in the logjam."[22]

Initially, then, Roosevelt's perception of German strength was deeply ambivalent. While he recognized that the Nazis were clearly acquiring the power to do some damage beyond their borders, he detected numerous signs below the surface that Hitler's rearmament program was engendering political and economic difficulties. FDR naturally hoped that the Führer might soon become a victim of these internal stresses and strains. But if he did not—if he remained in charge and continued to build arms and consolidate the Axis alliance—then this raised the problem of what exactly were Hitler's goals. How, in particular, did the Führer intend to use these new armed forces?

In this period, this was also a question to which the president had no clear answer, again largely because the available evidence was either murky or somewhat contradictory. Thus, in 1933 FDR received a copy of *Mein Kampf*, but he felt that the translation had been "so expurgated as to give a totally false view of what Hitler is and says—the German original would make a very different story."[23] Thereafter, he frequently worried that the willingness of top Nazis to boast that "that Germany intended to pay no attention to treaties" might denote that their goals were neither conservative nor limited.[24] But at the same time Roosevelt remained fairly optimistic that perhaps the Nazis only wanted to revise the most objectionable clauses of the Versailles Treaty. In these years, this was what Hitler himself declared in public. And for all his rapid rearmament, he had yet to engage in an overt action that could not be explained away under the guise of seeking either equality of arms or national self-determination.

Unable to clearly identify the scope or nature of the German problem, Roosevelt was naturally somewhat ambivalent when it came to formulating proposed solutions. Occasionally, he was inclined toward ideas whose central thrust was to block Hitler, such as a direct appeal to the German people or a quarantine that would bring the fragile Nazi economy to its knees.[25] But at this stage, Roosevelt's attention was not focused purely on containment. Instead, although vividly aware of the potential perils of appeasing untrustworthy "gangsters," FDR before October 1938 refused to abandon all hope that Hitler had relatively limited aims that could be satiated by negotiation—and if an agreement was in the offing he was determined to be, if not a leading player, then at least an enthusiastic spectator.[26] This explains why he endorsed the Welles Plan in the winter of 1937–38, which aimed partly at giving a boost to British negotiations with Germany and Italy. And when this proved a nonstarter, the president even intermittently expressed some sympathy for the British attempts at appeasement, stating that he "would be the first to cheer" if Neville Chamberlain succeeded in clinching a deal with Hitler.[27]

Roosevelt's fragile faith in the efficacy of appeasement did not long outlast the Munich crisis of October 1938, however. In Asia, war had erupted between Japan and China the previous summer, providing the Japanese army with the opportunity to launch a series of offensives that placed it in control of most of China's major cities. In Europe, Hitler then sparked a series of crises throughout 1938, unilaterally uniting Austria with the Reich in March, before pressuring Czechoslovakia to cede the German-speaking Sudetenland the following fall. At the Munich Conference in October, Britain and France sanctioned Germany's acquisition of the Sudetenland in a desperate attempt to avoid war. But Hitler refused to be appeased. The following March, he shocked the democracies by forcibly annexing the rump of Czechoslovakia. In response to this blatant violation of the Munich agreement, Neville Chamberlain grudgingly moved to protect Hitler's next likely victims, and Europe again prepared for war.

On the back of these events, FDR finally became convinced that Hitler's actions were part of a conscious and planned attempt not only to transform the European status quo but also to make inroads into Africa, Latin America, and even the United States. In January 1939, he told the Senate Military Affairs Committee that the administration now had "rather definite information as to what the ultimate objective of Hitler was," namely, "world domination," which would proceed step by step until Germany had effected "the gradual encirclement of the U.S. by the removal of its first line of defense."[28] Hitler's actions during the Czechoslovak crisis—his obduracy in negotiations, his aggressive speechmaking, and his decision to ignore the Munich agreement by marching into Prague—also confirmed that negotiating with such a character was pointless and futile.[29] Soon after the cession of the Sudetenland to Germany, FDR began to express second thoughts about having urged Hitler to "sit down around the table and make peace." A year later, when told of Hitler's claim that the Polish issue was his last demand, and that after solving it he would retire from public life and simply paint, Roosevelt's reaction was one of astonished disbelief. "The president," one top official recorded, "related this in an amused tone and said that the report was so unique that he had put it in his private files."[30]

But did Hitler now have the capabilities to achieve his ambitions? By 1939 Roosevelt was starting to recognize symbiotic relationship between Nazi success and German power, for Hitler's every move clearly seemed to bolster his confidence. He also felt that events such as the *Anschluss*, the carving up of Czechoslovakia, and now the invasion of Poland were severely disrupting the distribution of power in Central Europe, thereby making it all but inevitable that this region's remaining states would join the bandwagon behind Germany.[31] And he feared too that all these gains were providing the Nazis with the ability to place pressure on Latin America, both economically, by threatening to cut off their exports to Europe, and covertly, through the use of agents in those countries with large German immigrant populations.[32]

Still, the Nazi threat remained distant, largely because Britain and France were now willing to stand up to Hitler. In March 1939, Chamberlain finally offered a guarantee to Poland, and when Germany invaded this country on September 1 both London and Paris duly (if reluctantly) declared war. As FDR began to contemplate the possible outcome of this conflict, he reached the tentative conclusion that defense would prevail on land.[33] With a stalemate likely to develop on the western front—with the Germans unable to overcome the Maginot line and the French unable to penetrate the German frontier—the two vital theaters would be the sea and the air. In the former, Roosevelt felt that Britain and France would control the Atlantic and Mediterranean, thereby strangling supplies to Germany, with all that this implied for the politically and economically vulnerable Nazi regime. In the air, however, he recognized that the Germans enjoyed a distinct advantage, mainly because of Hitler's early start in rearming. But even here, he was hopeful that, if the Allies were allowed access to U.S. resources, they could quickly catch up.[34] He was also confident "that the morale of the German people would crack under aerial attacks much sooner than that of the French or the English." As this statement reveals, the final weapon in Roosevelt's armory remained the persistent hope that Hitler's ambitions would be thwarted by Germany's internal vulnerabilities. The president's "own hunch," one official recorded in September 1939, "was that by June 1940 the Germans either will have gained ascendancy over the French and the English, or there will be a revolution inside Germany itself."[35]

Of course, by June 1940 it was Hitler who was ascendant. On May 10, the Wehrmacht, Germany's efficient new army, launched a devastating blitzkrieg through Holland, Belgium, Luxembourg, and northern France, crashing through the French defenses on the Meuse near Sedan and cutting the Allied forces in two within a week. After remnants of the British army managed to escape at Dunkirk, it only took the Germans another two-and-a-half weeks to overcome the last French resistance. An armistice was then concluded on June 25.[36]

This dramatic change in fortunes greatly heightened Roosevelt's fear that Hitler now had the ability to menace the Americas directly. Initially, he worried that the French fleet might fall into German hands.[37] Then, after the British reduced this danger by destroying the great French naval base at Mers-el-Kébir, his focus shifted to the prospect that many South American states might defect to the Nazi camp, particularly because "40 percent of the normal exports of Latin America have been lost due to the war" and thus they would benefit economically by leaning toward Germany.[38] Finally, during the winter and spring of 1940–41, as the Wehrmacht seemingly marched at will through the Balkans and the Mediterranean, Roosevelt started to fret that a German triumph in North Africa, especially in the region around Dakar, might open a path for an invasion across the South Atlantic, or perhaps even a long distance bombing campaign against the United States itself.[39] By May 1941, this final worry was even disturbing the president's sleep patterns; as he told a group of aides, his recent nightmares had been dominated by images of the Luftwaffe bombing New York and his being forced to shelter in a bomb-proof cave "until a squadron of German planes" had passed over.[40]

Yet even during the darkest months of 1940 and 1941 Roosevelt's optimism never faded entirely. This was partly because the fall of France had not eliminated all the obstacles in Germany's way, for Britain remained stubbornly in the fight and in June 1941 Hitler added to his growing list of enemies by attacking the Soviet Union. Admittedly, there were times in the summer of 1940 and the spring of 1941 when Roosevelt worried that a beleaguered Britain was on the verge of disaster, but for the most part he felt that, with Winston Churchill at the helm, Britain could withstand the Nazi onslaught and thereby block Hitler's path to complete control of the Atlantic and Mediterranean.[41] He was also relatively confident that the USSR would come out on top after Hitler launched his invasion on June 22, 1941. As he explained in a revealing comment just four days later, "now comes this Russian diversion. If it is more than just that it will mean the liberation of Europe from Nazi domination—and at the same time I do not think we need to worry about any possibility of Russian domination."[42]

Although sometimes frustrated by signs of the German people's enthusiastic reaction to the Wehrmacht's victories, Roosevelt also remained hopeful that the Nazi regime was internally vulnerable. In particular, with Hitler's empire now encompassing much of continental Europe, the president thought the Third Reich would find it difficult to digest its enormous territorial gains; as he put it on one occasion, "The economic and organizational stresses and strains of taking over Eastern Europe will make the going increasingly hard."[43] Thus, even in the midst of Hitler's incredible success, FDR remained eager for information that pointed to internal weakness and unrest. During March and April 1941, he read with interest the variety of reports that repeatedly stressed that "the standard of living of the German people has lowered by nearly one fifth since 1938" and that the Third Reich was suffering from labor shortages and transport problems.[44] Of course, there was still the danger that such internal vulnerabilities might encourage Hitler to lash out even more aggressively—in January 1941, for example, FDR passed on to Churchill a report that suggested that "Germany will have to find food for the occupied countries and will [thus] move into [the] Balkans and possibly [the] Ukraine."[45] But even after these moves had come to fruition, reports of Germany's internal woes persisted, replete with indications of "despair" and "misery," of morale deteriorating as the Wehrmacht failed speedily to defeat the Red Army, and of workers revolting under the pressure of British bombs.[46]

So even with Hitler apparently at the height of his power, Roosevelt's image of Germany remained complex and ambiguous. Although he clearly feared Germany's capabilities and Hitler's ambitions, at the same time he generally remained confident that there were elements within the Reich who were more peacefully inclined than their leaders, that those forcibly occupied would eventually rebel, and that, in any case, dramatic rearmament would ultimately lead to an internal economic collapse. But if these were FDR's underlying assumptions, what were his policy preferences? If he had been able to base policy purely on his own inclinations, what courses would he have favored?

One important consideration was the relative importance to be accorded to the Nazi danger. By the end of 1940, Roosevelt was increasingly convinced that the world was polarizing into two camps, with a monolithic Axis bloc menacing U.S. interests in Asia as well as Europe and the Mediterranean.[47] But which of the three Axis powers posed the greatest danger? Which one should America seek to counter first?

Italy was of no great concern. In Roosevelt's opinion Mussolini was a shameless opportunist, anxious "to play the role of jackal to Hitler's lion." But Italian morale, especially in its armed forces, was far too fragile to sustain a long war of aggression. As FDR ungenerously remarked at the start of June 1940, Italian soldiers would fight tolerably well while they were on the offensive, but "once they were stopped, they were through, and if the line were ever turned, they would run like rabbits."[48]

The Japanese, however, could not be dismissed so lightly. FDR had long feared that Japan, like Germany, was in the grip of dangerous militarists, its own "Junker crowd," who were bent on rearmament and expansion. He was particularly disturbed by the ferocious and savage war this group was waging in China. More ominously, if the Japanese were allowed to continue in this vein, especially by expanding into Indochina and the Dutch East Indies, then the president was concerned that this would have negative repercussions for the U.S. economy, for the Japanese would undoubtedly seek to exclude all American trade from this region so they could exploit it for their own narrow ends.[49] But as with Germany, Roosevelt's image of Japan was not purely negative. He also believed this nation was plagued by its own internal problems. Economically, Japan was clearly dependent on the United States for vital raw materials. Politically, the president recognized that the civil government in Tokyo had no real control over the Japanese army in China. He was also keenly aware of the serious splits within the Japanese armed services over how best to proceed in Asia.[50]

Roosevelt therefore viewed both Germany and Japan through a similar framework of fears and hopes, but with one vital difference: in his opinion, the Japanese threat clearly paled next to the danger posed by Hitler and the Nazis, who aimed at world, rather than regional, domination. Unlike the Japanese, the Nazis also had a military machine impressive enough to directly menace the Western Hemisphere, especially if Britain or the USSR were to collapse. Moreover, although the Third Reich was undoubtedly plagued by its own internal problems, Roosevelt felt that Japan's weaknesses, especially in the economic sphere, were far more acute. As a result of all these calculations, the president strongly believed that Nazi Germany posed the most powerful threat to U.S. interests and that America's energies had to be directed principally at this danger. Wherever possible, the conflict in Asia had to be contained and dampened so that scarce U.S. resources would not be diverted away from Europe.[51]

By the end of 1938, Roosevelt had also reached the conclusion that Hitler and the Nazis were such a threat to European stability that an enduring peace could only be achieved after "Hitlerism" had been totally eradicated. After the Munich crisis it certainly seemed pointless to negotiate with a regime that habitually violated treaties and used any respite from conflict to regroup for a new round of fighting. The president therefore abandoned any last lingering hopes in appeasement. Indeed, although he sent Sumner Welles on a "special mission" to confer with Hitler, Mussolini, and the other key European leaders in February 1940, FDR no longer seriously entertained the prospect of brokering a peace deal; rather, the aim of the Welles mission was merely to obtain information about European conditions and silence critics at home.[52] The following year, the president's adamant opposition to anything that smacked of appeasement was clearly revealed in a letter sent to a close aide. "You were quite right," he informed Admiral William D. Leahy, "in expressing the opinion that this country will not join any effort to bring about a negotiated peace with Nazism. This attitude of our[s] should be clear by now to all the world."[53]

But how to defeat the Third Reich? FDR's clear preference was to use all methods short of direct U.S. involvement in the fighting. Even in 1940 and 1941 he remained confident that an internally fragile regime might be eradicated relatively cheaply by blockade, bombing, and psychological warfare. But increasingly, the president's central goal was to extend U.S. aid to all those fighting Germany. Before May 1940, when Roosevelt was relatively confident that France and Britain would emerge victorious, this policy was unproblematic. Thereafter, as the president's fears and hopes waxed and waned, so did his belief in the efficacy of sending material abroad.

The president was particularly pessimistic during the dark days of June and July 1940, as the French sued for peace and Churchill's new government frantically prepared for a German invasion. For a brief period, he was even reluctant to gamble on Britain's survival, fearing that if he guessed wrong he would not only "further enrage Hitler" but would also be in effect handing the Germans some of America's very limited military material. It was only in August 1940, after the British neutralized the French fleet at Mers-el-Kébir and began to demonstrate that they might hold out against the Luftwaffe, that FDR began referring to his "'hunch'—not necessarily based on cold figures, that [Britain had] . . . turned the corner."[54] By the following spring, after the series of debacles in Greece, Crete, and North Africa, together with mounting shipping losses in the Atlantic, he was again anxious about Britain's prospects.[55] And this time it took the German invasion of the USSR to raise his spirits. Not only did Roosevelt believe that Stalin and communism paled in comparison to the very real danger posed by Hitler and the Nazis, but (especially in July and August 1941) he was also confident that the Red Army would hold out and eventually defeat the Wehrmacht. As a result, he was willing to extend U.S. aid to the Soviets and was soon prodding the War Department to hasten delivery of key equipment.[56]

Whenever Roosevelt was confident that his proxies could sustain the struggle against the Nazis, there was little need for more drastic action. Essentially, this was the case right up until the fall of 1941, since, for all the waning optimism of June–July 1940 and April–May 1941, the defeat of Britain was never at any stage imminent. He could therefore move one step at a time—extending limited amounts of material in the fall and winter of 1940, making the more comprehensive commitment of Lend-Lease the following March, and then seeking to ensure that these supplies reached their destination during the summer—in the belief that each move might be enough to win the war. Not until September–October 1941 was it necessary to think in terms of additional measures. And then, with the Wehrmacht breaking through Red Army lines in the vicinity of Moscow, it suddenly appeared that methods short of war were no longer sufficient. This was certainly the view of Harry L. Hopkins who now was "all for" America's direct involvement in the conflict, because "I . . . don't believe we can ever lick Hitler with a Lend-Lease program."[57] Roosevelt's personal opinion is more difficult to discern, but there are a number of indications that he probably agreed with his closest adviser.

In theory, the president was not violently opposed to America's formal involvement in the war, if it was absolutely essential to U.S. security. As early as September 1939 he had contemplated the various dangers to the United States, especially the prospect that the Germans might "establish a naval base in the Atlantic islands, say the Azores," and had concluded that it would be foolish to pledge publicly that the United States would definitely stay out of the conflict.[58] Then in May 1940 he had mentioned to the treasury secretary, Henry Morgenthau, Jr., that the United States could well be at war within two or three months.[59] During 1941, moreover, while he tried to contain and dampen events in Asia, Roosevelt was determined to take steps to protect the Atlantic from the U-boat danger, well aware that policies such as "shoot on sight" carried the distinct risk of war.[60] And on at least seven occasions during the first half of 1941 he even intimated that he would welcome a German retaliation in the Atlantic, since he could then use this to justify more belligerent American action against the Nazis.[61]

Roosevelt also had no fundamental aversion to the idea of sending American troops abroad. This was apparent in his decision to authorize talks between American and British military planners in the first months of 1941. Although keen to keep these meetings secret, the president knew what conclusions were reached and was undoubtedly aware that their main recommendation was to "build up the necessary [land] forces for the eventual offensive against Germany."[62] During the spring and summer, FDR then talked about the desirability of organizing a 75,000-man American Expeditionary Force (AEF) that could be used outside the Western Hemisphere. He also favored deploying U.S. forces overseas, in areas ranging from the Azores to Iceland.[63] Finally, the president's recognition of the need to deploy American ground troops against the Wehrmacht was demonstrated right after Pearl Harbor, when he quickly became a champion of using U.S. troops, commenting to Churchill on December 22 that "he was anxious that American land forces should give their support as quickly as possible wherever they could be most helpful."[64]

By the fall of 1941, therefore, Roosevelt was not only increasingly fearful of the danger posed by Nazi intentions and capabilities, but he also had no fundamental aversion either to war or to U.S. troops fighting in it. In this context, it seems likely that he now deemed it desirable for the U.S. to become fully and formally engaged in the conflict.[65] In other words, had FDR been able to work in a domestic vacuum, then his burgeoning fears would have encouraged him to advocate a mixture of measures, centering around the use of land troops but backed up with subsidiary tools to weaken the fragile Nazi state.[66] But, of course, Roosevelt was not simply free to act on his personal proclivities. He also had to take into account the views of the American public. We therefore need to look at the president's sensitivity to the domestic environment—the role he thought it *ought* to play in the foreign-policy process—and to examine the mechanisms he employed to gauge it, the content that these channels conveyed, and the impact that these perceptions actually had on the choices taken and the speeches made.

The "Great Debate": Public Opinion and Nazi Germany before Pearl Harbor

Although Roosevelt sometimes mused about the desirability of working in an environment free from prying journalists or the fluctuating moods of the masses, he was nevertheless acutely aware that, in actuality, the domestic mood could not merely be ignored.[67] This stemmed largely from his belief that a president's ability to decide on a course of action and then shape opinion behind it was strictly limited. "The public psychology," he frequently stressed, "cannot, because of human weakness, be attuned for long periods of time to a constant repetition of the highest note in the scale"; thus, in a country where "there is a free and sensational Press people tire of seeing the same name day after day in the important headlines, the same voice night after night on the radio."[68] FDR also recognized that even on those select occasions when mass opinion was prepared to listen and take note of what their leaders said, many groups would not meekly accept each and every course that was proposed. He was therefore mystified whenever anyone suggested that he ignore public opinion and act like a "dictator." "Can you see the expressions on the faces of the Congress or on the Editors of the *Boston Transcript* and *Boston Herald*," he remarked on one occasion. "I am not even considering what the Boston Irish or the Kansas New Englanders would do." Small wonder, then, that Roosevelt believed that domestic developments had to be monitored, that it was vital "to watch Congress and public opinion like a hawk."[69] But what were his channels for doing so? And how reliable did he deem each different source?

The president always paid particularly close attention to the shifting attitudes of opinion makers, especially media figures such as journalists, editors, and commentators. These individuals commonly hold an ambiguous position, since their role is split between reflecting and forming the opinions of others. Newspaper editors, for instance, are often divided between the need to sell papers, and hence to tell their readers what they *want* to hear, and the desire to pedal their own beliefs, and thus to tell their readers what they *ought* to hear.[70] Roosevelt's attitudes toward the media starkly reflected this ambiguity. On the one hand, as a majority of newspaper proprietors started to turn against the New Deal with a vengeance, FDR became increasingly convinced that the pages of around 85 percent of the press were full of malicious misrepresentations, with the worst offenders being the triumvirate of powerful newspaper barons: William Randolph Hearst, who controlled around 13 percent of *all* American dailies, as well as thirteen magazines, eight radio stations, and two motion picture companies; Colonel Robert R. McCormick, who owned the influential *Chicago Daily Tribune*; and Cissy Patterson, who published the *New York Daily News*.[71] In Roosevelt's eyes, these owners were simply out to "pervert" and "attack" every administration move in an attempt to "confuse the public mind." The one saving grace, he thought, was that their organs "do not carry any particular weight of expression of public opinion."[72] "I have closer contact with the people than any man in this room," he told the American Society of Newspaper Editors in April 1938, not only because most "papers are regional, [and] often tend to have [a] parochial, local bias," but also because many journalists tended simply to echo the viewpoints and prejudices of their bosses.[73] Moreover, as he repeatedly pointed out, for all their attacks on the New Deal, publishers and owners had been spectacularly unsuccessful in shifting mass opinion. After all, FDR had won in a landslide in the 1936 election, despite the overwhelming opposition of the media. If anything, he felt that his most vehement newspapers critics "so overdid it that the public saw through it," and thus their "attacks gained us votes."[74]

Yet, for all these expressions of disgust about the biased tone of press coverage and for all these declarations of doubt that newspapers reflected the views of the wider public, Roosevelt not only remained inordinately sensitive to press criticism but also could never entirely rid himself of the thought that perhaps the press's views *did* matter. An avid newspaper reader, he scoured the *New York Times* and *Herald Tribune*, the *Baltimore Sun*, *Chicago Tribune*, *Washington Post* and *Times Herald*—with special attention to the editorial page—before beginning his official working day.[75] From March 1941, the president was also interested in receiving a weekly survey of editorial opinion, written in a somewhat fawning tone and fuzzy style by Alan Barth, an employee initially in the Treasury Department and later in the Office of Facts and Figures (OFF).[76] Then in July 1941, he asked Lowell Mellett, a White House aide and director of the Office of Government Reports (OGR), to prepare a weekly final screening of editorial opinion. Thereafter, the OGR began compiling the "Weekly Analysis of Press Reaction," which employed basic statistical techniques to monitor editorials in more than three hundred newspapers, journals, and magazines across the country.[77]

While Roosevelt had access to a variety of media surveys, these were not his only source for gauging opinion. The president was also keen to monitor both the opinions of prominent groups and the mood in key regions. To this end, he established informal "back-channel" connections with figures like John Franklin Carter, a New Deal journalist and author, who headed a special intelligence-gathering unit for the president, and Morris L. Ernst, a prominent lawyer and civil libertarian, who gathered gossipy "tidbits" from his informal parties with the prominent opinion makers and then reported them back to the White House. Both were colorful figures who strove to present their findings in a lively and engaging manner. And their output tended to appeal to a president always on the lookout for information that provided color, shade, and the hidden human dimension that was so often lacking from dour conventional sources.[78]

Roosevelt also reveled in personal contact. During an average day he spent a quarter of his fourteen working hours on the phone, engaged in four to six hours of appointments with between ten to fifteen people, and still found time for biweekly press conferences and regular meetings with congressional leaders. Like Abraham Lincoln seventy-five years earlier, FDR viewed many of these discussions as akin to a "public opinion bath" —an opportunity to discern what reporters, legislators, and prominent individuals thought on the key issues of the day.[79] His wife's tireless trips around the country performed a similar function. For a president confined to a wheelchair since a polio attack in 1921, it was undoubtedly useful to receive interesting snippets of firsthand information from Eleanor on conditions and trends in important states, especially since they were invariably tinged with her passionate concern for the poor, the underprivileged, and the unemployed.[80] Finally, the White House also received five to eight thousand letters a day. Believing this to be a good measure of the issues on which people felt intensely about, the president, as the White House mail clerk later wrote, "always showed a keen interest in the mail and kept close watch on its trend."[81]

By September 1939, however, all these sources were declining in tandem with FDR's increased exposure to public opinion polls, a device that purported to show not what particular regions or groups thought, but what "the entire population as a unit believed."[82] In the late 1930s, new "scientific" techniques, pioneered by George Gallup and Elmo Roper, had revolutionized opinion polling, helping to banish the memory of the 1936 *Reader's Digest* straw poll that had confidently predicted a Republican presidential victory, only to see Roosevelt sweep the country with the largest landslide in American history.[83] Of course, even by 1939, despite their new status as a scientific measurement, polls were not entirely reliable. Not only did the possibility of massive error remain (as was demonstrated by the Truman-Dewey miscalculation of 1948), but the pollsters themselves recognized that polling on matters of *fact*, such as the number of people who had listened to a Roosevelt fireside chat, was far more accurate than results on *attitudes*, what people actually thought of the broadcast. In particular, pollsters were less able to measure the depth of feeling, the intensity with which individuals held beliefs, and thus were unable to conclude with any certainty whether public attitudes on a particular issue were firmly fixed or merely transitory.[84] Our problem, however, is not so much with the reliability of the data being produced at this time; rather, we are essentially concerned with the extent to which the president accepted these poll findings as accurate. How sensitive, then, was he to these new data?

Initially, FDR was a somewhat ambivalent recipient of these new "scientific" polls. From September 1939 he was certainly intrigued both by Elmo Roper's findings, sent to him directly by *Fortune* magazine, and by data obtained from newspaper proprietors like Eugene Meyer of the *Washington Post*.[85] But as the 1940 election neared, he was also increasingly suspicious and skeptical of one particular polling agency: George Gallup's American Institute of Public Opinion (AIPO). This was because Gallup was a Republican supporter who had underestimated FDR's vote in 1936 and was now "known to be very strongly for Willkie." Given this track record, during the summer and autumn of 1940 Roosevelt began talking about the prospect that Gallup would rig his findings so as to create a false momentum that would boost the GOP's electoral hopes.[86]

Distrustful of Gallup, Roosevelt started to shun his findings, but he did not give up on polling data altogether. For a start, the president remained "interested" in *Fortune*'s results, viewing them as "more nearly accurate than the Gallup poll."[87] More importantly, from the beginning of August

1940 he began utilizing the services of Hadley Cantril, who with financial help from Gerald C. Lambert had established the Office of Public Opinion Research (OPOR) at Princeton University. Unlike Gallup, Cantril was an ardent liberal and known supporter of the president's policies. Although he used some of Gallup's facilities, Cantril was not tarnished by this connection, as FDR's aides were anxious to point out that—"the replies are not seen by the Gallup organization," Mellett stressed in August 1940, "and the tabulation is made by the professors themselves." In a further attempt to make Cantril more appealing, Mellett added that Cantril used more extensive sampling techniques than his Republican-leaning colleague.[88] Roosevelt was soon convinced. That summer he met with the pollster, described his "special" polls as "extremely interesting," and even began submitting questions that he wanted surveyed.[89] In return, Cantril went to great lengths to supply his results promptly, in a clear and concise manner. Very soon he had become one of FDR's chief channels for gauging the mood of the American people.[90]

Although Roosevelt was satisfied that one pollster provided an accurate portrayal of mass opinion, increasingly he also wanted to supplement this information with additional reports from the OFF, a bureau established in October 1941 partly to monitor the domestic environment.[91] Within two months, the OFF's Bureau of Intelligence (BoI) started to compile a more comprehensive analysis of mass attitudes: the Survey of Intelligence Materials. The BoI frequently using findings from other polling agencies, but it attempted more than a simple regurgitation of their conclusions. Its 126 employees also monitored reaction to the administration's main information campaigns, provided detailed and sustained examination of public attitudes on specific issues, and most importantly, analyzed the attitudes of both the general public and specific groups "carefully correlat[ing] . . . one set of opinion with others" in an attempt to judge the "intensity with which opinions are held, their susceptibility to change, the degree to which they conform to social pressures, and the extent to which they are spontaneous and genuine."[92] Roosevelt was deeply interested in these reports, and even requested back copies when there were any omissions from his files. And as the president's interest grew, so did the sophistication of the BoI's output. By February 1942 it had been expanded from its original cursory four or five pages of general comment, to fifteen to twenty pages of more careful and comprehensive analysis on the public's response to specific foreign-policy issues.[93]

These, then, were the varied and extensive channels for monitoring American attitudes that the president had developed. But what did they convey? What were Roosevelt's broad perceptions of mass sentiment toward Germany in the period before December 7, 1941?

In October 1933, Cordell Hull remarked that editorial comment on foreign affairs combined "a wide resentment against the Hitler Government (as distinguished from the German people) together with a unanimous opinion that we must not allow ourselves to become involved in European political developments."[94] In this one sentence, Roosevelt's secretary of state neatly summarized the main strands that were to characterize American opinion toward the Third Reich throughout the 1930s.

For a start, an overwhelming majority of the public clearly detested the Nazi regime, both for its internal brutality and external bellicosity. Jewish-American groups were naturally appalled and horrified by the Nazis' treatment of Jews and in 1933 quickly instigated a boycott of German products. They found a measure of support within Congress, where Samuel Dickstein launched an investigation into Nazi propaganda in the United States in 1934 and a number of leading legislators condemned the Nazis' early acts as "sickening and terrifying." Opinion makers on the spot overwhelmingly agreed. Some of the best reporting in these years was conducted by a group of highly talented journalists, including Edgar Ansel Mowrer, William L. Shirer, and Frederick T. Birchall, whose antipathy toward the Nazis was sharpened by the daily grind of living in the Reich, with all its oppressive restrictions, clumsy repressions, and burgeoning militarism. Whenever opportunity and censorship permitted, these reporters hastened to tell Americans of the litany of crimes and misdemeanors committed by Hitler and his cronies, from the bullying and suppression of opponents at home to the bullying and annexation of enemies abroad.[95] Increasingly, it was a record that few editors dared to ignore. By 1939, even the *Chicago Tribune*, one of the most vehemently anti-Roosevelt and isolationist papers, was attacking the Nazis, declaring that "it would be a strange man indeed who could stomach their creed and their attitudes."[96]

By this benchmark there were indeed few "strange" people in the United States, for the first "scientific" polls clearly revealed a widespread dislike of the Nazi regime. This was particularly evident during the winter of 1938–39, in the wake of Munich and the infamous *Kristallnacht* pogrom, when pollsters found that 77 percent of Americans felt German demands on the Sudetenland to have been unjustified, 92 percent refused to believe Hitler's claim that he had no more territorial ambitions, and 94 percent strongly disapproved of the Nazis' treatment of the Jews.[97] A year later, when the president began to receive copies of the *Fortune* poll, the results were similar. From the very start of the war in Europe, 83 percent wanted the Allies to win; a mere 1 percent favored Hitler and the Nazis.[98] A clear majority also had no doubt that the current conflict had been caused by "Hitler's greed for land and lust for power," while only 6 percent maintained it was the result of "England and France . . . trying to stop Germany from becoming a really strong power." As *Fortune* informed the president, almost all Americans regarded "this as Hitler's personal war, and the guilt as mostly his."[99]

Yet at this stage, American detestation of the Führer did not translate into a deep-seated dislike of the German people. In fact, American attitudes toward Germany and the Germans had undergone a profound change in the years since 1917. During the Great War, George Creel's Committee of Public Information (CPI) had successfully whipped up a mass hysteria against all things German, disseminating dubious atrocity stories and propagating the notion that the Germans were an inherently aggressive and warlike people.[100] In the intervening years, however, passions had slowly cooled. This was partly because there had long been an ambivalence at the heart of the American image of Germany.[101] Although from the turn of the century, many Americans had perceived Kaiser Wilhelm II's Reich to be excessively militaristic, authoritarian, and arrogant, not everyone had felt this way.[102] Conservative Germanophile academics, for instance, had frequently stressed how "the Teutonic character was in good part responsible for modern democracy," progressive publicists had periodically highlighted Germany's much-vaunted penchant for efficiency, and Wilsonian liberals had sometimes been willing to distinguish between aggressive authoritarian leaders and the more pacific German public. Most of these positive images had been briefly submerged beneath a wave of anti-German hysteria in 1917 and 1918, but, after the Great War ended, Creel's vigorous crusade against all things German had gradually been discredited. In the 1920s, it was revealed that much of this wartime propaganda had been exaggerated, and in some cases even blatantly manufactured. In the 1930s, popular revisionist historians and a congressional investigation by the Nye Committee helped bolster the view that American involvement in the Great War had not been the product of aggressive and brutal actions by the German "Hun." Instead, Nye and his cohorts singled out American businessmen and British propagandists, whose devious machinations had maneuvered the United States into a conflict that, by implication, barely threatened the nation's interests.[103]

Faced with such evidence, many opinion makers held a relatively benign view of the German people. One of the most influential columnists was Walter Lippmann, whose razor-sharp reflections on topical issues appeared in around 160 newspapers with an estimated circulation of about 8 million. Lippmann, of Jewish descent, naturally disliked the new Nazi regime, but he was nevertheless quick to remind his readers that the Germans were "a genuinely civilized people."[104] So did many others. Throughout the 1930s, even vehement Nazi haters emphasized the Germans' apathy, perhaps even opposition, to Hitler's deeds. Thus William Shirer, in his popular broadcasts from Berlin, repeatedly pointed to the absence of war fever and the desire for peace amongst the masses, while the prominent columnist and commentator Walter Winchell informed the president that "Hitler does not represent the true will of the vast civilian population of Germany."[105] Little that happened after the outbreak of war shook this conviction. As Barth reported to the White House in August 1941, almost all the media still maintained that any "peace must not be punitive. As yet there is little disposition in the U.S. to blame the German people for the crimes of their Nazi Government."[106]

POLL (NOVEMBER 1939)

Which of these statements comes closest to your own idea of Germany?

The German people are essentially peace loving and kindly, but they have been unfortunate in being misled, too often, by ruthless and ambitious rulers. (66.6%)

The German people have always had an irresponsible fondness for brute force and conquest which makes the country a menace to world peace so long as it is allowed to be strong enough to fight. (19.6%)

The needs of Germany's expanding population compel her to seek to conquer because other jealous powers try to keep her from expanding in a normal way. (4.2%)

The best way for peace in Europe is to allow Germany, with her great organizing ability, to integrate the small nations of Europe. (1.8%)

Don't know. (7.8%)

Source: Fortune (December 1939), pp. 118–20, attached to Yorke to Early, November 21, 1939, OF 3618, FDRL.

Polls suggested widespread popular support for this sentiment. According to *Fortune*, in October 1939 two-thirds of the population was "anti-Hitler rather than anti-German." "It would surely take a tremendously cogent propaganda campaign," the magazine therefore concluded, "plus a number of frightful German blunders, to induce a state of mind as we suffered in 1917, when German music was banned from the opera and to bear a German name was to risk ostracism."

A host of other polls bolstered this conclusion. In October 1939, for instance, the White House received data indicating that a plurality clearly viewed German-Americans as the best foreign-born citizens.[107] Two months later a *Fortune* poll revealed little support for a harsh peace. While more than half the population wanted to "crush Hitler but not the Germans," only 19 percent opted for partition and a mere 14 percent favored Germany's complete disarmament.[108]

Like their president, then, in the period before Pearl Harbor a majority of Americans viewed the Third Reich with a degree of ambiguity, detesting the Nazi regime but refusing to extend this to a hatred of all things German. Increasingly, however, the debate within the United States did not center purely on images of the Third Reich. Far more important was the question of whether or not Nazi Germany actually posed a direct threat to the country. And here the consensus quickly broke down.

The 1930s were the high-water mark of American isolationism. Preoccupied with day-to-day economic issues, disillusioned with America's involvement in the Great War, and concerned lest U.S. participation in another foreign conflict irrevocably destroy the nation's constitutional and social fabric, until 1940 much of the population shared a number of core convictions, each of which seemed to suggest that the Nazis, for all their internal brutality and external bellicosity, presented no direct threat to the United States.[109]

The first was a keen faith in American impregnability. In the past, the Atlantic and Pacific oceans had offered an almost impenetrable barrier to potential aggressors. During the 1930s, despite Hitler's rearmament program and aggressive designs, many Americans still thought it highly doubtful that the Third Reich could ever directly menace the United States. For one thing, the Nazis would have to overcome both the French army and British navy, and throughout the winter of 1939–40 a clear majority of mass opinion optimistically believed that the two democracies would prevail and defeat Germany. Even if the aggressive dictators were to blast their way past these obstacles, most Americans remained so confident in their country's natural security that they felt this would have few tangible repercussions for the United States. This explains why as late as January 1939 only 46 percent of respondents were willing to use U.S. military power to protect the Philippines from armed invasion. Astonishingly, a mere 27 percent thought Brazil worth defending with force, a figure that only rose to 43 percent when it came to neighboring Mexico.[110] As such figures demonstrate, a significant section of the public apparently deemed the country to be so strategically immune that U.S. colonies and the Monroe Doctrine could both be abandoned with impunity.

While strategic invulnerability meant the United States could remain aloof from external events, an overwhelming desire to remain at peace coupled with a fear of foreign entanglements suggested to many that this course should be adopted. Throughout the 1930s, a vast majority of the public was appalled by the very prospect of involvement in another faraway war, even if it was to contain the aggressive Hitler. This was clearly demonstrated in 1936, by one of the very first straw polls, which found that 95 percent wanted to stay out of any conflict. As Roosevelt correctly acknowledged, he was up "against a public psychology of long standing—a psychology which comes very close to saying 'Peace at any price.'"[111]

For Americans desperate to remain out of any future conflict, it also seemed vital to avoid any needless political entanglements. The neutrality legislation enacted between 1935 and 1937, with its prohibitions on the sale and shipment of arms and munitions to belligerents, was just the most obvious manifestation of this desire for a unilateralist foreign policy. Another was the continued preference for some form of "impartial neutrality" even after the outbreak of war. As *Fortune* informed Roosevelt in November 1939, only 20 percent clearly favored a policy of aiding the democracies short of war, while more than 54 percent advocated the selling of goods to both sides—the Nazis as well as the Allies—on a cash-and-carry basis.[112]

The president, increasingly convinced of the need to contain and eradicate nazism, was palpably disturbed by the persistence of such attitudes.

"The country as a whole," he complained in December 1939, "does not yet have any deep sense of world crisis." "What worries me, especially," he wrote that same month, "is that public opinion over here is patting itself on the back every morning and thanking God for the Atlantic Ocean (and the Pacific Ocean)."[113] Yet even as FDR spoke, Hitler was planning a series of dramatic moves that would soon shake, and in some cases erode, much of the population's faith in the core tenets of the isolationist creed.

The first to be affected was the complacent sense of American impregnability. In June and July, in the immediate aftermath of Hitler's dramatic and stunning blitzkrieg through Scandinavia and Western Europe, polling data revealed a sharp increase in respondents who believed they would be personally affected by the war, up from 48 percent in March, to 67 percent in July, and 71 percent by the following January.[114] In July, Roosevelt also learned that 55 percent pessimistically thought Germany would go to war with the United States within the next ten years, a figure that rose to 61 percent by September.[115] A poll conducted in August 1940 also informed him that many Americans suddenly regarded more areas as vital to U.S. security, including Bermuda, Brazil, and Mexico.

Another immediate impact of this new mood of heightened insecurity was a clamor for increased preparedness at home. In the shock that followed the fall of France, Congress appropriated all the funds, and more, that the president and his military advisers asked for, allocating $3 billion to the armed forces in June, when in April legislators had been reluctant to even approve military expenditures of $853 million.[116] Amongst the mass public, support for compulsory military service also shot up, from 39 percent in October 1939 to 50 percent June 1940.[117] And if worst came to worst, and Germany did emerge triumphant in Europe, 88 percent of Americans wanted the United States to "arm to the teeth," while only 8 percent thought the United States could get along peacefully with the Third Reich.[118]

But should America do more? Should it seek to supply aid to those countries already fighting the Nazis? What about actually entering the war? In the eighteen months leading up to Pearl Harbor, these were the questions that sparked the vitriolic "great debate." On one side of this heated and often acrimonious exchange stood a significant minority of congressional, elite, and mass opinion, opposed to any steps that *might* result in American involvement in the war. Although most of these diehard isolationists were not overtly sympathetic to the Nazi cause, Roosevelt was constantly on the lookout for information that linked mainstream leaders, like Gerald P. Nye, Burton K. Wheeler, Charles Lindbergh, and Hamilton Fish, to out-and-out pro-Hitler extremists like the American Bund, the Silver Shirts, and Father Charles Coughlin.[119] He also thought that, at best, these figures were acting as a "transmission belt" for Nazi propagandists.[120] After all, isolationists were keen to stress that Germany posed no threat to the United States; they also espoused the view that communism was a far

POLL (JANUARY 1939–AUGUST 1940)

If a major foreign power actually threatened to take over any of the following countries by armed invasion, would you be willing to see the United States come to its rescue with armed forces?		Jan. 1939 (%)	Jan. 1940 (%)	Aug. 1940 (%)
Canada	Yes	73.1	74.2	87.8
	No	17.3	14.6	6.8
	Don't know	9.6	11.2	5.4
Hawaii	Yes	—	55.1	74.0
	No	—	25.3	12.5
	Don't know	—	19.6	13.5
The Philippines	Yes	46.3	54.0	62.5
	No	37.2	26.4	20.3
	Don't know	16.5	19.6	14.2
Mexico	Yes	43.0	54.5	76.5
	No	40.6	28.4	12.5
	Don't know	16.4	17.1	11.0
Brazil	Yes	27.1	36.8	54.7
	No	53.7	40.0	24.9
	Don't know	19.2	23.2	20.4
Bermuda	Yes	—	33.9	60.3
	No	—	39.9	19.1
	Don't know	—	26.2	20.6
Belgium	Yes	—	7.9	—
	No	—	72.5	—
	Don't know	—	19.6	—

Sources: Compiled from *Fortune*, undated, received by the White House, December 28, 1939, OF 857, FDRL; *Fortune* (August 1940) OF 3618, FDRL.

greater menace than Hitler and the Third Reich. More importantly, they refused even to accept the need for aiding Britain, since, in their opinion, this would not only denude the United States of vital equipment but would also drag the country directly into the conflict. Rather than getting involved in European squabbles, they advocated building up America's own defenses.[121] Some even pushed for a negotiated peace between the warring parties, regardless of either Hitler's past record in respecting agreements or the fact that this would ratify large territorial gains for Germany.[122]

Roosevelt, though, was increasingly aware that isolationists no longer dominated the political scene. During 1940, interventionist groups like the Committee to Defend America by Aiding the Allies (CDAAA), the Fight for Freedom Committee, and the "warhawks" of the Century Group also began to organize. Most remained in close contact with the administration and were employed by it to counter the main tenets of the isolationist

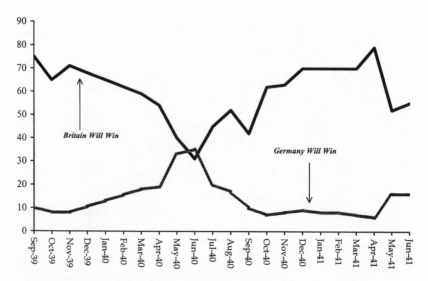

Who Will Win the War? U.S. Public Opinion, September 1939 to June 1941.

creed.[123] Their central claim was that the Nazis posed a direct threat to the United States, one that was certainly far more pressing than the specter of communism.[124] As a result, not only did they believe that a negotiated peace with the perfidious Hitler was out of the question but they also pushed vigorously for a policy of all aid to Britain.[125] Beyond that, however, there was less consensus. Some, like the CDAAA's chairman, William Allen White, only supported aid to Britain because they saw it was a way of keeping the United States out of the war, while others (most notably in the Fight for Freedom Committee after April 1941) wanted the United States to enter the conflict as a full belligerent.[126]

As this "great debate" unfolded, Roosevelt soon recognized that the sheer force of events was encouraging most Americans to adopt a moderate interventionist stance. Apart from a brief blip after news of the French armistice in June, most certainly remained remarkably optimistic that Britain would survive and prevail. Confident that arms sent to Britain would not simply end up in Hitler's hands, many also quickly abandoned their support of "impartial neutrality" Thus in September polls indicated that 62 percent of Americans favored supplying destroyers to Britain, while 56 percent supported sending more airplanes.[127]

This was the climate surrounding the 1940 presidential election campaign. Both candidates were essentially products of the international crisis. In Roosevelt's case, it enabled him to bypass the two-term tradition. In Willkie's, it propelled him from an unknown outsider, supported by only 3 percent of the population on May 7, to the GOP's nominee six weeks later, preferred to the inexperienced Dewey and the isolationist Taft.[128]

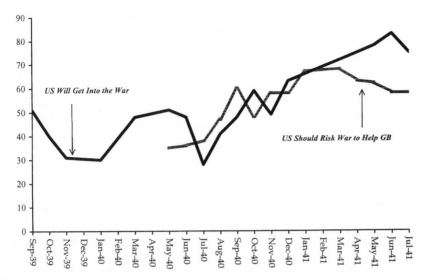

*Should the U.S. Risk War to Aid Britain? U.S. Public Opinion, September 1939
to July 1941. Both graphs compiled from, Cantril, worksheet, January 24, 1941;
"America Faces the War: The Reaction of Public Opinion," undated, both in
OF857, FDRL. Also Cantril to Rosenberg, April 18, 1941; "Analysis of Reasons for
Attitude Toward War," May 31, 1941; "Summary of American Public Opinion
Concerning the War, June 3, 1941, all in PPF1820, FDRL.*

Wendell Willkie began his bid for the presidency as an avowed interventionist, anxious to stress that he was "in agreement with many of the
basic international objectives of this administration at the present time."[129]
Detesting nazism and recognizing that a victory for the Third Reich would
place the United States in mortal danger, he initially attempted to distinguish himself from the incumbent only by charging that a Republican president would do a much better job of stimulating arms production, aiding
Britain, and forging a national consensus.[130] Unfortunately for Willkie,
however, such a message failed to dent Roosevelt's lead in the polls, and by
October the desperation of Republican party bosses was forcing him to
make a dramatic shift in emphasis. The last weeks of the campaign were
therefore marked by increasingly bitter and partisan charges, as Willkie
began to claim that Roosevelt's aid-to-Britain policy would mire the
United States in the conflict. "On the basis of his past performance with
pledges to the people," he declared on October 23, "if you re-elect him
you may expect war in April 1941."[131]

According to the polls, Americans seemed ready to accept this last
charge by a very small margin. In August, 28 percent thought the Republicans would keep the United States out of the war, compared to 26 percent
who believed the Democrats would. But by the same token, 39 percent also
felt the incumbent was better equipped to build up American defenses,

POLL (OCTOBER 1939–JULY 1940)

What should the U.S. do?	Oct. 1939 (%)		Dec. 1939 (%)		July 1940 (%)	
Enter the war at some stage	16.8	}36.7	17.2	}26.1	26.9	}67.5
Help the Allies, but don't enter the war	19.9		8.9		40.6	
Impartial neutrality—sell goods to both sides on a cash-and-carry basis	54.0		67.4		26.0	
Help Germany	0.1		0.2		0.2	
Other/Don't know	9.2		6.3		6.3	

Sources: Fortune (October 1939), PPF 1820, FDRL; Fortune (December 1939), attached to Yorke to Early, November 21, 1939, OF 3618, FDRL; ibid., June 21, 1940.

while only 26 percent supported Willkie on this issue.[132] Most voters were also far clearer about Roosevelt's policy preferences on the key foreign-policy issues.

With the electorate more confident in Roosevelt's ability to administer aid to Britain, with many in lower-income brackets still supporting the architect of the New Deal, and with some internationalists switching to the Democratic ticket and helping to offset the defection of Italian-, Irish-, and German-Americans who opposed the president's foreign-policy stance, FDR was reelected for an unprecedented third term in November.[133]

Buoyed by this fresh mandate, Roosevelt quickly turned his attention toward offering more concrete aid to Britain, secure in the knowledge that this policy enjoyed broad levels of support. In March, he obtained passage of the Lend-Lease Act, helped by Willkie who dismissed his previous jibes at the president as mere campaign rhetoric. Thereafter, the president recognized that most Americans endorsed extending aid to Britain, even if it meant risking war. He was also confident that there was little support for appeasing Hitler. As Cantril informed the White House in the summer of 1941, despite a peace drive by isolationists, only 38 percent supported negotiations, while 50 percent now rejected the idea out of hand.[134]

With the war clearly starting to assume global proportions, FDR was increasingly heartened by the fact that most Americans seemed to share his sense of priorities. This was particularly true after Germany's invasion of Russia, when neither the media nor the mass public seemed tempted to support Hitler's anticommunist crusade, despite the anti-Soviet rumblings emanating from many isolationist quarters. According to Cantril, although there was little enthusiasm as yet for sending U.S. materiel to the Russians, 73 percent of those polled did favor a Soviet victory (a figure that only

POLL (1940 ELECTION)

Which of these things do you think Roosevelt will favor, and which do you think Willkie will favor?	Will favor (%)	Will not favor (%)	Don't know (%)
Selling naval vessels to Britain			
Roosevelt	82.0	3.7	14.3
Willkie	42.3	11.7	46.0
Beginning compulsory military training			
Roosevelt	91.2	1.4	7.4
Willkie	47.1	9.1	43.8
Not letting any South American country establish a pro-Hitler government			
Roosevelt	83.9	4.3	11.8
Willkie	65.2	3.7	31.1

Source: *Fortune*, undated, PPF 5437, FDRL.

dropped to 65 percent among Catholics), while a mere 4 percent wanted Germany to win.[135]

Equally pleasing was the fact that most Americans seemed to endorse Roosevelt's view that Japanese posed a distinctly secondary threat. True, since 1932 the American press had universally denounced Japanese actions in Manchuria, and since the outbreak of the Sino-Japanese war in 1937 a clear majority of mass opinion had expressed sympathy for the Chinese cause. When prodded by pollsters, most respondents had also advocated stiff action to halt and contain Japanese aggression, supporting measures like sanctions or an arms embargo by large margins.[136] But at the same time, the public's desire for action in Asia did not run very deep. As early as 1938, while war raged in China but Europe remained precariously at peace, popular attention remained fixated on the Czech crisis and the Nazi persecution of the Jews. In a poll of the most interesting news stories of that year, these two European events clearly came out on top, with the struggle between China and Japan relegated to ninth place, behind the World Series and a New England hurricane.[137] Thereafter the media, while lavishing column space and editorial judgments on the dramatic and newsworthy stories flooding in from Europe, tended to treat the Sino-Japanese war as a distant sideshow, of little direct importance to American security. Even as late as July 1941, Barth reported that the press was failing to take Japan seriously. "The prevailing editorial judgment," he concluded, "is that four years of warfare has exhausted the Japanese, undermined their economy, and revealed them as a second-rate power. . . . A great many commentators cherish the conviction that the American Pacific fleet would polish off Japanese sea power between daybreak and breakfast—with the Atlantic fleet tied behind its back, at that." Nor did the mass public seem overly concerned with events in Asia. In one poll conducted during December 1940, Cantril found that 45 percent of respondents had no idea where Singapore was, while 41 percent had no opinion when asked the simple factual question of whether Japanese seizure of the Dutch East Indies would greatly improve its oil supply position.[138]

With America's gaze directed firmly toward Europe, in the months leading up to Pearl Harbor there was certainly no clamor for U.S. resources to be directed toward containing, controlling, or defeating the Japanese. Nor was there any real support for doing more in Europe than extending aid to those fighting Hitler. Even in 1941, with Britain suffering a series of reverses in the Mediterranean, the public retained an overwhelming confidence, verging on complacency, that Britain would ultimately prevail on its own.

Indeed, to many Americans the danger still seemed so remote that they saw no need to make any real sacrifices. Most certainly refused to believe that it was necessary to get directly involved in the fighting. As Cantril found in January, only 14 percent of the public said they would vote for a declaration of war. This figure then edged up slowly to 22 percent in April and to 29 percent in June, but it only ever remained less than a third of the total.[139] Small wonder, then, that the president told the British ambassador the following October that "his perpetual problem was to steer a course between the two factors represented by: (1) The wish of 70 percent of Americans to keep out of [the] war; (2) The wish of 70 percent of Americans to do everything to break Hitler, even if it means war."[140] Put another way, FDR clearly recognized that Americans were now prepared to help Britain, whatever the risks. But he also knew that they remained adamantly opposed to a direct, unlimited, and formal involvement in the conflict.

It remains to be seen how the president reacted to this situation. What attempts did he make to mould popular opinion and to what extent did these mass attitudes wield a decisive influence over policy outcomes during this period?

Cautious in Deed: FDR, Public Opinion, and Nazi Germany before Pearl Harbor

Faced with a public that did not really comprehend what was going on overseas, Roosevelt privately admitted that he was "in the midst of the long process of education," attempting "slowly but surely" to jog the American people out of their lack of concern with foreign affairs.[141] To accomplish this difficult and thankless task, he had at his disposal a variety of opinion-persuading channels. Since the very start of his presidency, FDR had been holding regular press conferences. Every Tuesday and Friday about a hundred reporters would cram so tightly into the Oval Office that some had to squeeze up close to the president's cluttered desk. Roosevelt always strove to create a relaxed and easygoing atmosphere in these sessions. Before the conference officially began, he would engage in small talk and banter with journalists. On the signal "all in," the president would sit back in his chair, cigarette holder clenched between his teeth, and wait for the interrogation to start. Having abolished the old convention of formal written questions, which had made many of his predecessors' press conferences dull and predictable affairs, FDR could in theory be quizzed on almost any matter. But he was rarely caught unprepared or off guard. Before each conference, his press secretary, Stephen T. Early, himself a highly experienced newspaperman, thoroughly briefed the president on possible lines of inquiry; occasionally, Early even went as far as to plant questions with friendly journalists. More often than not, Roosevelt would then try to set the agenda by announcing a breaking news story. Journalists would be handed a press release, which clearly staked out the government's position, while FDR went on to place his own particular spin on the issue, normally peppering his comments with tips on how it could best be written up. Once the questioning was underway, the president proved himself a master at evading sensitive or thorny matters, sometimes refusing to speculate on "iffy" questions, sometimes professing not to have read the relevant documents, and sometimes cracking a timely joke that distracted everyone's attention.[142]

Although Roosevelt kept a tight rein over his press conferences, reporters continued to flock to these sessions in droves. Some may have suspected that they were being skillfully used by the president to propagate the administration's message, but the vast majority appreciated the fact that, as FDR put it, they were "welcomed as gentlemen, not suspected as spies." Journalists also recognized the obvious news value of these conferences. Not only was each meeting shrewdly scheduled to cater for newspaper deadlines, but the president invariably went out of his way to explain complex issues and policies in simple, straightforward language that made great copy. And then there was Roosevelt's charisma. Even after two terms of office, the president could still put on the greatest show in town; as one top editor told him in 1939, "for box office attraction you leave Clark Gable gasping for breath."[143]

Opinion makers also appreciated the other, less visible, White House innovations. Every morning, Steve Early met with reporters to inform them of the president's schedule and to forewarn them of stories that were likely to break that day. Early also had a wire service telegram machine installed in his office so he could monitor the earliest press service reports and then step in to correct falsehoods and respond to criticisms. And when there were no major news stories on the horizon, Early's office made sure that it had numerous smaller items on hand that journalists could use to fill up column space.[144]

A presidential press conference, 1939.

The president, meanwhile, intermittently sought to establish more informal relationships with key media figures. From time to time, he would correspond or meet up with influential publishers, such as the Arthur Sulzberger of the *New York Times* or Eugene Meyer of the *Washington Post*. On other occasions, he would invite columnists like Arthur Krock, Anne O'Hare McCormick, and Walter Winchell to the White House or Hyde Park, where he would provide them with an exclusive interview—much to the chagrin of the rest of the press corps. FDR's goal was to try to convert these top opinion makers into consistent administration supporters, but he was not always successful. Krock, for instance, continued to pursue a fiercely independent line, much to the consternation of the president who by 1940 was referring to him as someone who "never in his whole life said a really decent thing about a human being without qualifying it by some nasty dig."[145]

As this comment suggests, despite all his attempts to influence the media's output, Roosevelt never lost his deep-seated distrust of the press —his firm conviction that the vast majority of publishers, editors, and columnists were out to get both him and the New Deal. Only by speaking directly to the American people did he believe it was truly possible to bypass this perceived bias—"give them all the facts," he once said to an aide,

Steve Early and FDR, 1941.

"and I would rather much trust the judgment of 130,000,000 Americans than I would that of any artificially selected few."[146] In an average year, the president therefore made between three and four informal "fireside chats," delivered a couple of addresses to Congress (including the annual state of the union message), and also spoke before a host of smaller and more specialized audiences in Washington and across the country. About twenty-five of these would be broadcast directly to the nation.[147]

Before each speech, Roosevelt and his aides would collect a wealth of information, from polls to press clippings and letters, on the various subjects to be tackled. By 1940, the president generally relied on three men to sort through these and fashion them into a rough draft: Samuel I. Rosenman, a New York state judge who had worked for FDR since the late 1920s; Robert E. Sherwood, the staunchly pro-interventionist playwright; and Harry Hopkins, Roosevelt's closest confidant who lived and worked in the Lincoln Bedroom on the second floor of the White House. A few days before a keynote address, the three men would gather in the Cabinet Room adjacent to the president's Oval Office, using the large table to arrange the array of suggestions that had to be fitted into the text. Ten or more drafts would then go to the president for discussion, revision, and finally approval. Fortified by Coca-Cola, beer, and the odd glass of bourbon, the team would often work late into the night, carefully scrutinizing each phrase to ensure that it carried the desired message and hit the correct note. It was always the president, however, who had the final word. And it was frequently Roosevelt who would be responsible for the speech's most striking imagery or its more pungent passages.[148]

When it was time to deliver the speech, especially if it was a fireside chat, Roosevelt would be wheeled into the Diplomatic Reception Room on the ground floor of the White House. Seated behind a desk, surrounded by microphones, technicians, and guests, the president would then begin to speak in slow, measured tones, averaging about one hundred words a minute. By common consent, his versatile voice was ideally suited to the radio.[149] The public certainly flocked to their sets in huge numbers to listen to him. By the start of the 1940s there were 60 million radio receivers throughout the country, which meant that 90 percent of the American people could be reached directly in their homes.[150] Whenever Roosevelt took to the airwaves, more than two-thirds of households would huddle around their radios, anxious to hear the president's interpretation of the worsening international situation.

While there was no doubting that the charismatic president was the administration's star performer, Roosevelt never had the stage entirely to himself. To deal with the depression and now the international crisis, FDR had created a host of new government departments and agencies, and each one was anxious to disseminate its own particular message to the American public. Roosevelt quickly realized the dangers this presented, for if different factions within the administration began emitting discordant noises then this could easily drown out, confuse, or obscure his own carefully crafted message. In an attempt to minimize this risk, the White House decreed that all statistical data had to be released centrally. Increasingly, cabinet officials were also encouraged to clear major policy statements with Early's press office, while the president was always exceedingly anxious to plug unofficial leaks. On more than one occasion, he lectured his cabinet members on the dangers of discussing matters informally with the press; from time to time, he even gathered information on the social activities of subordinates in order to monitor the relationships they developed with reporters.[151] Behind the scenes, then, the Roosevelt administration may well have been an unwieldy amalgam of competing individuals and interests, but the president at least tried to ensure that it presented a fairly united front to the outside world.

In the years before Pearl Harbor, full of "dread that my talks should be so frequent as to lose their effectiveness," the president used these channels selectively, reserving them for two broad purposes.[152] On a variety of oc-

Ratings for FDR's Fireside Chats, 1941–42

Date	Subject	Homes Listening	% of Total Homes
5/27/1941	"National Emergency"	53,800,000	69.8
9/11/1941	"Freedom of the Seas"	50,100,000	67.0
12/9/1941	"War with Japan"	62,100,000	79.0
2/23/1942	"Fighting Defeatism"	61,365,000	78.1

Source: Hooper Ratings Chart, accession 42-102-22, FDRL; McIntyre to Hassett, March 16, 1942, OF857.

casions, he sought to mobilize opinion behind a specific initiative. This was particularly important because the practicalities of aiding a Britain lurching from crisis to crisis ran into one congressional hurdle after another, and FDR realized that legislators were more likely to support a particular policy if surveys and polls showed it to be widely popular. Thus, between September and October 1939 he made a concerted effort to sell neutrality revision so that weapons could be supplied to the democracies on a cash-and-carry basis. Then, from January to March 1941 he lobbied extensively on behalf of the Lend-Lease bill. And finally, in the fall of 1941 he again tried to garner popular support for neutrality revision, this time so that merchant boats could be armed.

Aware that events were the most powerful persuader of mass opinion, Roosevelt also periodically used fireside chats to drive home the full implications of any change in the external environment, so as to further erode the public's complacency about European developments. This was especially true in May and June 1940, when he sought to sharpen the growing fear that Germany might be able to threaten the United States. As he commented at the time, events have "at least . . . given me the opportunity to bring home the seriousness of the world situation to the type of American who has hitherto believed, in much too large numbers, that no matter what happens there will be little effect on this country."[153] This motive was also uppermost in his mind in September 1941, when he used news of the sinking of the USS *Greer* to denounce the Nazis for piracy on the high seas and to announce that the U.S. Navy would begin shooting German U-boats on sight.[154]

Prior to Pearl Harbor, the content of Roosevelt's public message was a complex synthesis, which partly reflected the president's private hopes and fears and partly responded to perceived public pressures, with the balance fluctuating over time. Until the fall of France, the prevailing isolationist mood made it difficult for FDR to engage in little more than the most cautious attempts at education. From time to time, he certainly endeavored to make Americans more aware that the globe was shrinking, that there was "a solidarity and interdependence" about the modern world, and that they could not simply "close all doors and windows" and ignore external developments. He also talked publicly about his concern over the growth of "deadly armaments," as well as the trend away "from the observance both of the letter and the spirit of treaties."[155] But, recognizing that Americans overwhelmingly opposed any entanglement in European affairs, the president was always careful to retain a public veneer of impartiality. Not once did he actually name the aggressors; instead, he only alluded to the fact that these tended to be "those nations where democracy has been discarded or has never developed."[156] Nor was he anxious to outline measures for dealing with these expansionist powers. Even after delivering his famous quarantine speech in October 1937, in which he spoke of peaceful nations coming together to tackle the "present reign of terror and international lawlessness," FDR was quick to describe this as an "attitude" not a program.[157] Just over a year later, having made the decision to supply airplanes to the democracies, he then went to great lengths to keep this secret, and even after the news crept out he refused to acknowledge directly that his policy was "to assist or facilitate France in buying planes in this country."[158] It was a similar story after war finally erupted in Europe. Although the president rejected Woodrow Wilson's example of twenty-five years earlier and failed to ask Americans to be neutral in thought, he nevertheless refused even to speculate on who was to blame for starting the war, indicating that this was best "left to the historians."[159]

Rather than go out on a limb in his set-piece public addresses, Roosevelt preferred to use more indirect channels to convey his own increasingly "un-neutral" thoughts. In off-the-record meetings with congressmen and reporters during 1939, the president made no bones about his opposition to nazism and his desire to support Britain and France. He also had no qualms about encouraging others to take on the burden of indicting the Nazis. Within the administration the most vocal opponents of Hitler were Harold L. Ickes, the pugnacious secretary of the interior, and Henry Morgenthau, Jr., the aggressive if somewhat inarticulate secretary of the treasury. Both were anxious to inform the public of the Nazi danger. Sometimes they even went too far; on one occasion toward the end of 1938, for instance, Ickes caused a minor diplomatic incident when he made a particularly bitter denunciation of Hitler's ideas and methods.[160]

As soon as the war started, the White House also began to encourage other prominent opinion makers to take up the fight against neutrality. The president, anxious for bipartisan support, was especially keen to forge tacit alliances with key Republicans, such as Henry L. Stimson, Frank Knox, and William Allen White. Not only did he keep in touch with such figures, encouraging them to make aggressive speeches and then praising their efforts, but in June 1940 he also appointed Stimson and Knox to the positions of secretary of war and the navy, in a bold attempt to boost the bipartisan and interventionist image of his cabinet.[161]

Roosevelt was playing a typically complex and subtle game. Publicly, his stance was exceedingly cautious. In all his main speeches he was careful to avoid "scaring the American people into thinking that they are going to be dragged into the war."[162] But behind the scenes the president was certainly not idle. Instead, he increasingly went to great lengths to encourage other opinion makers to say and do things that were thought too controversial to emanate directly from the White House.[163]

It was not until the turbulent months of May and June 1940, with Hitler's stunning victories in Europe suddenly making FDR's bid for a third term feasible, that the president's own speeches suddenly became somewhat bolder. Both these developments certainly gave Roosevelt the opportunity and motive to heighten the public's concern about the war, for if Americans became convinced that they needed an experienced leader to see them through this crisis, then his reelection chances would undoubtedly grow. The president was therefore quick to start talking about the implications of the German victory, pointing out on May 26 that "the past two weeks have meant the shattering of many illusions," especially to those who thought the United States was safe behind its Atlantic barrier. Not only was it now possible for air power to strike quickly across this body of water, but, if democracies continued to perish then America might soon be in the position of a prisoner who, in FDR's words, is "handcuffed, hungry, and fed through bars from day to day by contemptuous unpitying masters."[164]

Roosevelt also avidly seized on the new lines of argument to deploy against his political opponents. Back in the early 1930s, he had often lumped Republicans together with "economic royalists," blaming both for the advent of the depression. Now he sought to equate isolationist Republicans with fifth columnists and appeasers. Republicans, he insisted on May 16, 1940, had the same leadership record "of timidity, of weakness, of short-sightedness that governed the policy of the confused, reactionary governments in France and England before the war."[165]

Yet even now, Roosevelt's cautious instincts were never far from the surface. Throughout the summer and fall he still habitually refused to name the offending aggressors. Of course, it was never difficult to recognize the aggressive dictatorial threat that FDR constantly referred to. But before December 29, 1940, he only employed the term *Nazi* on five occasions, and two of these were in a speech on October 26, 1939, that dealt with the New Deal's internal opponents. Essentially, this caution stemmed from electoral concerns, especially the fact that the Italian-American community had reacted angrily when on June 10 the president had fiercely attacked Mussolini for his cowardly invasion of France. Although FDR had been elated by this speech, relieved that "for once" he had been able to state "what was really on his mind," he was also aware that if such candor was extended to the Führer he could well alienate another bloc of voters. Unwilling to take such a risk before November, he persisted with his strategy of not naming the enemy.[166]

As the presidential campaign started to heat up after Labor Day, Willkie's dramatic claim that Roosevelt would soon lead the country into war also forced the president to tailor his public message to electoral needs. In the first weeks of the campaign, Roosevelt was reluctant to enter the fray, preferring to cultivate the image of an elder statesman preoccupied with weighty matters of defense and security. By the start of October, however, as Willkie's charges became more extravagant and his polling figures improved, the president decided it was time to take to the stump. He began by lambasting his political opponents for importing "certain propaganda techniques, created and developed in dictator countries," into the current campaign—including the constant repetition of falsehoods. In the eyes of Democratic party bosses, Willkie's depiction of FDR as a "warmonger" was the biggest "falsehood" of all; they also worried that this charge might be disastrous to the president's election chances. In complete agreement, FDR decided to respond. On a number of occasions, he had already repeatedly pledged to keep the United States out of the war, but always with the caveat "except in case of attack." Just days before the election, he decided to omit this important qualification. "Your boys," he starkly and (in)famously told a large audience in Boston on October 30, "are not going to be sent into any foreign wars."[167]

The president continued to repeat this pledge even after he secured re-election. "Our national policy is not directed toward war," he maintained toward the end of December. "Its sole purpose is to keep war away from our country and our people." With the election safely behind him, however, Roosevelt felt freer to abandon some of his old circumspection. With Britain in desperate need for more concrete aid, he also thought the situation demanded a far more forthright and aggressive statement of the danger posed by the Nazis. On December 29, 1940, the very evening that London endured one of its worst bombing raids, FDR launched into his first direct and sustained public attack on the Third Reich in a dramatic fireside chat. "The Nazi masters of Germany," he declared, "have made it clear that they intend not only to dominate all life and thought in their own country, but also to enslave the whole of Europe, and then use the resources of Europe to dominate the world." Negotiating with such a danger was patently pointless. "The experience of the past two years," he continued, "has proven beyond doubt that no nation can appease Nazis. No man can tame a tiger into a kitten by stroking it. There can be no appeasement with ruthlessness. There can be no reasoning with an incendiary bomb. We know now that a nation can have peace with the Nazis only at the price of total surrender."[168]

As the "great debate" reached its pitch, Roosevelt was not slow to encourage other opinion makers to support his efforts. Close links were forged with interventionist pressure groups, such as the CDAAA, the Century Group, and the Council for Democracy. Influential columnists, including Dorothy Thompson and Walter Winchell, also helped out with the preparation of administration speeches or acted as "semi-official" government spokespersons. In December 1940, the North American Newspaper Alliance even offered the White House a column that could be used to rally support for its foreign policy. Inside the administration, the deeply cautious State Department also started to join in the chorus of disapproval against the Third Reich. Until the end of 1940, Cordell Hull had consistently refused to aggressively lash out against the dictators and had often attempted to tone down the utterances of other officials. During 1941, however, Hull finally started to speak out, both in a series of addresses and in testimony before Congress in support of Lend-Lease and Neutrality revision.[169]

The message enunciated through all these channels was simple: Hitler and the Nazis posed a clear and immediate danger to U.S. security. During the course of 1941 FDR mentioned Hitler and the Nazis by name on more than 150 occasions. He also left his audience in little doubt that the Third Reich was qualitatively different from any other danger that Americans faced. "Although Prussian autocracy was bad enough," he declared in the spring, "nazi-ism is far worse. Nazi forces are not seeking mere modifications in colonial maps or in minor European boundaries. They openly seek the destruction of all elective systems of government on every continent—including our own; they seek to establish systems of government based on the regimentation of all human beings by a handful of individual rulers who have seized power by force."[170]

By contrast, Roosevelt only made four references to Japan in the eleven months leading up to Pearl Harbor, largely because he did not want the public's attention to be diverted away from Europe. And even after September 1940, when Germany, Italy, and Japan tightened their relationship by signing the Tripartite Pact, the president only deployed the term *Axis* very sparingly.

But how to eradicate this Nazi menace? From June 1940, the president began to make it clear that the United States would use its productive capacity to supply Britain with the tools for fighting Germany. America, he famously declared, would become the "arsenal of democracy."[171] Yet such claims continued to arouse isolationist suspicions that methods short of war would be insufficient and that FDR's real aim was to get the United States directly involved in the fighting. In response, Roosevelt went out of his way to emphasize his private hope that nazism might simply implode of its own vulnerabilities. "The spiritually unconquered," he declared in a nationwide broadcast on May 27, not only "Austrians, Czechs, Poles, Norwegians, Dutch, Frenchmen, Greeks, Southern Slavs," but "even those Italians and Germans who themselves have been enslaved . . . will prove to be a powerful force in the final disruption of the Nazi system."[172] The Allies, he stressed five months later, would not have to defeat the Third Reich militarily; containing it would be enough "because dictatorship of the Hitler type can live only through continuing victories and increasing conquests. The facts of the year 1918 are proof that a mighty German army

Who Is the Enemy? A Quantitative Content Analysis of FDR's Speeches, 1937–1941

	2H 1937	1H 1938	2H 1938	1H 1939	2H 1939	1H 1940	2H 1940	1H 1941	2H 1941
Unnamed/ dictatorship	2	2	6	4	4	16	24	31	7
Hitler/Nazism	—	—	—	—	2	—	13	42	110
German(y)/ German people	—	—	—	—	—	—	7	19	16
Mussolini/Fascist/ Italian govt.	—	2	2	—	2	9	1	—	1
Italy/Italian people	.	—	—	—	—	—	1	—	—
Japanese govt.	2	—	—	—	—	—	—	—	—
Japan/Japanese people	—	—	—	—	—	1	—	—	4
Axis	—	—	—	—	—	—	11	5	7

Source: Compiled from FDR, *Public Papers*, vols. 6–10.

Notes: This table is compiled only from FDR's speeches and addresses; his remarks in press conferences and before congressional leaders have not been included.

"Unnamed/Dictatorship" category includes references to an unspecified enemy: i.e., "nations" engaged in international lawlessness (October 5, 1937); "the new philosophies of force" (January 4, 1939); "anti-Christian forces" (October 28, 1940); and the "mighty forces of aggression" (October 25, 1941).

The "Germany" category does not include references to Germany as a geographic location, (i.e., when something was happening "inside Germany"), nor does it include those instances when the Nazi regime is distinguished from the German people (i.e., "the Nazi masters of Germany" [December 29, 1940] is only counted under Nazism).

and tired German people can crumble rapidly and go to pieces when they are faced with successful resistance."[173]

By the fall of 1941, both in order to jog the American people out of their complacency and to mobilize support for particular policies, Roosevelt had therefore developed a public message that not only stressed the expansionist, perfidious, and brutal nature of the Nazi regime, but also pointed to its internal fragility. By doing so, the president had not engaged in a vigorous crusade, which aimed to manipulate public opinion by over-selling the danger. Nor had he "unwittingly" cultivated the impression that only the Nazis—and not the mass of Germans—were to blame.[174] Far from it. To start with, convinced that attempts at education had to be sporadic, concerned before May 1940 about scaring "the American people into thinking that they will be dragged into the war," and anxious before the election not to further alienate the German-American community, Roosevelt had been persistently cautious in his public utterances. Only after external events had helped to shift the basic contours of the popular mood, as they increasingly did after the fall of France, and only after electoral concerns had not become so pressing, did he abandon such prudence. But even then, FDR neither exaggerated nor masked the extent of the danger; rather, by 1941 he was at last making public the private fears and hopes he had long entertained about the menace posed by Hitler and his cohorts.

But what about the other side of the equation? What role did public opinion play in determining policy during this period? As we have seen, Roosevelt was not simply an ardent Germanophobe who had long wanted to use America's full strength to defeat this inherently aggressive threat and had only been restrained from doing so by a more prudent and pacific public.[175] Instead, for much of the period up to September 1941 both the president and the public remained generally hopeful that measures short of war would be sufficient to defeat the Third Reich, and as a result the domestic environment only played a role at the margins. It was not until the fall of 1941, when FDR's fears started to grow but most Americans remained opposed to full and formal involvement in the war, that public opinion began to have a decisive impact on the most important policy question of the period: should the United States fully and formally enter the war?

By this stage, hardly any of the president's national security advisers were opposed to American belligerency in Europe. Gone were the old struggles between the army and navy over whether Germany or Japan presented the greatest threat. Largely absent, too, was the bureaucratic chaos that seemed to mark so many other areas of policy making in the Roosevelt administration. In fact, whereas FDR normally sought to divide and rule —shunning a neat hierarchical bureaucratic structure in which each agency and individual had a clearly delineated function and preferring instead to give the same task to competing bodies—in this "decision-making universe" the lines of authority were relatively clear. In September 1939, FDR had placed the Joint Board under his direct authority in the Executive Office, giving him the chance to monitor and control the activities of army and navy planners.[176] As the international crisis deepened, he then began to meet regularly and informally with the navy top brass, largely because he wanted to keep a close eye on fleet deployments as the Battle of the Atlantic started to unfold. Although his relations with the army were always more distant and less relaxed, the president increasingly came to admire both Henry Stimson, the aging but highly experienced secretary of war, and George C. Marshall, the cold and somewhat aloof chief of staff. More and more, he also relied on Harry Hopkins, his closest adviser, as a conduit to the military to convey messages, iron out misunderstandings, and coordinate the proliferating problems with strategy and supply.[177]

By 1941 all these officials agreed that Germany was the main enemy and that to beat it would, in Marshall's words, "evidently" require "large ground forces." As early as November 1940, Harold Stark, the chief of naval operations, had stressed in his famous "Plan Dog" memorandum that Germany could only be defeated by "military successes on shore, facilitated possibly by over-extension and by internal antagonisms developed by the Axis's conquests." "Alone," he concluded, "the British Empire lacks the man power and the material means to master Germany." It was a point endorsed the following September by the Joint Board planners. "Germany and her European satellites can not be defeated by the European powers fighting against her," they insisted. "Therefore, if our European enemies are to be defeated, it will be necessary for the United States to enter the war, and to employ a part of its armed forces offensively in the Eastern Atlantic, in Europe, or Africa."[178]

America's two "quasi-Allies" wholeheartedly concurred. From the start of his premiership, Winston Churchill's strategy for victory had rested firmly on the hope that the United States would enter the war. During 1941, as the cords that bound Britain and America became "thicker, more tangled, and more secure"—with the proliferation of correspondence between prime minister and president, Harry Hopkins visiting London to discern the condition and needs of the island kingdom, and the two leaders consummating their budding relationship by meeting at Placentia Bay—Churchill became ever more ardent in his calls for American belligerency. In August, he even warned Roosevelt that if by the spring of 1942 the United States had still not entered the war and the Soviets had been compelled to sue for peace, then hope would undoubtedly die in Britain and he "would not answer for the consequences."

Signals emanating from Moscow were equally disturbing. In August, the president sent Hopkins to the U.S.S.R. to assess its chances for survival. Although he was deeply relieved by Hopkins's conclusion that the Soviets would survive the German onslaught, within weeks this optimism seemed somewhat misplaced. With the Wehrmacht pushing ever deeper into Soviet territory, capturing Smolensk and Kiev and menacing Leningrad and Moscow, Stalin was soon making the first of his many requests for a second front. In evident desperation, the Soviet leader even began to emit strong hints that the U.S.S.R. would make peace unless America entered the war and the British launched an invasion of Western Europe.[179]

The president was therefore under pressure from both advisers and allies to plunge America directly into the war. Given his own mounting fears, it also seems likely that had Roosevelt been free to act he would probably have favored a balanced response to the Nazi danger, based primarily on the use of U.S. land power and only supported by bombing, blockade, and psychological warfare. After all, with the Wehrmacht marching from success to success, it seemed increasingly difficult either to maintain that Germany would be thwarted by Britain and the U.S.S.R. or to insist that it might collapse of its own accord. Nor was FDR fundamentally opposed to war or the deployment of American ground troops overseas.

Yet between September and December 1941 the president was not willing to act on either his own preferences or the demands of his aides and allies. In July, he instructed Hopkins before his trip to Britain and the U.S.S.R. that there should be "no talk about war." Then in November, when asked by the press whether the time had come to end diplomatic relations with Germany, he responded that "we don't want a declared war with Germany because we are acting in defense—self-defense."[180]

What is more, for all his desire after December 7 to get U.S. troops quickly involved in the action, during the second half of 1941 Roosevelt's musings were constantly skewed in favor of lesser means of defeating Hitler. In the summer, Hopkins recorded that FDR was increasingly "a believer in bombing as the only means of gaining victory." The president, as Morgenthau discovered, seemed convinced that if the British "sent a hundred planes over Germany for military objectives that ten of them should bomb some of the smaller towns that have never been bombed before." "That," he stressed, "is the only way to break the German morale."[181]

On a host of other occasions during 1941, Roosevelt also intimated that propaganda and psychological warfare would play a vital role in undermining the Nazis' fragile rule. Thus, he not only prodded his officials to devise ways of getting more news broadcast to occupied Europe, but also created the Office of Coordinator of Information in order to initiate "an effective psychological attack . . . against the Axis." Just days after the German invasion of the U.S.S.R., he then sent a questionnaire "to all Consuls who have been thrown out of Axis or Axis-occupied territories," asking them to report on prospective "means for lowering morale," "times when bombing would be most effective," the state of food supplies and housing, the effectiveness of British propaganda, and the "vulnerability of Party and leaders and means for taking advantage thereof."[182] Apparently confident that such measures would be sufficient on their own, in September Roosevelt briefly contemplated *reducing* the size of the U.S. Army.[183] That same month, he even told Stimson that an official Allied decision to invade and crush Germany would be counterproductive, since this would harden the German people's support for their regime and thereby clash with the logic underpinning the use of bombing and psychological warfare.[184]

Why was Roosevelt still so reluctant to enter the war formally and so willing to express confidence in means short of direct involvement? Such assertions of optimism were certainly not congruent with the desires of military advisers and alliance partners; increasingly, they did not even reflect the president's own perception of the international environment. Instead, FDR's caution stemmed partly from America's patent lack of preparedness and partly from pressing domestic constraints.

In stark contrast to Hitler's Germany, which had been rearming since 1933, the United States had only seriously started to build up its military forces after the shock of the French collapse. Much progress had been made in the intervening months, but by the fall of 1941 Roosevelt was only too aware that the United States lacked the men and materiel to make a decisive difference on the battlefield any time soon. Not only was a mere 15 percent of the nation's industrial capacity devoted to defense, but the shipping shortage was so acute that war planners estimated that there was only enough capacity to move fifty thousand men with their supplies and equipment to an overseas theater. The U.S. Army was also small and untrained. Whereas Hitler had launched 149 battle-hardened divisions against the Soviet Union in June, Roosevelt could only expect to have 20 divisions ready by the end of the year. Given the many competing demands on U.S. resources, from sending aid to Britain and the U.S.S.R. to deterring the looming Japanese threat in the Pacific, it was hardly surprising that, in the words of one top official, the president believed "he simply did not have enough butter to cover the bread."[185]

America was also mentally unprepared to enter the war, and this was probably the decisive reason for the president's caution in 1941. Isolationist groups, although in a steadily declining minority, remained vociferously opposed to any additional involvement in the conflict. As Roosevelt recognized, if he came out in favor of full belligerency he would undoubtedly face a stubborn and well-organized minority determined to undermine domestic unity at a time when harmony was vital for a successful war effort. The president also realized that the mass public was opposed to the deployment of troops abroad unless the United States was directly attacked. As early as November 1938 he had remarked that sending a large army abroad was "politically out of the question"; a year later he was again worried about increasing troop levels because the public would not accept a large rise "without undue excitement."[186] After November 1940, Roosevelt's caution on this point was dramatically reinforced by his categorical pledge not to send U.S. troops abroad. It was probably heightened, too, by the discontent emerging from the military training camps, where the poor morale of the new recruits was increasingly filtering into newspaper articles and legislative debates.[187]

But above all, Roosevelt still could not escape the stark reality that there was little popular support for America's formal involvement in the conflict. Any declaration of war would have to go before a Congress that in August only authorized an extension of the military draft by one vote and in November only narrowly revised the Neutrality Act.[188] And legislators were hardly likely to vote for a declaration at a time when opinion polls demonstrated that less than a third of the populace supported such a course. Small wonder, then, that FDR continually alluded to the fact that "the American people as a whole desire now to remain out of the war."[189] As he remarked to Lord Halifax in October, even "if he asked for a declaration of war he wouldn't get it, and opinion would swing against him. He therefore intended to go on doing whatever he best could to help us," believing that "declarations of war were . . . out of fashion."[190]

Aware that without a dramatic threat to U.S. security public opinion was fundamentally averse to both a formal declaration of war and the deployment of ground troops abroad, Roosevelt believed it impossible to push for such a course. In the fall of 1941, this overwhelming popular opposition also encouraged FDR to overemphasize his hopes at a time when such optimism was being profoundly shaken by the Wehrmacht's continued victories. After all, it was far easier to stress that bombing, psychological warfare, and the use of proxies would defeat the fragile Third Reich when the alternative — the direct and unlimited involvement of the US in the European war — was unacceptable to a majority of mass and congressional opinion.

From September to December 1941, public opinion therefore acted as an important constraint when it came to the final policy choice of taking America into the war. Indeed, in these anxious and frustrating months, FDR still felt it would take at least one more dramatic incident to change the popular mood and enable him to lead a united and determined America into the war.

The president did not have long to wait.

2

America's
Phony War

Reports from many points indicate a growing parallel between the attitude of the American public today toward the war and the attitude of the French public in 1939. The French knew they were at war and theoretically realized that an all out effort was necessary, but the war was something on the other side of the Maginot Line. The American public is losing its first up-surge of feeling after Pearl Harbor, and increasingly thinks of the war as something on the other side of the Atlantic and Pacific Oceans. Long-term educational programs should correct this, but in the meantime specific steps should be taken from time to time to overcome the apathy in plants and elsewhere.

—Committee of War Information
Meeting, January 19, 1942

The first Japanese planes swooped in low over Pearl Harbor shortly after 7:30 A.M., local time. Within minutes bombs and torpedoes were raining down on American battleships, cruisers, and destroyers, as they sat inert and largely defenseless, moored so closely together that they offered the most inviting of targets. By the time the attack was over, the carnage left by the Japanese was appalling: eighteen U.S. naval vessels had been sunk or severely damaged, 180 aircraft had been destroyed, and 2,403 men lay dead with another 1,178 wounded. By any standards it was a disaster of the first magnitude.

Franklin Roosevelt was eating a quiet lunch at his desk with Harry Hopkins when he first heard the news. For the past few days the atmosphere in the White House had been tense, as officials anxiously awaited word of the next developments, not just in Asia where the Japanese seemed poised to make a decisive move, but also in Russia where the Germans were closing in on Moscow. Now the waiting was over. With Stalin having just launched a desperate defensive counterstroke on the outskirts of Moscow, the Japanese had—in the most brazen, violent, and unexpected of fashions—finally ended all the uncertainty in Asia.

On hearing word of the Japanese attack, the White House immediately erupted into a frenzy of frenetic activity. Aides hurried to and fro, clutching the latest dispatches. Cabinet officers and congressional leaders descended on the Executive Mansion, desperate for the most up-to-date information. Everyone seemed nervous and agitated—everyone, that is, except the president. As he sat quietly at his desk trying to come to terms with the scale of the disaster, Roosevelt's mood was a complex blend of horror and relief—horror that the navy had been so disastrously "caught unawares," but relief that at long last the momentous decision of whether or not the United States should enter the war had been made for him. Torn between these conflicting emotions, FDR called Steve Early and calmly dictated a statement informing the American people of the attack. He wanted it released immediately.[1]

The news quickly filtered out. Soon radio stations were hastening to interrupt their scheduled broadcasts, journalists were frantically preparing special editions, and Americans across the nation were hurrying to inform each other of the first sketchy details of the attack. Everywhere the first reaction was one of stunned shock, but soon this gave way to a mood of angry determination. Within days, a survey by *Time*, *Life*, and *Fortune* found an America "deeply resentful of the treachery. Vengeance-bent, confident of victory, dazzled by cataclysm," the nation now demanded war, with "little second thought yet of the cost."[2]

Even former isolationists shared this view. In Congress, all but one voted for declarations of war against Japan, Germany, and Italy, while the Republican leadership pledged to support the war effort and offered to adjourn politics "for the duration." Outside the capital, the America First organization disbanded four days after Pearl Harbor, and one of its most prominent members, Charles Lindbergh, privately conceded that he could "see nothing to do under the circumstances except to fight." "If I had been in Congress," he continued, "I certainly would have voted for a declaration of war."[3] Summarizing the abrupt change in mood, Alan Barth noted that "commentators of all political hues are in agreement that the first Japanese bomb dropped upon Hawaii wrought suddenly the miracle which no amount of logic or persuasion had previously been able to achieve." Isolationism, he therefore believed, "was the initial casualty of the war."[4]

Although the public now seemed united behind the war effort, the president's public opinion problems were by no means over. Pearl Harbor had undoubtedly generated widespread support for full and formal in-

volvement in the war, but it had also diverted the public's gaze toward
Asia; all of a sudden Japan, not Germany, seemed to be the number one
enemy. Moreover, when it came to the European conflict, many Americans
still seemed to be afflicted by a "Maginot mentality"—a defensive mindset
underpinned by a complacent optimism that the war could be easily won.[5]
According to some surveys, there even appeared to be a worrying ignorance about the true nature of the Nazi enemy and the threat it posed to the
United States. This chapter focuses on one dimension of the government's
response to these problems: the information campaign it designed to
counter these moods by educating the populace about the danger posed by
Hitler's Germany.

Public Opinion and Nazi Germany, December 1941 to June 1942

With the United States formally and fully in the war, Roosevelt was more
determined than ever to monitor mass attitudes. In January, he expressed
delight when the head of the OFF, Archibald MacLeish, sent him opinion
surveys, and within weeks he was even requesting copies of all the bureau's
main reports. According to one official, OFF data were so valued at the
White House because it was "based on what was regarded as the best available information about the thinking of the American people."[6]

At the outset, at least, these surveys confirmed that Pearl Harbor had
removed the one major constraint that had shackled the president during
the second half of 1941. "An overwhelming majority of the press," the
OFF concluded in January, now "accepted the prospect of an American
Expeditionary Force (AEF) as wise and necessary." "In the press as a
whole," Barth declared a few weeks later, "the defensive psychology
which prevailed before Pearl Harbor has now largely disappeared. There is
no longer a myopic watching of the ramparts . . . [but] a desire to strike the
enemy on his home ground."[7] Opinion polls reinforced these somewhat
vague musings. In March, 56 percent of Americans favored sending the
U.S. Army abroad, while only 36 percent opposed such a course. A month
later, in a survey of the "specific grievances" held by residents in five main
cities, the rural Midwest, and the rural South, "misgivings about AEF"
came fifth in a list of eight, behind anti-British, anti-Russian, and anti-labor
sentiment, and was a concern of only 23 percent in the cities, 23 percent in
the Midwest, and a mere 16 percent in the South.[8]

While most officials were naturally pleased by such findings, some
were concerned that these changing attitudes were merely a transitory phe-
nomenon. As early as December 29, the Committee of War Information
(CWI)—a body consisting of members from all main departments whose
task was to co-ordinate the administration's domestic propaganda efforts—
began to worry that the "emotional upsurge following Pearl Harbor will

not last forever." "There is [an] immediate danger," it fretted, "that the public will relapse into a defensive psychology."[9] The president agreed. Moving speedily to counter such a possibility, he proclaimed on January 6 that "we cannot wage this war in a defensive spirit." The United States had to keep the enemy "far from our shores," he told a congressional and national audience, "for we intend to bring this battle to him on his home grounds. American armed forces must be used at any place in all the world where it seems advisable to engage the forces of the enemy."[10]

For a growing number of Americans, the Pacific suddenly appeared to be the one place that U.S. troops were most needed. This calculation was based partly on a desire for vengeance after Japan's sneak attack on Hawaii. But increasingly it was also a reaction to the appalling series of defeats suffered by the Allies in the wake of Pearl Harbor. In the last weeks of 1941, Guam, Wake Island, and Hong Kong were all lost to the marauding Japanese, as were the two main pillars of British naval power in the region, the battleships *Prince of Wales* and *Repulse*. The New Year brought even worse news. In the middle of February, Singapore, the centerpiece of Britain's defenses in Southeast Asia, fell after only token resistance, rounding off what *Time* termed the "worst week of the century." In March, the situation deteriorated still further with the loss of Java and Rangoon, the latter threatening the supply route to Chiang Kai-shek's Nationalist government in China, while in May the Philippines finally succumbed when General Jonathan M. Wainwright capitulated on Bataan. The fate of ABDA, the command structure for the Americans, British, Dutch, and Australians in the region, symbolized the extent of the catastrophe. Formed on January 15, it was dissolved 40 days later in the midst of the apparently irrepressible Japanese advance.[11]

Stunned by this string of disasters, the media swiftly abandoned its previous neglect of the Pacific conflict. Between December and March, editorial coverage of the Japanese war began to far outweigh the interest shown in the conflict with Germany. Newspapers across the political spectrum also started to express the view that Japan rather than Germany offered the most immediate danger to the United States. Not only did formerly isolationist newspapers such as the *Chicago Tribune* now argue that "for the present, at least, our single war aim must be the crushing of the Japanese," "the principal and proximate enemy," but mainstream organs like the *New York Times* also believed that the Japanese drive had to be halted. Smaller newspapers, such as the *Denver Post*, chipped in too, with a racist rationale, asserting that "Japanese power must be destroyed so completely that the Pacific Ocean will be a white man's ocean from now on."[12]

At first glance, the mass public did not seem to share the press' conviction that Japan was the main enemy. In April, when pollsters asked a national sample who they considered to be the "number one enemy," 46 percent said Germany and only 35 percent said Japan. But, as the OFF quickly realized, initial impressions could easily mislead. Indeed, although a plu-

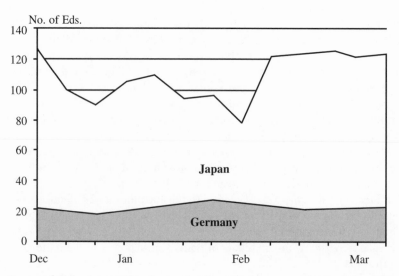

Survey of Editorial Opinion: Interest in War with Germany and Japan, December 1941 to March 1942. From Statistical Services, Report No. 96, March 11, 1942, Hopkins Papers, box 139, FDRL.

rality now thought that Germany was the main enemy, when the question was altered to the more important, Who should the United States concentrate on fighting? then there was a dramatic change in the result. On this issue, 62 percent believed the United States should focus on Japan, while only 21 percent wanted to direct men and materiel against Germany. Confusingly, then, more people viewed Germany as the main enemy, but most favored attacking "Asia first," largely because, as the OFF concluded, Americans looked upon Japan as the more immediate threat, and there was a hard core of racially motivated antipathy.[13]

To a president firmly convinced of the need to fight "Germany first," this was a disturbing development. But it was by no means the only problem he now faced. Accompanying the defeats on the battlefield was the reappearance of isolationist sentiment, or "divisionism," as the administration now liked to label it. In April, a concerned OFF began to note that "perhaps as much as one fifth of the American people, or approximately 17 million adults," were still willing to follow the lead of traditional "Roosevelt haters" like Hearst, McCormick, and Patterson. "It is no accident," it reported, "that this group is similar in composition, though not equal in size, to that portion of the population which, prior to American participation in the war, constituted the isolationist bloc."[14]

The administration employed the term *divisionist* "to designate all those persons who, from various motives and with varying degrees of intensity, oppose and obstruct" the prosecution of the war against the Axis.[15] Although a far smaller group than the isolationists of 1940 and 1941, offi-

cials believed these individuals still clung to many of the outmoded shib-
boleths that had proved so popular with a stubborn minority before Pearl
Harbor. One was a belief that every effort should be focused on defending
the continental United States. As Japan now appeared to offer the greatest
menace to the mainland, divisionists felt that American strength should be
accumulated on the West Coast. Moreover, turning away from Europe
would also have the advantage of halting U.S. aid to two of America's true
enemies: Imperialist Britain and Bolshevik Russia. Isolationist enmity toward the former was reawakened both by reports of Indian pressure for independence during the spring, which sharpened the traditional American
distaste for the British Empire, and by the series of military defeats, which
seemed to demonstrate Britain's liability as an ally.[16] But the Soviet Union
was by far and away the divisionists' main concern. With the Red Army
resurgent at the gates of Moscow in December and January, pushing back
the Wehrmacht more than 200 miles in some places, a number of isolationist papers even began to paint "the Russians as being on the road to
victory." "This picture," the OFF noted on March 2, "has manifestly been
presented in an effort to instill a fear that Communism will spread over the
whole of Europe, and to make us feel the Nazis are no longer a menace."[17]

Fearing bolshevism more than nazism, many divisionists even advocated a negotiated peace with Germany that would leave not only the Third
Reich but also its conquests essentially intact. Far from rejecting such an
idea out of hand, a significant minority of the mass public ominously appeared to support such a course. In January one poll found that 30 percent
of Americans would be willing "to end the war and discuss peace terms
with the German army, if it were to take over the reins of government from
Hitler." Of these, "slightly more than one-tenth" indicated that "they
would favor the acceptance of a peace offer made by Hitler *on the basis of
the territorial and political situation existing at that time.*" In this context, the
OFF feared that "efforts are now being inaugurated to make such a course
palatable to the American people by calling it a 'negotiated victory.' The
rationalization offered is that further fighting can produce only defeat or at
best stalemate."[18] Roosevelt shared this concern. "The real trouble," he remarked privately in March, comes from "a gang which unfortunately sur-
vives—made up mostly of those who were isolationists before December
Seventh and who are actuated today by various motives in their effort to instill disunity in the country. . . . The hearts of these people are not in unity
and some of them still want a negotiated peace."[19]

That the mass public might be susceptible to this divisionist pressure
was deemed all the more likely given the growing evidence that American
confidence was sagging. The defeats of late winter and early spring did not
merely embolden the isolationists; they also helped create a general growth
in pessimism, embodied in the feeling that, as the *New York Herald Tribune*
put it, "The War Can Be Lost."[20] This was demonstrated in a OFF report,
which found that mass opinion was generally less confident, with a rise

POLL (MARCH 2, 1942)

	Dec. 26–30, 1941 (%)	Feb. 16–23, 1942 (%)
a. There is no question that the U.S. and her Allies will win the war and be able to write the peace terms.	68.5	54.6
b. We will win the war all right, but the losers will be strong enough so *we* will have to make some concessions too.	22.4	30.8
c. We won't be defeated, but neither will the Axis—the war will end in a draw.	3.9	6.5
d. I am afraid the Axis powers will have a pretty good chance to win the war.	0.9	3.9

Source: "Survey of Intelligence Material," No. 12, March 2, 1942, PSF (Subject): OWI, FDRL.

among both those who felt that the victory might not be completely decisive and those who thought the result would be stalemate.

The reemergence of isolationism and pessimism, though, were only two elements of the problem. The other was far less tangible, but affected a larger portion of the populace and was soon creating even greater anxiety. This was the appearance of a vague and inchoate popular mood described variously as apathy or complacency. It was, as Barth reported in February, a difficult concept to define. "It may amount to smugness—and, on the other hand, to a mere absence of hysteria or defeatism." More commonly, it was applied to the "conviction that the American people as a whole do not appreciate the seriousness of the situation confronting them today."[21] Essentially, then, it was far removed from the pessimistic feeling reported by many pollsters. After all, pessimism denoted a belief that the war could or would be lost, while complacency implied that the war would be won so easily that there was little need for any extra effort. One looked fearfully at the power and success of the enemy; the other remained blasé and over-confident about America's own strength. Yet these two separate strands were commonly linked together by an administration fearful that anything that smacked either of defeatism, pessimism, or complacency might "lead to a great enlargement of the divisionist ranks."[22]

Although all three strands were frequently lumped together under the heading of morale, it was the last of these moods, complacency, which leapt to center stage in the minds of most opinion makers during the first weeks of 1942. On February 8, the *New York Times* asserted that "the country is too complacent, too overconfident about the war," and backed up this claim with a poll that showed an overwhelming majority felt America was already doing enough to defeat the enemy.

POLL (FEBRUARY 8, 1942)

Do you think the U.S. is doing all it can to win the war?	All Voters (%)	Republican Voters (%)	Democratic Voters (%)
Yes	78	69	82
No	17	24	15
Don't know	5	7	3

Source: New York Times, February 8, 1942.

"Many other newspapers echo this theme," Barth noted, "urging the public to be on guard against overconfidence or the expectation of an easy victory."[23] The president himself became directly aware of the press' new preoccupation on February 10, when he was asked to comment on the welter of reports about "complacency . . . in the face of bad news in the Pacific."[24]

What lay behind such sentiments? According to many OFF reports, the combined problems of divisionism, defeatism, and complacency were all being fuelled by one final problem: a pervasive ignorance about the true nature of the enemy and the reasons for fighting the war. This is not to say that Americans had suddenly gone soft on the Nazis. Far from it. Only at the extreme margins of U.S. society was there any sympathy for Hitler and his cronies—and even here, the likes of Father Coughlin, Gerald L. K. Smith, and the American Bund would soon be either silenced or imprisoned by the government. Rather, the problem was more complex. As officials began to scratch below the surface of American attitudes they started to find a worrying lack of real knowledge about the nature, aims, and capabilities of the Nazi enemy.

In the first days and weeks after Pearl Harbor, the president and his officials tried their best to rectify this. Roosevelt, for his part, frequently referred to the catalogue of aggressive deeds committed by Hitler since 1933. He also repeatedly stressed that the war was being waged not against the German people but against the insidious Nazi regime. In Germany, he declared, power was imposed from above on an inert and enslaved mass: "With them it all comes from the top. It is done only on order from the Ruler. It is carried out by uniformed servants of the Ruler. It is based, in great part, on direction, compulsion, and fear. And the Rulers are not concerned with human beings as human beings but as mere slaves of the state—or as cannon fodder."[25]

The president's efforts were also supplemented by the work of the OFF, part of whose remit was to "facilitate a widespread and accurate understanding of the status and progress of the national defense effort." Under Archibald MacLeish, who was anxious to pursue a "strategy of truth" by releasing information that "neither perverted nor colored" the war news, the OFF quickly expanded its functions to encompass not only the coordination of all major administration speeches but also the dissemination of its own message.[26] For this latter task, MacLeish used FDR's utterances as his "information blueprint." Dissecting the president's words, he devised three themes that Roosevelt had stressed and that could be developed by the OFF to provide the public with a clearer picture of the enemy, namely, a "statement of U.S. objectives," including an assessment of the impact that Axis militarism would have on "every day American life"; the "nature of the enemy," particularly the fact that the Nazis were bent on world domination; and the Allies' "counterstrategy," especially the need to stop the Wehrmacht with vigorous offensive operations. MacLeish's aim was to get other officials to deliver speeches, or to produce OFF posters, pamphlets, and radio programs, which the media could repeat, republish, and rebroadcast. Once furnished with such material, MacLeish hoped that journalists would echo the government's themes and thereby disseminate the official message to a wider audience.[27]

In the first months of 1942, however, despite Roosevelt's speeches and MacLeish's aspirations, the OFF doubted that its message was getting through. Part of the problem was that these efforts were still in their infancy, and so most posters, pamphlets, and radio programs had yet to reach a wide audience. But the OFF was also hampered by a distinct lack of authority. While it sought to develop its own message, it had little power over the press releases issued by other departments—a weakness that was only made worse by the president's decision to give the army and the navy the task of determining what war-related news could be released.[28] Nor did the OFF really have the resources to carry out its tasks. MacLeish himself tried hard to combine his leadership of the government's propaganda efforts with his other duties as the librarian of Congress. But only supported by a staff of about four hundred, who had a wide array of tasks, from monitoring popular attitudes to coordinating the government's output, it soon became apparent that the OFF was seriously undermanned.[29]

Given these problems, it was hardly surprising that the administration as a whole provided fewer cues on the nature of the enemy than MacLeish and the OFF would have liked. In February, for instance, other government departments (excluding the White House) issued forty-two speeches and statements. But only seven of these focused on America's objectives in the war, three on the nature of the Axis conspiracy, and five on the allies' counter strategy. "Some progress has been made toward familiarizing the American people with the fundamental themes enunciated by President Roosevelt in his great message on the State of the Union," the OFF concluded in March. "But the treatment of these themes by Government spokesmen appears to have been uneven and, in some instances, wholly inadequate."[30]

Without much of a lead from the government and preoccupied with events in the Pacific, the OFF quickly concluded that the media was ig-

OFF Objectives in the Press, February 15 to March 15, 1942

OFF Objective	Feb. 15–21	Feb. 22–28	Mar. 1–7	Mar 1–15	Total
U.S. objectives	29	65	30	1	125
Nature of Nazi conspiracy	45	56	54	101	256
UN counter strategy	47	79	77	36	230
Total	121	191	161	138	611

Sources: OFF, "Survey of Intelligence Material," No. 18, April 8, 1942, PSF(Subject) OWI, FDRL; and No. 19, 15 April 1942; OFF, "Media Trend Report," No. 1, March 31, 1942, Entry 171, box 1844, RG44, NA

noring its halting and sporadic efforts. During February and March, an examination of 415 newspapers found less than two hundred stories each week on the administration's three main themes. This lack of interest continued into April, May, and June, when these same papers ran only slightly more than one hundred editorials a week on subjects relating to the enemy.[31] To make matters worse, throughout March there was a similar paucity of coverage by radio commentators, with only thirteen stories reiterating America's goals, thirty-two calling for an offensive strategy in Europe, and one emphasizing the basic traits of the Nazis. Nor were the newsreels any different. Although about 80 percent of the 160-plus stories that appeared each month on MGM, Fox, Paramount, Pathé, and Universal were related in some way to the war, only one of these dealt specifically with the enemy in April, two in May, and none in June.[32]

Even those few articles that did discuss Nazi Germany during this period were nevertheless a disappointment to the OFF. "The press evaluation of the enemy is fuzzy," complained Barth. "There is no sharp-focus picture. Rather the enemy is presented as a composite of barbarisms, an intangible entity." Indeed, sometimes the Nazis were portrayed as treacherous and deceitful, at other times as brutal and ruthless; until the middle of June there was also a tendency to depict Axis leaders as madmen, fools, or maniacs.[33] According to the OFF, the isolated newsreel stories on this subject were similarly ambiguous and superficial. "The newsreel treatment of the enemy," declared one survey, "is unfortunate in that it lends itself to an easy optimism. Either the enemy is not mentioned at all, or he is obviously silly and inept, with musical comedy names, or is greatly inferior to us. . . . Who are we fighting? Scarcely a mention and never a sober statement is made about enemy strength, of the risks involved, or what we must undergo to subdue our strong adversaries."[34]

In the absence of concentrated and consistent leads from either the government or the mass media, the OFF believed that the mass of people remained "badly informed." In one report that circulated within the agency, officials expressed concern that the public "do not know the enemy; they do not realize his strength, his deceit, his utter disregard of decency and humanity; they still do not grasp the fact that he can win, nor the horrors

that await us if he does win."[35] Such worries naturally found their way into
the surveys that gravitated up to the White House. In January, one poll revealed that only 23 percent of those questioned had even heard of the Atlantic Charter, the list of war aims announced by Roosevelt and Churchill
the previous August, and less than a third of these could identify one of its
eight points.[36] Six months later, the OFF found that only 48 percent admitted they had any notion of the war's significance. Those uneducated
about the nature of the enemy, concluded another report, were "inclined to
take a shorter view of the war, to think less of the ultimate menace of Hitler
and more of settling scores with the Japs in the Pacific."[37]

During the spring of 1942, top officials were again preoccupied with a variety of public opinion problems. Admittedly, these were not of the same
order as those that had plagued the president before December 7. There
was no longer an overwhelming opposition to formal involvement in the
war, nor was there a basic antipathy to deploying a land army overseas;
even "Asia-first" sentiment might well prove to be ephemeral, a product of
temporary reverses in the Pacific. Yet, for all these caveats, the administration was deeply concerned. After all, complacency, defeatism, and ignorance might breathe new life into the waning isolationist movement; they
might also hamper, perhaps even destroy, the war effort by encouraging
workers to slacken or by prompting citizens to favor a negotiated peace.
The government's principal worry therefore stemmed from the possible
future ramifications of these different public opinion trends—the prospect
that, although only budding difficulties at present, they might blossom into
fully grown problems in the future. It therefore decided to make a more
concerted effort to educate mass opinion. On February 12, Roosevelt wrote
to MacLeish, remarking that the "difficulties the American people must
face in following and understanding this war have been constantly on my
mind."[38] At a cabinet meeting three days later "the question of morale was
raised and complaint made of our failure to do something about it."[39] A
month later the OFF, grumbling that there still "appears to be a conspicuous neglect of the important information objective referred to as the 'nature
of the enemy,'" concluded that "emphasis on this theme seems a prerequisite to understanding the need for all-out fighting." It therefore felt the
time was ripe to devise a comprehensive educational campaign aimed at
promoting "a balanced awareness of the war's significance as a whole."[40]

Defining the Nature of the Nazi Enemy: The Administration's Information Campaign, February to November 1942

One obvious method of jolting Americans out of their complacency and
educating those unaware of the nature of the enemy was to foster a deep ha-

tred of all things German. This was the claim of a number of influential figures, both inside and outside the government. On January 15, for instance, General Henry J. Riley told a large audience on NBC Blue's *America's Town Hall Meeting of the Air* that the United States could only win the war if it hated the enemy. The German-born Swiss emigrant historian, Emil Ludwig, made a similar point in a widely read article. "Americans feel they are fighting against Hitler and not the German people," he asserted. "This is a false and dangerous belief, which will lead to the same deceptions as the last war. . . . Hitler is Germany."[41]

At a cabinet meeting on April 11 both Henry Morgenthau and Harold Ickes took up this issue in an attempt to change the government's information policy. Morgenthau began by arguing "with great force and earnestness that our people ought to be taught to 'hate Germany.' . . . 'If we do not hate the Germans we will end by hating each other.'" And when the secretary of agriculture, Claude Wickard, "raised the question of whether it was the Germans or Hitler we should hate," Ickes first "snorted" and then "blurted out that there was no difference between the German rulers and the German people; that this had been the true from the times of Caesar." "The goose-step," he concluded, "was a perfect expression of the German character."[42]

Roosevelt was not convinced, however. At cabinet, he did not tackle Morgenthau and Ickes head on, but, as the latter complained, simply "allowed the discussion to trail off into nothingness."[43] Then, in subsequent weeks, rather than shift the emphasis on to hatred of the Germans as a whole, he drew the distinction between the people and regime even more starkly than before, albeit with the caveat that the Germans were being hoodwinked or enslaved by their rulers. Indeed, as an OFF content analysis of presidential and State Department speeches discovered, in the period from April to August FDR used the terms "Hitler(ite)" and/or "Nazi(s/ism)" 25 percent more than ambiguous term, "German(y)." And this conclusion was confirmed by a qualitative analysis of presidential statements. In a fireside chat on April 28, for example, Roosevelt pointed out that "in the German and Italian peoples themselves there is a growing conviction that the cause of Nazism and Fascism is hopeless—that their political and military leaders have led them along the bitter road that leads not to world conquest but to final defeat," while on June 14 he asked "the German people, still dominated by their Nazi whipmasters," whether they were happy with "the mechanized hell of Hitler's new order."[44]

At this stage, Roosevelt was also deeply reluctant to engage in any activity that might be construed as anti-German. In the winter, not only did he tactfully refuse to meet with Emil Ludwig—even though Ludwig had spent some time in the White House during the 1930s researching what was to become "a most friendly and sympathetic" biography of the president—but he was also distinctly lukewarm about the idea of employing this Germanophobe in the OFF.[45] In stark contrast, FDR had no qualms

Who Is the Enemy? A Quantitative Content Analysis of Speeches by Top
Officials, December 1941 to July 1942

	Roosevelt	Wallace	Hull	Welles
Hitler/Nazi	55	20	7	33
Germany	33	11	3	18
Berlin	5	—	1	—
Hirohito/warlords	5	—	6	2
Japan	105	5	4	35
Tokyo	6	—	1	—
Mussolini/Fascist	6	3	1	—
Italy	14	1	2	3
Rome	3	–	—	—
Dictators	1	—	—	—
Axis	26	—	3	24
Militarists	1	—	—	—

Sources: FDR, *Public Papers*, vols. 10–11; Lyness to Pettee, "Who Is the Enemy? Peoples?
Or Regimes?" August 11, 1942, entry 171, box 1849, RG 44, NA.

about attempting to locate the "more than twenty-four former members of
the German Reichstag now living in the U.S." He thought they might
"make a very good publicity story," one that would no doubt emphasize
that many "good" Germans detested the Nazis.[46] Meanwhile, when it came
to the mass of German-Americans, Roosevelt's attitude was crystal clear:
he adamantly opposed any campaign to hound or roundup the 314,000-
strong German-American community, on the basis that this would have a
very "bad effect on morale."[47]

Roosevelt's clear rejection of a hate campaign stemmed from a variety
of concerns. One was the distinct lack of popular support for pursuing such
a course. Throughout 1942, Ludwig, Morgenthau, and Ickes were lonely,
isolated voices, for the vast majority of Americans continued to make a
sharp distinction between evil Nazis and the mass of the German population. This was reflected in the fact that only one editorial out of the three
hundred monitored by the OGR actually endorsed Ludwig's anti-German
stance. When the British ambassador, Lord Halifax, also called publicly for
a harsher peace than that imposed on Germany in 1919, the media simply
ignored his speech altogether.[48] The mass public was similarly uninter-
ested; as MacLeish concluded, Americans were just not prepared to support
a race war against the entire German nation.[49]

But Roosevelt was not merely pandering to public opinion. At this
stage, distinguishing between Nazis and Germans also reflected his own
private image of the enemy. America's entry into the war had not dented
FDR's hopes that many Germans opposed or were apathetic toward
Hitler's regime. "There must be in Germany elements," he remarked privately toward the end of 1942, "now thoroughly subdued, but who at the

proper time will, I am sure, rise, and protest against the atrocities, against the whole Hitler system."[50] Largely for this reason, Roosevelt remained optimistic that the Nazi regime would be vulnerable to a psychological-warfare campaign. As he stressed in May, the time was now ripe to "make a distinction between the Nazi gang and the German people," in order "to accelerate the process of political change there."[51] The following month he acted on this belief by bringing Ernst "Putzi" Hanfstaengl to the United States. Confident that this ex-Nazi and former associate of Hitler might be able to devise a propaganda message that would undermine the Third Reich, the president installed Hanfstaengl in a farmhouse just outside Washington, provided him with a short-wave radio and numerous creature comforts, and then asked him to devise messages that would appeal to the mass of Germans.[52]

When it came to foreign propaganda, the president and his advisers were in complete agreement that the bulk of Germans had to be distinguished from the "fascist cliques."[53] Of course, the government's domestic information campaign did not have to reflect foreign propaganda imperatives. But Roosevelt, clearly believing in the existence of "good" Germans, saw no reason to whip up American hatred against the entire nation. Along with some of his top officials, he also realized that, as a practical matter, it would be all but impossible to keep the foreign and domestic campaigns distinct, because the press could easily monitor the message being relayed to occupied Europe and then quickly publicize any differences between the two. Propaganda was therefore deemed to be something of a double-edged sword, with both a domestic and foreign component. More to the point, the president recognized that it was both undesirable and impractical to disseminate widely differing messages in these two spheres.[54]

For Roosevelt, then, America's entry into the war, together with the problems of complacency, defeatism, divisionism, and ignorance, did not necessitate any change in his public depiction of the enemy. The Nazis not the Germans were still painted as the central culprits. But how much coordination was there with other officials? To what extent were the president's utterances echoed or obscured by the output of other departments and agencies?

This question is important because during the course of 1942 the dynamics of Roosevelt's relationship with the press began to change ever so slightly. The war certainly increased the president's preoccupation with security. Immediately after Pearl Harbor he became more and more determined to withhold information, fearing that any slip or careless phrase might provide the enemy with vital intelligence. In a February fireside chat, Roosevelt attempted to justify his growing reticence, commenting that the public had to realize that "in many cases details of military operations cannot be disclosed until we are absolutely certain that the announcement will not give to the enemy information which he does not already possess." But this did not change the fact that his press conferences were becoming less informative than before. "Getting nowhere fast" was now a more common refrain amongst frustrated journalists faced with the president's skillful stonewalling.[55]

Slowly but perceptibly FDR also started to reduce his exposure to the press and public. Although concerns about security were partly to blame for this as well, the enormous presidential workload increasingly took its toll. In the last weeks of December and the first weeks of January, Roosevelt was preoccupied with a full-scale military conference in Washington with Churchill and the British. The prime minister journeyed to Hyde Park and Washington again in June, and on each occasion he invariably managed to exhaust the president with his tremendous energy and idiosyncratic sleeping habits. Also taxing were the myriad of problems that continued to flood into the Oval Office—questions of grand strategy and supply, problems of labor and race relations, and quarrels between the variety of new agencies that sprung up to administer the war effort. Each one demanded a response and each one ate in to the president's day. Roosevelt increasingly craved periods of peace and quiet away from the pressures of Washington. At the start of the year he began to escape more frequently to his family home in Hyde Park. From the summer he also started to use a retreat named Shangri-La (now Camp David) in the Maryland woods, while in September he took a long and ostensibly secret train ride around the country to inspect the nation's booming war industries.[56]

All of these excursions certainly helped the president to recharge his batteries, but they also meant canceling a number of press conferences. In February, *Time* noted that FDR had not been able to make two recent sessions and had cut a third down to a cursory three minutes. Unlike in previous years, Roosevelt also refused to play a prominent part in the midterm congressional election campaign, preferring to appear aloof, as a national war leader above petty party squabbles.[57] This is not to say that the president was invisible or mute during 1942; in fact, he made three prominent fireside chats and still held around seventy press conferences. It was more a case that, with the pressure of work and the demands of the war, he was gradually becoming more selective in his public appearances.

As Roosevelt receded ever so slightly into the background as opinion persuader, his place was partially filled by the newly established Office of War Information (OWI). Throughout the spring, MacLeish, for all his efforts to produce radio shows, pamphlets, and posters, had become increasingly frustrated with his agency's lack of authority over coordinating day-to-day news and had therefore pressed for the creation of a new bureau. Journalists were also directing their fire at this aspect of the OFF's work, especially the dearth of material released on military reverses and the duplication of information disseminated on more mundane matters.[58] As pressure for reform mounted, FDR responded in June by creating the OWI under the leadership of the highly popular radio commentator, Elmer Davis. With more than two thousand employees situated in 112 regional offices, the OWI was charged not only with coordinating "the war informational activities of all Federal departments and agencies," but also with formulating and carrying out, "through the use of press, radio, motion pictures and other facilities, information programs designed to facilitate the development of an informed and intelligent understanding, at home and abroad, of the status and progress of the war effort."[59]

In practice, this meant that one of the OWI's main tasks was to define how the enemy would be portrayed to the American public. Back in March, top officials in the OFF had already discussed "whether the policy of the Government should [be to] differentiate between the Hitler government and the German people," only to defer the matter when "extreme difference[s] in point[s] of view were expressed."[60] Two months later, however, when the Committee of War Information also debated "whether or not the government should seek to develop hatred of the Germans," the main paper submitted on this subject concluded that "there are more arguments con than pro." These included the probability that mass hatred will have "unfortunate results at the peace table" and that "a campaign to arouse hatred might easily backfire, simply because there is such a mistrust of atrocity propaganda."[61]

Throughout the summer and fall, the OWI effectively endorsed this rejection of a hate campaign. This was partly because, as one memorandum contended, it would be far easier to establish a durable postwar order if hatred was not directed at each and every German. "Indiscriminate hatred may be a mighty weapon," it stressed, "but it is likely to be impeding to a satisfactory peace."[62] But above all, the OWI recognized that the president clearly opposed a hate campaign. Although the White House had issued no specific guidelines, even the most cursory glance at FDR's speeches demonstrated his conviction that the "enemy is not the German people . . . but the militaristic and fascist cliques."[63]

Determined to follow the president's tacit lead, the OWI quickly singled out Hitler and his cohorts as the main enemy. As it hastened to tell radio networks, "the American people must have a clear picture of the Nazis, the ruthless planned route by which they came to power, their cold dismissal of every humanitarian principle, the subjugation in all things of the individual to the state."[64] The OWI's own radio series, "You Can't Do Business With Hitler," unambiguously made the same point throughout 1942.[65] So did a series of speeches by top presidential advisers, cabinet members, and State Department officials. "First and foremost," announced Harry Hopkins in a typical comment, "we are fighting to destroy completely Hitler's power." "How long the German people will be able to bear up under this offensive from their own government," declared Francis Biddle, the attorney general, "is as much one of the unpredictables of this war as the military engagements."[66]

At the heart of the administration's indictment of nazism was an emphasis on the fundamental clash between Hitler's ideology and the most cherished principles of American life. This was a central point of a series of thirty-minute radio dramas produced by the OWI, entitled "This Is Our Enemy." Aired throughout 1942, this show sought to demonstrate how in Germany churches had been destroyed, private life had been abolished, justice had been perverted, and emphasis had been given to a racial and not civic brand of nationalism. "Our enemy," remarked the narrator in one episode, "holds these things to be self-evident; that all men are created unequal, that they are endowed by their creator with inalienable virtues if they be Germans, and that they are fit only for slavery if they not be Germans"—even though the "Nazi theory of German racial superiority is completely false to scientific fact."[67] This Nazi challenge to Americanism became a central theme in government films, too. In *Price of Victory*, for instance, a fifteen-minute short released in 1942, Henry Wallace described 160 years of progress stemming from the American Revolution of 1776, which the Nazis now wanted to completely reverse.[68]

Yet this desire to focus on the ideological nature of the enemy raised one very awkward problem: the country currently shouldering the greatest burden in the struggle against Hitler was not a bastion of democratic virtue but Stalin's own form of totalitarian dictatorship. The administration never devised a coordinated or planned response to this dilemma. But noises emanating from a variety of sources did nevertheless create the impression that, at the very least, the Soviet menace paled in comparison to the Third Reich; they also left no one in any doubt that the Red Army was a valued ally in the struggle against Hitler. This was certainly the thrust of Joseph E. Davies's bestseller, *Mission to Moscow*, which was published in 1942 with the permission of the State Department. Davies, a former ambassador to the Soviet Union and occasional confidant of the president, hastened to tell his readers that, unlike the fascists, the "Russians did not seek to revolutionize the world, but [wanted] rather to create an egalitarian society in which all men would be governed according to ethical principles." Roosevelt was instrumental in getting this book turned into a full-length movie—apparently he told the boss of Warner Brothers, "Jack, this picture *must* be made."[69] At the start of 1942, the president also made great play of the fact that the Soviets had signed the UN Declaration (a series of principles that were supposed to unite and guide all those fighting the Axis). As he was keen to advertise, by doing so Stalin had pledged "to defend life, liberty independence, and religious freedom, and to preserve human rights and justice in their own lands . . . in a common struggle against savage and brutal forces seeking to subjugate the world."[70]

While the president and his close associates attempted to minimize the Soviet danger, the OWI sought to establish that the Nazis were the only real threat to the United States—that only Hitler had the intentions and the capabilities to truly menace the Western Hemisphere. Driving home this

point was vitally important, because isolationism had long been predicated
on the conviction that America was essentially impregnable behind its Atlantic barrier; now, divisionism, complacency, and "Asia-first" sentiment
also seemed to be rooted in a similar optimism that faraway European
countries posed no immediate danger to the Western Hemisphere. One
way to erode this dogged faith was to demonstrate once and for all that
Hitler actually intended world, and not merely European, domination, and
that he hoped at some stage to launch an invasion of the United States. This
task was taken up by the radio series "You Can't Do Business With
Hitler," which detailed Hitler's over-all plan to conquer the Americas. It
was also at the heart of the OWI's *Information Guide*. In this set of instructions, officials were told to stress that the "enemy wants what we've got.
. . . He wants all our manpower to work for him in the way he tells it to. He
wants all our factories making goods for him. He wants all the natural resources of America—its coal, iron, lumber—so he can become rich and
more powerful."[71]

With Nazi intentions established, the OWI turned next to the Third
Reich's capabilities, the means it could employ to achieve this end. The
OWI began by repeating Roosevelt's old refrain that technology was shrinking the globe. As the *Information Guide* put it, "the enemy faces us across
two oceans that are not so wide as they used to be. . . . Today there is no
such thing as faraway."[72] Officials also emphasized the importance of geo-
politics in Nazi thinking. The OWI, for example, prodded publications
like *Collier's* to publish articles on this subject, while Hadley Cantril used
the *New Republic* as a platform to talk of Hitler's "elaborate system of geo-
politics," which "aims to divide the world's resources and peoples into a
great system of production and distribution for those who are at the foun-
tainhead of the German empire."[73]

According to the OWI, the Nazis also had a powerful weapon closer
to home: fifth-column agents and Quisling collaborators, who first sought
to engender and exploit a mood of complacency and defeatism within target states and then acted as Hitler's stooges once the Nazis emerged victorious. Here, the French example played an important role in the government's efforts. After all, the swift French collapse in June 1940 had not
only been one of the most shocking, unexpected, and pivotal events of the
war, it also appeared to provide a number of parallels to America's present
position. To start with, France in 1940 and the United States in 1942 both
seemed to be plagued by poor morale—not just by complacency and defeatism, but also by a "Maginot mentality," an unwarranted faith that the
country was safe behind a defensive barrier. In France, traitorous collaborators had then apparently capitalized on this apathy and pessimism in order
to pave the way for Hitler's stunning victory. What lay in store for the
United States?

As early as May 1940, Roosevelt had publicly alluded to the dangers
presented by these fifth columnists. Throughout 1941 and 1942, although

the president and the State Department were keen to maintain diplomatic relations with Marshal Philippe Pétain's Vichy regime, both nevertheless made periodic attacks on the worst of the French collaborators, describing Pierre Laval and Admiral Jean-François Darlan as Nazi stooges who had delivered their countries "politically, economically, socially, and militarily to Hitler."[74] The OWI now sought to build on this. In the two main pamphlets it published during 1942, these "hirelings of the 'New Order'" were condemned not just for laying the groundwork for the Nazis' military successes but also for carrying out much of the Führer's dirty work. From here, of course, it was but a short step to stress that America had its very own fifth columnists—the divisionists who were attempting to exacerbate the public's apathy and pessimism in order to "destroy our national unity, create unrest in all groups of the population, and deflect us from our major purpose—the defeat of the Axis."[75] Nor was it too difficult to start smearing everyone who grumbled and complained as "sixth columnists"—as misguided individuals "who spread the propaganda, wittingly or unwittingly, originated by the fifth columnists."[76]

In addition to demonstrating that Hitler had the ability to threaten the Western Hemisphere, the OWI was also keen to illuminate the prospective dangers to the United States if the Third Reich did emerge victorious, mainly by highlighting the brutal methods the Nazis and their cohorts were employing in the countries they had already overrun. Officials certainly had a wealth of information at their fingertips, especially now that the first unconfirmed and sporadic reports on the mass destruction of Jews in Russia were starting to arrive. Within the administration, however, there was an acute awareness that atrocity stories had to be treated with extreme caution.[77] On the one hand, because the current conflict had been raging for almost three years, some officials feared that the public was becoming desensitized to the horrific acts being committed in Europe. Conversely, others felt that the scale of Nazi brutality was so great as to be beyond the scope of most people's understanding; as the OWI *Information Guide* put it, "the recitation of enemy atrocities is often so horrible that decent Americans find it hard to believe that they really happen."[78]

To make the public truly aware of the extent of Nazi acts, the government took great pains to make its atrocity stories comprehensible. For the most part, it hoped to achieve this by dramatizing particular events. Often, these were anniversaries of notorious acts, such as the May 1933 burning of books.[79] But far more important was the decision in June 1942 to "immortalize" Lidice, the town eradicated by the Nazis in retaliation for Reinhard Heydrich's assassination. "For ten years or more," began MacLeish in a fact sheet distributed to radio stations, "Americans have heard and read the stories of Axis terror East and West. The shooting of innocent hostages has become such a regular commonplace that we look for it in our papers as if it were the daily box score. But that was before Lidice! In that single act the Nazis brought home to the American people the full frightfulness

... the utter immorality ... of the Nazi system."[80] To bring it home still further, officials went into high gear throughout June, issuing press releases and posters, sponsoring radio programs, and even encouraging the formation of the Lidice Lives Committee, under the chairmanship of Joseph E. Davies, which enlisted nearly 120 prominent persons as sponsors, including Albert Einstein, Eduard Benes, William O. Douglas, Thomas Mann, and Rex Stout.[81]

Using specific events like Lidice as a symbol of Nazi brutality also bypassed another problem. Most officials recalled that during the Great War the Bryce Commission had catalogued numerous German acts of savagery in Belgium only to see its work condemned as a tissue of lies in 1922.[82] The result of this, as one OFF memorandum put it, was that Americans were now skeptical of the veracity of barbarity reports.[83] Officials therefore had to find a method of detaching their efforts from any connection with the tainted activities of World War I; in other words, they had to ensure that their atrocity stories were not only comprehensible but also believable.

To achieve this, the OWI used four main techniques. First, its radio programs and films enlisted experts who were intimately associated with a particular field. Thus, the radio series "You Can't Do Business With Hitler" was hosted by Douglas Miller, who had been in Berlin for fifteen years as U.S. commercial attaché, while an OWI radio special, "The Nature of the Enemy," had Gerhart H. Seger, a former member of the German Reichstag, discussing the Nazis' use of slave labor, and the Reverend Henry Smith Leiper, American secretary of the World Council of Churches, talking about the Nazis' desecration of religion.[84] Second, all those officially involved with highlighting Nazi brutality were told to avoid exaggeration. "Report atrocity stories straight," they were instructed by the OWI's *Information Guide*. "Don't overdramatize or give them added horror."[85] Third, because at this stage many officials were themselves skeptical about evidence that suggested the systematic destruction of the Jews, the OWI focused instead on Nazi atrocities against civilians in the occupied countries. Here, the figures were in the hundreds, and so were more likely to be deemed credible by the public than claims that the Nazis were slaughtering thousands, even millions, in specially constructed death camps.[86] These lesser acts were also emphasized because they were based on the Nazis own figures; the pamphlet *Unconquered People*, for example, pointed out that the Germans themselves had admitted shooting "117 persons in Yugoslavia, 18 in Poland, 5 in Belgium."[87] Indeed, a fourth tactic was to indict the Nazi leadership with its own words and statistics. The Lidice massacre had first been publicized by Heinrich Himmler, the head of the SS. In fact sheets to radio stations MacLeish continued to use "quotations from Nazi officials and Nazi sources [to] reveal the established Nazi ideology toward conquered people." Himmler, for instance, had also made no secret of his desire "to eliminate non-Germans in the occupied eastern territory to prevent the 'weakening' of the German strain."[88]

Of course, emphasizing the Nazis' brutal acts in occupied Europe carried the implication that the guilty would have to be punished. This goal was made explicit by the president in two statements in the late summer, the background to which also revealed many of Roosevelt's deeper convictions about his administration's information campaign. For a start, FDR was well aware of the double-edged nature of propaganda, the fact that it had both a foreign and domestic component. Hence, he decided in August, and again in October, that the time was ripe to make "an authoritative presentation of the atrocities committed by the Germans," not merely "to deter those committing the atrocities by naming their names and letting them know that they are being watched by the civilized world," but also because this would further "help to keep the people of the U.S. informed of the nature of our enemies, spurring us to renewed efforts to defeat them."[89] Although anxious to make a public stand against war crimes, the president was also keen to retain the distinction between Nazi leaders and the German people. In August, Roosevelt therefore announced that he had evidence "concerning the barbaric crimes being committed against civilian populations in occupied countries, particularly in the continent of Europe" and revealed that the Allies would establish a Commission for the Investigation of War Crimes. But while he advocated meting out "just and sure punishment" to the ringleaders, he also emphasized that "the number of persons eventually found guilty will undoubtedly be extremely small compared to the total enemy populations." "The president," explained Welles, "believes it essential that a clear cut statement of this character be made to prevent the implication that the Allied Governments intend to undertake mass executions."[90]

In the administration's information campaign, then, there was no mistaking who the European enemy was: it was clearly confined to the ideological menace posed by Hitler and his Quisling partners in crime. When it came to Asia, however, officials found it far harder to depict the enemy in such narrow terms. Some certainly tried. Throughout 1942, the president's keynote speeches were peppered with phrases separating the Japanese people from "their savage lords of slaughter."[91] MacLeish also spoke for a number of officials in both the OFF and then OWI when he stressed that "the enemy is not the German people or the Italian people *or the Japanese people*, but the militaristic and fascist cliques in control of the destinies of these three countries."[92] Ambassador Joseph S. Grew, the most prominent official spokesman on Japan during the latter half of 1942, made a similar point. Grew, who arrived back in the United States in June after more than ten years in Japan, made no bones about the long, bloody struggle that lay ahead. But he also repeatedly alluded to the existence of moderates within Japanese society, of liberal elements, some of whom he "admired, respected, and loved."[93]

Yet increasingly this distinction between Japanese militarists and mod-

erates was largely drowned out by the overwhelming tendency of government spokesmen to indict each and every Japanese person. Part of the
problem was the lack of a ready symbol, a Hitler or a jack-booted Nazi,
that could be used as shorthand for the Japanese leadership. Throughout
1942 certain formulations were tried, including "warlordism" and "Nip-
ponism," but none ever caught on. As a result, officials from the president
down often found it easier to talk about "the Nazis, Fascists, and Japanese"—to conflate the European enemy with the "brutal Nazi" but inflate
the Asian menace to the "wily Jap."[94]

But, of course, there was more to it than a lack of ready terminology.
Outrage at the sneak attack on Pearl Harbor combined with a knee-jerk
racist antipathy to the "yellow peril" also encouraged many officials to believe that Japan was a monolithic entity—that, as one top general put it, "a
Jap is a Jap."[95] Despite the OWI's initial good intentions, even this organization found it increasingly difficult to resist the temptation. "Our line has
not tended to differentiate much between the Japanese people and the militarists," one of its policy directives explained toward the end of the year,
"mainly because there is presently no group or class of any importance in
Japan opposed to the war."[96] The president also fell into the same habit.
Between December and July, he singled out the "emperor" or the "warlords" five times. But this was greatly overshadowed by the fact that he
used the blanket (if somewhat ambiguous) terms Japan or the Japanese on
no less than 105 occasions.[97]

In the atmosphere of shock and outrage that greeted news of Pearl
Harbor, the general thrust of official utterances was largely in tune with the
dominant public sentiment. Indeed, the media was already employing
crude racial stereotypes to depict the Asian enemy. *Time*, for instance, hastened to teach its readers about the telltale racial attributes that distinguished the Chinese ally from the "Jap" enemy, including the Japanese inclination toward dogmatism and arrogance and a tendency to "laugh loudly
at the wrong time." Hollywood films were no different; invariably, they
employed epithets such as "Japs, beasts, yellow monkeys, nips, or slant-
eyed rats" to describe the perpetrator of Pearl Harbor.[98] Throughout the
West Coast as a whole, there was also mounting pressure to round-up and
incarcerate the 100,000-strong Japanese-American community—pressure
that the administration notoriously caved in to. In February, Roosevelt
signed Executive Order 9066, which paved the way for Japanese-Ameri-
cans to be herded into the ten "relocation centers," where they would be
forced to sit out much of the war in primitive and depressing conditions.[99]

Although shocking in retrospect, this relocation of Japanese-Ameri-
cans caused barely a ripple of protest at the time, because much of the mass
public seemed prone to agree with the anti-Japanese sentiment that underpinned this action. True, polls often appeared to paint an ambivalent picture. Thus, in one survey conducted in April a plurality of 41 percent
thought that the Japanese would "always want war" (which was hardly a

ringing condemnation), while in another poll published in September three-fifths of Americans deemed the Japanese government, rather than the people, to be the main enemy. But such figures were treated with care by many in the administration. The BoI, for one, was keen to point out that Americans had a far more benign attitude toward the Germans—only 21 percent, for instance, felt that the German people were inherently warlike. More importantly, as soon as pollsters scratched below the surface, they detected the very distinct likelihood that American attitudes toward Japan were about to harden. As one survey put it, there seemed to be a "dangerous possibility that American animus will be directed exclusively, on racial grounds, against the Japanese" in the very near future. Because "many already believe the 'the Japs aren't like us,'" stressed another report, "the present feeling of tolerance may flare into a hatred of the Japanese more readily than it would in the case of Italians and Germans."[100]

Indicting the entire Japanese nation therefore seemed likely to play well with the public. But its very popularity also highlighted a clear danger inherent in this course: the probability that the administration's own efforts might fuel, rather than dampen, the growing public desire to pursue an "Asia-first" strategy. After all, the more Americans became aroused by the racial and monolithic nature of the "yellow peril," then the more they might be tempted to press for extra resources to be directed toward the Pacific.[101]

One way of responding to this problem was simply to drop all references to the Asian war. This had been Roosevelt's strategy during the first eleven months of 1941. Now, it was the course often adopted by the OFF and OWI. Throughout the spring and summer, as both organizations began to devise their own pamphlets, posters, and radio shows, officials were definitely quick to fix the spotlight firmly on Hitler rather than the Japanese. Thus, both *Divide and Conquer* and *The Unconquered People*, the two main pamphlets released in 1942, focused purely on the Nazis' means and ends. Likewise, of the numerous radio shows the government produced during 1942 and 1943, only a very small minority examined events in Asia; almost all explored Hitler's intentions, Germany's capabilities, and the Nazis' brutality.[102]

Although the president himself may have preferred to continue with his old policy of publicly ignoring developments in the Pacific War, after Pearl Harbor there was just no way he could escape talking about Japanese aggression in Hawaii, the Philippines, Malaya, and Burma. So instead of remaining silent, Roosevelt decided to counter "Asia-first" sentiment by downplaying the intentions and capabilities of this Asian enemy. In his public speeches, the president now frequently referred to the Japanese as a perfidious and aggressive foe. But he was also at pains to point out that they were only junior partners in a global enterprise directed from Berlin. By focusing on this Axis conspiracy, with Nazi Germany clearly in the vanguard, prodding and encouraging the other members into military expansion, the president hoped to bring home the global nature of the war. He also wanted to encourage Americans to focus on defeating the ringleader first, despite the string of disasters in the Pacific.

This new emphasis was evident just days after Pearl Harbor. The Axis, FDR declared on December 9, "is a collaboration so well calculated that all the continents of the world, and all the oceans, are now considered by the Axis strategists as one gigantic battlefield." This alliance, moreover, had only one clear leader. "Your Government knows," he continued, "that for weeks Germany has been telling Japan that if Japan did not attack the United States, Japan would not share in dividing the spoils with Germany when peace came. She was promised by Germany that if she came in she would receive the complete and perpetual control of the whole Pacific area." This point was reiterated on numerous other occasions. A month later, for instance, Roosevelt declared to a large national audience that

> The dreams of empire of the Japanese and Fascist leaders were modest in comparison with the gargantuan aspirations of Hitler and the Nazis. Even before they came to power in 1933, their plans for that conquest had been drawn. Those plans provided for the ultimate domination, not of any one section of the world, but of the whole earth and the oceans on it. When Hitler organized his Berlin-Rome-Tokyo alliance, all these plans of conquest became a single plan.[103]

Unlike Nazi Germany, Japan also lacked the strength to win the war, let alone to truly menace the Western Hemisphere. This was a point FDR was anxious to make even at the depths of Allied fortunes in Asia. America, he insisted, clearly had the far "greater resources," which would enable it to "out build Japan and ultimately overthrow her on sea, on land, and in the air."[104] Frank Knox, the secretary of the navy, put it far more colorfully. As he told an audience in Boston in June, Japan simply did not have the power to achieve her immense ambitions. "As my mother used to say to me at the dinner table—'his eyes are bigger than his tummy.' The Jap will never eat his dinner; he'll wish he had never ordered it!"[105]

By the summer and fall of 1942, as the administration began to develop and expand on these themes, officials began to detect a growing media interest. The president was certainly adept at captivating the nation. Whenever he took to the airwaves, his speeches not only continued to reach a huge mass audience—estimated at approximately 70 percent of the population for his February 23 broadcast[106]—but were also widely reported and discussed in newspapers and on the radio. After his February fireside chat, for instance, 382 editorials discussed the speech, while a majority of the 224 editorials that commented upon his April broadcast applauded the president for his "stirring and inspirational summons for all-out effort."[107]

The OFF and the OWI enjoyed similar success when they released pamphlets depicting the enemy. In March, the OFF was inundated with 1.6

million requests for *Divide and Conquer*, "the most astonishing response in such a short space of time for any government pamphlet ever published." It was also able to persuade the three wire services to carry extensive stories on the booklet, which ensured an additional audience estimated at more than 20 million.[108] When the OWI published a follow-up, *The Unconquered People*, four months later, the response was equally impressive, with fourteen metropolitan newspapers, including *PM Daily*, the *Washington Post*, and *New York Times*, devoting a total of 833 inches of space to this story of the European struggle against Nazis and their Quisling cohorts.[109]

According to government surveys, this increased coverage was having a profound impact on media and mass attitudes, so that a clear majority of both were now starting to share more fully the administration's conception of the enemy. Of course, Americans had long detested nazism. With the government continuing to distinguish between the Nazi leadership and the bulk of Germans, it was hardly surprising that Hitler and his cohorts were still singled out as the main enemy. In July, for example, only two editorials out of more than three hundred monitored by the OGR subscribed to the view that the German nation was beyond the pale.[110] Polls indicated that the mass public clearly shared this view. Throughout the summer, when Americans were asked whether they felt the "chief enemy is the German people as a whole or the German government," an overwhelming majority of 74 percent were quick to blame the "government only," while just 5 percent blamed the people, and only 18 percent blamed both. Other surveys gave further substance to this verdict. The BoI, for instance, found "a marked tendency among Americans to believe, even today, that the German army and people are disloyal to their government," while among the small minority who thought that "the German people are behind Hitler, the most common explanation offered in support of the opinion was that they are forced to be, or are afraid to be otherwise."[111]

Although this basic antipathy toward the Nazis was not new, the administration did notice a perceptible change in the volume and depth of media coverage. "Editorials are now making use of almost every bit of news which can serve as a springboard for attacking the Axis," the BoI's Media Division concluded on September 5, "and the volume of such comment continues to grow."[112] The press was certainly quick to pick up on the administration's attempt to make Lidice an "immortal" symbol of Nazi brutality. Prodded by a barrage of press releases, fact sheets, and posters, editorial coverage of Nazi savagery shot up, from an average of 100 a week before June 10 to more than 270 a week after, when "the story of Lidice was told and re-told."[113]

The government's preoccupation with making atrocity material both intelligible and believable paid especially rich dividends. "Perhaps the reason for the emotional impact of Lidice's fate," explained a *New York Herald Tribune* editorial on June 20, "is that it was restricted enough to be comprehensible. . . . Lidice was Hitlerism in capsule form—very real, very terrible."[114] The media also had no qualms about using government-produced material because the source for the story—Himmler's own words and deeds—was clearly unimpeachable. As a result, journalists flocked to use OFF press releases, which in turn helped to ensure that the basic portrayal of the enemy conformed closely to the administration's view.[115]

Bombarded by such stories from both the administration and the media, the mass public now seemed to have a deeper awareness of what the Third Reich really stood for. As the OWI informed Roosevelt in September, "the number of people believing that they have a grasp of the war's significance has increased markedly since the early part of June."[116] One indication of this was the fact that a growing portion now acknowledged that the Nazis had global aspirations, demonstrated by an OPOR poll that found that 66 percent of respondents now agreed that Germany and Japan "will divide the whole world between them, including the United States."[117]

By the fall, Americans also appeared to have few illusions about the savagery of the Nazis. True, as the first sketchy reports filtered out from occupied Europe that Jews were being slaughtered in vast numbers, only a small cross-section of the public, consisting largely of Jewish leaders, union bosses, and liberal intellectuals, really took much notice.[118] But the outrage at Lidice did penetrate deeply into the national consciousness. In the wake of the administration's attempts to highlight this massacre, the BoI was able to inform the president that "Americans appear to have a vivid awareness of the ruthless treatment which Germany has meted out to the conquered countries of Europe." When asked to describe how people in these countries were treated, almost all responded with terms such as "cruelly," "as slaves," or "killing them."[119] An overwhelming majority also had no illusions about the harsh treatment that would be in store for the United States if the Nazis were to emerge victorious: 95 percent thought they would extract reparations, 88 percent thought they would kill America's political and business leaders, and 72 percent thought "they would take our food away so they could starve us."[120]

The public generally blamed Hitler and a few Nazis for such deeds, but there was also a growing recognition that the Führer had willing accomplices throughout occupied Europe. During 1942, many opinion makers from across the political spectrum began to lavish attention on the Quislings, Lavals, and Darlans who actually carried out so much of the dirty work. As the BoI pointed out, Laval was widely loathed by the American press and "was commonly portrayed in the form of a mustached rat or diminutive Führer."[121] A number of journalists were also beginning to question why the United States still retained formal relations with the Vichy regime. In the week ending April 9, for instance, only 11 editorials opposed the "continued appeasement of Vichy." But two weeks later, after Laval returned to power, this figure had jumped to 272, with almost all calling for a "re-examination of policies toward Vichy."[122] As Barth put it, "many commentators now urge tough tactics in dealing with the Vichy government; they regard it as being in the Axis camp beyond redemption."[123]

When it came to dealing with those responsible for all the brutality, redemption was not a word that sprang readily to many American minds. As Roosevelt was informed in September, a majority of Americans now favored "harsh" treatment for top Nazis, with almost a half wanting to "kill them; do away with them." Hardly anyone, however, advocated harsh treatment for the mass of Germans. According to one OWI survey, Americans still felt little rancor toward the German people as a whole. "The overwhelming belief was that they should be kept under control and prevented from re-arming, but that they should be treated with kindness."[124] The comparison with popular attitudes toward Japan was especially marked. Demonstrating the public's far greater hatred of the Asian enemy, one survey found that "roughly seven times as many Americans say that we can get along better with the Germans after this war as say we can get along better with the Japanese."

Lingering Public Opinion Problems, February to November 1942

During the summer and fall, then, a series of polls and surveys indicated that the press and public basically accepted the image of the enemy developed by the president and the OWI. Yet, despite all these reassuring indications, the administration was not entirely satisfied that it had solved all its public opinion problems. Morale was one area that continued to be a particular cause for concern. Of course, the very nature of the complacency issue meant it was likely to linger, because any official who claimed that the public was no longer complacent was likely to be condemned for being too sanguine! But as military fortunes ebbed and flowed, so Roosevelt continued to worry about, and try to react to, this and other perceived morale difficulties.

Throughout much of 1942, Allied fortunes appeared to be on a downward trajectory. During the winter and early spring, with Japan on the march throughout the Pacific, the news from the fighting fronts was almost uniformly bad. Not until May and June, as the U.S. Navy halted the Japanese tide in two battles at Coral Sea and Midway, was there any reason for good cheer, and this was soon dampened by developments in Europe and North Africa. In May, the Germans won yet another overwhelming victory against the Red Army, this time around Kharkov, which provided them with an ideal launching pad to begin their summer campaign—a highly ambitious attempt to drive southwest toward Stalingrad and into the Caucasus. In June, Erwin Rommel then scored a stunning victory in North Africa, capturing Tobruk and pushing into Egypt. Desperate defensive battles subsequently helped to hinder the German offensives in southern Russia and North Africa, as well as holding up the Japanese incursion onto Guadalcanal. But all in all, the first ten months of 1942 were a depressing time for Allied arms.

Mr. Overoptimist. © *1942,* The Washington Post. *Reprinted with permission.*

Although the news from the fighting fronts was generally bad, American morale tended to fluctuate feverishly between optimism and pessimism—much to the president's exasperation. Roosevelt certainly did his best to try to smooth out the peaks and troughs. In February, when faced with the twin problems of complacency and defeatism that greeted Japan's marauding advances, he focused firmly on the very real hardships ahead and the need for Americans to give their all to the war effort.[125] By the spring, however, as news filtered through of successes at Coral Sea and Midway, FDR's worries shifted somewhat, and he now attempted to caution against excessive mood swings. "In a war," he lectured the press on

POLL (JUNE TO SEPTEMBER 1942)

How do you think the war is going now?	June 29 – July 18 (%)	Aug. 10 – Aug. 29 (%)	Aug. 31 – Sept. 12 (%)
War going well, improving	19	35	40
Badly, slowly	51	35	21
Sometimes well, sometimes badly	7	5	5
Don't know, nervous confused	6	7	7
Don't know/not ascertainable	17	18	27

Sources: "Intelligence Report: Realism and the Offensive Spirit," October 21, 1942, PSF (Subject): OWI, FDRL. See also "How the War Appears to be Going: Trends—July to September 1942," September 29, 1942, entry 162, box 1784, RG 44, NA.

May 22, "public opinion—and news—goes up and down with things which look big at the moment that actually are merely a part of a war. All we can do to prevent those ups and downs the better it will be for the war effort. It is going to be a long war, and there is no reason for being over-optimistic one week and over-pessimistic the next week."[126]

As if to back-up FDR's prediction, by the start of July the OWI suddenly noted "a dramatic shift from ebullience to gloom." This new "realism," it fretted, "coming so suddenly on the heels of pervasive over-confidence, contains elements which may be disturbing to national morale."[127] Yet within weeks Roosevelt received other surveys revealing that more people thought the war was going well than badly, even though the German campaign on the Eastern Front was still rolling inexorably forward toward the Volga and the Caucasus.[128] Deeply frustrated, the president had to turn his attention back toward complacency. The press, he grumbled in August, was far "too optimistic," for its reports were holding out "too great [a] hope of Allied success against superior forces both in men and materiel."[129]

Despite all his efforts to keep popular opinion on an even keel, Roosevelt was acutely aware of his inability to prevent the press and public from reading too much into each and every event. But this was not the only aspect of the problem. Trying to improve morale also complicated certain elements of the administration's nature-of-the-enemy campaign.

This first became evident in January and February. In the first few weeks after Pearl Harbor, a central component of the government's educational message had been that the Nazi regime was so mendacious, brutal, and expansive that a negotiated peace was out of the question. The Allies' only possible goal, Roosevelt repeatedly declared, was "complete and total victory." By the start of the New Year, however, the president suddenly deemed it prudent to play down the prospects of victory and to drop any references to the postwar world. His reasoning was simple: with the public suffering from excessive complacency, FDR shied away from any phrase that might create the impression that the war would soon be over. So not only were calls for "complete and total victory" promptly expunged from his public utterances, but the president was now especially reluctant to get involved in any public discussion about war aims at this stage, admonishing journalists to focus on winning the war "before we start determining all the details of geography and the forms of government, and boundaries and things like that."[130]

Roosevelt and his officials were also convinced that complacency could best be dampened by highlighting the very real danger the Nazis posed to the United States. As MacLeish stressed in April, it was vital to make the public aware that "we *can* be defeated," that "America *can* lose," and that "It *Can* Happen Here!"[131] But complacency was only one aspect of the morale problem; from time to time officials also worried that the public might be excessively defeatist. Consequently, any talk of the Nazis being able either to invade the United States or to win the war had to be handled with extreme care. Indeed, such themes could not be used too frequently, for fear that they might tempt a defeatist public to give up the fight altogether and opt for a compromise peace. How this served to complicate the government's information campaign was best illustrated by an episode in April. At this stage, the president was anxious to fire the public's imagination by asking them to find a name for the current conflict. Roosevelt favored the label, "Survival War," since he felt that excessive optimism might be dampened if people realized that the stakes were nothing less than "the survival of our civilization, the survival of our democracy, the survival of our hemisphere." But he was soon backing away from this suggestion because, as his speech writer, Samuel Rosenman, pointed out, at a time of one military setback after another, "some of us feel that the term the 'War of Survival' is somewhat defeatist in nature."[132]

Compounding these difficulties was the lack of a coordinated government response to the cluster of morale problems. Whereas the OWI and top officials had effectively followed the president's lead in indicting the brutal and expansionist Nazis, when it came to reacting to the peaks and troughs—to fine-tuning the public mood so that it overreacted neither to defeat nor victory—the administration's efforts were not so harmonious. Essentially, this was because the OWI, like the OFF before it, was unable to gain complete authority over the daily news output of executive branch. Not only did other departments continue to issue their own press releases, "often [being] careless in their clearance with OWI," but the army and navy also retained a tight grip on the release over casualty figures and news of U.S. battles. In the navy's case this meant that often very little was made public; as Elmer Davis later complained, he always suspected that the navy's "idea of war information was that there should be just *one* communiqué. Some morning we would announce that the war was won and that we had won it."[133] With the OWI unable to fulfill its promise of releasing truthful information that gave "the public a clear and accurate picture of ... the war," it was hardly surprising that the press now began to turn the tables on the government, accusing *it* of engendering complacency. The most common criticism among both friendly and opposition newspapers, noted the OWI, was that the administration deliberately withholds bad news.[134]

Underpinning the administration's continued concern about the state of morale, and especially the public's penchant to be overoptimistic, was the feeling that, although mass opinion might now have a basic awareness of the main characteristics of nazism, this might not be held with any great intensity. In other words, officials were fearful that, while the people might be familiar with the brutal and expansionist nature of the Nazi regime, their complacency nevertheless implied that they had doubts that the threat was imminent and a misplaced confidence that defeating Germany would be easy. Even now, there appeared to be a continued detachment, passivity, perhaps even apathy about the whole war. As one OWI report to the president put it, the government's information campaign had convinced the people, "on an intellectual level, that it is sensible to fight fascism. But it has not kindled their imagination."[135]

A number of other trends appeared to reinforce this lack of fervor. One was the fact that media and mass antipathy toward the Nazis was not yet fierce enough to engender consistent support for a "Germany-first" strategy. By July, polls were suddenly indicating yet another distinct shift in mass opinion, so that a plurality of Americans now shared Roosevelt's view that U.S. resources should be concentrated against the Wehrmacht. But just as complacency and defeatism still oscillated in response to external events, so the OWI also felt that this rekindled desire to focus against the Third Reich was merely a product of battlefield fortunes. As it reported to the president in September, the American people have "tended to demand the strongest action against the member of the Axis which is on the attack."[136] This in itself was troubling, for it meant the new support for "Germany first" might only be transitory and could easily be reversed if battlefield fortunes changed, regardless of the fact that the government had expended much time and effort attempting to convince the people of the need to focus on the Nazi threat to America's very existence.

Another sign of a general lack of zeal in the public's opposition toward Germany was the persistence of sentiment in favor of a negotiated peace. Here, too, the evidence initially suggested widespread support for the government line. In September, one opinion poll revealed that 58 percent of the population was opposed to discussing peace terms with the enemy, while in October a number of the Republican congressmen seeking reelection signed a manifesto stating that they would oppose any attempt at a negotiated peace and would instead seek to prosecute the war vigorously until "complete decisive victory is won."[137] But again, officials were less

POLL (MARCH TO JULY 1942)

Which one of these do you think the U.S. ought to do now *in the war against Germany and Japan?*	Mar. 28 – April 7 (%)	May 6 – May 17 (%)	July 1–11 (%)	July 20–27 (%)
Concentrate on Japan	62	33	22	21
Concentrate on Germany	21	22	34	40
Concentrate on both	—	27	28	23
Withdraw to home	—	7	7	8
Not ascertainable	17	11	9	8

Source: "Intelligence Report: Trends in American Public Opinion Since Pearl Harbor," September 11, 1942, PSF (Subject): OWI, FDRL.

concerned with such surface facts; rather, what caught their attention was not that most opposed negotiation but that so many favored it. On September 14, in a confidential report sent to the president, Cantril highlighted the growing support for a compromise peace, if the German army was to "overthrow Hitler and agreed to stop the war and discuss peace." A third of all Americans would be willing to talk with the German generals; and of these, 60 percent identified the German army with the German people.[138]

Of course, administration rhetoric had hardly helped to dissuade such sentiment. Not only had Roosevelt and his officials continued to separate the regime from the people, thereby creating the impression that if the Nazis were overthrown then negotiation might be possible, but they had also paid scant attention to the more subtle distinction between the German army and the German people. At this stage, however, officials ignored this possible side effect of their own information campaign and blamed such attitudes on two familiar villains. "A willingness to accept a negotiated peace," asserted one report that filtered up to the White House, "is symptomatic of unhealthy morale," and those who held such opinions "apparently fail to grasp the issues and the purposes of the war or to visualize the consequences of defeat."[139] Negotiated-peace sentiment, the president complained, was merely a product of machinations by divisionists and "Roosevelt-haters," those who only wanted to win the war "(a) if at the same time, Russia is defeated, (b) at the same time, England is defeated, (c) at the same time, Roosevelt is defeated."[140]

As this statement demonstrates, even after ten months of war FDR remained concerned about the dogged persistence of divisionism. Once more, a cursory glance at the opinion polls hardly seemed to confirm the president's anxiety. In two surveys that caught the attention of top State Department officials it was clear that internationalism had grown markedly since Pearl Harbor, with almost three-quarters of the public now in favor of U.S. participation in an international organization. Such results, however, obscured the tenor of much political discourse undertaken throughout the summer and fall, both by FDR's opponents in the press and by Republican congressional candidates. As one report sent to Welles in July reported, the Hearst-Patterson-McCormick newspapers were continuing a "policy of obstructing, beclouding, and misrepresenting the aims of the government."[141] More importantly, for all the indications that the Republican Party was about to embrace interventionism, the isolationist bloc remained remarkably resilient in November's congressional election. "Isolationism" gloated the GOP party organ after the results were all in, "laid a very large egg." Of "115 members of the House of Representatives who survived the primaries and who were selected for purging by the 'interventionist' groups, 110 were elected and only 5 were defeated."[142] This reaction was shared by other conservative newspapers. The *Detroit News*, for example, called the election result "a protest against stumbling and fumbling," while the Scripps-Howard press declared that "the people at the polls were protesting inefficient, ankle-deep conduct of the war."[143] For these journalists, then, complacency, the persistence of isolationism, and a general unease about the course of the war had apparently filtered through to the one opinion poll that really mattered: the ballot box.

After nearly a year of war, Roosevelt and his top officials still feared that the American people were by no means united behind the war effort. In that time, the administration had made numerous efforts to counter five specific problems: "Asia-first" sentiment, divisionism, defeatism, complacency, and ignorance. In seeking to educate the public about the nature of the Nazi enemy, it had also been able to coordinate its response. While the president had provided few explicit leads, the OFF, OWI, and most top officials had all been willing to echo his central theme: namely, that Hitler and the Nazis, because of their expansionist and brutal goals, were the true number-one enemy. But despite this clear depiction of an ideological menace, the government had hardly been engaged in a vigorous crusade aimed at manipulating public opinion by exaggerating the danger. For one thing, the president and his propagandists had constantly rejected appeals to foment hatred against all Germans; Roosevelt, in particular, had simply been content to repeat his private image of the enemy, publicly emphasizing his hopes as well as his fears. When highlighting the savage or aggressive nature of nazism, the OWI had also been anxious to make its comments comprehensible and believable. But it had failed to inform the public about the true extent of the Third Reich's heinous conduct. Most conspicuously, of course, it had remained silent about the genocide of the Jews that was now starting to unfold across occupied Europe.

In response to these concerted, coordinated, but somewhat restrained efforts, there were indications that most Americans were now more acutely aware of the danger posed by Hitler and his cohorts. But while most continued to believe that nazism was beyond the pale, that it was so brutal and dangerous that appeasement would be pointless, not all drew the same implications from this conclusion. Indeed, partly because the administration had been keen to emphasize the danger from the Nazi leadership rather than the German people, a significant minority felt that negotiation would be desirable if the Hitler state was ever overthrown. Officials also feared that this emerging consensus on the nature of the Nazi enemy was not intensely held. They were especially preoccupied with the fact that public attitudes still tended to fluctuate in line with battlefield fortunes, so that on many issues popular opinion remained confused and confusing.

Ultimately, then, the government clearly recognized that it could not mould popular opinion at will. It might be able to bolster the public's existing hatred of nazism, pointing out the intentions and capabilities of Hitler and his ilk. But it could not generate sustained and deep-seated support for a "Germany-first" strategy, nor could it prevent the ebbs and flows in morale. As the president's attention turned toward the problems of grand strategy, he was therefore acutely aware that he faced a stubborn and persistent set of public opinion problems that still had the potential to hamper, and perhaps even endanger, the nation's war effort.

3

Planning
Germany's Defeat

DECEMBER 1941 TO NOVEMBER 1943

Apparently our political system would re-
quire major operations this year in Africa.
——General George C. Marshall,
July 14, 1942

Winston Churchill was at Chequers on
Sunday, December 7, 1941, relaxing at
the prime minister's official retreat with
John G. Winant, the American ambassador, and Averell Harriman, the president's envoy. After a somewhat subdued dinner, the three men gathered
around the radio set to catch the BBC's
nine o'clock news. As the announcer
began to recount the first sketchy details of a Japanese attack on Hawaii,
everyone in the room was stunned, for
it seemed scarcely credible that the
Japanese would be foolish enough to launch a direct assault on U.S. territory. Churchill, desperate for additional information, immediately placed a
transatlantic call to the White House. "It's quite true," the president soon
confirmed. "They have attacked us at Pearl Harbor. We are all in the same
boat now." When he put down the phone, Churchill was ecstatic. Confident that American power would prove decisive in the struggle against the
Axis, he now deemed victory to be certain. "All the rest," as he later put it,
"was merely the proper application of overwhelming force."[1]

Yet Churchill's burst of optimism greatly minimized the problems that
lay ahead. While there was no doubting that the Allies had far more raw

strength than the Axis, it was by no means clear exactly how this over-whelming force could best be applied. Should it be deployed against Germany or Japan first? Should American power be translated into a large land army or should the United States remain the "arsenal of democracy"? When should the first attacks be unleashed? And where was the best location to launch any assault? Even with America plunged directly into the war, these were questions that would continue to plague Allied leaders.

As President Roosevelt struggled to the find the answers, he never for one moment forgot about the phony war mentality that still afflicted many of his fellow countrymen—the brittle morale, the fragile support for "Germany first," the lack of real awareness about the Nazi menace. But while the president remained deeply sensitive to the vagaries of the popular mood, this did not mean that there was a simple correlation between public opinion and policy outcomes. It was not merely the case of the president bowing to a popular clamor for an immediate second front. Nor was he purely preoccupied with launching an invasion before the impending congressional elections. In fact, when it came to grand strategy, public opinion only entered Franklin Roosevelt's calculations in a highly subtle and complicated manner.

Toward the First Offensive: FDR, Public Opinion, and Grand Strategy, January to October 1942

On December 12, less than a week after the Pearl Harbor attack, Winston Churchill and a retinue of advisers boarded the *Duke of York*, bound for the United States and a full-scale military conference with the new belligerent. On arriving in Washington, the prime minister was immediately installed as a guest in the White House. From here, he soon pitched in to help FDR with his information campaign, appearing unexpectedly at a presidential press conference on December 23 and delivering an impassioned address to a joint session of Congress three days later.

Churchill, like Roosevelt, had a natural flair for publicity, and his efforts played exceedingly well with the press and public. But when it came to the mechanics of decision-making it soon became clear that the two men had very different styles. The prime minister always seemed to be at the hub of a great deal of activity and noise, reeling off missives, dressing down subordinates, rushing off to be wherever the action was. The president, however, preferred to work at a more leisurely pace and needed frequent periods of rest and relaxation. The prime minister was also a hands-on administrator, who liked to meet frequently and regularly with his military chiefs, bombarding them with suggestions and intervening in their problems both large and small. The president, however, tended to remain in the background, a more remote figure, whose views were often difficult to fathom but who rarely bothered subordinates with detailed questions about operational or tactical problems.[2] Moreover, the prime minister generally conducted the bulk of his business in writing, developing his thoughts in verbose but articulate memoranda and sending off instructions in precise and detailed minutes. The president, however, had a distinct aversion to writing anything down, and not only discouraged his officials from taking notes in meetings but on one occasion even asked top aides to falsify the documentary record so as to obscure the record for future researchers![3]

With the two men living and working in such close proximity, their contrasting styles and clashing egos occasionally surfaced. Churchill, for instance, "would slump in silence" whenever the president dominated the conversation: he was not accustomed to being upstaged. Roosevelt, meanwhile, would sometimes get overly tired as the conversation extended into the early hours of the morning: he was not used to such late-night sessions. But on the whole, the time the two spent together over Christmas and New Year helped to cement both their friendship and the alliance. The president even began to recognize the merits of some of the prime minister's working habits. Roosevelt was certainly impressed by the way Churchill was kept informed of the very latest military developments, and soon had a map room installed in the White House so that he too could receive the most up-to-date information and intelligence.[4] FDR also recognized that he would need a new organization not just to coordinate military planning more efficiently but also to deal with the British military chiefs on an equal footing. In January, he therefore created the Joint Chiefs of Staff (JCS), consisting of General Marshall; Henry "Hap" Arnold, the air chief; and Ernest J. King, the new chief of naval operations.

Yet for some of the president's top advisers, these innovations did not address the real problem. With the Allies suffering one defeat after another, they worried that the president's style was particularly ill suited to the demands and complexities of determining grand strategy. Roosevelt's reluctance to meet formally with the Joint Chiefs as a body seemed to be one handicap. But even worse, the president (like the press he often lambasted) sometimes appeared to get too easily distracted by news of each and every fluctuation in Allied fortunes. Marshall, for one, frequently despaired of FDR's "cigarette-holder gesture," his tendency to muse casually about new operations in response to the latest change on the battlefield. Stimson agreed. "The same qualities which endear him to his countrymen," he grumbled in May, "militate against the firmness of his execution at a time like this."[5]

Marshall and Stimson certainly had reason to be upset with the president, for in 1942 they were vehemently opposed to many of his central policy preferences. But their specific criticisms about the damaging effects of Roosevelt's administrative style were wide of the mark. FDR undoubtedly liked to work in a relatively calm, relaxed, and informal manner, but this did not mean he was either too detached or overly indecisive. Indeed, he may have shied away from scheduled and structured meetings with the JCS

FDR and his senior military advisers. From left to right, King, Leahy, FDR, Marshall. General Laurence S. Kuter is on the extreme right.

as a whole, but he still invited the navy top brass to the White House on a regular basis (Admiral King was a visitor at least forty-two times during 1942). He also continued to use Harry Hopkins as his liaison with Marshall and the army, and from July he had his own personal chief of staff, in the guise of Admiral William D. Leahy, who was not only a full member of the Joint Chiefs but was also charged with the task of being the president's "leg man, a collector of military advice, a summarizer."[6] More to the point, FDR may have had an infuriating propensity to let meetings and discussions wander off the point, but as soon as he began to focus his mind on the core problems of grand strategy, no one could doubt that he had a clear and firm grasp of exactly what he wanted and why he wanted it.

Since the late 1930s, Roosevelt had been convinced that Nazi Germany was the most powerful and dangerous of America's enemies. As soon as Churchill arrived in the White House, the president wasted no time in agreeing with the British that Germany was the prime enemy and its defeat was the key to victory. Until the Third Reich was defeated, Allied troops would have to remain on the defensive in Asia.[7]

During the dark, depressing winter of 1941–42, some inroads were made into this "Germany-first" principle. This was the period when the Japanese were on the rampage, overrunning Allied positions in Malaya, the Philippines, and the Dutch East Indies, and so merely defending an area from Australia to the Aleutian islands required a seemingly endless supply of Allied men and materiel. Roosevelt, increasingly concerned that "the Japanese were getting awfully close to home," quickly bowed to the logic of the situation. By June, the president and his military advisers had agreed to send 245,000 troops to the Pacific, which was already 15,000 more than the War Department had planned to have in this theater by the end of the year. During the spring, FDR then endorsed a token bombing attack on the Japanese mainland, the so-called Doolittle Raid, in an attempt to take the war to the perpetrator of Pearl Harbor. And at the same time, he was also aware of the great strides being made by the navy after the debacle of December. In May, the reorganized Pacific Fleet managed to fight a creditable draw against the Japanese in the Coral Sea; a month later it won a decisive victory at Midway.[8]

Yet for Roosevelt, these early deployments were only ad hoc and defensive ripostes to the unfolding military threat. Although they took valuable resources away from the European theater, in his opinion they did nothing to undermine the commitment to launch America's first major offensive against the Germans. Increasingly, however, the president faced intense pressure to reassess his thinking on this subject. Admiral King, the hard-bitten, blunt-talking new commander of the U.S. Fleet, was especially keen to see even more resources directed to Asia, fearing that any delay in dealing with the Japanese would give the enemy the opportunity to "drive hard" at the remaining Allied outposts. Douglas MacArthur agreed. Having ignominiously escaped the military disaster engulfing the Philippines in March, MacArthur was now desperate to use his new base in Australia to strike back at the Japanese. During the summer, he got a measure of support from a surprising source. In July, General Marshall, up to now an ardent partisan of a "Germany-first" strategy, briefly got the Joint Chiefs to endorse an "Asia-first" policy, if the alternative was to fritter away American resources in secondary sideshows like North Africa.[9]

Significantly, in their attempts to prod the president to backtrack from "Germany first," these military men all contended that a majority of Americans strongly favored such a course. The United States, declared MacArthur on May 8, should take the offensive against Japan at "the earliest possible moment" in order to "satisfy American public opinion by providing an adequate effort in the only theatre which is charged exclusively to the U.S." "Decisive action against Japan," noted Marshall on July 10, "would be highly popular throughout the U.S., particularly on the West Coast."[10]

The president refused to agree, however, and brushed off such claims as a "red herring."[11] In large part, this was due to his perception of the military situation. "It seems unwise to attempt a major offensive in the Pacific

area," he wrote to his top advisers on July 29, "because of the time involved—one to two years—and the total lack of effect on Germany of
such a major offensive."[12] To ignore the Third Reich for this length of
time would also provide the Wehrmacht with a perfect opportunity to destroy the Red Army, and, as he remarked in June, "Germany would be
very strong if Russia collapsed"—certainly stronger and more dangerous
than Japan was ever likely to be. The Atlantic area, he therefore believed,
"calls for essentially offensive operations," for this was the best method "of
aiding Russia in the destruction of as many Germans and German material
as possible."[13]

But FDR also ignored the arguments of his military advisers because
he was aware they were using "public opinion" instrumentally, to bolster
their arguments, and were not championing a widely popular cause. Indeed, contrary to the claims not only of MacArthur and the JCS but also of
many subsequent historians, Roosevelt was *not* at this stage deeply concerned "that public pressure for a Pacific-first approach was reaching dangerous proportions."[14] True, between January and March, with the Japanese army rampant, he was told that "the pendulum of editorial attention"
had increasingly swung from the Atlantic to the Pacific, while in April and
May the OFF informed him that almost two-thirds of mass opinion wanted
to focus U.S. resources against Japan.[15] But at the same time, he was also
aware that such views were not held with any intensity. As early as April,
a clear plurality of Americans still viewed Germany as "the number-one
enemy," while over the spring and summer, in the wake of Japanese defeats
and German victories, the remaining support for "Asia-first" strategy also
started to wane. Thereafter, although the mass attitudes remained a worry,
with public approval for "Germany first" likely to crumble as soon as battlefield fortunes changed, there was by no means the popular furor, the
overwhelming public pressure, that would have been necessary for the
president even to contemplate reassessing such a deeply held conviction.[16]
As a result, by May FDR could confidently proclaim "that Hitler was the
chief enemy," and that although "it had been difficult to put that view
across, . . . in his opinion, it was now accepted."[17]

If Roosevelt's first aim was to focus U.S. efforts against the Third
Reich, his second goal was to deploy American ground troops against the
Wehrmacht. This is not to say that the president's old hopes that the fragile
Hitler state might be eradicated relatively cheaply had entirely vanished. In
May, he agreed with one adviser that "there was beginning to be a consciousness of defeat and [the German] people were beginning to look
around for the next thing." In July, he remarked in a similar vein "that reports from inside Germany continued to be bad" and that it was his "conviction that if Russia can hold out and if the Middle East can hold out, Germany cannot successfully pass another winter."[18]

But while the president remained somewhat sanguine about the
prospects of an internal collapse, he no longer saw this as a central method

In 1942, FDR's focus was firmly fixed on Europe.

of eradicating nazism. Instead, abandoning his pre–Pearl Harbor aversion to sending U.S. troops abroad, FDR began to favor a more balanced approach to defeating the Third Reich. This retained subsidiary means such as air power or propaganda to loosen the Nazis' grip on power, but the principal emphasis was now on the use of U.S. ground troops to defeat the powerful German army. As Roosevelt remarked on May 28, while the "State Department is in receipt of many dispatches from the neutral capitals of Europe telling of the steadily deteriorating position of the Axis," and "while the indications were hopeful, nevertheless 'We can't . . . win this war by hoping that Germany will lose it.'"[19] "Propaganda or other measures designed to break down morale within the enemy ranks are important elements in the conduct of the war," he stressed on another occasion. "It will, however, be through the force of our ever-growing strength of arms that the enemy wherever he be shall and will be thoroughly defeated."[20] In practice, this meant that, whereas in September 1941 the president had contemplated reducing the size of the U.S. Army, by January 1942 he agreed to the War Department's plan to increase troop levels to 3.6 million by the end of the year, and also contemplated increasing the army to 5 million by July 1943 and 8 million by July 1944.[21]

FDR's views on the means required to defeat Germany had undergone a distinct shift. But what explains this newfound desire to construct a large army and send it abroad? What variable had changed between the fall of 1941 and the beginning of 1942? Roosevelt's sudden conversion can hardly be attributed to the fluctuating dictates of alliance politics, because both before and after December 7 Churchill and Stalin had been anxious for the United States to throw its full weight onto the scales. Nor did it stem from shifting bureaucratic pressures, since the bulk of FDR's military advisers had also long been convinced of the need to send U.S. land forces abroad. It was not even the product of a mounting pessimism that the Hitler regime might *not* implode internally and that bombing and psychological warfare might not therefore suffice. After all, as the Red Army drove the Wehrmacht back from the gates of Moscow during the winter, Roosevelt received numerous reports stressing that "many Germans are nervous and worried," that "discord between the Party and population is growing," and that "Hitler and other officials of the Nazi Party are having difficulty with the army."[22] As we have seen, he also remained firmly inclined to accept the accuracy of such information.

The only variable that changed markedly during this period was public opinion. Put simply, in the fall of 1941, FDR's public and private utterances had been skewed exclusively toward propaganda and bombing because of the overwhelming popular opposition to sending American troops abroad. Now that Pearl Harbor had removed this controlling constraint, the president suddenly felt free to place primary emphasis on the use of ground troops, confident that such an approach "will work out in full accord with [the] trend of public opinion here."[23]

With the president's blessing and few overt signs of public dissatisfaction, the U.S. Army began to grow in dramatic fashion during 1942. Millions of new recruits headed south, destined for one of the 242 training camps where they would receive basic training, indoctrination about Allied war aims, and then more specialized instruction in radio communications and the use of different types of weapons. By the end of the year, many of these soldiers had been organized into thirty-seven new divisions.

As America finally developed the fighting capacity to confront the Wehrmacht, the president and his advisers turned their attention to when and where these troops should be deployed. Throughout the spring and summer, Roosevelt's concentration was firmly fixed on the problem of timing. Indeed, by this stage the president was not content merely to endorse the use of ground troops. He also fervently and repeatedly stressed the need to get the army into battle against Germans at the earliest possible moment. "It is of the highest importance," he instructed Marshall, King, and Hopkins in July, "that U.S. ground troops be brought into action against the enemy in 1942." "The necessities of the case," he declared on another occasion, "call for action in 1942—not 1943."[24] But what necessitated such prompt action?

Again, there were sound military reasons underpinning FDR's convictions. Most obviously, with the German army deep inside Soviet territory, and driving south into the Caucasus and toward the Volga by the end of June, something had to be done to aid a Red Army that, according to the president, was "killing more Germans and destroying more Axis material than all the twenty-five united nations put together."[25] To discuss exactly how America could help, the president invited Stalin's foreign minister, Vyacheslav Molotov, to Washington toward the end of May. The Russian proved a difficult guest. Not only was his distrust of foreigners so great that he kept a pistol under his bed at night, but he also remained conspicuously immune to Roosevelt's charm. According to one contemporary joke Molotov only knew four English words—"yes," "no," and "second front"—and his meetings in the White House certainly seemed to bear this out. After four days, the president was in doubt that the one thing the Soviets craved was an immediate cross-channel attack to draw German divisions away from the Eastern Front. At a time when the Red Army was in the throes of yet another military disaster, this time around Kharkov where the Germans captured nearly 240,000 soldiers, Roosevelt was anxious to oblige. On June 1, he therefore gave the Soviets a promise, albeit qualified with some doubts about feasibility, that the United States would do its utmost to open up a second front in 1942.[26]

A few weeks later the British arrived in town. Like Molotov, Churchill and his advisers hoped to prod the Americans into an active role as soon as possible, but preferably in the Mediterranean where British military fortunes had just reached their nadir with the fall of Tobruk. The surrender of this vital port was a tremendous blow to the prime minister, and back in London moves were already afoot to stage a vote of no confidence on his handling of the war. Characteristically, Churchill wasted no time in trying to shore up his position. Using his proximity to the president, he began by lobbying for U.S. tanks to be sent to the Middle East to bolster Britain's ailing defenses. The Americans duly obliged, but the prime minister was not content to leave matters there. He was also angling for an Anglo-American invasion of Northwest Africa, in the firm belief that this would present an acute threat to the entire Axis position in the Mediterranean.[27]

The president was therefore under intense pressure from both his main allies to hasten the deployment of U.S. ground troops, and this might well have resulted in a decision for action in 1942, even had no other factors been involved. But alliance diplomacy was not the president's only concern. Public opinion also entered into his calculations and greatly reinforced his desire to get Americans fighting Germans as quickly as possible.

It is worth examining in some detail exactly how domestic politics shaped Roosevelt's actions, because there was no simple and direct relationship between popular opinion and government policy. In the first place, it was not simply the case that "the public was screaming for a second front" and that FDR bowed to this pressure.[28] To be sure, throughout the spring and summer the president was aware that more and more newspapers were lobbying for immediate offensive action. Whereas the OFF monitored only fourteen editorials supporting such a course in the week ending April 9, this had risen to twenty-seven for the week ending June 25 and to forty-three for the week ending July 16.[29] At the start of July, even divisionist organs like the *Chicago Tribune* and *Washington Times-Herald* began calling for a second front. Within two weeks they were joined by mainstream papers like the *New York Times* and *Washington Post*, who jumped on the bandwagon when it became clear that the Wehrmacht was now heading swiftly toward the key city of Stalingrad.[30] Monitoring these trends for the president, by July 29 the OWI began to note that the treatment of the news was becoming "feverish," with "demand for vigorous offensive action against Germany [now being] voiced by the nation's outstanding commentators."[31]

Yet it seems doubtful whether this mounting popular pressure had any direct bearing on Roosevelt's decision to seek prompt action in 1942, since the media's second-front campaign only began in earnest *after* the president's mind had already been made up. Indeed, FDR had expressed a desire to get U.S. troops quickly into action against the Wehrmacht throughout the spring, long before the nation's editors started to grasp this issue.[32] The decision to act in 1942 was then basically taken on June 21, a month before the media's treatment of this issue became "feverish."[33]

It was also clear to Roosevelt that pressure for a second front lacked intensity. Although most opinion makers were discussing this subject by the end of July, the president was dismissive and scathing about their conclusions. Public opinion on strategic matters, he remarked at one point during the summer, "is made largely by the commentators and columnists who had little understanding" of these matters "and are for the most part rather shallow thinkers."[34] As if to confirm FDR's skepticism, the press' interest in the whole matter also ebbed quickly during August and September, as Red Army resistance stiffened around Stalingrad and the Allies launched an ill-fated raid along the French coast at Dieppe. According to one OWI survey, by the end of September most newspapers were almost completely ignoring the broad aspects of this issue.[35] Moreover, while demand for action from opinion makers was belated and brief, the attitude of the mass public was permissive rather than pressurizing. "They have been taught that the road to victory must be opened by offensive action," the OWI concluded in October, in the only survey received by the White House that closely monitored popular opinion on this subject. But most Americans were hardly calling vehemently for an immediate attack; on this subject mass opinion remained far from fervent.

While direct popular pressure therefore played a minimal role in Roosevelt's calculations, a desire to shape the outcome of the November congressional poll was also a subsidiary concern. Of course, the president was not oblivious to the electoral rewards that might be reaped by a successful attack. During July and August he therefore pushed constantly for an offensive to be launched by October 31, so that it would occur before polling day. For a brief period he also considered reducing the military personnel

POLL (SEPTEMBER 1942)

---

*Do you think in the next two or three months
the Allies should try to land an army on
the continent of Europe for a real invasion?*

Yes (57%)

No (25%)

Don't know (18%)

Source: "Intelligence Report: Realism and the Offensive Spirit," October 21, 1942, p. 1, pp. 4–5, PSF (Subject): OWI, FDRL.

involved by one-third when told that sufficient shipping was not available for a swift attack.[36] And on one occasion when Marshall went to the White House for a consultation about operational planning, the president even jokingly "held up his hands in an attitude of prayer and said 'please make it before Election Day.'" But although FDR naturally preferred a preelection offensive, believing that this might rally voters behind the Democratic party, this was not a controlling factor. As Marshall later testified, when it became clear that because of the time-consuming process of converting ocean liners into troop ships the earliest possible date for an invasion would be five days after the congressional poll, the president "never said a word." He simply left the military alone to take care of the necessary tactical planning and to come up with their own timetable.[37]

Roosevelt's desire for action in 1942, then, was neither a product of intense popular pressure for a second front nor principally the result of electoral politics. Instead, the president's motives on this question only become clear in light of his perception of public opinion, both his old difficulties dating back to before Pearl Harbor and the current problems that his information campaign had failed to resolve. On the one hand, FDR had not forgotten that throughout 1941 the poor morale of conscripts in military camps had quickly become a subject of national debate. When combined with his fear that the public's new-found desire for offensive action might prove ephemeral, the president was naturally anxious *not* to retain vast numbers of troops in training camps throughout the United States, where their continued discontent might well provide divisionists with an opportunity to fuel the public's traditional distrust of large standing armies. Instead, Roosevelt preferred to send the GIs abroad quickly. As he remarked in June, rather than having "a serious political problem of having a vast army here in this country trained and ready to fight," he wanted it made clear "that our government was insisting upon our taking an appropriate part in the war, not only by sea and air but by our ground forces as well."[38]

But by sending the army off to fight in 1942, Roosevelt was not merely seeking to remove a potential object of divisionist criticism. He was also attempting to set the agenda, to create an incident that would alter the main contours of public opinion. He had, after all, long been aware that important external incidents such as France's fall or Pearl Harbor had had a profound impact on popular attitudes. And in the first months of 1942, with both morale and support for "Germany first" fluctuating in line with military fortunes, it was again apparent that events were a powerful persuader. Given these lessons, it was hardly surprising that FDR was convinced that prompt action could well help to solve his lingering public opinion problems. In particular, if GIs were fighting the Wehrmacht, this would undoubtedly dominate media coverage and the minds of the mass public, thereby leading to a relative decline in interest in the Asia conflict. As a result, popular support for "Germany first," which had previously depended on the intensity of fighting in the respective theatres, might well become more firmly ingrained. Furthermore, stories and pictures of Americans in mortal combat with German soldiers might also engender a greater awareness about the war in Europe, while a string of victories would undoubtedly assuage the closely related morale problems of apathy and defeatism. Small wonder, then, that as FDR remarked in one meeting with Churchill, it was "very important to morale, to give this country a feeling that they are in the war, . . . to have American troops fighting somewhere across the Atlantic." Or, as Marshall later conceded, "the leader in a democracy has to keep the people entertained."[39]

For Roosevelt, it was essential to begin this task of entertaining the people as soon as possible. On June 11, he therefore used the occasion of Molotov's visit to publicly announce that the Allies had reached a full understanding "with regard to the urgent tasks of creating a second front in Europe in 1942." Almost two weeks later, on the first anniversary of Hitler's invasion of the Soviet Union, Harry Hopkins then publicly reiterated this commitment, declaring that the United States would establish a second, third, and fourth front if necessary. On the back of such pronouncements, the press was not slow to speculate on the significance of General Dwight D. Eisenhower's appointment to head the newly created "European Theater of Operations for U.S. Forces" based in London. According to the nation's media, this was nothing less than a "second front staff," a sure sign that U.S. troops would soon be on the move against the Nazis.[40]

But where exactly? By July, Roosevelt's determination to use a land force against the Germans in 1942 had effectively decided this final problem. Given the logistical problems of mounting an invasion on the French coast, especially the lack of transport ships, which made it possible to land only six to eight divisions to face far greater German forces, any cross-channel assault in 1942 would be an extremely hazardous operation.[41] In FDR's opinion this left North Africa as the most viable alternative. But before he could carry this point he had to confront staunch opposition from his military advisers. The root of the problem was that, while Roosevelt was concerned primarily with timing, for Marshall and Stimson the top priority was location. Both greatly preferred opening a second front in France.

This would confront the Germans in a vital area and would consequently force Hitler to divert resources from the Eastern Front. It would also avoid the dissipation of American men and material to marginal regions. "To defeat the Germans," Marshall believed, "we must have overwhelming power, and Northwest Europe was the only front on which this over-whelming superiority was logistically possible. It was, therefore, sound strategy to concentrate on this front and divert minimum resources only to other fronts."[42]

The president was not initially opposed to a direct attack on the European continent, but he was increasingly concerned about the risks involved. "A second front against Germany," he remarked on April 19, "should not be opened rashly but it should be done if it offered a reasonable chance of success."[43] He was also worried about the time it would take to launch an attack in France, becoming more and more convinced that a successful invasion could not be undertaken in 1942.[44] But Churchill, not Roosevelt, was the most outspoken opponent of any immediate landing in France, since Britain would have to provide the bulk of the troops for such a risky undertaking at this time, and the prime minister was extremely reluctant to meet the Wehrmacht head-on before a peripheral strategy had considerably worn down German strength.[45] Churchill, after all, faced his own domestic problems and, having just survived a vote of no confidence in the wake of Tobruk's fall, he was not anxious to send British troops off on a sacrifice mission across the channel, where in all likelihood they would either be slaughtered or be forced into another humiliating Dunkirk-style evacuation.

By July, the respective positions were clearly drawn. On one hand, Churchill was firmly against a cross-channel invasion in 1942, instead favoring an offensive in the Mediterranean where the bulk of Britains's offensive had been directed since 1940. On the other hand, the JCS were prepared to abandon Europe altogether, preferring an "Asia-first" strategy rather than see American resources dissipated in a marginal area.[46] Roosevelt, meanwhile, remained adamant that U.S. troops should be brought into action against Germany in 1942. With Britain opposed to sacrificing their troops in an invasion of France that year, he worked hard to push his Joint Chiefs into accepting the North African alternative. For a start, he argued in a series of discussions at the beginning of July, "Asia first" was an unrealistic option. Not only were there no detailed plans on which to base such a dramatic shift in policy, but as he told Marshall, this "is exactly what Germany hoped the United States would do following Pearl Harbor." FDR also believed that a North African invasion had its advantages, repeatedly stressing that it would forestall Nazi penetration into Dakar, an area that provided Germany with its best opportunity to launch an attack against the Americas.[47]

Bombarded by the president's arguments, and unable to shift British opposition in a series of meetings between July 18 and 24, the Joint Chiefs finally succumbed and the decision was taken to launch an offensive in the fall against Morocco and Algeria under the code-name Operation TORCH. "I am, of course, very happy in the result," Roosevelt wrote to Churchill three days later, and "I cannot help feeling that the past week represented a turning point in the whole war."[48]

By the late summer, planning for Operation TORCH was proceeding apace. Public opinion had played a role in this first major decision of American World War II grand strategy, but not in a simple or straightforward manner. Roosevelt was not merely preoccupied with electoral politics, since he ultimately accepted that the invasion would have to be launched after polling day. Nor were his decisions congruent with direct popular pressure for a second front, because this largely came in July, at least a month after his mind had already been made up on this issue. Instead, public opinion only entered presidential calculations in three distinct and subtle ways. First, when it came to deciding who was the main enemy, Roosevelt was basically able to ignore popular support for an "Asia-first" strategy, aware that mass attitudes were far from firm and tended to fluctuate in line with battlefield fortunes. Second, on the subject of what means to employ, FDR had initially been faced with a far different domestic environment. Indeed, before December 7 he was acutely aware of the intense and overwhelming opposition to the use of land troops, and thus in this period public opinion acted as a controlling constraint. Only as the domestic environment became more permissive after Pearl Harbor did Roosevelt begin to explicitly advocate the need for land forces to defeat the Third Reich. Finally, on the question of when and where to launch the first attack, the president's decision to push for prompt action, although partially a product of a desire to aid the ailing Soviets, was also reinforced by a need to solve his lingering public opinion difficulties. Instead of simply reacting to opinion, FDR was hoping to shape it. His aim was to employ American troops against the Wehrmacht as a method of finally eradicating the lingering problems of apathy, defeatism, and weak support for a "Germany-first" strategy, and North Africa was the only feasible area for such action in 1942.

"A Revolution in Political Sentiment"?
Public Opinion and the Aftermath of TORCH,
November 1942 to May 1943

In the early morning of November 8, sixty-five thousand U.S. and British troops waded ashore at Casablanca, Oran, and Algiers to begin the first major American offensive of the war. Despite its hazardous nature, the possibility that "the Allies might find themselves in a long campaign fought for very secondary objectives at the end of tenuous supply lines which ran across submarine-infested seas," the attack proceeded smoothly. The Atlantic remained calm, the landings were mostly unopposed, and key air-fields and installations were soon under Allied control.[49] As Roosevelt had hoped, the initial success of Operation TORCH also had a tremendous impact on mass attitudes. Just as in May 1940, when the Wehrmacht's attack on the Low Countries and France ended the period of European Phony War, so now the North African invasion seemed to have brought the American Phony War and its attendant public opinion problems to a hasty conclusion. As one report to the president concluded, there has been "a revolution in political sentiment toward you and your conduct of the war since the African coup."[50]

Essentially, this "revolution" had three main components. In the first place, the morale problem seemed to dissolve. The administration, long preoccupied with the twin concerns of complacency and defeatism, now felt there was an almost universal optimism about the course of the war. Opinion makers were especially quick to depict TORCH as part of a global and coordinated Allied offensive that was pushing back the Axis on every front—from Stalingrad to El Alamein to Guadalcanal. The press had already been fixated on the struggle in Stalingrad since late summer, lavishing great attention on the street-by-street battle and praying that the Soviets could hold on as the German effort reached its height in mid-October. When the Red Army then launched its counteroffensive just eleven days after TORCH, almost all editorial writers believed the two events to be inextricably linked.[51] Coming on the heels of British success at El Alamein and the stout defense by U.S. troops at Guadalcanal, many even stressed that these victories heralded the ultimate demise of Nazi Germany. As the *Christian Science Monitor* concluded, the combined impact of all four battles would change the fortunes of war dramatically. "Whereas Berlin once planned the moves and did the conquering, today it is the United Nations who have gained the sword of initiative and who have set German divisions shifting back and cross the map of Europe in an attempt to plug a dozen more invasion holes."[52] A few weeks later, the first anniversary of Pearl Harbor provided another opportunity to focus on this swift reversal of fortune. Editorial writers, noted the OWI, were now in the process of reviewing the first year of the war, and were "conclud[ing] that it had turned out well. The United Nations were held to be on the march—wresting the offensive from an enemy which a year ago had been on the attack."[53]

Optimism and confidence were now suddenly the main ingredients of the popular mood. In the middle of November, an administration study of major headlines in twenty metropolitan centers indicated that "78 percent of them blazoned good news stories from one or another fighting fronts. Editorial comment was scarcely less buoyant."[54] Most elements of the mass public also seemed to have discarded any defeatist thoughts. By late November, almost three-quarters now believed that the United States was winning the war, compared to less than half in mid-October. A similar

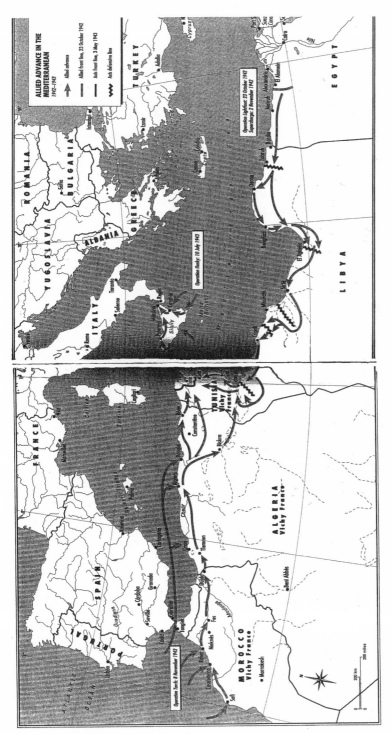

ALLIED ADVANCE IN THE
MEDITERRANEAN
1942–1943

→ Allied advance
▬▬▬ Allied front line, 23 October 1942
▬▬▬ Axis front line, 3 May 1943
〰〰 Axis defensive line

Operation Lightfoot: 23 October 1942
Supercharge: 2 November 1942

Operation Husky: 10 July 1943

Operation Torch: 8 November 1942

Reprinted by permission from A War to be Won: Fighting the Second World War *by Williamson Murray and Allan R. Millett, pp. 264–65, Cambridge, Mass.: The Belknap Press of Harvard University Press, Copyright © 2000 by the President and Fellows of Harvard College.*

POLL (DECEMBER 4, 1942)

Which one of these statements comes closest to the way you think the war will end?	July (%)	Late November (%)
a. There is no question that the United States and her allies will win the war and be able to write the peace terms.	58	73
b. We'll win the war all right, but the losers will be strong enough so *we* will have to make some concessions too	28	19
c. We won't be defeated, but neither will the Axis—the war will end in a draw	6	3
d. I'm afraid the Axis powers have a pretty good chance to win the war.	3	0
Don't know	5	5

Source: "Intelligence Report," No. 52, December 4, 1942, PSF(Subject) OWI: FDRL.

change was recorded on the question of whether the United States would ultimately emerge victorious.

As well as boosting morale, TORCH also seemed to generate further support for a "Germany-first" strategy. Most newspaper analysts were certainly quick to picture the North African landings as the harbinger to a real second front, which they speculated might lead to a direct Anglo-American assault on "Hitler's soft southern flank." Even habitual "Asia-first" partisans like the *Denver Post* now echoed this line, predicting that when the North African campaign was won by the Allies they would then "be in a position to strike and strike hard at the most vulnerable link in the Axis chain—Italy."[55] There seemed to be a growing acceptance too of the administration's view that Germany was the main enemy, and that as soon as it had been defeated Japan would be isolated and hence doomed. As the OWI put it, the "prevailing disposition" amongst commentators was that, "as for Japan—it would be just a matter of time, once the Germans had been knocked out."[56]

The final effect of the November successes was to weaken support for isolationism. Just four days after the start of TORCH, John Franklin Carter informed FDR that even die-hard "Roosevelt haters" now suddenly appreciated the war's significance. In a report filled with the kind of anecdotal evidence the president usually liked, Carter wrote of a crusty old Republican hack who had no love for the administration. Previously, the journalist admitted, he had done "little real serious thinking about the war." But now, with his son in Africa, the journalist had for the first time "begun to do some really independent thinking about this whole mess" and was even

contemplating volunteer work in the civilian services, perhaps even signing up with the military.[57]

The administration had long felt that distrust of America's two main allies had been a main pillar of divisionist sentiment, but this too appeared to
be changing. The previous February, for instance, at the height of the isolationist resurgence, the OWI found that "no more than 49 percent of the
American people were willing to credit the British with making an all-out
war effort." Now, with the Eighth Army's success at El Alamein, with Roosevelt anxious to inform reporters that "Montgomery's army [was] only
equipped in a 'minor' way by the U.S.," and with British soldiers also fighting alongside GIs in North Africa, this mood quickly changed.[58] By the end
of November, almost three-quarters felt that Britain was pulling its weight,
and for the first time "the approval expressed for the British war effort
equaled that expressed for the United States." Attitudes toward the Soviets
followed a similar course, with respect also replacing mistrust. According
to the OWI, the "deep admiration people feel about Russia's valiant resistance to Nazi aggression is having its effect." A majority of 51 percent now
believed that, after the war was over, the Soviet Union could "be depended
upon to co-operate with us," up from 38 percent in February.[59]

The president and his top advisers were naturally pleased by these
changes. FDR, Hull, and Welles, although recognizing that "every administration had to be watchful not to get too far in advance of its public opinion," were definitely not about to mourn the apparent passing of isolationism.[60] Nor were they overly concerned by the public's prevailing
optimism, since, unlike the old complacent attitude, this seemed to be
based on a realistic assessment of concrete achievements. As the OWI succinctly put it, "the growth of optimism registered by these opinions is not
necessarily unhealthy by any means."[61]

By the start of 1943 it therefore seemed that planned events like
TORCH could indeed have a tremendous and immediate impact on mass
attitudes. But this did not mean that the administration's public opinion
problems were now over. Most obviously, there remained the very distinct
likelihood that a series of unforeseen incidents might well intervene and
undo all the good work.

In February 1943, Madame Chiang Kai-shek became the latest in the long
string of foreign visitors to the White House. In the middle of the month,
the Chinese leader's wife clearly betrayed the underlying purpose of her
visit when she went before a joint session of Congress to criticize those
strategists who considered "the defeat of the Japanese as of relative unim-
portance and that Hitler is our first concern."[62] At a time when the Red
Army was capitalizing on its Stalingrad victory by pushing the Germans
back more than four hundred miles to Kharkov, Madame Chiang's analysis seemed particularly persuasive to anyone worried that America's exces-

sive focus on Europe would inadvertently help to spread communism. In the spring, William Bullitt explicitly expressed this concern to the president, writing that if Germany were defeated first, and "if we have a hard fight against Japan while the Soviet Union is at peace and Great Britain is fighting only conservatively, we shall have no decisive voice in the settlement in Europe."[63] Almost coincidentally, the White House received evidence that the Japanese had executed American aviators captured during the Doolittle Raid. Roosevelt quickly realized that by publicizing this information he would provide further ammunition to those clamoring for more action in the Pacific. But, "deeply stirred and horrified" by this incident, and determined to warn the Japanese that the United States would bring those responsible to justice, he never contemplated suppressing it. Instead, on April 21 he issued a statement calling this act "barbarous" and declaring that "it will make the American people more determined than ever to blot out the shameless militarism of Japan."[64]

For many Republicans, emboldened by their gains in the 1942 midterm elections, this series of events seemed to offer the perfect opportunity to revive calls for an "Asia-first" strategy. They certainly took little time in mounting what, according to Raymond Gramm Swing, was "by all odds the best promoted campaign that Washington has ever been subjected to."[65] Their first wave of attacks came in the middle of February, when the OWI noted that "the ex-isolationist press took Madame Chiang's remarks as support for their position that Japan should be regarded as our prime enemy."[66] Then, in April and May numerous congressmen from across the political spectrum went on record calling for the eradication of the nation that was slaughtering U.S. airmen.[67]

As Congress turned up the heat, the White House became increasingly concerned about the wider political implications underpinning this campaign. On March 11, Carter reported to Roosevelt that top members of the GOP were intending to use the "Asia-first" issue as a centerpiece in the following year's presidential campaign. They planned to argue that while "the Democrats (you) are specialists in and preoccupied with European affairs[,] . . . the Republicans (Willkie, Luce, & Co.) are specialists in Pacific and Asiatic affairs; therefore, in 1944, with the defeat of Hitler imminent, it will be sound policy to switch from the war-administration of the European-minded Democrats to a war administration of Asiatic-minded Republicans."[68] Such a political strategy seemed feasible not only because of the noises emanating from Capitol Hill. Toward the end of March, Cantril forwarded to the White House a poll result suggesting that MacArthur was the strongest potential presidential contender in 1944, with a favorable rating of 43 percent, 17 points more than his closest rival, Senator Robert Taft.[69] If the general did become the Republican candidate in a year's time, there was little doubt that greater effort in the Pacific would be a pivotal issue in his campaign.

To make matters worse, during February and March this possible political threat became intertwined with a controversy in Congress over the size of the U.S. Army. Roosevelt had long been worried by the public's deep-seated aversion to a large standing army. Polls published during 1942 had hardly helped to allay these concerns, for they revealed that a majority of Americans continued to oppose inducting eighteen- and nineteen-year-olds into the army. By the start of February, with the new Republican intake helping to spark six separate congressional investigations into the allocation of American manpower resources, Senator John Bankhead then led a high-profile attack against the administration's decision to build up a large army. These men, he declared, would be better used to produce weapons that could then be distributed to those allies who desperately needed them, most notably China. To bolster his arguments, Bankhead even argued that America's first major defeat by the Germans, at Kasserine Pass on February 14, was principally a product of the administration's determination to build up an oversized and poorly equipped army, at the expense of production.[70] Divisionist organs were predictably quick to support such claims, but during the first weeks of February the OWI also found "a three-to-one majority" in the press in favor of reducing the planned size of the army. Even more ominously, liberals were starting to join the bandwagon, claiming that the creation of a large army might well condemn the United States to an excessively militaristic future.[71]

Faced with such pressure, Roosevelt decided to take the offensive. In January, he became the first sitting president to fly when he made the long and arduous journey to Casablanca to meet with Churchill and the British. On his return, FDR hastened to point out to reporters the deeper implications of this trip, especially the new proximity of the Mediterranean and European theatres in an age of air power. In a press conference on February 12, before speaking of the "direct threat" a German takeover of Dakar would have posed "against Brazil and this continent," he revealed how quickly he had covered this distance. "It's an amazing thing," he informed reporters; "Wednesday in Liberia, Thursday in Brazil! And I *don't* like flying!" Later that same day, in a nationally broadcast speech he then pointed out that America's main priority remained the launching of "actual invasions of the continent of Europe," and took pains to stress that the United States had "definite offensive plans for offensive operations" in Asia. A week later, in a joint press conference with Madame Chiang, he also told reporters that he was trying to "find ways and means" to increase aid to China, albeit with careful emphasis on the enormous logistical problems involved.[72]

Other officials and prominent individuals helped to bolster the president's efforts. Military leaders were quick to testify before Congress on the need for a large army, pointing out that a force of 8.2 million by the end of the year was essential if planned operations were to be successful. They also promised to ensure that these men would be employed as efficiently as possible. In March, Stimson then decisively supported this message in a nationally broadcast speech, which documented how the United States had sufficient manpower to meet both production and military targets.[73] When it came to combating the "Asia-first" campaign, Marshall prevailed on the president to release a statement in February, publicly praising General MacArthur's "tremendous and remarkably efficient bombardments" of the enemy and stressing how these have "made a great impression on our people."[74] Winston Churchill also stepped into the breach. Addressing a joint session of Congress in May, the prime minister made a bold and successful attempt to undo Madame Chiang's efforts by clearly restating the reasons why the Allies sought to strike at the Nazis first.[75]

While in public the administration moved to dampen criticism, in private the president never wavered in his commitment to focus on the defeat of Germany. In February, aware that Madame Chiang was a focal point of the "Asia-first" campaign, he remarked to the British ambassador that he was "scared stiff" of the Generalissimo's wife and informed Morgenthau that he was "just crazy to get her out of the country."[76] Then, at the third Washington Conference with the British in May, he not only reaffirmed his adherence to the "Germany-first" principle but also came out staunchly in favor of launching a cross-channel attack at the earliest possible date, probably in the spring of 1944.[77] The Asia lobby had therefore failed miserably in its attempt to pressure the president. But why was Roosevelt able to brush off this campaign so easily?

Part of the answer stems from FDR's perception of public opinion. For all the intensity of their efforts, Republicans and divisionists enjoyed little success in generating widespread support for their cause. Even in the days immediately after Madame Chiang's speech, the OWI concluded that "comment, in general, concurred in the desirability of providing additional supplies for China, but avoided commitment as to the relative importance of the European and Asiatic fronts."[78] "American sentiment," according to a *New York Times* editorial, typical of many, "is in favor of sending to China everything that can possibly be delivered now, [but] it concentrates on Germany for the moment . . . because greater forces are massed in Europe and there is a better chance of beating Hitler first."[79] Although polls were somewhat sparse, their findings indicated that on this issue mass opinion remained far from fervent. In February, a Gallup poll revealed that 53 percent of respondents considered Japan to be the "number-one enemy," but by June this figure had dwindled to a paltry 18 percent, whereas 38 percent advocated focusing on Germany.[80] Again, there was hardly the overwhelming and intense opposition that would have been required if the president was even to consider abandoning this fundamental principle.

Nor did the pressure to scale down the size of the army amount to much in the end. This was partly because Stimson made such a persuasive case in a radio address in March. According to the OWI, within days of this performance most of the media had been quickly converted into supporters of the administration's stance on this issue. Such an about-turn in the press probably helped inject a note of caution into the debates on Capitol Hill. But legislators were also extremely reluctant to go against the expert testimony of the president's top military advisers. As the War Department's head of public relations succinctly put it, "despite all the talk, Congress isn't sure, and members will not risk their political necks by taking a position where they might be charged with sabotaging the war effort."[81]

Yet the nature of this popular opposition was only part of the reason why the president paid so little heed to it. He was also well aware that the current course of the conflict was itself starting to weaken his opponents' more extreme claims. After all, by this stage the United States was not completely ignoring the war in the Pacific. The defeats in the first months of 1942 had already sucked in large numbers of troops. In July, the JCS then sanctioned CCS 94, which in light of the postponement of a cross-channel attack in favor of Operation TORCH permitted certain "readjustments . . . for the purpose of furthering offensive operations in the Pacific."[82] Throughout the fall and winter American forces had also been mustered in order to halt and then defeat the Japanese at Guadalcanal, while at the third Washington Conference in May 1943 planners deemed that the Allies would soon have sufficient resources to contemplate an attack on the Solomons, the Marshalls, and the Carolines.[83] Consequently, even though Europe remained the principal focus, the exigencies of actually fighting the war had led to an impressive accumulation of American power in the Pacific. And this in turn was serving to weaken the assertions of those who charged the administration with neglecting this theater altogether.

Taking the War to the Heart of the Reich, January to November 1943

At the start of the New Year, with TORCH well underway and Roosevelt's gaze still fixed firmly on the European war, the president, prime minister, and their military staffs journeyed to Casablanca to discuss their next moves. Both leaders could hardly wait to escape to this "comfortable oasis in the desert" in the midst of a wartime winter, and the whole excursion had something of a holiday feel to it. The president certainly appreciated the opportunity to meet up with his two sons who were serving in the North African theater. He also reveled in becoming the first president since Lincoln to visit a war zone and took every opportunity to inspect the front-line troops, no doubt well aware that photographs of the commander-in-chief saluting GIs, meeting with the flamboyant General George S. Patton, and eating an open-air lunch with officers would soon be appearing in every daily newspaper.[84]

Yet, despite all the opportunities for relaxation and publicity, Roosevelt could not escape the problems of grand strategy for long. At Casablanca, the central question he faced was how to follow up TORCH.

FDR (with Patton on extreme right) reviewing troops in North Africa, January 1943.

When it came to land operations, the simple answer was that it remained too early to tell. With Eisenhower's army still bogged down in North Africa, the Combined Chiefs decided to defer any firm commitment about when and where to attack the European mainland until the battlefield situation was clearer. The only operation they approved was an invasion of Sicily, tentatively scheduled for July.[85] In the interim, it was clearly desirable to do something more. But what exactly? The British were already engaged in a full-scale bombing campaign of the Reich, attempting to weaken both its fighting capacity and its morale. What did the Americans think about extending this still further?

The president's position was never in any doubt. During 1942, Roosevelt continued to allude to the merits of an air campaign, remarking in September that "if the U.S. bombers were able to continue effectively to bomb Germany during daylight, and the RAF during the night, . . . [then] Germany was in for 'a hot time for the rest of the war.'"[86] At Casablanca, when air chiefs raised the possibility of a combined bombing offensive, Roosevelt did not hesitate to proffer his full support. Along with Churchill, he sanctioned an air campaign aimed at "the progressive destruction and dislocation of the German military, industry and economic systems, and the undermining of the morale of the German people to a point where their capacity for armed resistance is fatally weakened."[87] Soon thereafter, the American Air Force (AAF) used this directive to begin stepping up preparations for daylight raids on the Reich. With the British already engaged in nighttime area bombing, by the summer the two air forces were pounding Germany's industrial heartland around the clock. The apogee of their efforts came on July 22–23, with a sustained attack on Hamburg, which left more than forty thousand civilians dead.

The president closely monitored the fruits of his Casablanca decision. Most days he would pay at least one visit to the White House Map Room, a small, low-ceilinged room on the first floor, where large charts of the various battle zones adorned the walls and kept him up-to-date with the very latest developments in the war. By July 26, FDR was in no doubt as to the scale of the Allies' unfolding efforts, for incoming intelligence clearly detailed how more than 2,300 tons of bombs had been dropped on Hamburg, starting "many large fires [that] merged into a conflagration covering the whole city."[88] Yet this catalogue of death and destruction left him largely unmoved. Rather than expressing any qualms about the slaughter, he privately commented with satisfaction on the efficacy of modern air power. "The complete destruction of Hamburg," he remarked at the start of August, "is an impressive demonstration of what can be done by long-range bombing."[89]

Roosevelt's lack of remorse should come as no surprise. Although the AAF was keen to experiment with daylight precision bombing, with its focus on Germany's industrial base, the president had always been more inclined toward area bombing, which targeted civilians. This was largely because the hopeful strand in his image of the enemy encouraged him to think that air power might quickly exacerbate the latent tensions between the people and their regime. By depressing morale, he even hoped that it might set the scene for an internal revolution.[90]

Yet FDR had failed to make such subtleties clear to the American public. Instead, on numerous occasions he had merely pointed out that the Nazis were the culpable criminals, while the mass of Germans were simply their innocent victims. It was not beyond the realm of possibility, therefore, that popular opinion might start to recoil in disgust if faced with a strategy that was brazenly based on the slaughter of huge numbers of blameless civilians. To make matters worse, back in September 1939 FDR had explicitly made this link when appealing to belligerents to eschew aerial bombing. This form of "inhuman barbarism," he had asserted, would simply target "hundreds of thousands of innocent human beings who have no responsibility for, and who are not even remotely participating in, the hostilities which have now broken out."[91] In 1940 and 1941, as the Luftwaffe went into action over the skies of Western Europe and Britain, Roosevelt had then used the fate of Rotterdam and Coventry to highlight the ruthless barbarity of Nazi war making. As a result, Americans might now start to wonder if their own Air Force was acting in a manner little different from their savage Nazi counterparts.

In this context, Roosevelt's concerns about a possible adverse public reaction to Allied bombing become clear. He was hardly worried about the state of current opinion, because media surveys and opinion polls indicated that at present there were few signs of protest. As early as the first week of May 1942, as the RAF's efforts had begun to gather pace, more than a hundred editorials had "hailed" the continuous RAF bombing of German industrial areas. Three months later, 109 editorials had even urged a more intensive bombing campaign against Germany, in the belief that "salvation of Allies may lie in all-out air attacks."[92] Once the round-the-clock raids got underway, the OWI continued to note that press and radio comment considered them effective, "both in disrupting German production and in undermining German morale." A number of commentators even pointed out "with obvious satisfaction that the raids were greater than any ever made on England by the Luftwaffe."[93]

However, the president did remain troubled by the possibility of future opposition if Americans thought the Allies were callously targeting civilians. He was especially convinced that there would be little popular support for, and perhaps much mass opposition to, terror bombings and reprisal raids. As he remarked on one occasion, "although the people of the U.S. [were] deeply incensed at the barbaric treatment which the Nazis are meting out, . . . I am nevertheless convinced that they are not prepared to resort to such measures as the indiscriminate bombing of the civilian population of enemy countries."[94]

Given this conclusion, Roosevelt trod carefully when portraying the Allied effort to the American people. Whereas in private his rationale for bombing rested on targeting civilians in order to provoke a political implosion by depressing morale, in public he now emphasized that the Americans and British were specifically targeting industry in order to precipitate an economic collapse by depriving manufacturers of key raw materials. As he declared in one speech, "We are not bombing tenements for the sheer sadistic pleasure of killing, as the Nazis did. We are striking devastating blows at carefully selected, clearly identified strategic objectives—factories, shipyards, munitions dumps, transportation facilities, which make it possible for the Nazis to wage war."[95] Such claims were eagerly backed up by air leaders, who had long been preoccupied with the need to cultivate mass support for bombing in order to improve their chances of achieving independent status as a separate branch of the armed services. AAF chief of staff, Henry "Hap" Arnold, was especially anxious to go on record describing terror bombing as "abhorrent to our humanity, our sense of decency." He also warned his aircrews that careless bombing would "intensify feelings of hatred in the 'victim populations,' poisoning relationships between countries after the fighting ended."[96] Meanwhile, the OWI sought to reassure the public about the efforts of both the AAF and RAF. In its factual radio program "This Is Official," which aimed at educating the American public about various aspects of the war effort, the question

was asked in July: "In what way does the present Allied air offensive on
Germany differ from the Germans bombing of Britain back in 1940?" The
answer was crystal clear. Allied Air Forces "accurately and scientifically"
planned only to destroy targets "of military or production importance in a
strict order of priority." Allied bombing was also "more accurate, whether
it be the daylight bombing of the AAF, . . . or the night 'Area bombing'
with the RAF's giant blockbusters." Modern methods, it mendaciously
claimed, made Allied efforts "so accurate that industrial sections of cities
can be wiped out, area by area."[97]

While Roosevelt saw an air campaign as an ideal way to soften up the
Reich, he no longer viewed bombing as a central method of winning the
war. Indeed, his thinking on the means required to defeat Germany had
evolved considerably since the summer of 1941. With the U.S. Army total-
ing around 8 million and with the public no longer adamantly opposed to
deploying these troops abroad, the president now firmly believed that victory would only come after a full-scale invasion of Europe. But this still
raised that fundamental question: when and where should the next blows
be landed?

As Roosevelt began to ponder this problem during the spring of 1943,
he was quick to recognize the profound change in the public's attitude toward the war. TORCH had clearly worked its magic. Over the winter,
America's first offensive had not only helped to undermine defeatism and
apathy, it had also generated a greater interest in the European conflict, as
well as confining "Asia-first" sentiment to a divisionist minority with no
"real public opinion behind them."[98] Now, with Eisenhower's armies finally emerging victorious in May, capturing Tunis and around 240,000
Axis soldiers by the middle of the month, Americans were quick to lavish
praise on the president and his strategic vision. In June, when the Democratic National Committee conducted a survey in a string of key congressional districts, it found that a vast majority of voters strongly endorsed
FDR's "leadership and courage in running the war." Overwhelming numbers also expressed their approval for the general way in which the war was
being handled on the military fronts.[99]

Basking in the afterglow of military victory, Roosevelt soon reached
the conclusion that public opinion was no longer such an important consideration when it came to the timing of the next offensive. Unlike 1942, he
no longer deemed it so essential to speed up aggressive action in order to
arouse the American people from a phony-war style torpor. But this was
not his only calculation. The president also felt he could safely ignore public opinion when it came to the location of America's next assault. What lay
behind his confidence on this issue?

To a large extent, it was not new. Even in 1942, FDR had only fretted
about the popular mood when it came to the timing of the first campaign.
His general attitude had been that Americans were not worried whether

the United States attacked France, North Africa, the Middle East, or Norway; all they craved was action soon.[100] Now, he had a number of concrete indications that the public remained agnostic on this issue. One was the obvious fact that most opinion makers were not calling fervently for action in any particular region. Quite the opposite: most still seemed content to leave this matter in the hands of those with the requisite information and authority.[101] Polling data that percolated up to the White House also continued to suggest that popular attitudes were permissive rather than pressurizing. Polls published in June, for instance, revealed that 62 percent of Americans thought an invasion of Europe would be necessary to defeat the Germans, while 63 percent believed that such an attack would now succeed. But pollsters conspicuously failed to specify exactly where in Europe this attack should come. In fact, not one single survey addressed the problem of whether the United States should opt for a cross-channel assault rather than a Mediterranean offensive.[102] Small wonder, then, that Roosevelt believed he had a good deal of freedom on this subject. At the start of May, when the Joint Chiefs had the temerity to suggest that the American people would only support the use of U.S. troops in particular regions, he was certainly quick to dismiss their arguments out of hand. Such claims, he colorfully replied, were pure "spinach."[103]

Actually it was quite fortunate that the president felt he could safely ignore public opinion when it came to the timing and whereabouts of the next offensive, because although TORCH increased room for maneuver on the domestic front, it had precisely the opposite effect on short-term military planning. Indeed, the decision to attack North Africa in 1942, together with the subsequent failure to defeat the Germans quickly, drastically narrowed options for 1943. By May, with the Mediterranean already containing twenty-five Allied divisions and with time rapidly running out for launching an alternative campaign that summer, there seemed to be little alternative to continuing in same direction for the time being. In July, the precariousness of the internal situation in Italy also encouraged the Allies to continue probing at Hitler's "soft underbelly." When Mussolini was overthrown toward the end of the month, the opportunity to knock one of the three main Axis powers out of the war was just too good to miss. Even General Marshall, long suspicious of channeling U.S. forces into the "suction pump" of the Mediterranean, now supported an invasion of Italy. With Roosevelt and Churchill wholeheartedly endorsing the decision, on September 9 Allied troops landed on the Italian mainland at Salerno, just south of Naples.[104]

Operations for the remainder of 1943 were thus a natural outgrowth of TORCH. But what should the Allies do in 1944? Should they pour more resources into the Mediterranean, or should they husband men and materiel in Britain for a large-scale assault on the French coast? This key question precipitated much heated debate between the three allies throughout 1943. Stalin, in particular, still had very definite views about where the

Anglo-Americans should concentrate their efforts. Already deeply skeptical of the merits of TORCH, in March the Soviet leader made it perfectly clear that he did not consider an attack on Sicily to be a substitute for a cross-channel invasion. In July, when it was obvious that no assault of France would be forthcoming that year, Stalin recalled his ambassadors from the United States and Britain.[105] These developments had a considerable impact on Roosevelt's thinking. In his opinion, America and Britain now had to begin planning for a second front in France in the spring of 1944, since this was clearly the only way of truly placating the increasingly suspicious Stalin and thereby cementing a dangerously fractious alliance.

Underpinning the president's decision to opt for a cross-channel invasion was also the stark fact that America now had sufficient resources to engage in such an operation. Gone were the old days of 1941 when unpreparedness had bolstered Roosevelt's reluctance to get directly involved in the war. Gone too were the days of 1942 when the lack of trained troops and shipping meant that a cross-channel assault had not been feasible. American industry was now in high gear, churning out a staggering eighty-six thousand aircraft and almost thirty thousand tanks during the course of 1943.[106] The U.S. army was also generating enough divisions available for an attack in 1944, and hopefully there would soon be sufficient landing craft to get these troops to France with all the necessary equipment. As FDR cheerfully remarked in August 1943, "our available means seem to fit in pretty well with our plans." The president was even optimistic that the United States now had sufficient resources to carry out a second front on its own, in the event of a British refusal to participate in such an operation.[107]

And for much of 1943 it seemed all too likely that the British might well be reluctant to participate. Churchill was clearly still less than enamored with the prospects of attacking the French coast. Whereas the president and the Joint Chiefs wanted the campaigns in Sicily and Italy to be strictly limited so that enough resources could be mustered for an attack on the French coast in the spring of 1944, the prime minister eloquently and doggedly advocated a more flexible course. Not only did Churchill want to make any attack on France dependent on the decline of German strength but he also wanted to make sure that the Allies were in a position to exploit any opportunity that arose in the Mediterranean. This difference of opinion reached such a pitch at both the third Washington Conference in May and the first Quebec Conference in August that in some meetings subordinates had to be cleared from the room so that the Combined Chiefs could air their disagreements "off the record." Tentative compromise agreements were nevertheless hammered out on both occasions. Even so, a firm British commitment to a second front remained highly elusive. The whole matter was therefore left in abeyance until the first Big Three meeting at the end of November.[108]

Roosevelt arrived in Tehran determined to build up a close personal rapport with Stalin. Indicative of the president's general attitude was his decision to move into secure (and undoubtedly bugged) accommodation in the Soviet compound, after reports emerged that there were Axis assassins in the city. When it came to problems of grand strategy, however, the portents for a U.S.-Soviet understanding were somewhat ominous. In recent weeks, Soviet officials had suddenly and mysteriously become more lukewarm on the whole idea of an attack on France. To make matters worse, Marshall, long the most articulate American champion of a cross-channel assault, went missing on the afternoon of the vital first plenary meeting. After a scheduling mix-up, he had gone sightseeing around the Iranian capital with "Hap" Arnold.[109]

But if the president entered the first Tehran meeting with a feeling of trepidation, this was not to last. As soon as Roosevelt asked whether the Soviets preferred a cross-channel invasion or further campaigns in the Mediterranean, it was clear that Stalin would cast the deciding vote in favor of the American position. An invasion of the French coast, the Soviet leader unequivocally declared, was "still the best" method of striking right at heart of the Reich. Churchill, never one to give up without a struggle, did his best to argue and complain, but to no avail. Outvoted two-to-one, the British had no choice but to succumb. In one swift moment, Stalin had put an end to almost two years of strategic wrangling. With Eisenhower soon to be appointed supreme commander, detailed planning could now begin in earnest for Operation OVERLORD, the Anglo-American invasion of northern France.[110]

At long last the central question of grand strategy in Europe had been agreed on. With Germany now patently on the defensive, not only in the east and south but also in the sea and air, attention turned quickly toward victory. On their way back from Tehran, the Combined Chiefs even indulged in an informal guessing game of when the war would end. In a straw poll conducted by Marshall, the consensus was "that if Germany does not crack at the end of the winter, she will not until [the] fall [of 1944]."[111] For military leaders, then, victory might not be imminent, but it was certainly inevitable. In a similar mood of confidence, the president also turned his attention from war to peace, and especially to the pressing question: what to do with postwar Germany?

4

The Politics of
Unconditional Surrender

Secretary Hull . . . hoped that in your speech tonight you could include a paragraph which would rebut the charge sometimes made that we are planning to deliver Europe to the Fascists.

—Adolf A. Berle to FDR,
February 12, 1943

Sunday January 24, 1943, the last full day of the Casablanca Conference, dawned warm and sunny. Around midday Roosevelt and Churchill went onto the lawn just outside the president's villa. A short while later, the newspapermen who had made the long trek to North Africa were invited to sit down and make themselves comfortable. As they huddled around the two leaders, most reporters probably expected to hear nothing more than the normal platitudes of a wartime press conference. After all, the president and prime minister, desperate not to give anything away to the enemy, were only likely to talk in vague generalities about the need to help the Soviets or to get more troops into action against the Axis. To most, it probably seemed that the lead story would be the exotic location of this third wartime meeting, rather than anything the two leaders were about to say.

Then Roosevelt dropped his bombshell. Invoking a loose and inaccurate historical analogy about how Ulysses S. Grant had dealt with Robert E. Lee at the end of the Civil War, the president revealed, in no uncertain terms, his "determination that peace can come to the world only by the total elimination of German and Japanese war power. . . . The elimination of German, Japanese, and Italian war power," he added with a flourish, "means the unconditional surrender by Germany, Italy, and Japan." To drive the point home, he ended by imploring journalists to depict the Casablanca Conference as "the 'unconditional surrender meeting.'"[1]

Roosevelt's casual pronouncement before a few reporters on a sunny afternoon in North Africa has long been the subject of controversy. Quite apart from the vexed question of whether this formula prolonged the war by encouraging the Germans to resist more fanatically, historians have been unable to reach a consensus on FDR's motivation for making this statement at this particular time. In his memoirs, Winston Churchill's only contribution was to downplay any complicity in the whole affair.[2] Subsequently, a number of writers have posited a link between the president's action and the domestic outrage over the so-called Darlan deal—the arrangement made in November 1942 to stop French forces in North Africa from fighting the Allies.[3] Many others have altogether ignored this connection, however.[4] And even among those who believe the Darlan deal was crucial, there has been little assessment of why FDR waited until the end of January to make the announcement, more than two months after the deal had been struck and exactly one month after Darlan had been removed from the scene by an assassin's bullet. Previous works have also tended to neglect the role that other public opinion trends might have played in this decision and almost all have remained silent about why Roosevelt constantly reiterated unconditional surrender during 1943 and 1944.[5] This chapter aims to clarify this episode and rectify these omissions, as well as to examine how much weight should be ascribed to the domestic environment when explaining Franklin Roosevelt's deeply controversial Casablanca proclamation.

Defusing the Debate over "Darlanism," November 1942 to February 1943

That Roosevelt was privately inclined to favor unconditional surrender comes as no surprise. Ever since the Munich crisis of 1938 he had been convinced of the futility of even talking to the perfidious Hitler. It was hardly unexpected, therefore, that when State Department planners from the Subcommittee on Security Issues came to him in May 1942 and stated "that nothing short of unconditional surrender by the principal enemies, Germany, and Japan, could be accepted," the president did not dispute their decision.[6] The puzzle, then, is not why FDR favored unconditional surrender, because it clearly stemmed directly from his image of the Nazi enemy; rather, it is in the timing of the announcement: why did he decide to enunciate it explicitly at the Casablanca Conference in January 1943?

One contributing but subordinate factor was the president's fluctuating assessments of the complacency problem. Put simply, whenever overoptimism was *not* a worry, Roosevelt was always more inclined to talk publicly about the prospect of defeating the enemy. This was the case between December 1940 and January 1942 when, untroubled by the possibility of fueling overconfidence, he had made at least fifteen public references to the perils of appeasement and the consequent need to utterly destroy the Hitler state. For a brief period after Pearl Harbor, he had even been prepared to declare that America's central objective was "victory, final and complete," which meant the "smashing of militarism imposed by warlords upon their enslaved peoples."[7]

Yet from February 1942, as Roosevelt's fears of overconfidence mounted, such talk about the prospects of peace and the postwar world rapidly dropped out of the president's public repertoire. From February to September 1942, FDR made only three indirect and rather feeble excursions into this territory, and then merely to state that the Allies, not the Axis, "will make the final peace," that "victory is essential," and that "this great war effort must be carried through to its victorious conclusion."[8] As he told one official in May, "the whole attitude ought to be talk on the pessimistic side, lest anyone get the idea that the war would be easy."[9] Officials on the Committee of War Information wholeheartedly agreed. As one of its members put it, "the theme to the country should be based on the assumption that we would not talk too much of peace and the world thereafter, until the war was won."[10] Thus, for much of 1942, with the administration shying away from mentioning any war aims in public, Roosevelt was naturally not tempted to start talking about his support for unconditional surrender.

Only with the spate of Allied victories and the resulting change in the popular mood did this constraint ease. After November 1942, the president often continued to adopt a cautious posture, informing a press conference that he did not want to induce overoptimism by speculating about the probable end of the war and telling the *Herald Tribune* forum that "there can be no coasting to victory."[11] But at the same time, with America on the offensive, defeatism assuaged, and public confidence justly reflecting Allied success, he also believed that the moment was ripe to start talking again about the prospects of defeating the enemy. "Today," he therefore declared just three days after TORCH, "we know and they [the Axis] know that they have conquered nothing. Today, they face inevitable, final defeat." German superiority, he reiterated six weeks later, "has gone—forever. Yes, the Nazis and the Fascists have asked for it—and they are going to get it."[12] More importantly, Roosevelt also started to offer certain hints about "the victorious peace which surely will come."[13] In November, he suggested that Clark Eichelberger, a prominent internationalist, float "a trial balloon" on his plan that "four policemen" patrol the postwar world and enforce disarmament. In his keynote speeches, Roosevelt also began to return to the theme of smashing the Axis. Our task in 1943, he declared on New Year's Day, is "to press on with the massed forces of humanity till the bandit assault on civilization is completely crushed."[14]

But while the "revolution in political sentiment" that accompanied TORCH and the victories at Stalingrad and El Alamein helped to create a permissive environment that enabled the president to start talking tentatively about victory and war aims, this was not the only significant development at this time. Back in October, both Washington and London had decided that to neutralize, or at least minimize, French opposition to their North African attack, they would have to supplement the military campaign with some form of political maneuver. For this reason, the Americans dispatched General Mark Clark to Algiers in an attempt to persuade French general Charles Mast not to oppose the Allied landings. They also brought in Henri-Honoré Giraud, in the hope that French forces would rally behind this anti-German general who had only recently escaped from a Nazi prison. More ominously, the administration contemplated negotiating with Admiral Jean-François Darlan, commander-in-chief of all Vichy forces and number-two figure in the Vichy government, who happened to be visiting his ill son in Algiers. In the immediate aftermath of the Allied landings, when it quickly became apparent that both Mast and Giraud had little standing with the French forces in North Africa, and that only Darlan had the requisite authority to conclude a cease-fire, General Clark began discussions with Darlan. On November 13 the so-called Darlan deal was struck, by which the Allies accepted Darlan as the head of civil administration in North Africa and in return Darlan agreed to a cease-fire that stopped the fighting in French Morocco and Algeria.[15]

For Clark and his superior officer, General Eisenhower, this development was perfectly compatible with instructions received from Washington. They also believed it offered important military advantages, since it effectively nullified a potential enemy that was more than double the size of the Allied force.[16] Yet, for all its practical benefits, dealing with Darlan raised obvious problems. In particular, the administration had long depicted Quisling collaborators as "diminutive Führers" who simply aided the malevolent Axis cause. And Darlan seemed to be very much of this ilk, having held numerous positions in the Vichy government. As Bullitt advised the president, "his acts as head of Pétain's governing apparatus hung like an albatross around his neck. He cannot get it off." The military, too, conceded as much, for in the pep talk given to U.S. troops landing in North Africa, Darlan was described as a "Nazi rat" little different from the likes of Laval.[17]

It would not have been surprising, then, if a public told to treat Nazi collaborators as brutal archenemies quickly began to recoil in disgust at this deal. The initial popular reaction, however, was remarkably mild. On November 15 and 16, noted the BoI, "press and radio commentators revealed perplexity and, in some cases, dismay over the political maneuvers in North Africa." But while "the position of Darlan was widely questioned," at this early stage most remained guarded in their criticism, unwilling to condemn a deal that could well reduce casualties. As the popular broadcaster, Raymond Gram Swing, put it: "It all comes down to . . . the decision to save American and British and French lives, and to save invaluable manpower for the real enemy, and to save time."[18] The nation's legislators, meanwhile, remained preoccupied with thorny domestic issues, much to the president's relief. As he remarked on November 18, "luckily for me the Congress has been interested in the Poll Tax matter, so I have had no repercussions about the Darlan affair from that body."[19]

Exceptions to this relatively mute and moderate reaction came from just two sources, but both were to prove extremely important. On November 15 CBS reporter Edward R. Murrow broadcast to America from London. After revealing his astonishment at the deal, he accused Darlan of having adopted "Gestapo methods." The admiral had "intensified anti-Semitic measures" in France, argued Murrow. "His police force [had] helped the Germans round up Alsatian refugees. . . . And now this man is given political dominion over North Africa, with American support." "Wherever American forces go," he concluded, "they will carry with them food and money and power, and the Quislings will rally to our sides if we permit it."[20] Two days later, in a memorandum sent to both Cordell Hull and the War Department, Walter Lippmann concurred with this analysis. For Lippmann, the deal called into question America's war aims. "What we do with the first country liberated by American arms will obviously have the profoundest influence as an example and as a precedent upon all other occupied territory in Europe. It is self evident," he asserted, "that we must dispel any idea that we shall recognize and uphold Quisling governments."[21]

Although such bitter criticism was not widespread, with most commentators merely acting perplexed rather than outraged, the administration's perception of public opinion was very much shaped by the arguments of these two opinion makers. Henry Morgenthau was particularly distressed by Murrow's broadcast, and on November 16 phoned Sumner Welles for an explanation.[22] Pressure was building from other quarters, too. Elmer Davis and Cordell Hull both wanted Roosevelt to make a statement on the matter, while Davis hurried to inform Henry Stimson that Wendell Willkie was due to give a radio address at the *Herald Tribune* Forum, in which he intended to castigate the administration for appeasing Quislings and would describe Darlan as "Hitler's tool."[23]

Well aware that "a lot of people have gotten quite upset about our dealings with Darlan," the president decided to respond through a combination of censorship and persuasion.[24] To begin with, on November 16 he gave Eisenhower his "complete support," but was careful to warn him "that we do not trust Darlan" and "that it is impossible to keep a collaborator of

Hitler and one whom we believe to be a Fascist in civil power any longer than is absolutely necessary."[25] That same day FDR's subordinates were also busy. While Marshall sought to placate potential critics on Capitol Hill, his staff not only asked the press to refrain from commenting on the political situation in North Africa but also prevented the release of movie footage containing pictures of Eisenhower and the French Admiral on the basis that "less said about Darlan the better."[26] In a similar vein, Stimson called Willkie just an hour before he was scheduled to make a keynote radio broadcast and prevailed on his fellow Republican to drop any references to Darlan. A relieved FDR then listened to the speech and later congratulated Stimson for this prompt action.[27]

But it was also clear to the president that a complete news blackout would probably engender as much critical comment as it would allay. The next day Roosevelt attempted to clarify the situation, by persuading his more vehement critics of its temporary nature. He began by calling in Morgenthau and assuring him "that there have been no promises of any kind made to Darlan as to the future, and they [the military] can throw him overboard any minute they want to."[28] Then in a press conference he stressed to reporters that the deal was "only a temporary expedient, justified solely by the stress of battle"— one that had been improvised by soldiers on the ground in order to save American lives and would be jettisoned as soon as the military situation improved. To drive home the point, he quoted the old Balkan proverb: "My children, you are permitted in time of great danger to walk with the Devil until you have crossed the bridge."[29]

In the first days after this press conference most newspapers were willing to go along with this "walk with Devil" because of Roosevelt's assurance that it was a one-off temporary expedient based purely on military calculations. Thus, two of the most influential daily newspapers, the *New York Times* and *Washington Post*, both supported the president, arguing that his statement ought to "clear the air of misconceptions and misunderstandings that have arisen as a result" of this whole episode.[30] Far more importantly, FDR also appeared to have placated Walter Lippmann. In his column on November 19, Lippmann still warned against making Darlan a permanent ally, since this would set a dangerous precedent. But, accepting that the deal was only a temporary expedient, he now saw the whole episode in a new light and even praised the administration for the "unplanned but wisely improvised fashion" by which it had brought "to an orderly end the power of Vichy France in Africa."[31]

Yet the media's support for the Darlan deal remained highly fragile. On one hand, Roosevelt was hardly reassured by the fact that his most vociferous support was coming from the ranks of conservatives and divisionists. As the BoI noted, "reactionaries" were encouraged by "proof that we are real politicians after all—fighting for our own interests not for Wilsonian ideals," while anticommunists were reassured by what they felt to be the administration's abandonment of the moral high ground. "This proves," wrote one isolationist commentator, "that our alliance with Russia is not so ideological as we feared, but opportunistic just as in the case of Darlan."[32] On the other hand, middle-of-the-road newspapers and liberal commentators were only willing to accept the present arrangement as long as it did not set a precedent, and they were particularly sensitive to any sign that the United States was abandoning its hatred of nazism and Nazi collaborators. Thus, indications either that Darlan's position was permanent, or that he was a harbinger of things to come, were apt to rekindle the controversy. As the *New York Times* clearly warned: "One Darlan may have been necessary. But one Darlan is enough."[33]

It was in this context that a second wave of press protest and indignation, more intensive and widespread than the first, started to mount. The backdrop to this was a series of reports in December that not only demonstrated that Darlan was consolidating his position in North Africa but also told of the War Department's attempt to set up an Austrian Legion with allegiance to the Hapsburg dynasty. The press was also busy publicizing an arrangement that the State Department had concluded with Vice-Admiral Georges Robert "under which this fascist-minded man, this admirer of Pétain, remains in power for the duration and, apparently all the French democrats on Martinique remain in jail."[34] In his *New York Times* column, Arthur Krock had already raised suspicions that the administration was about to abandon its crusade against nazism and instead seek to end the war by a whole series of tawdry deals with Fascist elements, when he revealed that an anonymous administration official had informed him that the "war has forced us idealists and democrats to quantitative rather than qualitative, morality as the test. If, for example, Göring should offer to come over with a few planes, we don't want him. He will cost more than he will contribute. But if he can bring the Luftwaffe with him we'll receive him."[35] Other newspapers were now quick to express their concern that the United States was contracting "a Darlan habit," with Henry Luce's *Time* providing perhaps the most lucid rendition. "The U.S.," it pointed out,

> was doing business, if not with Hitler, with one of his stooges, Admiral Jean-François Darlan. The invasion of North Africa was the first great political-military adventure of the United States in World War II. Its tone would set the tone for others to come. How could the U.S. Government, opponent of fascism, exponent of the Atlantic Charter, explain this? Was not freedom to come in the wake of Americans? If Norway were invaded, would the United States thenceforth move to strengthen the hand of Vidkun Quisling?[36]

And, it might have added, by the same token if Germany were invaded, would the United States thenceforth move to strengthen the hand of Hermann Göring?

It was therefore the implications of these arrangements for the future, rather than the initial Darlan deal, that fueled the mounting furor. This was demonstrated most clearly by the events of late December and early January. On Christmas Eve, Darlan was assassinated by a young French royalist. Although this appeared to remove the major irritant from the scene, the administration enjoyed only a brief respite, for within two weeks popular protest had not merely been rekindled but had reached its apex. This time, the cause was Marcel Peyrouton's appointment as governor general of Algeria. Unlike the original Darlan deal, which the administration had been able to portray as an improvised affair only made possible by the admiral's fortuitous presence in Algiers, Peyrouton had been specifically brought to North Africa by Robert D. Murphy, the U.S. minister to French North Africa. Moreover, Peyrouton's record as Vichy interior minister marked him as one of the most vicious and brutal of all French collaborators.

These two points were quickly picked up by the press, and as the OWI noted they brought media "anxiety to a ferment." While the *Washington Post* called the Peyrouton deal the "last straw," Walter Lippmann, relatively quiet since the middle of November, soon seized upon a story in the *American Mercury* magazine. This purported to elucidate Hull's belief that "there are likely to be other deals with other Darlans in other conquered and Axis-dominated countries," perhaps even with Germans who overthrew "the Nazi gang." Rejecting this as totally unacceptable, Lippmann suggested that "nothing ought to suit us better . . . than unconditional surrender."[37] Both Lippmann and the *Washington Post* were especially "severe" in their condemnation of Murphy, whom they held responsible for the disastrous appointment of Peyrouton. "It was high time that Murphy was removed from his job," the *Post* editorialized on January 15, "where his lack of understanding of the realities, his readiness to appease the time-serving and double-dealing Vichy bureaucrats, and his general incompetence make him a very dangerous man to have in a highly difficult spot."[38]

In contrast to the rather lackluster popular response to the initial Darlan deal, the White House mailbag began to bulge with letters of protest over Peyrouton. Typical of many was the wire sent by the Washington Heights Republican Club, denouncing the appointment as "a disgrace and a contradiction of every noble aim."[39] Likewise, the OWI was inundated with spontaneous and unsolicited comments from its correspondence panels. "I am convinced," declared one letter writer "that the government is not aware of the intensity of the feeling of vast numbers of people, and more particularly, of those people who have supported the war from the beginning and the president from the days of his 'quarantine' speech [of 1937] in Chicago and before."[40]

By the beginning of December this persistent criticism was beginning to take its toll on top officials. Cordell Hull, whose State Department was bearing the brunt of the press's disapproval, "was very much exercised" by Walter Lippmann's initial attack, and in a series of press conferences throughout December and January he berated the media for ignoring the main issues.[41] By all accounts Roosevelt, too, was stung by the media's repeated assaults. Rosenman, his speechwriter and long-time friend, could not remember a time when the president was so deeply affected by a political attack. On occasion, he later recalled, FDR would refuse to discuss the matter at all, while at other times, he would bitterly read aloud the press's criticisms.[42] At one cabinet meeting he even flew into a rage when the North African situation was broached, stating that "there had been altogether too much power-grabbing and back-biting" by his top officials.[43] Finally, on December 11, in an attempt to escape from this mounting indignation, and perhaps even quell it with a dramatic gesture, Roosevelt decided to meet with Churchill in North Africa. "I have just made up my mind," he cabled the prime minister, "to go along with the Africa idea—on the theory that public opinion here will gasp but be satisfied when they hear about it after it is over." "Incidentally," he continued, "it would also do me personally an enormous amount of good to get out of the political atmosphere of Washington for a couple of weeks."[44]

But before he could escape the hostile environment of the capital, Roosevelt had another problem to handle. For the past six months FDR's "back-channel" operative, John Franklin Carter, had been dealing with Ernst "Putzi" Hanfstaengl, a former friend of Hitler who had fled to Britain in 1937 and had been transferred to North America four years later. With Roosevelt's approval, Hanfstaengl had been supplying the administration with information about Nazi Germany under the code-name "Sedgwick." On December 1, for example, in response to a specific request from the president on "how word could effectively be brought to reach the German people . . . that we do not propose a general massacre of the Germans," Hanfstaengl reported that he believed an internal revolution was likely and that "we might find a German Darlan . . . in addition to people like Schacht and Neurath to end it all." Given the political climate at this time, particularly the press's sensitivity to anything that smacked of negotiation with Nazis or Nazi sympathizers, the president was obviously anxious to keep this "S-Project" secret, and all the relevant documentation was accordingly marked "very confidential." At the turn of the year, however, news leaked to Hearst's *Cosmopolitan* magazine of Hanfstaengl's presence in the United States. Roosevelt acted promptly. He called in Carter and gave him verbal instructions to "make a quick deal with the editor of *Cosmopolitan*." Subsequently, the magazine agreed to put the story on hold for a month, thus providing the administration with time both to defuse the current wave of criticism over its deals with Nazi collaborators and to brief the press about Hanfstaengl's connection with the government. Carter then moved to assure selected reporters that Hanfstaengl "is devoid of political or diplomatic significance in terms of German political life" and so "none of the issues involved in North Africa can arise in this connection." This seemed to work. Indeed when, on January 28, Carter finally referred publicly to Hanfstaengl, the media's reaction was surprisingly mild.[45]

As well as acting behind the scenes to defuse this potential problem, Roosevelt also made more public attempts to dampen the existing furor. On December 16, responding to the second wave of press criticism, he issued a press release that argued that the people of North Africa "have definitely allied themselves on the side of liberalism against all that the Axis stands for."[46] On January 7, he then made another effort to reassure his critics, this time in his high-profile annual message to Congress. The war, he declared, was essentially between two ways of life, "between those who put their faith in the people and those who put their faith in dictators and tyrants." Further negotiation with such tyrants, he continued, was out of the question. We have learned "that if we do not pull the fangs out of the predatory animals of this world, they will multiply and grow in strength— and they will be at our throats again once more in a short generation."[47]

Two days later Roosevelt began the eight-thousand-mile journey to Casablanca. On arrival, the president found that the political pressure in the United States had not died down, despite both his reassurances to the press and Darlan's death. On January 14, for example, Hull cabled to the absent president a lengthy paraphrase of a United Press article that blamed Eisenhower "for public confusion on the situation in French North Africa."[48] A note wired to Casablanca by Elmer Davis was even more explicit. "Most urgently hope Peyrouton will be excluded from any post or trust or authority," he pleaded to the president. "Would find it extremely difficult to explain to the American people."[49] Even though Roosevelt had initially been unaware of the arrangement to bring Peyrouton to Africa, he was not willing to bow to such pressure. Instead, acutely aware that "at home the newspapers have been making such a mountain out of rather a small hill," the president looked for another way of reassuring his critics that further "walks with the Devil" were not being contemplated.[50]

Publicizing his support for unconditional surrender seemed an obvious choice. Once in Casablanca, FDR soon broached the subject to Churchill, who then hurried to consult with his War Cabinet back in London. Roosevelt also got Harry Hopkins to prepare some background briefing notes, which expanded on and defined the formula. The president was therefore fully prepared and primed by the time he met with reporters on the lawn outside his villa on January 24. He began proceedings at this fateful press conference by pointing out that while unconditional surrender was an idea we have all had "in our hearts and heads before," it was now time to express it openly. Retaining the distinction between the enemy leaders and their peoples that had characterized his rhetoric since the start of the war, he declared that "unconditional surrender means not the destruction of the German populace, nor the Italian or Japanese populace, but does mean the destruction of a philosophy in Germany, Italy, and Japan which is based on the conquest and subjugation of other people." The Casablanca Conference, he dramatically concluded, should therefore be "called the 'unconditional surrender meeting.'"[51]

Public opinion had therefore played an important role in Roosevelt's enunciation of unconditional surrender. To start with, the success of the North African invasion in alleviating the morale problem had removed a major constraint. Whereas previously the administration had been reluctant to talk about the possibility of total victory for fear that this might encourage complacency, after November, with the new mood of confidence based on solid Allied victories, the president now deemed the time ripe to start talking about postwar plans. But the TORCH invasion also raised a new and unexpected issue: did the Darlan and Peyrouton deals demonstrate that the administration was prepared to abandon its crusade against nazism for a whole series of tawdry arrangements with Fascist elements? Faced with a barrage of "liberal" criticism on this subject, Roosevelt did not simply back down, change course, and disassociate himself from the actions of Eisenhower and Murphy.[61] Rather, he first attempted to alleviate liberal concern by insisting that the Darlan deal was only temporary. Only when this was belied by the Peyrouton episode did he then seek a bold new initiative, and announcing his long-held support for unconditional surrender was the ultimate result.

On this issue, the president's perception of what constituted "public opinion" was quite narrow. Rather than receiving a series of polls on the matter of "Darlanism"—which, incidentally, might well have reached the same conclusion as the British Embassy, namely that the "man in the street" tended to express either ignorance or approval of these developments—FDR was only exposed to the sentiments of a few columnists and journalists.[62] Ironically, the most prominent and influential of these was Walter Lippmann, who in 1942–43 was less concerned about a public incited to "paroxysms of hatred" being intolerant of calculated compromises, and more preoccupied with lambasting the administration for its various deals with a vicious and brutal enemy. In fact, there is an interesting paradox here between Lippmann the philosopher of American diplomacy who became an outspoken critic of his country's penchant to launch vigorous crusades resulting in the total destruction of the foe, and Lippmann the influential columnist who in these months played an instrumental role in prodding FDR to enunciate unconditional surrender.

But while public opinion, as defined by the president, was an important motivation for the unconditional surrender announcement, how does Roosevelt's reaction to this liberal criticism compare to his response to other public-opinion problems in 1942 and 1943? The president clearly paid more attention to these political attacks than he ever did to the equally vociferous but far more organized efforts of the Asia-first campaign. This was partly because in this instance his critics were only attacking a series of ad hoc arrangements made by generals in a confusing and hazardous situation, whereas "Asia firsters" were directing their attention at a deeply held and long agreed upon tenet of Allied strategy. More importantly, the detractors over Darlan were generally liberals, many of whom had previously

*Despite the Darlan deal, FDR stood by Eisenhower. FDR and Eisenhower in Sicily,
December 1943.*

been among the president's fiercest supporters, whereas the opponents of
"Germany first" tended to be the divisionists, those whom FDR knew
would attack him regardless of the rights of the case. And Roosevelt always
found it far easier to dismiss the criticism of long-term opponents than that
of his traditional supporters.

But there were some interesting parallels between FDR's decision to
launch TORCH and his unconditional surrender pronouncement. Of
course, they were two very different types of policy decisions. Whereas the
former was deliberative, in the sense that it was made after months of debate, the latter was more reflexive, made speedily after other attempts to defuse liberal opposition had failed.[63] Whereas the former revolved around
the vexed question of where to send American troops into battle, the latter
was merely concerned with the announcement of a single war aim. Yet, despite these obvious contrasts, there were nevertheless similar processes at
work in each instance. Popular opinion clearly influenced the timing of
both, generally hastening the adoption of measures that FDR was already
inclined to favor. Roosevelt also believed that by speeding up certain initiatives he could deflect the public's attention from other matters. Specifically,
to combat complacency and lukewarm support for the Germany-first strategy, he advocated throwing U.S. troops into combat against the Wehrmacht
at the earliest possible date. Then, when the resulting invasion was in

turn accompanied by the furor over "Darlanism," he again looked for a way both of distracting attention from this issue and of reassuring the public that such arrangements would not be repeated when it came to Germany. Ultimately, therefore, public opinion not only helped determine the timing of Roosevelt's first two wartime policy initiatives, but by expediting both TORCH and the announcement of unconditional surrender, the president also hoped to set the agenda for public debate and thereby influence what the media covered and what the American people thought about.

Though the unconditional-surrender proclamation, like TORCH, was therefore congruent with Roosevelt's reading of public opinion, how much weight should we ascribe to this one factor? Were other non-public-opinion influences also at work? For a start, a number of alternative explanations can quickly be ruled out. Although State Department officials had earlier informed FDR of their support for unconditional surrender, and although Hull pressed for a reiteration of the formula on February 12, there was no pressure from either diplomats or military advisers to make the major announcement of January 24; in fact, as one of the main planners later stressed, "the president's enunciation of the policy of unconditional surrender at Casablanca . . . reflected no recommendation by the [State] Department; none had been made."[64] Nor did the British play a vital role. Churchill, to be sure, was initially concerned about the possible ramifications of the Darlan deal and in November had pressed FDR to inform the public that it would only be a temporary arrangement.[65] But by the time of Casablanca he was no longer so preoccupied with this issue, and he merely acquiesced in Roosevelt's decision to make the announcement, albeit with some reservations about its applicability to Italy.[66]

In fact, the only other consideration that entered the president's calculations was a desire to mollify the Soviets. FDR deemed this to be necessary for several reasons. Despite attempts to portray the North African landings as a true second front, Stalin remained unconvinced and by December he was again pressing for a fulfillment of the May promise to Molotov. Moreover, although the Soviet leader had sound military reasons for not leaving Moscow while the Stalingrad counteroffensive was still raging, his refusal to come to Casablanca was nevertheless a deep disappointment to Roosevelt, since it seemed to indicate Stalin's continued suspicion of the West.[67] Finally, even the Red Army's resurgence was not without its potential problems. In particular, intelligence estimates were now starting to suggest that Hitler might be willing to make peace and that Stalin might be prepared to accept such an overture. There were also signs that even if the war on the Eastern Front persisted the Soviets might halt at their prewar borders.[68] It was in this context that Roosevelt remarked to the JCS on January 7 that "he thought that Mr. Stalin probably felt out of the picture as far as Great Britain and the U.S. was concerned." He therefore felt it necessary to reassure the Soviets, remarking that he was "going to speak to Mr. Churchill about the advisability of informing Mr. Stalin that . . . [the Allies] were to continue on until they reach Berlin, and that their only terms would be unconditional surrender."[69]

While the president's decision to make this announcement at Casablanca was thus consistent both with a desire to quell liberal criticism over "Darlanism" and a need to encourage and placate the increasingly distrustful Soviets, there are a number of signs that suggest that public opinion was the more crucial variable. One was the manner in which Roosevelt unveiled the formula. Significantly, the president chose not to include any mention of unconditional surrender in the letter that he and Churchill sent to Stalin at the end of the conference. Instead, FDR announced it at a press conference, where journalists could naturally be relied on to wire the news back home quickly, thereby weakening the force of those editorials that were still attacking Peyrouton.[70] Another indication of the close and vital link between unconditional surrender and liberal attacks over "Darlanism" was the president's decision to reiterate the formula in the weeks and months after Casablanca. This was clearly the case in his February 12 speech; it was also true throughout 1943 and the first half of 1944.

Reassuring the "Liberals": FDR and Unconditional Surrender, February 1943 to June 1944

In the weeks after Casablanca and the February 12 speech, a number of critics, including Walter Lippmann and the *Nation*, expressed satisfaction with the president's unconditional surrender proclamation.[71] Yet the carping never completely ceased. Most ominously, in March, Willkie, still upset about the administration's efforts to silence him back in November, published *One World*, an account of his trip to the various fighting fronts, which contained numerous criticisms of the administration's handling of political matters. "Too often," he insisted in one typical passage, "as in North Africa, ... we perform in terms of old power politics and purely military operations, in terms of expediency and apparent practicalities. We too frequently forget what the war is about and we abandon our ideals."[72]

During the summer, events surrounding Mussolini's fall appeared to support Willkie's charge. On the evening of July 24–25, King Victor Emmanuel II deposed Il Duce and replaced him with Marshal Pietro Badoglio. The new premier had not held any position in the Fascist government since 1940, but he had nevertheless commanded Italy's forces in the notorious invasion of Abyssinia in 1935.[73] It was hardly surprising, therefore, that as the Allies moved to negotiate with Badoglio in an attempt to encourage Italy to defect from the Axis, a section of the media quickly began to express its unease. According to the CBS commentator, Cecil Brown, Americans were starting "to wonder if we are fighting Fascism" and pressed the administration to "set the American people straight on this one important question." "In short," feared Mark Sullivan in the *New York Herald-Tribune*, "the present incident is a pre-glimpse of the postwar."[74]

Sumner Welles's resignation at the start of September, although essentially the result of a personality clash with Hull, was seen by critics as further evidence that the State Department was in the grip of conservatives and appeasers now that one of its more liberal members had been jettisoned. Drew Pearson, who led the attack, even accused Berle of stating that "it had now become the official policy of the U.S. to work with Admiral Horthy in Hungary, Count Ciano and Victor Emmanual [*sic*] in Italy, together with certain Fascist leaders in Central Europe."[75] Also in September, the influential weekly *Time* gave nationwide currency to William Shirer's indictment of "the frightened, timid little men who make our foreign policies." They were "prepared to traffic with a miserable little Italian king or his reactionary henchman Badoglio," he continued, just as they "once trafficked with a Pétain, a Darlan, a Peyrouton, to avoid 'revolt' or 'trouble.'" Such views were widely echoed, especially by journals such as the *New Republic*, *Nation*, and *Common Sense*.[76]

Both Roosevelt and Hull remained deeply sensitive to charges that they had either negotiated with Nazis and Fascists or were now about to abandon American principles and war aims. According to Dean Acheson, the secretary of state was not only "all broken up" and in "a very low state of mind" in March, he was also totally preoccupied with Darlan and Peyrouton, so that "whatever subject one takes to the secretary, in a few minutes he finds himself listening to an anguished harangue about North Africa and exposition of Hull's mental sufferings."[77] In the summer, the president was quick to notice the liberals' unease at the arrangement with Badoglio. He was especially anxious to refute the charge, made by erstwhile supporters such as Dorothy Thompson, that the State Department always "seems to pop up on the wrong side, with the Fascists." Such comments, he insisted, were "false, malicious, and libelous."[78]

Faced with these problems, throughout 1943 FDR remained anxious to reassure the public that the precedent of "Darlanism" would not be applied to America's principal enemy. In private, he even began to abandon his old hopes that Germany might speedily collapse, realizing that such an outcome would simply give his liberal critics more ammunition. Thus, he now became adamantly opposed to anything that smacked of negotiation with German elites. This was evident in November 1943, when he was informed that a former OWI operative, Theodore Morde, had been talking to Germany's Turkish ambassador, Franz von Papen, with the blessing of the U.S. intelligence chief, William J. Donovan. Von Papen, whom Morde considered "a German Badoglio," was apparently willing to organize Hitler's overthrow before engaging in peace talks with the United States. Deeply alarmed, Roosevelt instructed that these discussions be terminated immediately and that Morde be denied a passport, to prevent him seeing von Papen again. Since Morde now worked for the *Reader's Digest*, the administration was also quick to send a government official to the editors of this magazine "in order to give them some understanding of the foreign policy of the government," lest they felt tempted to publish a story on this incident and thereby precipitate another furor.[79]

Even if Germany did collapse before Allied armies reached its borders, the president now made it clear that the United States would not stand idly by while confusion racked the Reich and speculation abounded at home. Instead, he supported Operation RANKIN, whose objective was "to occupy, as rapidly as possible, appropriate areas from which we can take steps to enforce the terms of unconditional surrender imposed by the Allied Governments on Germany." In this plan, the troops' role would be to police and control Germany from the outset, especially "to take any action to overcome any resistance to our terms, to take punitive action against local disorder, and to be a reminder to the German people of the main strategic bomber force which will be based in the U.K."[80]

As events started to unfold in Italy, the president also made more public attempts to defuse any criticism. By the end of July he was keen to let the American public know directly of his determination to avoid past mistakes. "We will have no truck with Fascism in any way, shape or manner," he declared in a fireside chat. "We will permit no vestige of Fascism to remain." Having decided to negotiate with Badoglio, he then told reporters that this was acceptable because he "isn't a definite member of the Fascist government."[81]

But for Roosevelt, unconditional surrender remained the most potent tool to reassure his traditional supporters that "Darlanism" was not the shape of things to come. Well before Mussolini's overthrow he made it clear both to reporters and subordinates that "we could not get away from unconditional surrender" and that any new Italian government "would, of course, not include any form of Fascism or dictatorship."[82] At the third Washington Conference in May he also contemplated issuing a statement clarifying unconditional surrender, which would have precluded the possibility of negotiating an armistice with the Nazi regime, the German High Command, or any other organization within Germany.[83] During July and August, he then publicly repeated his commitment to unconditional surrender on at least three occasions, while in numerous other speeches he firmly declared that there could be no compromise with the enemy.[84] Finally, as an additional guarantee that there would be no deals with any German Darlan or Badoglio, in September FDR also decided to add Prussian militarists to the list of those beyond the pale. The forum he chose was a message to Congress detailing the progress of the war. Taking close care of this speech, which was carefully crafted in six drafts, the president declared that "when Hitler and the Nazis go out, the Prussian military clique will go with them. The war-breeding gangs of militarists must be rooted out of Germany if we are to have any real assurance of peace."[85] A week later Elmer Davis reiterated this theme, warning that we may likely, before the war is over, see a phony revolution in Germany, put over by a sham opposition—by Nazi leaders or by military leaders who would be willing to cut the throats of any of their old associates if they could thereby save not only their own necks, but the substance of German military and industrial power. But the object of such a revolution would be a compromise peace, which would leave Germany still strong enough among her shattered neighbors—a peace which would be only the beginning of a German preparation for the next war. That kind of victory would be no victory at all.[86]

While Roosevelt therefore saw the reiteration of unconditional surrender as a way of dampening liberal criticism, initially at least his actions were also congruent with a continued desire to placate the Soviets. This remained vital during 1943, because as the Red Army started to take the offensive—first by ending the last German resistance at Stalingrad, later by repulsing the Wehrmacht's attack on Kursk, and finally by pushing the Germans back to the Dnieper and beyond—so its relations with the West also began to deteriorate. In March, the U.S. Ambassador in Moscow, Admiral William H. Standley, publicly berated the Soviets for ingratitude over Lend-Lease; a month later, Stalin broke off diplomatic relations with the Polish government-in-exile over the Katyn graves affair. By August, the Soviet leader was not only angrily denouncing the West for its continued failure to launch a second front, but had also decided to recall his ambassador back from Washington for consultation. In this context, Roosevelt undoubtedly still viewed the combination of unconditional surrender and his refusal to make any contact with German opposition groups as a method of placating Stalin. By offering him reassurances that the West was determined to fight to the finish, the president hoped to dissuade the Soviet dictator from pursuing his own separate peace with the Germans

Yet increasingly, this factor became far less important. After the Moscow and Tehran Conferences in October and November, FDR was confident that any lingering distrust between the Allies had been dispelled. He was also well aware that the Soviets were now "bent on the complete destruction of Hitler and nazism," and as a result he was less concerned about the possibilities of a separate German-Soviet peace. More to the point, during and after Tehran the Soviets themselves started to express deep reservations about the whole concept of unconditional surrender.[87] As Hull informed the president in January 1944, Stalin wanted to publicize "some definition" of the surrender terms, believing this "would deprive the enemy of . . . [a] propaganda advantage and consequently weaken the morale of their armed forces and people."[88]

By this stage, moreover, both the British ally and Roosevelt's advisers were joining the chorus of disapproval over unconditional surrender. London, for instance, was pushing for the principle to be "abandoned in the case of the Axis satellite states . . . for the purpose of both propaganda and peace feelers."[89] Hull, meanwhile, not only repeatedly forwarded Soviet and British misgivings about the formula to the White House but also expressed his fear that America's rigid adherence to unconditional surrender would open it up to the charge "of having rendered more difficult the Soviet military task."[90] More importantly, as plans gathered momentum for the Anglo-American invasion of France, the military began to view with alarm anything that might compound its hazardous mission. In March 1944, the Joint Chiefs expressed concern that "the unconditional surrender formula in its present form has apparently enabled the Nazis to invoke the specter of annihilation and thus has stiffened the German will to resist." A month later Eisenhower intimated that a re-formulation would be "highly desirable in view of the accumulated evidence that the German population is interpreting the words 'Unconditional surrender' to strengthen the morale of the German army and people."[91]

Yet despite all this pressure, in the first months of 1944 Roosevelt refused to budge. "Frankly," he informed Hull, "I do not like the idea of conversation[s] to define the term 'unconditional surrender.'" "I want at all costs," he wrote on another occasion, "to prevent it from *being said* that unconditional surrender has been abandoned."[92] But "*being said*" by whom? Not by the British, the Soviets, or his military and diplomatic advisers, since they all would have been perfectly happy for him to change this doctrine in some way. Instead, the only people who were likely to indict the president if he began to backtrack were those domestic liberals who had constantly attacked the administration for dealing with Nazis, Fascists, or their sympathizers. So by this stage, Roosevelt did *not* view unconditional surrender as a "lowest common denominator" that would keep a potentially fractious alliance together, since both Britain and the U.S.S.R. had their doubts about it.[93] Rather, his sole motive for reiterating the formula was to reassure erstwhile domestic supporters that for all the day-to-day maneuvering required to win battles the major aim of the war remained the complete defeat of Hitler and nazism. By the start of 1944, then, the constant enunciation of unconditional surrender was principally a product of internal American politics, a method of defusing the continued debate over the perils of "Darlanism."

Postscript: The Summer of 1944

At 12:42 P.M. on July 20, 1944, a loud explosion ripped through the conference room in Hitler's Wolf Lair compound in East Prussia. Just minutes before, as Hitler and his top generals discussed the latest developments on the Eastern Front, Colonel Claus von Stauffenberg had pushed a bomb under the conference table, set the timer, and hastily departed from the scene. Stauffenberg then made his way to Berlin, from where he hoped to direct a coup against the Nazi regime. But his plans were soon in disarray, because amazingly Hitler had survived. Although his hair was charred, his back bruised, and his hearing impaired, the Führer moved swiftly to re-assert his authority. In a broadcast to the German people, Hitler assured everyone he was alive. He then turned his attention to the rebels. The lucky ones, like Stauffenberg, were executed by firing squad that night; others were hanged slowly with piano wire, their death throes filmed for the Führer's enjoyment.[94]

Only a month before, Roosevelt had once again contemplated the possibility of a German "crack-up," and especially the likelihood that any German peace proposals would "come via the Vatican."[95] Back in 1942, of course, he had hoped for such a collapse. But now, more keenly aware of the political complications that were certain to ensue, FDR moved promptly to head off such an outcome. On June 11, he sent Myron Taylor off to Rome, with instructions to dissuade the pope from acting as a peace broker. A week later, when Taylor met the pontiff, he was confident that he had dispelled "any hope that a negotiation leading to an armistice could be anticipated." A relieved Roosevelt then thanked his envoy for "correct[ing] false impressions and present[ing] with such force and clarity our fundamental policy that Germany shall be compelled to sue for unconditional surrender."[96]

Now in July, on hearing word of Stauffenberg's coup attempt, the president remained determined to avoid any action that could be construed as "Darlanism." Privately, he told an aide that there was very little chance of getting "unconditional surrender from any responsible German government"—even one that had overthrown the Nazis.[97] He then ignored a request from his intelligence operatives that some form of aid be given to the rebels, while in public he left no one in any doubt that the lessons of the past had been learned. "Unconditional surrender still stands," he assured reporters. "Practically every German denies the fact they surrendered in the last war," he insisted, "but this time they are going to know it."[98]

Well into 1944, then, unconditional surrender remained at the heart of Roosevelt's rhetoric, largely because it was an ideal way of reassuring liberals that no deals would be concluded with the enemy. But while this formula clearly had its domestic uses, when it came to planning Germany's future it was only a starting point. It highlighted the fact that the Allies would only accept complete military victory, but it gave no indication as to what would replace the Axis regimes. It clearly stated that the goal was the eradication of Hitler and everything he stood for, but it gave no hint about how deep the Allies would need to go in order to root out the evil.[99] Roosevelt recognized this, and throughout 1943 and 1944 he began to ponder what additional measures would be required to prevent Germany from again disrupting the peace. As he did so, the unconditional surrender announcement would continue to impact on his thinking—but often in an unexpected and strangely paradoxical manner.

5

Hardening Thoughts, Unchanging Rhetoric

Too many people here and in England hold to the view that the German people as a whole are not responsible for what has taken place—that only a few Nazi leaders are responsible. That unfortunately is not based on fact. The German people as a whole must have it driven home to them that the nation as a whole has been involved in a lawless conspiracy against the decencies of modern civilisation.

—FDR, August 1944

As Franklin Roosevelt's thoughts turned from planning Germany's defeat to planning its future during the course of 1943, his image of the enemy—the basic framework he had long employed when analyzing the German problem —changed dramatically. Gone were the old fears and hopes that had encouraged him to think in terms of a difference between the brutal Nazis and the more peaceably inclined population. They were replaced by a greater tendency to conceive of the German nation as a monolithic whole in which everyone shared a degree of culpability. Thus, whereas in December 1942 Roosevelt had still been willing to believe that there were elements within Germany who might still "rise, and protest against the atrocities, against the whole Hitler system," a year later he was starting to stress that there were few differences between Germans and their leaders. "Fifty years ago, there had been a difference," he told Stalin at Tehran, "but since the last war it was no longer so."[1] Similarly, whereas in 1941 and 1942 he had wanted to reassure respectable Germans that they would be treated equally after the war, two years later he was beginning to advocate punishing the entire nation. "We have got to be tough with Germany," he commented on one occasion, "and I mean the German people, not just the Nazis."[2]

At the same time, however, Roosevelt made few attempts to inform the public of his changing views. Instead, for much of 1943 and the first half of 1944, he continued to define the enemy narrowly, still singling out the Nazis while exempting the mass of Germans from any direct culpability for the war. With no new cues from their president, it was hardly surprising that most Americans refused to abandon their long-held conviction that the Nazis, rather than the German people, were the sole enemy. But why did Roosevelt act in this way? Why did his beliefs suddenly start to stiffen? And why was there such a growing disjunction between his private thoughts and public utterances?

Fears, Hopes and Tentative Peace Plans: FDR and the Problem of Postwar Germany, 1941–42

Until the start of 1943, two recurring elements lay at the heart of Roosevelt's image of the German enemy—a fear of Hitler's aggressive intentions, Germany's growing capabilities, and the Nazis' brutal methods, combined with a lingering hope that the Third Reich was internally fragile and that an implosion was always possible. During 1941 and 1942, both strands exerted a powerful influence whenever the president briefly pondered policies for postwar Germany.

Vividly recalling that Hitler's path to expansion had begun when the Nazis walked out of the Disarmament Conference, reintroduced conscription, and created the Luftwaffe, in the first years of the war FDR looked for ways of preventing a future rogue German leader from pursuing a similar course. "As you know," he wrote an old associate in November 1942, "I dream dreams but am, at the same time, an intensely practical person, and I am convinced that disarmament of the aggressor nations is an essential first step."[3] As Roosevelt's mind turned toward how to ensure disarmament, he began to develop the idea of surveillance by the great powers, reinforced by two long-cherished notions: the blockade and air power. "As soon as any of the other nations was caught arming," he declared, "they would be threatened first with quarantine and if the quarantine did not work they would be bombed."[4]

While Roosevelt's fears encouraged him to advocate disarmament, his hopes prompted him to enumerate relatively soft terms in other spheres. Specifically, the president's belief that an internal revolution was possible led him in two different but complementary directions. First, if the Nazis could be eliminated, Roosevelt believed a large ingredient of the problem would be solved. As a result, he felt it would be relatively easy and quick to reintegrate Germany into a multilateral economic framework. As the British ambassador recorded in April 1941, FDR favored a united economic system to which all states, "not excluding Germany on good behavior, might adhere." Four months later, at the Atlantic Conference, this idea emerged again. Our enemies must be guaranteed free access to raw materials, Roosevelt told Churchill. "This point was of very great importance," he continued, "as a measure of assurance to the German and Italian peoples that the British and U.S. Governments desired to offer them, after the war, fair and equal opportunity of an economic character." The word "assurance" is critically important here and reveals a second strand of FDR's thinking. By demonstrating to the German people that they could expect relatively soft terms, his aim was to encourage them to ditch their leadership. The president "evidently had in mind," noted the British ambassador after discussing these ideas in April 1941, "the psychological effect within Germany of the knowledge that this sort of thing was in the process of taking shape."[5] For these two reasons, the overall tenor of the broad war aims agreed on at the Atlantic Conference tended toward the benign. The Allies, for example, would seek "the final destruction of the Nazi tyranny," but they would also ensure "that *all men in all lands* may live out their lives in freedom from fear and want," as well as providing all states, "*victor or vanquished*," with equal access "to the trade and to the raw materials of the world which are needed for their economic prosperity." As one close aide noted in November 1942, "the Atlantic Charter pretty nearly rules out a punitive peace in the normal sense of the term."[6]

Hardening Thoughts: FDR's Changing Image of the Enemy, 1943

Yet, just two months after this comment had been made, notions of a punitive peace, far from being ruled out, were increasingly starting to dominate the president's thinking. According to conventional wisdom, the reason for this was simple: Roosevelt's inclination for harsh postwar measures was a clear reflection of his deep-seated Germanophobia, an overt manifestation of his persistent hatred of Germany that dated back to his earliest experiences in the Reich.[7] How accurate is this claim?

During 1943 and 1944, FDR certainly went out of his way to create the impression that he had always been aware of Germany's penchant for militarism and aggression. On one occasion, he insisted that the incubus of militarism had first entered the German bloodstream in the late 1880s, with the advent of Kaiser Wilhelm II; before then, he maintained, Germany "was not a military nation," but thereafter even railroad workers and schoolchildren wore uniforms. "The president recalled his earlier travels to Germany," an aide noted another time, pointing out that "passports came in with militarization of Germany under Kaiser Wilhelm [II] and the consequent growth of suspicion and government intrigue and treachery." "The president began with an account of his boyhood studies in Germany," recorded yet another official, "when, he said, he grew fond of the German people as they were [then]. . . . The president said that four years later he visited Germany again and found a great change in this respect— the students had started wearing uniforms and were marching in formation. Militarism took the ascendancy from then on."[8]

Yet these statements need to be treated with care. Although they indicate that Roosevelt was *now* willing to equate current German behavior with militaristic traits dating back to the 1890s, they do not prove that he had *always* thought this way. As we have seen, despite his claims in 1943–44, there had been numerous occasions in the past when FDR had been far from convinced that the entire nation was irredeemably aggressive. During the 1930s, in particular, he had frequently been willing to identify reliable and respectable elements within the Reich, never intimating for a moment that they might have been inculcated with the militaristic bug during their Wilhelmine school days. By 1943, moreover, Roosevelt was not just conveniently forgetting his previous attitudes and assumptions; he was also starting to create an imagined past that had little basis in fact. To take two examples: first, while in conversation FDR now gave the impression of an extensive personal experience of Germany, in actuality he had only been to school in the Reich for a brief period, and this "superficial" experience hardly furnished him with sufficient evidence to claim a growth in both militarism and "government intrigue and treachery." Similarly, while he now talked of the fundamental change he had seen at first hand with the advent of Wilhelm II, in reality he had first visited Germany in 1891, three years after this kaiser had come to power, and so had no direct knowledge of the pre-Wilhelmine period and no way of knowing whether there had been a sudden transformation with the demise of Wilhelm I and Bismarck. In short, then, Roosevelt's "reminiscences" were not an accurate reflection of how he had always viewed Germany. In fact, they are best seen as a symptom, an overt manifestation, of his *new* and developing animus toward Germany.[9]

During 1943, this animus largely developed in response to four important changes in the international and domestic context. The first was linked directly to the liberal criticism over "Darlanism." During 1943, the persistent carping over Peyrouton and Badoglio not only prodded FDR to enunciate unconditional surrender; it also encouraged him to think about all the possible ramifications of a German implosion. After all, events in North Africa and especially Italy had demonstrated that any revolution was most likely to be effected by elites with close connections to the existing regime, rather than by the entire population. This naturally begged the question: what if the same thing happened in Germany? Specifically, how would the American public react if a leading German general or member of the conservative establishment emerged as the head of a new regime and sued for peace? It was now glaringly obvious that liberals would be outraged by any deal with a German Badoglio or Darlan, and this in turn would leave the administration facing an exceedingly difficult problem. As one top State Department official put it, if a military government was to take over in Germany "and then turn to us and say, 'You were fighting Mussolini and Hitler. We deposed them and got rid of them. You said you were fighting against ideologies and were against Fascism and Nazism. We have dispensed with them. Now we have peace with Germany and we are ready to make peace with you.' That would leave us in a very bad position. Psychologically it would be very hard to explain."[10]

Roosevelt agreed. To avoid such an awkward situation, he decided that it was far more prudent to focus solely on the complete military defeat of Germany. Abandoning his old hopes, he therefore started to comment that when it came to the Third Reich "we must not place our hopes on such a collapse but . . . we must continue to exert every effort to compel unqualified surrender."[11]

Yet public opinion, in the guise of liberal criticism, was only one small reason why Roosevelt's attitudes started to stiffen. Equally important was the content of intelligence information now flooding into the White House. By 1943, this was clearly starting to indicate that most Germans supported their criminal regime. On the way to the Cairo Conference in November, "Hap" Arnold briefed FDR about a survey completed by leading scholars (including Carl Becker, Henry Steele Commager, Edward Mead Earle, and Dumas Malone), which stressed that "the complete and highly organized control of the Nazi party gives no encouragement to the hope that any political upheaval can be anticipated in Germany in the near future."[12] Such a conclusion was supported by both the American and British intelligence communities, who in September asserted that "no organized opposition exists" inside Germany and that disaffected Germans would never accept unconditional surrender.[13] It was bolstered, too, by a series of reports indicating that Allied tools such as bombing and psychological warfare were failing to have the intended effect of undermining morale and exacerbating tensions within Germany. In a memorandum from J. Edgar Hoover that Roosevelt deemed important enough to forward to George Marshall, one informant revealed that even those with little loyalty to the Nazi regime were becoming hardened to the damage inflicted by the Allied air forces and "can think of nothing but revenge."[14] Finally, by this stage Roosevelt was also made aware that many Germans, far from being peaceably inclined, were instead showing signs of having completely imbibed the Nazi ethos. As the head of intelligence informed the White House in October, interrogations of German prisoners of war demonstrated that, despite almost universal war weariness and acceptance that defeat was inevitable, the vast majority remained far from repentant. "Eight-five percent," he concluded, "have no conception of democracy."

In lengthy discussions "many come to admit that 'democracy is a wonderful thing but impossible for Germany'"; their preference instead was for a polity akin to the present system that revolved around the whims of one powerful individual—"If Hitler is a bad leader," was a common refrain, "then we must find a better leader."[15]

The third change related to alliance diplomacy. During the course of 1943, Roosevelt became convinced that a firm anti-German stance would help to cement his fragile relationship with Stalin. It was now clear that, as the British foreign secretary informed FDR in March, Stalin had a "deep-seated distrust of the Germans and . . . he will insist that Germany be broken up into a number of states."[16] Since Roosevelt was already inclining toward an anti-German stance, he found it easy to agree with Stalin on this matter. But other dynamics were also at work to reinforce this tendency. For one thing, by encouraging the punitive aspects of Stalin's thinking, Roosevelt hoped to safeguard against the possibility of a separate Soviet-German peace, for if Russian leaders went on record as being willing to treat the entire nation harshly then the Germans would have little incentive to look to Moscow for a negotiated settlement. In the longer term the president also believed that U.S.-Soviet cooperation would be an essential cornerstone of an enduring postwar peace structure. If he could assuage Stalin's security concerns by assuring him that Germany would be kept weak, then he hoped that this might smooth the way for a high degree of postwar cooperation amongst the Big Three.[17]

The fourth and final transformation was in the nature of the German problem itself. In the past ten years, FDR had principally been preoccupied with discerning the growth of German power and the extent of Hitler's ambitions, as well as with finding ways of containing and then eradicating this menace. As the Nazis went from success to success, it was perhaps easier to focus on the prospect that the Third Reich might suddenly collapse, for this avoided having to contemplate the huge manpower and economic sacrifices that would be required in any full-scale invasion of Western Europe. In 1941, FDR's hopes certainly enabled him to square the circle of advocating Hitler's defeat at a time when the American public was overwhelmingly opposed to sending an AEF abroad; the following year, when the western Allies were then unable to muster sufficient forces to mount a cross-channel attack, clinging to the belief that Germany would crack held out the prospect that the United States could win the war without a large-scale and costly battle on French beaches against a full-strength Wehrmacht.[18] By 1943, however, such considerations were no longer germane. After all, the tide of battle was turning against Germany with its defeat at Stalingrad, the United States and Britain were garnering the forces to launch an offensive in Europe, and the decision was about to be made to launch a second front in France in the spring of 1944. Consequently, Roosevelt could now view the whole German problem in a very different light. In particular, with nazism soon to be eradicated, it was increasingly anachronistic to think in terms of the shaky relationship between a dictatorship and the wider population; instead, FDR could ponder a prostrate nation, a clean slate on which the Allies could write whatever they wished.

Naturally, these stiffening attitudes exerted a profound influence over Roosevelt's preferred policy solutions. In short, the president no longer believed that once nazism had been eradicated then the German problem would essentially be solved; unlike 1941–42, he was no longer content simply to plump for disarmament and the overthrow of the existing regime. As FDR told the Joint Chiefs, he now firmly rejected proposals based merely on "a reconstituting of the German state which would give active cooperation apparently at once to peace in Europe. . . . [The] German philosophy cannot be changed by decree, law, or military order," he continued. "The change in German philosophy must be evolutionary and may take two generations."[19]

What did this mean in practice? During the winter of 1942–43, with his old hopes still at the fore, Roosevelt's attitudes toward Germany remained generally mild. At the start of December, he met with Jewish-American leaders. After confirming that the reports of Nazi genocide were sadly true, Roosevelt immediately emphasized that the Allies were "dealing with an insane man—Hitler, and the group that surrounds him represent an example of a national psychopathic case." But he was also keen to stress that it was "not in the best interests of the Allied cause to make it appear that the entire German people are murderers or are in agreement with what Hitler is doing." There must be some groups, he concluded, who will "at the proper time" rise up and protest against these grotesque atrocities.[20] If this were true, then such elements might conceivably form the nucleus of a new Germany soon after the war was over. That Roosevelt's mind was still thinking along these lines was indicated by another meeting he had in December, this time with the Canadian prime minister, where he made clear his opposition to dismemberment, the annexation of German territory, or anything that might "prevent her development in any way."[21] A short while later, still clinging to his Wilsonian faith in the pacific nature of the masses, FDR also mused about the possibility of establishing "Free Ports of Information." Because these ports would ensure that no one "could be denied access by totalitarian censorship to the same news that was available to all other people," the president was confident that they would prevent another Goebbels from hoodwinking and misleading a peace-loving public.[22]

It was not long, however, before Roosevelt finally came to the conclusion that such measures would be totally inadequate. Indicative of the president's hardening views was his decision to invite Emil Ludwig to the White House. Back in 1942, Roosevelt had been anxious to keep his distance from this prominent Germanophobe and had not liked the idea of employing him in the administration's propaganda agency. Now, however, on March 24 FDR granted Ludwig a lunchtime interview. He also made sure that Ludwig's stern-peace meditations were circulated within the administration. Anthony Eden, the British foreign secretary, even got a copy when he came to Washington in March for a series of preliminary discussions about the postwar world.[23] Over a period of more than two weeks, Eden and Roosevelt engaged in a series of relaxed and wide-ranging talks, surveying "the outstanding political questions of the entire planet, playing with borders, shifting governments like so many chess pieces, guessing at political shadings that would color the postwar map."[24] They soon came to the German problem.

The president began by pointing out that Germany would have to lose some of its territory to Poland. This was only fair because Stalin wanted to push his own borders westward, and Poland could best be compensated for this loss by obtaining East Prussia. "Poland," Hopkins dutifully recorded, "wants East Prussia and both the president and Eden agree that Poland should have it." But giving East Prussia to Poland raised the further question of what to do with the large group of ethnic Germans who would not only remain in this area but would also be likely to create trouble, as they had done in the months leading up to the outbreak of war in 1939. As much for this reason as for any other, the president began to comment that the Nazis were not the only dangerous element within Germany. "The Prussians," he declared, "cannot be trusted." Although "a harsh procedure," he advocated a mild version of ethnic cleansing—moving the Prussians out of East Prussia, "the same way the Greeks were moved out of Turkey after the last war." FDR was also a sudden new convert to the notion of dismemberment. "Germany must be divided into several states," he agreed with Eden, "one of which must, over all circumstances be Prussia."[25]

Over the next few months, ideas like these remained at the heart of Roosevelt's vision for postwar Germany. Time after time, he stressed that this country would have to be dismembered, that it would have to lose territory in the east, that it ought to be prevented from ever acquiring an air force, that its population would have to be reeducated out of their militaristic and authoritarian tendencies. But while there was no doubting that the president's preferences were now stern, until November there remained a hint of ambivalence in Roosevelt's private musings—an ambivalence that historians have often failed to pick up.[26]

FDR's equivocation stemmed partly from the fact that his image of Germany did not shift overnight but hardened gradually, so that for a time fragments of his old conception were still evident. Initially, for instance, Roosevelt remained convinced that there were profound divisions and cleavages within German society. He even based his early support for dismemberment on the fact that, while the Prussians had to be dispersed because they could not be trusted, in other regions there were "differences and ambitions that will spring up" and enable the Allies to base partition on consent rather than force. There might be a southern state, he suggested on a number of occasions, based on a shared Catholic identity and a north-western state founded on common Protestant characteristics. At this stage, the president was certainly quick to oppose "the methods used at Versailles and also promoted by Clemenceau to arbitrarily divide Germany." Instead, he hoped for "a division that represents German public opinion."[27]

Roosevelt was also keenly aware that the State Department was suspicious of proposals that were excessively harsh or vindictive, and during the fall he felt a particular need to tone down his comments whenever Cordell Hull was around. During the past decade, the president had never developed a close relationship with his secretary of state. As a general rule, he considered professional diplomats to be excessively conservative, invariably second rate, and far too likely to share government secrets with columnists and reporters. He tolerated Hull because of his influence and prestige on Capitol Hill, but he rarely took the secretary of state into his confidence and generally sought ways to bypass him. In fact, the president was always far more comfortable in the company of Sumner Welles, his undersecretary of state. It was Welles he had sent on a fact-finding mission to Europe in 1940, Welles who had accompanied him to the Atlantic Conference in August 1941, and Welles who was frequently called to the White House whenever the president needed advice. In September 1943, however, Hull at last gained his revenge, when, tired of having his authority usurped and concerned that Welles's alleged homosexual activities were a security risk, he finally forced the undersecretary's resignation.[28]

Roosevelt responded quickly to the loss of Welles by trying to mend fences with his secretary of state. In October, he agreed to send Hull off to Moscow, in order to smooth out relations with the Soviets in the wake of all the second front postponements and to raise Hull's spirits in the aftermath of the feud with Welles.[29] The president also deemed it prudent to temper his views about Germany whenever State Department planners were in earshot. So, aware that Hull adamantly opposed partition, in October he conceded that it might be a good idea if Germany's political fragmentation was accompanied by a degree of economic integration, to ensure that the three new German states remained "joined by a network of common services as regards postal arrangements, communications, railways, customs, perhaps power, etc." At the same time, the president also intimated that his attitude toward Germany was pragmatic rather than stern. There would obviously be a transitional postwar period, he pointed out, and "it may well happen that in practice we shall discover that partitions, undertaken immediately after the war, may have to be abandoned."[30]

Yet ultimately, these scattered concessions proved to be largely cosmetic. For one thing, Roosevelt still remained wedded to some form of dismemberment, despite Hull's insistence that "imposed partition would be little short of a disaster both for Germany and us."[31] For another, FDR had no doubt that the Moscow Conference would be little more than a talking shop for the three foreign ministers. All the big matters would have to wait until he, Stalin, and Churchill got together for the very first time.

Roosevelt left a cold and wet Washington late on the evening of November 11. He was hoping to relax during the long eight-day cruise across the Atlantic and was certainly looking forward to a week or more without any newspapers. But the journey was not to be without incident. On the second day at sea, a U.S. escort destroyer nearly ended the trip by accidentally firing a torpedo in the direction of the president's battleship; fortunately it missed by a couple of hundred feet.[32] Thereafter, FDR took time out to tour the ancient and modern battlefields of Carthage and Tunisia, with General Eisenhower as his expert guide. He also stopped off at Cairo for a five-day summit with the British and the Chinese, where plans for the next stage in the war against Japan were discussed. So it was not until November 27 that Roosevelt finally arrived in Tehran. The journey had been long and grueling, but the president was excited by the prospect of meeting Stalin at long last. The next day he quickly accepted an invitation to stay in the more secure accommodation inside the Soviet compound. Minutes after he arrived, a smiling Stalin ambled into his room. "I am glad to see you," FDR began. "I have tried for a long time to bring this about."[33]

The leaders soon got down to business. Discussions about Germany's future began at dinner that first evening. Roosevelt got the ball rolling by musing about the need for political reform, and especially his determination to see "the concept of the Reich" erased from the German mind and stricken from the German language. Stalin disagreed, however. "It was not enough to eliminate the word," the marshal averred; "the very Reich itself must be rendered impotent ever again to plunge the world into war." Warming to his theme, Stalin then dominated the dinner table talk, "constantly emphasizing that the measures for the control of Germany and her disarmament were insufficient to prevent the rebirth of German militarism." As the president's interpreter pointed out later that evening, Stalin obviously regarded all the measures proposed by either the president or Churchill for the subjugation of Germany as quite inadequate.[34]

On reflection, Roosevelt was greatly heartened by this turn of events, for he quickly recognized that he had a perfect opportunity not just to garner powerful support for his own harsh policies but also to improve his relationship with the suspicious and distrustful Soviet leader. The very next day, he wasted no time in accepting the need for a degree of economic control, agreeing with Stalin that a method had to be found to prevent Germany from converting its industries for warlike purposes. The president also revealed how heavily the public's opposition to American military involvement in Europe during 1941 still weighed on his mind. "If the Japanese had not attacked the U.S." at Pearl Harbor, he confided to the Soviet leader, then it was doubtful "whether it would have been possible to send any American forces to Europe." This naturally had implications for the postwar world, FDR continued, because in the absence of "another terrible crisis" it was highly unlikely that the great American public would agree to a lengthy future deployment of troops abroad.[35]

Roosevelt's recollection of past public opinion problems undoubtedly helped to reinforce his desire for stern measures. After all, in the absence of a long-term American occupation, alternative methods would have to be found to ensure that Germany did not again disrupt the peace—and what better way than to permanently eradicate its power to make war. The president was certainly in a harsh frame of mind on December 1, when he introduced his dismemberment proposals. In contrast to his earlier discussions with the State Department, he now spoke of partition into five (and not three) German states, as well as advocating two zones (the Kiel Canal and the Ruhr) to be under international control. The idea of economic integration was now conspicuously absent from FDR's presentation. As a shocked Churchill blurted out, "the president had said a mouthful."

But the president was still not finished. Such measures, he stressed, were vital because of the inherently aggressive nature of the German nation. Whereas his support for division had previously revolved around the premise that there were profound differences within Germany that would enable any fragmentation to be based on consent, now for the first time Roosevelt enunciated the notion that all Germans were alike, that few distinctions could be made between Nazis, Prussians, or the bulk of the population, and that all were equally to blame for the current conflagration. As the U.S. minutes recorded, "the president said he agreed with the Marshal, particularly in regard to the absence of differences between Germans. He said fifty years ago there had been a difference but since the last war it was no longer so. He said the only difference was that in Bavaria and the southern part of Germany there was no officer cast[e] as there had been in Prussia." Dismemberment, he now implied, had to be forcibly imposed to prevent the aggressive German nation from ever threatening future European security. As FDR told Stalin, "Germany had been less dangerous to civilisation when in 107 provinces."[36]

Clearly, then, the Tehran Conference marked a watershed in Roosevelt's thinking about postwar Germany, even though many of his ideas remained in an embryonic form. For instance, although FDR now talked about the need to prevent Germany from ever obtaining weapons again, he was only starting to recognize the difference between "direct" and "indirect" rearmament—the fact that it might be necessary not only to supervise the dismantling of arms manufacturing but also to keep an eye on, say, furniture or watch factories since, as Stalin argued, these could be quickly converted to produce airplanes or fuses for shells.[37] As a result, Roosevelt had yet to fully examine the possibility that extensive economic controls, perhaps even deindustrialization, would be necessary in order to truly ensure disarmament.

At this stage, the president was also reluctant to commit himself to too

The big three at Tehran. Stalin, FDR, and Churchill. Behind them, from left to right, Hopkins, Molotov, Harriman, Clark Kerr (the British ambassador to the U.S.S.R.), and Eden.

many specific proposals. As he wrote to Churchill in February, "I have been worrying a good deal of late on account of the tendency of all of us to prepare for future events in such detail that we may be letting ourselves in for trouble when the time arrives." Excessive planning, he concluded, should be regarded "as prophecies by prophets who cannot be fallible."[38] This probably explains why at Tehran, despite the meeting of minds between the president and Stalin, few concrete proposals for Germany were agreed in their final form. Instead, ideas like dismemberment were referred to the newly constructed European Advisory Commission (EAC) for further study.[39]

But despite these caveats, the overall drift in FDR's thinking was now clear. Unlike 1941–42, he no longer felt that denazification, disarmament, and then a quick reintegration of Germany back into the international fold would be sufficient. Rather, believing that each and every German was culpable, he deemed it essential to impose more stringent controls on the nation as a whole. As the president told both the cabinet and the congressional leadership in a series of hectic meetings on his return, this would entail occupation, division, political reorganization, and a measure of economic supervision.[40] Whether the wider audience of domestic public opinion would endorse such measures remained to be seen.

Unchanging Rhetoric: The Failure to Alter the
Nature-of-the-Enemy Campaign, 1943–44

Throughout 1943, as Roosevelt's private thoughts hardened, there was little evidence to suggest that the public's attitude toward Germany had altered in any meaningful way. In September, one poll found that less than a quarter of Americans thought that the Germans were inherently warlike— a figure that had changed little in the past eighteen months. A short while later, another survey revealed that 71 percent still felt "the German government is the chief enemy," with only 9 percent considering "the German people as our main foe"; almost two-thirds of the public also confidently believed that the Germans wanted to get rid of their Nazi masters.[41]

Support for relatively benign policies flowed naturally from this conception of the enemy. In May, a *Fortune* survey sent to the White House concluded that "the American people, up to now are inclined toward a reasonable rather than vindictive settlement with Germany.... A bloody retribution is called for by less than four percent of the people."[42] Basic minimum goals such as denazification, demobilization, and disarmament were widely popular, but once these had been secured most Americans thought that the German problem would be largely solved. As a result, they felt more stringent measures, like partition and deindustrialization, to be unnecessary, even excessive. This was confirmed by a January 1944 poll.

Rather than impoverishing a future Germany, a majority even favored its speedy reintegration back into the international fold. When pollsters asked, "Would you like to see our government *help* Germany get her peacetime industries going again after this war, or not," for instance, 51 percent said yes, 8 percent expressed qualified approval, and only 34 percent said no.[43]

For one small group of opinion pollsters and commentators, such benign sentiments were deeply disturbing, and they quickly called on the White House to take some corrective action. In September 1942, George Gallup sent FDR a confidential survey of American attitudes toward the war. This concluded that the administration's attempt to differentiate between Nazis and Germans was confusing the American mind. To correct this, he suggested, "the government should pursue a much stronger and more direct policy of arousing fear of Germany."[44]

Others agreed. Rex Stout, in a widely read article that appeared in the *New York Times Magazine* the following January, insisted that "We Shall Hate, or We Shall Fail." Stout, a popular author, had become closely connected with the government's information campaign through both his chairmanship of the War Writer's Board (WWB) and his appearances on numerous OWI-sponsored radio programs.[45] He now argued that "Adolf Hitler is nothing to be surprised at. A close student of German history, if sufficiently acute, might in the year 1900 have predicted a Hitler as the culmination of the deep-rooted mental and nervous disease afflicting the

POLL (JANUARY 1944)

We have listed a number of things that might be done with Germany when we are victorious. Do you think the UN should or should not:	Should (%)	Should Not (%)	Don't Know (%)
a. Abolish the Nazi party?	88	3	9
b. Completely demobilize the German Army and keep them from having an army again?	77	13	9
c. Govern Germany with an occupation force for several years?	73	11	15
d. Break Germany into smaller states?	29	41	30
e. Prevent the Germans from rebuilding their steel, chemical, and automotive industries?	31	53	16
f. Make German labor rebuild devastated areas in other countries at the rate usually paid to POWs?	46	32	22

Source: "Current Surveys," No. 36, January 5, 1944, entry 149, box 1715, RG 44, NA.

German people." Because all Germans, and not just their leaders, were the enemy, Stout believed it essential to develop among the American people "a feeling toward the Germans of deep and implacable resentment for their savage attack upon the rights and dignity of man, . . . of contempt for their arrogant and insolent doctrine of the German master race." He also argued that, far from undermining any prospective peace, such hatred was an essential prerequisite for a stable postwar order.[46]

Stout's view was endorsed by other prominent figures, including George Creel, the head of America's World War I propaganda agency, and James W. Gerard, a former American ambassador in Berlin. In letters to the American Mercury in April, the former declared that "Hitler is the German people," while the latter asserted that only partition and "an army of conquerors can restrain the German will to war."[47] At about the same time, Emil Ludwig made a similar case before the House Foreign Affairs Committee. Ludwig, like all these individuals, believed that the German people were to blame for the current conflagration. He therefore felt that American ire should be directed at the entire nation, rather than just a few Nazi leaders.[48]

Yet even among opinion makers such Germanophobia was not common during 1943. At the start of the year, Stout was quickly taken to task in a series of pamphlets, articles, and letters for seeking to engender a hatred, perhaps even a racism, that was no different from the "screaming frenzies" conducted by Hitler and Goebbels. Many also thought that Stout's call for an anti-German campaign would undermine the prospects for a lasting peace, as it had in 1919.[49] Both the mainstream *New York Times* and the divisionist *Chicago Daily Tribune* agreed.[50] And if additional corroboration was required, then it was provided by a digest of the views of prominent individuals that was sent to the president in October. This quoted the former president, Herbert Hoover, as stating that "we cannot have both revenge and peace. We must make such a setting as will give the decent elements in Axis peoples a chance to lead their comrades on the paths of peace." Other leading politicians also warned that "hate is not the answer to our problems; that by using it we can neither destroy anarchy nor build a better order."[51]

At this early stage, most opinion makers were reluctant to contemplate specific and detailed policies for postwar Germany. The main exception was Walter Lippmann, who in a series of columns published in April 1943 developed a rationale for a medium-term occupation, disarmament, Allied control of German industry, and the "reorientation" of German elites. But at this juncture, Lippmann was keen to point out that "the enemy is the historic German governing class" and not the German nation as a whole. He also gave short shrift to any thoughts of dismemberment, widespread extermination, or making the German people suffer over a long period of time.[52]

As Roosevelt kept a close eye on the attitudes of press and public, he must have realized that he had an acute problem, for the public clearly opposed most of the ideas he had mooted to Eden in March and to Stalin in November. But how could this be remedied? Perhaps FDR could start to educate popular opinion about the need for specific punitive measures. Perhaps he could lay the groundwork for the acceptance of a harsh peace by publicly talking about the guilt of the entire German nation. Or perhaps he could only wait until popular attitudes changed of their own accord.

As the first president to hold regular informal press conferences and to employ the radio to good effect, Roosevelt had always been innovative when it came to finding ways of getting his message across to the American public. Toward the end of 1942, with the phony war mentality starting to evaporate, he now thought the time was ripe to give the populace an indication of his thinking on postwar issues. But he also deemed it too early to issue a direct statement on this subject. What the president needed was a subtler channel to convey his preliminary ideas.

In December, FDR decided to invite Forrest Davis to the White House for the weekend. As soon as the journalist arrived, Roosevelt gave him an exclusive interview. In subsequent weeks, he then read and approved the article that Davis wrote, so that by the time it finally appeared in the April edition of the *Saturday Evening Post*, under the heading "Roosevelt's World Blueprint," there could be no doubt that it was intended to be an authoritative summary of the president's views. Davis began by publicizing the enormous importance that Roosevelt attached to the disarmament of aggressor nations. To enforce this, FDR would rely on a blockade or quarantine, for this would produce, "in the president's opinion, a sort of economic paralysis in a nation embedded, as is Germany, in the heart of Europe.... The effect of such segregation on the [German] public would not be less than alarming."[53]

Of course, such notions owed much to Roosevelt's old conception of the enemy, based as they were on a faith that economic weakness and the less belligerent nature of the German people could restrain a warlike regime. But when it came to going beyond this and discussing the more severe ideas he was now starting to embrace—ideas like partition, truncation, or reeducation—the president doggedly refused to comment. It was far too early to talk about such matters, he told inquisitive reporters on more than one occasion, for "we are still in the generality stage, not in the detail stage."[54] The Allies, he declared in a similarly evasive tone in July,

> are substantially agreed on the general objectives of the postwar world. They are also agreed that this is not the time to engage in an international discussion of all the terms of peace and *all* the details of the future. Let us win the war first. We must not relax our pressure on the enemy by taking time out to define every boundary and settle every political controversy in every part of the world. The all-important thing now is to get on with the war—and to win it.[55]

The Tehran communiqué released at the end of the conference was very much in this vein, for it revealed little of the minutiae of the Big Three discussions. On military matters, it merely insisted that "our military staffs . . . have concerted our plans for the destruction of the German forces." When it came to postwar issues, the communiqué was even terser. Roosevelt himself deleted an appeal to the German people, which would have modified unconditional surrender by reassuring the Germans that they would not be enslaved. All that was left after he, Hopkins, and Churchill had completed their editing, was the anodyne statement that the Big Three had promised to provide solutions that "will command the good will of the overwhelming mass of the peoples of the world, and banish the scourge and terror of war for many generations."[56]

The media's reaction to this reticence was mixed. On one hand, as Early wired to Hopkins on December 7, the "Tehran release [was] enthusiastically received by all except isolationist press and isolationist senators and representatives. Tremendous news play with strong headlines and vigorous editorial treatment emphasizing the meeting as 'Victory Conference.'"[57] Most opinion makers were quick to express their relief that the three leaders had finally met and almost all drew the implication that this display of Big Three solidarity spelled inevitable doom for Nazi Germany. "The big thing about the meeting," announced Raymond Gramm Swing on the Blue network, ". . . was, of course, the meeting itself. . . . The meeting signifies co-ordination in war and collaboration in peace." "The importance of Tehran" agreed Max Lerner in the *PM Daily*, "is that the three men did meet, and that they agreed enough to issue a warm statement."[58]

But at the same time, many columnists and editors were deeply dissatisfied with the continued lack of specifics. Opinion polls had already revealed that what to do with postwar Germany's was the one issue above all others on which the public craved more information. Now, Lerner, Lippmann, Krock, Shirer, and Thompson all complained about the absence of any details. "The clearest omission in the communiqué," grumbled Lerner, "is the failure to say anything about the kind of peace Germany can expect from us." Or as Dorothy Thompson pithily put it: "The three agreed to go on agreeing. But what they agreed to no one knows."[59]

Roosevelt, however, was scarcely in a position to weaken the force of such criticisms. In private, he was only just starting to grapple with the whole problem of Germany's future, the State Department was clearly opposed to ideas like partition, and although FDR and Stalin shared a common inclination to treat Germany harshly, no concrete agreements had been reached at Tehran and most subjects had been referred to the EAC for further discussion. As a result, it would have been jumping the gun to start informing the American people about proposals such as partition and economic control.

But the president did have another option: why not take the advice of Gallup, Stout, and Ludwig, and start to foster a new consensus around the notion that all the Germans, and not just a few Nazis, were to blame for the war? This would lay the groundwork for popular acceptance of a harsh peace, so that specific measures could then be publicized once alliance negotiations had been completed. Such a strategy would hardly have been novel, for the president was currently engaged in a similar process with respect to an international organization. Here, his aim was to carefully cultivate a consensus on the general principle of greater U.S. involvement in world affairs, while not revealing any details of what exact form a new League of Nations would take.[60] Such a strategy was also likely to enjoy a measure of success. After all, American hatred of the Japanese nation was now clearly starting to translate into support for a harsh peace in the Pacific; as one survey pointed out in November, "the public wants harsher treatment for Japan than Germany—a sentiment which is apparently linked to the belief of 62 percent of Americans that 'the Japanese will always want war,'" whereas only 22 percent felt the same way about the Germans.[61]

Yet Roosevelt consistently refused to launch a hate campaign against the German nation. Instead, in the first six months of 1943, he continued to use the terms "Nazi" and "Hitler" to characterize the enemy; and even on those less frequent occasions when "German(y)" was employed this tended to be in the context of, say, a comparison between American and German production or a vow to employ American air power over Ger-

Who Is the Enemy? A Content Analysis of the FDR's Speeches,
January–July 1943

	1/17/1943 State of Union	2/12/1943 Radio Address	5/2/1943 Fireside Chat	7/28/1943 Fireside Chat
Hitler/Nazi	5	10	3	9
German(y)	4	4	—	4
Berlin	2	2	—	2
Tojo/warlords	1	—	—	2
Japan(ese)	12	10	1	13
Tokyo	2	2	—	2
Mussolini/Fascist	2	3	1	10
Italy	2	2	—	4
Rome	2	1	—	1
Axis	9	5	—	1

Sources: Compiled from FDR, *Public Papers*, 12:21-34, 71-81; *FDR's Fireside Chats*, pp. 250–56, 258–66.

many, and so was not an attempt to develop the argument that the German people, or even the German generals, were the true adversary. In a fireside chat in May, for instance, Roosevelt emphasized that it was "Nazi machine-gun bullets" and Nazi land mines that were killing U.S. soldiers. The implication was clear: it was only the Nazis who would have to be defeated and then dealt with.[62]

During the fall and winter, Roosevelt did make a few amendments to this message. On two occasions, spurred on by the constant liberal criticism over "Darlanism," he added Prussian militarism to the list of America's true enemies. Then, in a fireside chat on Christmas Eve, the president went even further, declaring that "we intend to rid them [the German people] once and for all of Nazism and Prussian militarism and the fantastic and disastrous notion that they constitute the 'master race.'" For the first time in a public speech, he also pointed to the continuities in German aggression, stressing how after 1918 the United States had naively "hoped that the militaristic philosophy of Germany had been crushed; and being full of the milk of human kindness we spent the next twenty years disarming, while the Germans whined so pathetically that other nations permitted them — and even helped them — to rearm."[63]

Yet such passages soon turned out to be isolated exceptions rather than the start of a coherent new nature of the enemy campaign. Even the Christmas Eve broadcast was ultimately something of a damp squib. The original draft had been far more strident, indicting the German people "as a whole" for their enthusiastic support of Hitler and hinting that harsh long-term measures would be required to keep this nation in its place.[64] But as Roosevelt and his speechwriters went through the familiar ritual of revising and

FDR delivers a fireside chat, Christmas Eve, 1943.

editing, of carefully checking each phrase to ensure that it struck exactly the right note, the passages on Germany were gradually and significantly toned down. By the time the president delivered the speech, the odd anti-German comment remained. But this was now carefully cancelled out by FDR's declaration that he would not clamp down too harshly on the German nation. The Allies, he insisted, "have no intention to enslave the German people. We wish them to have a normal chance to develop in peace, as useful and respectable members of the European family."[65]

Over the winter, the president then slid back into his old habit of differentiating between Nazis and Germans. The war, Roosevelt declared in the 1944 budget message, was the product of "nations that have become tools in the hands of irresponsible cliques bent on conquests."[66] The slaughter in the occupied territories, he stressed two month later, was being conducted purely by the perverted Nazis. "Hitler is committing these crimes against humanity in the name of the German people," he concluded. "I ask every German . . . to show the world by his action that in his heart he does not share these criminal desires."[67] In an article for the January edition of the *American Magazine*, Harry Hopkins made a similar point. According to Hopkins, the Nazis were clearly the central culprits; consequently, as soon as they had been eliminated and the German people had evinced signs of good behavior, there would be no problem reintegrating this country quickly back into the international fold. "You can't do business with Hitler, it is true," he declared. "But we will do business with a disarmed German people."[68]

Roosevelt's reluctance to launch a hate campaign stemmed from a variety of concerns. One was his clear recognition, gleaned from the wealth of opinion poll data, that the American public was likely to be staunchly and stubbornly averse to anything that smacked of anti-German propaganda. Of course, the whole aim of any information campaign is to alter the popular mood so that the public rallies behind its government. But, as we have seen, Roosevelt had always been keenly aware of the limits of leadership.

Indeed, back in the period from 1937 to 1940, FDR had been acutely concerned about the threat posed by Hitler and his cohorts. But realizing that public opinion was opposed to any involvement in European squabbles, he had moved with great circumspection; until December 1940 he had even been reluctant to publicly name the actual aggressors. Instead, the president's strategy had been to wait, in the hope that incidents would force a fundamental shift in popular attitudes. When they did, when great external events like the fall of France started to undermine the appeal of isolationism, he then finally acted, changing the tenor of his message so as to further erode the public's complacency about European developments.

Faced with a comparable situation in 1943, it seems highly likely that the president chose to adopt a similar strategy. Rather than attempt to lead on an issue where the public was unlikely to follow, he probably thought it was better to sit tight. After all, the course of the war would probably throw up events that would stiffen American opinion. Once popular attitudes then began to change, FDR could move to prod them still further in their anti-German direction. One such opportunity almost occurred in January 1944, when information filtered out that the Germans were contemplating the execution of captured American airmen. Roosevelt felt that the public would undoubtedly react to such news as it had in April 1943, when the Japanese had committed a similar atrocity: with outrage, horror, and calls for retribution against the perpetrators.[69] This time, however, the story proved false and so the administration was not able to take any action. But Roosevelt's reaction is nevertheless instructive, for it suggests that, while his public utterances remained cautious, he was still looking to publicize any comprehensible and believable event that might harden American attitudes toward the enemy.[70]

While the president waited patiently for incidents that might encourage the public to turn against the German nation, the news from the fighting fronts was improving all the time. The war in the Pacific was going better than expected, with the U.S. Navy now accumulating the resources to strike at Gilbert and Marshall Islands. On the Eastern Front, the Red Army had halted the last great German offensive around Kursk in July, and by the end of the year was poised not only to end the long bloody siege of Leningrad—after almost a thousand days and a million casualties—but also to set foot on prewar Polish territory. Meanwhile, the battle of the Atlantic had swung decisively in the Allies' favor, removing the threat of starvation from the British Isles and enabling Marshall and Eisenhower to start

POLL (MARCH 1944)

	Roosevelt (%)	Dewey (%)	Undecided (%)
If the war is still going on and if President Roosevelt runs for the Democrats against Governor Dewey for the Republicans, how do you think you will vote?	51	32	17
If the war is over and Roosevelt runs for the Democrats against Dewey, how do you think you will vote?	30	51	19
Now suppose the war is still going on but the end of the war is clearly in sight. In that case, how do you think you will vote—for Roosevelt or for Dewey?	41	42	17

Source: Rosenman to FDR, and attached memorandum, Cantril and Lambert to Rosenman, March 17, 1944, PSF (Subject): Public Opinion Polls, FDRL.

congregating American troops in southern England for the cross-channel invasion. And in the air, Allied forces were finally achieving undisputed superiority, as new long-range escort fighters began destroying the Luftwaffe in the skies, while bombers wiped out German airplane factories on the ground.

These were heady days, but they soon threw up one difficulty that would just not go away: complacency. As early as February 1943, worried legislators and anxious officials at the OWI hurried to inform the White House that "the people as a whole are much too disposed to think that the war is about over" or that overoptimism was lowering "the general sense of urgency" and leading to "opposition to government calls for sacrifice."[71] FDR had always been acutely sensitive to this problem, but now his interest and concern was greatly sharpened by political self-interest. As Cantril informed him more than once, if Americans became convinced that the war would end by the autumn of 1944, they would vote overwhelmingly against "the Democratic candidate, even if he were Mr. Roosevelt."[72] This was confirmed by another poll conducted in March 1944.

Recognizing that such results would be political dynamite in the wrong hands, the White House promptly asked Cantril to keep them away from Gallup and out of the press.[73] FDR also decided that it was vital to drum home the message that the end of the war was *not* imminent. In a number of press conferences, he told reporters not to hope for an early German collapse. In October, he then prevailed upon Harry Hopkins to write an article for the *American* magazine, which insisted that there was no way the conflict would end before 1945—by which time, presumably, the president would have safely secured a fourth term.[74] But above all, the president's desire to combat complacency greatly reinforced his determination to remain silent about proposals for Germany's future, lest any talk about the postwar world started to foster the impression that the war would soon be over. So in July, when asked whether he intended to eliminate German power, FDR refused to comment. Such a question, he insisted, was a "waste of time" because "it takes people's thoughts off winning the war to talk about things like that now."[75]

By the winter, however, complacency was only one aspect of the morale problem. As in 1942, certain sections of the public also seemed to be excessively apprehensive and pessimistic; in some quarters, the mood even appeared to be verging on downright defeatism. The reason for this surprising pessimism was simple: although in most theaters Allied forces were going from strength to strength, in Italy little had gone right since Mussolini's overthrow back in July. Indeed, Hitler had quickly poured troops into the region, occupying the northern half of the country, establishing strong defensive positions, and even restoring Il Duce to power. Allied troops then slugged away at the German defenses throughout the winter, but little progress was made. In January 1944, Churchill was able to spirit away fifty-six landing craft from the OVERLORD preparations in order to launch a landing at Anzio, just fifty miles southwest of Rome. But instead of outflanking the German positions, this operation was halted by determined Wehrmacht resistance. "I had hoped that we were hurling a wildcat onto the shore," a frustrated Churchill remarked, "but all we had got was a stranded whale."[76] The fate of this operation did not bode well for the proposed Anglo-American invasion of France, which everyone now realized was likely to come in the spring. And as many started to fret about the likely outcome of the long-awaited second front, support even began to mount for some retreat from unconditional surrender.

This is not to say that Americans were suddenly clamoring for an immediate armistice with Hitler and the Nazis. Only at the very fringes of American society was there any desire to negotiate with the current German regime. Here, two groups led the way: the National Council for the Prevention of War, an organization consisting of religious and socialist pacifists, and Peace Now, led by the Columbia and Harvard professor, George W. Hartmann. For both, it was far more desirable to do a deal with the Third Reich than to incur huge casualties by fighting the Wehrmacht in France. In December, Peace Now even began lobbying Congress in an attempt to secure an "immediate and generous" peace with Germany. It also held a rally in New York City to raise the profile of its campaign and addressed an open letter to the president, stressing its opposition "to an Allied invasion of the continent of Europe—at least until such a public attempt to reach a reasonable basis of agreement is made." "A peace offensive," it insisted, "should be made before the order to attack is given. It is wrong to continue the slaughter of thousands of young Americans until we have made an honest attempt to adjust grievances and come to terms with all our adversaries."[77]

Peace Now may have been increasingly active over the winter, but it clearly had little influence on the vast majority of Americans. For one thing, the organization remained small; even in 1944, it had only around two thousand members. For another, Peace Now soon became the target of a scathing campaign of press vilification. The *New York Post*, for instance, hastened to condemn it for advocating "the surrender of this country to Nazism. . . . Peace Now is a demand, in fact, for unconditional surrender not to us, but by us." "It is particularly pernicious," agreed the *Philadelphia Record*, "to find so-called Americans urging a losers peace upon their country. . . . Either we win—or Hitler wins. There is no third choice. No compromise with barbarity, slavery and murder."[78] On Capitol Hill, meanwhile, rather than bow to pressure from Peace Now, the first instinct was to begin an investigation of the movement. This was conducted under the auspices of Martin Dies' Special Committee on Un-American Activities, and it eventually concluded that the organization was "an un-American group whose activities are calculated to interfere with the successful prosecution of the war." Not only was it "guilty of acts whose nature is clearly seditious and which tend toward the encouragement of treason," but it also clearly served the "interests of Goebbels' Nazi propaganda machine."[79]

Yet this was not the end of the story. Although there was only negligible support for a new appeasement settlement with the Nazis, the public was far more evenly divided when it came to the prospect of negotiating with other German elites. In May, Hadley Cantril compiled a graph that he felt "should be brought to the president's attention without delay." This demonstrated an alarming increase in support for a negotiated peace "if the German army overthrew Hitler and then offered to stop the war." More than 40 percent of the public now favored such a course, a figure that was even higher than during the nervous phony war months prior to TORCH.

Roosevelt was undoubtedly disturbed by such findings, but they were not his only problem. As apprehension about the prospective cross-channel invasion started to mount, many mainstream opinion makers also began to argue that the unconditional-surrender formula, while remaining a fundamental Allied goal, should be elaborated on or qualified in some way. Only by defining exactly what this concept meant, they claimed, could Roosevelt counter Hitler's repeated charge that an Allied victory would mean extinction for the German nation. Only by offering assurances that the Germans would be treated fairly, they insisted, could FDR weaken the Wehrmacht's resolve to fight.

FDR first became aware of this pressure to modify unconditional surrender while he was away in Cairo and Tehran. Each day, a pouch was flown out to the traveling president, containing the important items that had to be dealt with at once. Steve Early had the task of ensuring that a media digest was placed in the pouch, so that even in his absence Roosevelt

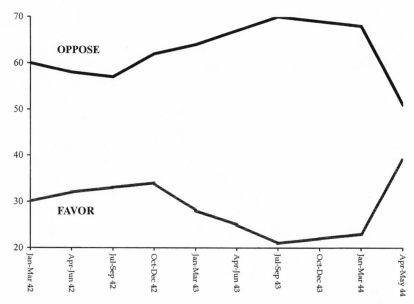

If the German army overthrew Hitler and then offered to stop the war and discuss peace terms with the Allies, would you favor or oppose accepting the offer of the German army? From Cantril to Walker, May 8, 1944, OF857, FDRL.

could monitor the popular mood back home. By the start of December, this digest was pointing out that on the MBS radio station Sam Balter had stressed that, while a negotiated peace was unacceptable, reiteration of the phrase "unconditional surrender" delayed rather than expedited the making of peace; likewise, on NBC Morgan Beatty had argued that the United States should emphasize to the Germans that there were supplementary terms to unconditional surrender.[80] When the Tehran communiqué failed to do this, criticism grew. As a *Washington Times-Herald* editorial stressed, the Big Three meetings "may have raised Allied morale," but "we think they must also have increased Axis determination to fight to the last ditch. Why not, when you have nothing to gain by quitting?"[81] A telegram from Clarence Poe, editor of the *Progressive Farmer and Southern Ruralist*, was even more explicit. "Millions of Americans," he wired the White House at the end of December, "hope that at this Christmas season you will say something that will make the innocent in Germany willing to trust our humanity and give Americans at home increased faith in the nobility of our purposes and that Christian principles will not be forsaken for pagan brutality when victory puts the vanquished in our power."[82]

With his allies and advisers both making exactly the same point, Roosevelt reluctantly decided to temper the content of his speeches. This is not to say that he ever contemplated dropping unconditional surrender altogether; in fact, as we have seen, it remained at the heart of his strategy to defuse the persistent liberal carping over "Darlanism." But FDR did realize that in order to placate both his domestic and foreign critics, he would have to reassure the Germans that unconditional surrender would not mean an excessively harsh peace. "The German people can have dinned into their ears what I said in my Christmas Eve speech," he told his aides in January; "in effect, that we have no thought of destroying the German people and that we want them to live through the generations like other European peoples on condition, of course, that they get rid of their present philosophy of conquest."[83] In practice, this meant that whenever FDR mentioned unconditional surrender, he now went out of his way to distinguish between the nation and the regime. "Except for the responsible fascist leaders," he declared in a typical comment, "the people of the Axis need not fear unconditional surrender. . . . [They] may be assured that when they agree to unconditional surrender they will not be trading Axis despotism for ruin under the UN. The goal of the UN is to permit liberated peoples to create a free political life of their own choosing and to attain economic security. These are the two great objectives of the Atlantic Charter."[84]

Ultimately, then, unconditional surrender had a paradoxical impact on the president's actions. In private, it helped to pave the way for his harsher view of the German enemy—not only because FDR now recognized that anything short of total military victory carried too many political risks, but also because unconditional surrender would obviously provide the Allies with a clean slate to work from. Yet in public it had precisely the opposite effect. This was because pressure from American opinion, advisers, and allies alike, all forced Roosevelt to elaborate on the formula in the months before OVERLORD. Instead of talking publicly about his harsher view of the German nation, this meant that the president had to offer reassurances to the German people that they would not be treated too harshly; instead of indicting the whole nation, in effect he had to continue making his old distinction between the criminal Nazi regime and the less culpable German people.

Seen in this light, there was *not* a clear, straightforward, and unambiguous line from unconditional surrender to a harsh peace.[85] Rather, Roosevelt's public refinement of the doctrine was actually placing a large obstacle in the way of stern postwar measures, for it prevented him from revealing to the American people his newfound conviction that the Germans were inherently militaristic and warlike.

While Roosevelt found it difficult to alter the basic thrust of his public utterances, in this period he was receding further into the background as an opinion persuader, largely as a result of ill health. On returning from Tehran, the president was laid low with what he called the "grippe." Thereafter, he frequently complained of feeling "rotten" or "like hell," of suffering from persistent headaches or drowsiness during the day. On March 28, he finally went to the Bethesda Naval Hospital for a thorough

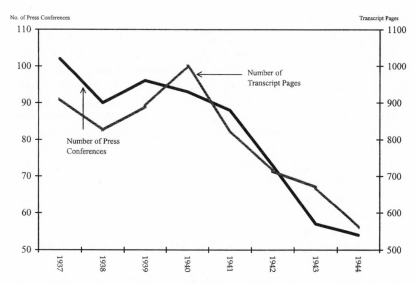

No. of Press Conferences   Transcript Pages

The Declining Frequency of Roosevelt's Press Conferences, 1937–1944. Compiled from FDRPC, vols. 9–24.

check up by Dr Howard Bruenn, a heart specialist. Bruenn was shocked by the president's condition; in his opinion, FDR was clearly suffering from congestive heart failure exacerbated by hypertension. Along with three other doctors, he prescribed digitalis, a low-fat diet, fewer cigarettes and cocktails, and above all plenty of rest. Roosevelt immediately complied with the last of these recommendations, going off to a secluded South Carolina plantation for four weeks from April 9 to May 6. He also shortened his working day to just four hours, interspersed with long rest periods at lunch and in the afternoon.[86] One practical result of this was that the president now had far less time to hold regular press conferences. Whereas in 1940 and 1941 he had attended about ninety sessions a year, in 1944 this figure dropped to just over fifty. Roosevelt also had to cut down on his public addresses. Between the Italian armistice of September 1943 and D-Day the following June, he only took to the airwaves twice, first to report on the Tehran Conference and later to deliver his annual state of the union message.[87]

Back in 1942, the OWI had taken up some of the slack left by the president's absences. Now, it briefly remained at the forefront of the government's information efforts, releasing films, radio shows, pamphlets, and posters. In May 1943, it even launched a "Nature of the Enemy" exhibit at the Rockefeller Plaza in New York City, replete with detailed photographic displays and accompanied by a series of radio shows hosted by Raymond Gramm Swing.[88]

To a large extent, the OWI used these channels to repeat the same old message. Time and again, the Nazis were still singled out as the central enemy, on the basis that their expansionist ideology was directly antithetical to everything that America stood for. Yet there were a few discernible shifts in emphasis. At the end of 1942, Mike Cowles replaced MacLeish as the head of the Domestic Branch. A publishing executive rather than a liberal intellectual, Cowles soon revealed a penchant for "splashy displays, short sentences, and simplified concepts"—much to the frustration and consternation of a group in the Writer's Bureau, who resigned in April because they thought that the OWI was now dominated by "high-pressure promoters who prefer slick salesmanship to honest information."[89] When it came to depicting Germany, moreover, the OWI also made one clear alteration to its new sound-bite message. Aware that the president was deeply irritated by the constant carping over "Darlanism," and concerned that the public might still be willing to support a negotiated peace if the Wehrmacht suddenly deposed Hitler, the OWI was now at pains to point out that "the German Army and the Nazi Party are one and the same thing."[90] On occasion, it even went slightly further. "Any 'peace feelers' revolving around alleged splits between the Army staff or industrial leadership and the Nazis themselves," its *Information Guide* instructed officials, "should be identified only as minor conflicts between the 'old imperialists' and the 'new imperialists.'"[91]

By the spring of 1943, the OWI had reason to be fairly pleased with its efforts. Although it had never been able to gain a grip over the daily output of war news, it had amplified the president's public themes, constantly reiterating the distinction between Nazis and Germans and later adding only selected German elites to the panoply of America's true enemies. This message had also resonated reasonably well with the American public. Yet the OWI was not without its critics. From within the organization, liberals were already concerned that its output was becoming too shallow and too populist. But from without, an even greater threat was looming, since Republicans and conservative Democrats, buoyed by their gains in the 1942 midterm elections, were now preparing to turn against the OWI with a vengeance.

Southern Democrats had taken particular umbrage to one OWI publication, entitled *Negroes and the War*, which emphasized the prospects for racial equality in postwar America. Republicans, meanwhile, had always been suspicious of a propaganda tool in the hands of a Democratic administration. Now, with a presidential election on the horizon and with one OWI overseas publication depicting Roosevelt as the "Champion of Liberty, U.S. Leader in the War to Win Lasting and Worldwide Peace," they increasingly perceived this bureau to be simply a vehicle for FDR's drive to a fourth term. When combined with other claims, such as Representative John Taber's description of it as "a haven and refuge for the derelicts" or Congressman Joe Starnes's charge that it "was trying to tell us, like we were six-year-old children, why we are at war," a cross-party coalition was easily forged in June 1943 to axe the OWI's budget. The Domestic Branch was left with a mere $2.75 million, which, as Elmer Davis noted, was just enough to avoid "the odium of having put us out of business, and carefully not enough to let us accomplish much."[92] The OWI was also prohibited from producing material for domestic consumption, and so it retained only the task of providing support and guidance to other departments and agencies.[93]

When added to the president's increasingly paltry efforts, the emasculation of the OWI might well have created a gaping hole at the center of the administration's information campaign had it not been for the fact that two other departments were starting to become far more active. Between April 1943 and July 1944, the Treasury Department quickly leapt to center stage, launching five concerted campaigns aimed at encouraging the U.S. public to purchase more war bonds.[94] These consistently reached huge audiences. The Second War Loan Drive, for instance, was comprised of 171 radio programs, 61,279 local radio announcements, and twenty-five national spot and regional network programs in the three weeks between April 12 and May 2, 1943.[95] In those weeks when it was active, the Treasury's efforts were actually far more intensive than anything the OFF or OWI had ever been able to sustain.

At the same time, the State Department also began to enjoy a higher profile. In part, this was a natural product of the shifting emphasis from military strategy to postwar political problems. But Hull, stung by the mounting criticism he had received over Darlan and Badoglio, was also anxious to develop more adequate channels for gauging and shaping opinion. In this task he was aided by the appointment of Edward R. Stettinius, who replaced Sumner Welles as undersecretary in September 1943. With Hull's approval, Stettinius quickly began a wholesale reorganization of the department, and as one writer put it at the time, "one of the most conspicuous features" of this reform was "the changes in the functions and organization relating to popular education." In January 1944, an Office of Public Information was set up, with a mandate both to analyze polling data and to build up relations with private groups and the wider public. Top officials were also encouraged to take to the airwaves more frequently, while in the first months of 1944 the State Department even produced its own radio series, entitled "The State Department Speaks," which attempted to inform the public about key foreign-policy issues.[96]

Initially, at least, there were some minor indications that these departments might be inclined to alter the basic tenor of the government's nature-of-the-enemy campaign. In April 1943, Kingsbury Smith of the *American Mercury* reported that the State Department was planning a relatively harsh peace for Germany. Apparently he had been told by officials that this would include the "total disarmament of the German nation," the "swift, merciless punishment of its war criminals," the "drastic decentralization of the country as a single powerful industrial and political unit, and the temporary restriction of its economic life to the minimum required for self-subsistence."[97] A month later, Adolf A. Berle, the assistant secretary of state, appeared to give credence to the thrust of Smith's claims. In a speech delivered to a crowd of more than twenty thousand in the Boston Garden, Berle leveled a stinging attack against the German people. "No group of rulers, no party, could have conceived, organized, and carried out a program of general civilian slaughter," he declared, "without at least the tacit acquiescence of a large part of the German people."[98]

Overall, however, such remarks proved to be isolated exceptions that were increasingly drowned out by the majority of official utterances. Other senior State Department employees, such as Sumner Welles (until his resignation in September 1943) and Joseph Grew, were certainly quick to counter Berle's indictment of the German nation. In a string of speeches throughout the year, both firmly emphasized the evils of "Hitlerism" and pointed out that "today we probably have spiritual allies among the German people."[99] In a similar vein, the Treasury's War Loan Drives focused clearly on Nazi rather than German perfidy, with radio commentators speaking of "the *Nazi* danger to our freedom," or officials being told to distinguish between "*Japan's* island chain of defenses in the Pacific" but *Hitler's* vaunted fortress in Europe.[100]

From time to time, the military also added to this continued cacophony of anti-Nazi rhetoric. The War Department, it is true, generated much anti-German material for training purposes, using hate to foster a fighting spirit among GIs and even employing "horror stories and pictures" to demonstrate to new recruits "the utter ruthlessness of the German military character."[101] But most of the output the U.S. Army released to a wider audience tended to eschew this harsher line in favor of the familiar old distinction between the regime and people. Thus Marshall, in a speech to the Governors' Conference in June, clearly declared that "we fight to destroy dictatorships, to guarantee freedom of speech and of the press."[102] Frank Capra's film, *Prelude to War*, famously made the same point. Originally designed as a training movie, it went on general release in May 1943, largely at the president's behest and with the OWI's aid.[103] Capra, with the help of a talented team (including Eric Knight, Anatole Litvak, and Anthony Veiller), sought to stress that the current conflict was between two ideological systems: the free world symbolized by American icons such as the Liberty Bell and Abraham Lincoln, and the slave world mired in darkness, whose aim was to reverse the years of progress since 1776. Admittedly, *Prelude to War* did point out that tyranny had found a fertile breeding ground in Germany, since the population had "an in-built national love of regimentation and harsh discipline." But its focus remained first and foremost on the Führer and his cohorts, whose gangster methods had led to the eradication of free speech, a free press, and freedom of religion.[104]

During the spring of 1944, in the face of mounting discontent over the government's reticence, State Department officials also decided to elaborate on their vision for the postwar world. Although shorn of details and specifics, their remarks were effectively a sharp refutation of Kingsbury Smith's claims that the administration was contemplating a stern peace. Instead, Hull and his advisers emphasized that the benefits of free trade and self-determination, as envisaged in the Atlantic Charter, would be accorded to victor and vanquished alike. In March 1944, for instance, the secretary of state released a document entitled the "Bases of the Foreign Policy of the U.S." In it, he stressed that the Allies "must exercise surveillance over aggressor nations until such time as the latter demonstrate their willingness and ability to live at peace with other nations." But he then implied that this would not take long and that thereafter Germany would be permitted the chance for "material advancements" and the ability "to decide for itself the forms and details of its governmental organization."[105]

The reasons for this reluctance to develop a new conception of the enemy are not difficult to fathom. At this stage, very few officials privately shared the president's opinion that the militaristic Germans would have to be treated severely.[106] On the contrary, most agreed with Henry Stimson, the venerable old secretary of war, who was convinced that there remained a group of "freedom-loving people in Germany" whom the United States could work with after the fighting had stopped.[107] Hull, in particular, envisaged the speedy restoration of Germany after the eradication of Hitler and his cohorts, while officials in the OWI had always been inclined to view the conflict as an ideological struggle against nazism, rather than a national or racial struggle against the Germans.

A direct presidential order might well have prevented top officials in the State Department, War Department, and OWI from simply enunciating their privately held views. But there was never even a hint that this was about to happen. Although the president informed the cabinet of his views immediately after Tehran, he then largely abstained from detailed bureaucratic discussions about Germany until the following August. This was partly because illness frequently hampered his ability to dominate the decision-making process during the first months of 1944. But even when he was at his desk, Roosevelt was preoccupied with other matters, from the preparations for OVERLORD to a battle with Congress over an economic Bill of Rights. With Harry Hopkins plagued by illness and Sumner Welles having resigned, the president was also without the two subordinates who had previously kept him in touch with developments in other departments.[108] Finally, even if Roosevelt had maintained closer control over his administration, he would hardly have been in a position to direct his subordinates to espouse a cause that he himself was reluctant to champion in the face of popular opposition and fears about the impact of unconditional surrender.

In the absence of any direct prodding from the White House, the Treasury was the only department that might have been willing to buck the general trend. After all, Morgenthau was the cabinet member most vehemently opposed to making any distinction between Nazis and Germans. In

April 1943, as the War Loan Drives started to gather momentum, there is some evidence that he contemplated using these as a platform to arouse the public's hatred of all Germans. According to one Treasury official, at this stage Morgenthau even proposed to make a speech that rejected the notion of a "good Germany" and instead referred to the "rotten bloodstained foundations" of the nation as a whole. However, Morgenthau's aspirations were soon frustrated. This was partly because the OWI retained the power to screen speeches made by top officials, and Davis and his colleagues adamantly refused to sanction Morgenthau's speech because it failed to differentiate between the people and the regime.[109] Moreover, even after Congress slashed its funds, the OWI continued to play an important role in coordinating the Treasury's War Loan Drives, and this gave it a further opportunity to temper the Treasury's output. Of course, Morgenthau could have complained to his close friend and neighbor in the White House. But one attempt in 1942 to get FDR to launch a hate campaign had already proved fruitless, and unaware that Roosevelt's views were now starting to harden, Morgenthau probably deemed it a waste of time to bring up this matter once again.

So as thoughts turned from war to peace, a growing chasm started to emerge between the president and public on how to solve the German problem. While Roosevelt's private image of the enemy was clearly starting to stiffen, most Americans continued to hold a relatively benign view of Germany. As late as May 30, 1944, the OWI reported that "on the whole the majority attitude toward the German people is still one of generosity. Only a minority believe that harsh postwar treatment will provide the answer to the question of national security." More specifically, polls continued to find that 64 percent believed the Germans wanted to get rid of their Nazi leaders, 72 percent thought Germany should be admitted into a "Society of Nations" soon after the war, and a mere 26 percent supported partition.[110]

In large part, of course, these persistently benign attitudes were a product of the administration's own efforts. In 1942, the government's initial campaign had merely emphasized Nazi and not German evil; now, despite the president's hardening private attitudes, the administration's public utterances had hardly changed. This was basically because Roosevelt, chary of getting too far in front of mass opinion and forced to elaborate on unconditional surrender, was continuing to reassure Germans that they would not be treated too harshly. But other departments continued to follow the president's lead—indeed, the State and War departments, largely kept in the dark about details of alliance negotiations, were perfectly willing to echo these arguments since they reflected their own private preferences, while the OWI, similarly unaware of the thrust of FDR's thinking, still reiterated its own old nature-of-the-enemy campaign, and also had some success in forcing Morgenthau and the Treasury to do likewise.

The president was acutely aware of this growing disparity between his own views and the attitudes of most Americans.[111] But he believed he had time on his side. After all, Germany had not been defeated, concrete agreements still had to be reached, and in the interim the course of the conflict might yet stiffen the public's mood toward the enemy. Nevertheless, Roosevelt's decision to sit back and wait was not without risk. In particular, if these punitive ideas leaked out before the government had a chance to lay the domestic groundwork for their acceptance, then they would undoubtedly become mired in political controversy. FDR's inaction might therefore come back to haunt him, especially since a presidential election was now imminent and the Republican party was feverishly looking for any stick with which to beat the three-term incumbent.

6

Planning Germany's Future

JUNE 1944 TO APRIL 1945

The president said that he did not think it would be an undue hardship to require Germany to revert toward an agricultural status such as she had enjoyed up to the latter part of the last century. She had shown she could not be trusted with all the facilities for making weapons.
—*FRUS: Conference at Quebec,*
September 1944

The president then stated that Morgenthau had made a great mistake in stirring this whole thing up during the campaign, and that the agrarian thing was absurd.
—*The Diaries of Edward R. Stettinius,*
December 22, 1944

On June 6, 1944, as Allied troops poured onto the Normandy beaches to open the eagerly awaited second front, Franklin Roosevelt led the nation in prayer. "Our sons . . . this day have set upon a mighty endeavor," the president began in his calm, measured, patrician voice, "a struggle to preserve our republic, our religion, and our civilization, and to set free a suffering humanity." "Their road will be long and hard," he continued. "For the enemy is strong. He may hurl back our forces. Success may not come with rushing speed, but we shall return again and again; and we know that by Thy grace, and by the righteousness of our cause, our sons will triumph."[1]

In the next few days, as Americans followed their president's example and flocked to pray for the success of the invasion, Allied forces swiftly secured a strong bridgehead in northern France, into which almost a million men and more than half a million tons of supplies were soon crammed. But thereafter the going was often painfully slow, as poor weather played havoc with supply lines and air support, while the Wehrmacht used the tricky *bocage* terrain to fight a stubborn defense. It was not until the start of August that the Allied armies were finally able to break free. And then, bottling up around thirty thousand Germans in the Falaise pocket by August 20, they moved rapidly forward, liberating Paris five days later and pushing into Belgium early in September. When combined with the fall of Rome and yet another series of stunning Soviet victories in the east, the summer months of 1944 were ultimately a period of heady success for Allied arms.[2]

This was significant for Roosevelt because the machinery for the presidential election campaign started to crank into action in June. At the end of the month, the Republican party held its convention and nominated Thomas E. Dewey; in July, the Democrats renominated FDR for a fourth term. At first glance, there was little to choose between the two candidates on the central foreign-policy issues of the day. The Republican platform, eschewing the party's earlier flirtation with isolationism, now unequivocally declared that America's "relentless aim" was both "to win the war against all our enemies" and to "keep the Axis powers impotent to renew tyranny and attack"; it also favored "responsible participation by the U.S. in [a] postwar cooperative organization among sovereign nations to prevent military aggression and to attain permanent peace."[3] But just because Dewey and FDR would be running on similar platforms, did not mean the campaign would be harmonious. On the contrary, because the two were so close on many of the substantive issues all but ensured that the tone would be acrimonious and bitter; after all, Dewey had to find some way of distinguishing himself from the three-term incumbent.

Actually, the Republican nominee would prove to be a formidable opponent: cold and calculating, formerly a shrewd and aggressive Manhattan prosecutor, Dewey was now a highly efficient governor of New York. As the campaigning season got underway, he quickly latched onto a variety of subjects. One was Roosevelt's health, especially the fact that the president and many of his top advisers now appeared to be "tired old men." Another was the close relationship that the administration had apparently developed with certain trade unionists, perhaps even with domestic communists, who Dewey depicted as the real power behind the throne.[4] Then in September, the Republican candidate was gifted a very real, very tangible foreign-policy issue. Although polls indicated that there was still little popular support for a truly punitive peace, word suddenly leaked out that the president had endorsed a radical plan to pastoralize and dismember the German nation. Both Dewey and the press seized on this story with alacrity, forcing Roosevelt to backpedal. Over the winter, in the wake of this new uproar, a chastened president then had to search around for a new formula for Germany that would satisfy both his own stern views and the relatively softer opinions of most Americans—a formula, in fact, that would conform more closely to the expectations that the administration had itself fostered in its information campaigns since 1941.

"A General Stiffening of Attitude toward Germany," June to September 1944

During the spring and early summer, with Allied troops at last poised to strike at the heart of the Reich, Roosevelt finally decided to make some slow, halting, and sporadic attempts to enlighten the public about what lay in store for postwar Germany. Even before the first Allied soldiers had set foot on the Normandy beaches, FDR had readily agreed with Churchill that, although the term "liberation" should be used to describe Allied operations in occupied Europe, when Americans entered Germany they should publicly proclaim their determination to act as invaders and not liberators. The implication of this would be crystal clear: the Allies would not seek to free the oppressed Germans from their despotic Nazi regime; instead they would come to occupy, supervise, and control the whole nation.[5]

After D-Day, the president intermittently expanded on this theme. In July, he attacked those "nice, high-minded people" who complained about unconditional surrender and who argued "that if we changed the term" then "Germany might surrender more quickly." He then went on to tell reporters that after Germany had been totally defeated it would be treated more harshly than other countries. "We don't believe in wholesale starvation," he insisted. ". . . But [this] doesn't mean that we will send the first spare food that we have into Germany. We will take care of our own and our Allies first."[6] A month later he confirmed to journalists that even if "Germany were to quit," the United States would still invade and then occupy the Reich. It would not be like 1918, he continued, because "if we let them get away with it this time the next generation will tell us they have won the war."[7]

While the president emitted a few broad hints about Germany's future, some of his subordinates also became a little bolder in their public statements. In August, Attorney General Francis Biddle testified at Senator Harley M. Kilgore's hearings on Cartels and National Security. In this forum, Biddle grasped the opportunity to level a stinging attack on German big business, describing German cartels as "departments of the German government," who aimed to weaken other states by hampering production, stealing technical knowledge, and engaging in industrial espionage. Because these criminal entities would try to pass themselves off as "ordinary commercial firms as soon as the war ended," Biddle maintained that the United States had to be ready to eradicate them, so that they would "no longer constitute a menace to the civilized world."[8] Other officials endorsed this position. A background report by the OWI, for instance, highlighted how the Reichswerke Hermann Göring had plundered Europe.[9] Then, in early September the president also had his say, no doubt well aware that the time was electorally ripe to tackle an issue whose antimonopolistic overtones would win warm praise from New Deal liberals. In a public letter, FDR declared that in Germany "cartels were used as governmental instrumentalities to achieve political ends. The history of the use of IG Farben trust by the Nazis reads like a detective story," he concluded, and because of the close relationship between the two institutions "the defeat of the Nazi armies will have to be followed by the eradication of these weapons of economic warfare."[10]

When compared to the extremely paltry efforts of the past eighteen months, these sporadic and scattered statements were clearly something of an improvement. Yet there was still little indication that the president was about to initiate an intensive information campaign. In fact, on a whole range of fundamental issues FDR and his subordinates remained tight-lipped and taciturn. This was certainly the conclusion of Morris Ernst, one of Roosevelt's back-channel operatives. In June, when Ernst scoured government statements to find material for an article in the *Reader's Digest*, he ended up complaining to the White House that "as to Germany I cannot find enough information to freeze the policy into simple terms." All he came up with was that problems like the "elimination of war industries, control of essential economy, control of raw materials, trial of culprits, re-education of youth" were up for consideration.[11] Nor did anyone seem eager to rectify this reticence. A month later, for instance, when the *New York Times* reporter, James Reston, asked Stettinius for any information on the administration's partition plan for Germany, the undersecretary was uncharacteristically brusque, brushing off Reston with the unhelpful reply that there was "nothing to be gained by discussing this matter in the press."[12]

Moreover, even when administration spokesmen did talk publicly about certain measures, they still left an awful lot unsaid. Roosevelt, for example, had clearly alluded to the need to occupy Germany and to treat it more harshly than any other area, but he had omitted to mention how long the occupation would last or what level of subsistence the Germans would be allowed. Similarly, when prodded by the Kilgore subcommittee the president and his subordinates had agreed that international cartels must be eliminated, but they had failed to broach the issue of what, if anything, would replace them; indeed, there was still no official word on whether Germany would be allowed to rebuild her industries and, if so, on what basis.

Nor was the president entirely consistent in his public words and deeds. Most obviously, Roosevelt's hints that the Germans would have to be treated more sternly than other Europeans were still not accompanied by a full-scale indictment of the German nation. In June, FDR even publicly depicted the extermination program as "but one manifestation of Hitler's aim to salvage from military defeat victory for Nazi principles—the very principles which this war must destroy unless we shall have fought in vain"; entirely absent was any attempt to establish the culpability of the German people. The contrast with Roosevelt's remarks about Japan remained particularly striking. Following the precedent he had established back in 1942, FDR continued to have few qualms about blaming both the Japanese warlords and the Japanese people for the Pacific conflagration. As he told a large radio audience in August, "whether or not the people of Japan itself know and approve of what their war lords . . . have done for nearly a century, the fact remains that they seem to be given hearty approval to the Japanese policy of acquisition of their neighbors and their neighbors' lands."[13]

Given the lackluster nature of the president's public utterances, many liberal commentators quickly latched on to his decision to appoint Robert Murphy as Eisenhower's political adviser, worrying that this was an ominous indication that the administration intended to be dangerously soft on Germany. After all, Murphy had been held responsible for the Darlan and Peyrouton episodes back in the winter of 1942–43. Now, numerous "liberal sources," from Edgar Mowrer to Cecil Brown, from the *New York Herald Tribune* to the *St. Louis Post-Dispatch*, wasted no time in repeating the "old charges of dealing with 'Vichyites' and 'reactionaries.'" In their considered opinion, Murphy's appointment "indicated a U.S. policy of 'improving the manners and brushing the teeth'" of nazism, but not of eradicating it once and for all. Perhaps, they surmised, Murphy intended to collaborate with German Darlans and Quislings. Perhaps, they predicted, he would seek to protect, pamper, and even advance the fortunes of a whole host of elites who had assisted the Nazis in their reign of conquest and plunder.[14]

Roosevelt remained deeply sensitive to these continued rumblings about "Darlanism," but he still found it difficult, if not impossible, to be more forthcoming about his preferences for Germany. The reasons for this were strikingly familiar. When it came to detailed policies, official reticence largely reflected the absence of concrete agreements. In the months since Tehran, there had been a lot of fruitless debate about whether the United States should have an occupation zone in the north or south of Germany. But few other questions had even been discussed in any great detail and almost nothing had been finalized. Small wonder, then, that administration spokesmen continued to have so little to say.

The president's cautious instincts were also greatly sharpened by the looming election campaign. For more than a year now, Cantril had kept the White House fully informed of the very close relationship that existed between the fortunes of war and the president's reelection chances. In July, the pollster again confirmed that "the chief argument for Roosevelt is his practical experience in handling problems created by the war—the administration's domestic record is a poor second by comparison." Put an-

POLL (JULY 1944)

What would you say are the strongest arguments for voting FOR Roosevelt for the next four years?

Superior ability to handle present and future situations (62%)
    Knows the war; has war experience (39%)
    Not time to change administrations (16%)
    Understands foreign affairs best (5%)
    Best man for postwar problems (2%)

Past record of handling internal affairs (19%)
    Has helped working man; helped labor (7%)
    Has done well all along; worked for country (8%)
    Has fine record; social security, etc. (2%)
    He's the best man (2%)

No arguments for voting for Roosevelt (15%)

What would you say are the strongest arguments for voting AGAINST Roosevelt for the next four years?

Poor domestic policies (42%)
    Wasteful spending; taxes too high (10%)
    Too much power vested in him (11%)
    Dislike New Deal tactics (5%)
    Too much coddling of labor (4%)
    Miscellaneous (12%)

We need a change; Roosevelt has been in too long (35%)

His health is failing; he is too old (5%)

No arguments for voting against Roosevelt (16%)

Source: Cantril, July 5, 1944, OF 857, FDRL.

other way, the public now clearly saw FDR as "Dr Win the War"; the achievements of "Dr New Deal" had long since been forgotten, overshadowed by the strikes, the unpopular rationing policies, the burgeoning tax rates of recent years.

When it came to the practical matter of devising a campaign strategy, these findings gave White House aides and Democratic party bosses a very delicate problem. On the one hand, it was clearly desirable to highlight the growing success of Allied arms in France. As Steve Early wrote to a top official at the Democratic National Committee, the party needed to focus the public's attention on "the great victory in northern France," especially "the Allied teamwork—the meticulous care in planning and preparation etc. After all, who but the president has made all this possible? Who but the president would have gotten the blame for it all if there had been a failure instead of a brilliant success?"[15] But at the same time, officials recognized that they had to tread very carefully, because polls showed that an electorate convinced that victory was imminent might not only slacken off but also vote for Dewey. Spokesmen therefore went out of their way to emphasize the fact that a long, hard struggle lay ahead. The president, for his part, continued to shy away from speaking too frequently about the postwar world, no doubt still fearful that a highly intensive public debate on the peace would foster an excessive complacency about the length of the war.[16]

In any case, over the summer Roosevelt had fewer opportunities to take to the stump. On July 21, he set sail on a long cruise to Pearl Harbor, where he would meet MacArthur, Nimitz, and others who "seem to feel a little neglected for to them the Pacific operations seem at least as important as those in Normandy."[17] The trip itself was heavy in symbolism, for the president undoubtedly hoped it would dispel any last lingering "Asia-first" sentiment. But there were also more therapeutic motives for undertaking such a long voyage, for FDR felt that another long break from the rigors of Washington might help to restore his failing health and refresh him for the coming campaign.

The sun, the sea, and the fishing definitely had some positive effect, and those who visited the White House on his return generally found the president "keen and alert," in an adequate condition to handle four more years in the top job.[18] Yet below the suntan and the breezy exterior, Roosevelt remained a very ill man—weak, listless, unable to cope with his old workload. Ominously, his growing frailty was now a significant handicap when it came to making speeches. This became particularly clear on August 12, when the president delivered nationwide broadcast aboard a destroyer, the USS *Cummings*, which turned into something of a disaster as high winds blew away portions of his script and the pitching boat almost knocked him over. "It looks like the old master has lost his touch," his supporters gloomily began to note. "His campaigning days must be over. It's going to look mighty sad when he begins to trade punches with young Dewey."[19]

Chastened by this experience, Roosevelt did not make another public address until the election campaign began to hot up six weeks later. But throughout this period, he was not completely idle. Instead, there were a number of indications that FDR was starting to employ a trusted old strategy: encouraging other individuals and organizations to say and do things that were deemed too controversial to emanate directly from the White House.

In the summer of 1944, Sumner Welles published *The Time for Decision*, a book that became a surprise hit with the public, selling nearly half a million copies and knocking Bob Hope's *I Never Left Home* off the top of the bestseller lists. Within the administration, not everyone was happy that Welles had embarked upon this project. Cordell Hull naturally viewed the whole book with profound disdain, not just because of the personal feud between the two men but also because Welles's views on subjects such as Germany's future were far more radical than anything envisaged by the State Department. One of Hull's associates even hastened to inform the president that the book was "inaccurate" and misleading, and suggested that "an attempt be made to counteract" its "harmful effects."[20] Yet Roosevelt disagreed. He had only reluctantly accepted Welles's resignation the previous September and he was now perfectly content to see Welles talk in strident terms about the German menace. Moreover, when it came to Welles's call for partition on the grounds that this "will do more than anything else to break the hold which militarism has on the German people," FDR probably recognized that this was largely an echo of what he himself had said privately on a number of occasions during 1943.[21]

While Welles gave public vent to his views on Germany, a new pressure group, the Society for the Prevention of World War III (SPWW3), also entered the fray. Headed by Rex Stout, the chairman of the War Writers Board (WWB), the SPWW3 quickly attracted the support of liberal commentators such as William Shirer and Cecil Brown, German-American authors like Emil Ludwig and F. W. Foerster, and prominent figures including George Creel, head of America's World War I propaganda agency, and Major George Fielding Eliot, a well-known military analyst.

SPWW3's aim was simple: to destroy the American habit "of setting the Nazis apart from the German people."[22] As Stout complained, there remained numerous

> moist-eyed sentimentalists who, when they are told that the Germans have murdered five million civilians, prattle of Beethoven and Goethe; those who, told that the Germans have plundered the rest of Europe to the tune of eighty billion dollars, murmur that German housewives have the cleanest kitchens in the world; those who, learning that the Germans have deliberately shelled our hospital on the Anzio beach, speak nostalgically of the romantic beauty of the Rhine.[23]

These sentimentalists included not only the majority of mass opinion who still supported relatively soft peace terms, but also the likes of Thomas Mann, Reinhold Niebuhr, Paul Hagen, and Dorothy Thompson, all of whom retained a misguided faith in a "good" Germany.[24]

For SPWW3, the central task was to educate this "misinformed" public about the true nature of the German beast. Its starting point was the claim that all Germans were alike, that all had militaristic and aggressive traits, and that the Nazis were consequently no different from an average member of the race. As George Creel wrote, "never, in the course of German history have 'good Germans' constituted anything but a pitiful, ineffectual minority." "There may be some Germans," agreed Cecil Brown, "who recoil from . . . barbarism. But they are too few to cut any ice, and the so-called good Germans in Germany always have been too few to affect the course of history."[25] As a result, there was no nucleus around which to construct a democratic Germany after the war. Quite the opposite. According to Louis Nizer, "a German Republic will be merely a protective cloak for the militarists." Soft measures, such as those envisaged by the Atlantic Charter, were therefore not applicable to Germany since they would simply "be utilized to facilitate a new attack against the moral basis of humanity."[26] Instead, stringent terms had to be imposed on the nation as a whole.[27] Emil Ludwig, for instance, devised "Fourteen Rules for the American Occupation Officer in Germany," which spoke of the need to treat the Germans with disdain, to "distrust everybody who has given you no proof of his [sic] honesty," and to "never forget that you are in an enemy country—even when all the secret arms and bombs have been destroyed."[28]

For the most part, Stout relied on his fellow SPWW3 opinion makers to disseminate these central themes to a wider audience.[29] But in April, he also took out a full-page advertisement in the New York Times, which warned that this was "no time for Americans to work on the manufacture of a device for Germany's escape."[30] In May, the SPWW3 then circulated 100,000 copies of T. H. Tetens's Know Your Enemy to legislators, newspapers, radio stations, colleges, and the clergy. In this book, Tetens collated statements by Germans of all political persuasions, in order to demonstrate how the German people have "always [been] ready to support the criminal policies of their governments."[31] That same month, Stout began a monthly bulletin, Prevent World War III, which provided a forum for SPWW3 members to propagate their anti-German sentiments and also reprinted the views of prominent figures, such as Walter Lippmann, Sumner Welles, and Lord Vansittart, whenever they were suitably vehement. Increasingly, SPWW3 members also took to the airwaves. In June, for instance, Ludwig spoke in a Blue Network "Town Hall Meeting of the Air" in favor of denying Germany immediate self-government after the war, while in September SPWW3 held a forum on the WINS station in order to address the question, "Is the German and the Nazi one and the same thing?"[32]

Roosevelt generally welcomed these activities. He certainly had no hesitation in inviting Stout to the White House on a number of occasions during 1944.[33] Nor did he mind that Stout and the WWB were in the process of producing a series of campaign pamphlets for the Democrats, some of which focused on the need for unconditional surrender and the militaristic nature of the German enemy.[34] At a press conference in August, FDR gave a further indication that he approved of SPWW3, when he told reporters that one of its members, Major Eliot, "is the best writer on the war," before launching into a monologue describing how, if he was Eliot, he "would write an article on the psychology of the Germans—not just the German people but the German command."[35]

While the president cautiously and tacitly supported the SPWW3, Elmer Davis leapt to Stout's defense. In May, Common Sense accused Stout of seeking to foster a "rampant racism" against each and every German.

The journal's editors were particularly incensed by the fact that Stout's position as chairman of the WWB meant that he was effectively acting as a government spokesman. The WWB, they complained, "has direct access to all media of mass communications. It co-operates with various official agencies; and the U.S. Government, through the OWI, maintains a liaison office for its use." "What," they therefore asked, "does Elmer Davis, a lifelong friend of the German people, propose to do? Does the hospitality and co-operation he gives the WWB through the OWI denote government approval of Mr. Stout's vendetta?"[36] Davis' response was unambiguous and clear. Far from being "a lifelong friend of the German people," Davis insisted that he preferred

> to be regarded as a friend of the ten other European peoples whom the German people have wantonly attacked and atrociously oppressed. No doubt you hold that it is not the German people but the Nazis who have barbarously subjugated western Europe, and would have done the same to us if they could. Well, there were not enough Nazis to do it all; the non-Nazis went right along with them, and I recall no evidence that any noticeable number of them ever displayed any dissatisfaction with the things their leaders were doing. . . . If the German people want anybody's friendship, they had better do something to earn it."[37]

The public's reaction to all this was mixed. On the one hand, by August the State Department's Office of Public Opinion Studies was starting to record "a general stiffening of attitude toward Germany."[38] This was partly because the administration's opinion-gauging channels were simply picking up the message that Stout and his cohorts were disseminating in the media. But a growing number of other reporters, columnists, and editors also seemed far more willing to weave an anti-German thread into their news stories. In June, in the wake of Germany's first V-bomb attacks on Britain, Walter Lippmann certainly grasped the opportunity to urge "a deep and drastic settlement with pan-Germanism and German militarism." This new weapon, he believed, was "sufficiently ominous in its future possibilities to put an end to all doubt and scruple among Allied peoples that Germany must not only be disarmed and demilitarized but reduced from her position as the strongest power of continental Europe."[39] After July 20, many commentators reached a similar conclusion when analyzing Stauffenberg's failed bomb plot. "The German people and their generals," declared CBS's Bob Trout, "had many years in which to revolt against Hitler. They did not do it. The generals joined in enthusiastically with him against the Allies. The people were ready enough to share the loot of conquest."[40] These officers, agreed Edgar Mowrer, were "not representative of a non-existent bunch of so-called 'decent' Germans panting to be liberated from 'Nazi tyranny.' Nine-tenths of the German people had no quarrel with the Nazi tyranny and the Nazi war as long as both were bringing in the loot from the conquered countries and promising to make Germans the lords of creation."[41]

A growing proportion of the mass public appeared to agree with these

POLL (AUGUST 1944)

Should we prevent the rebuilding of German industries possessing a war potential?	Jan. 1944 (%)	Aug. 1944 (%)
Should prevent	31	51
Should NOT prevent	53	38
Don't know	16	11

Source: State Department, "Public Attitudes on Foreign Policy: Treatment of Germany, August 1944," No. 33, September 9, 1944, Schuyler Foster files, entry 568J, box 1, RG 59, NA.

sentiments. Significantly, a week after the failed attempt on Hitler's life, Cantril found that support for a negotiated peace with the German army had suddenly plunged. Whereas before OVERLORD more than 40 percent of Americans had been inclined to endorse peace talks if the army overthrew Hitler, now 68 percent rejected this course out of hand and only 28 percent were in favor. Almost 80 percent of the public also recognized that if a deal was ever struck with the German army there would be a far "greater risk of being involved in another world war."[42]

In addition, mass support for a handful of harsh postwar measures now seemed to be on the increase. In August, one survey found that 73 percent wanted to keep Germany as a third-rate power, while 67 percent advocated an Allied reeducation program. A majority also opposed rebuilding any German industry that could be used for producing weapons.

Yet it would be a mistake to overemphasize the extent of this change, either among opinion makers or the mass public. For a start, even commentators who had no liking for Germany or the Germans, nevertheless opposed certain punitive measures because they believed these would be counterproductive. Thus, the MBS commentator, Arthur Gaeth, now felt that it would be essential to deal harshly with many segments of German society. But he vehemently opposed partition on the basis that this would simply result in revanchism, "for the Germans will strive to unite."[43] Sumner Welles and Walter Lippmann adopted a similar stance. During the summer, the two men engaged in a vigorous public debate over international security issues, with the liberal Welles emerging as the foremost advocate of a new collective-security organization, while the realist Lippmann countered that only a balance-of-power arrangement would ensure the future peace. When it came to Germany, however, both had a similar vision, inclining on the one hand toward stern measures such as political reform, reeducation, and, in Welles's case partition, but at the same time still favoring a benign economic settlement that would provide Germany with "free access to raw materials and a genuine opportunity to maintain the economic welfare of her population."[44]

POLL (AUGUST 1944)

---

*Should we continue food rationing several
extra months in the U.S. in order to
enable the German people to buy enough
food to maintain health?*

    Yes (70%)

    No (24%)

    Don't know (6%)

Source: State Department, "Public Attitudes on Foreign Policy: Treatment of Germany,
August 1944," No. 33, September 9, 1944, Schuyler Foster files, entry 568J, box 1, RG 59,
NA.

There remained a degree of ambivalence amongst the mass public, too.
Thus, a series of polls conducted throughout the summer found that only 42
percent favored partition, a plurality of 43 percent were opposed to reparations, while an impressive majority were "willing to inconvenience themselves" in order to ensure the German people had adequate food supplies.

Perhaps reflecting the government's halting efforts, the whole public
debate was also carried out in a vague and hazy manner. In particular, key
questions remained unasked, while many results were susceptible to a variety of interpretations. So, for instance, although 51 percent opposed the
rebuilding of German war potential, this offered no indication on whether
respondents meant just actual arms manufacturers or "indirect" industries
such as steel, chemicals, or airplanes. Similarly, although 73 percent advocated keeping Germany as a third-rate power, this could imply any number
of policies, ranging from complete deindustrialization at one end to demobilization and demilitarization at the other.

The public's reluctance to support a truly stern peace was thrown into
particularly sharp relief when compared to the popular view of the Asian
enemy. According to the polls, America's hatred of the Japanese nation still
burned brightly. Around half the population continued to believe that the
Japanese would "always want war"—whereas only about a quarter of
Americans felt the same way about the Germans. Moreover, almost 60 percent wanted Japan to pay reparations even after it had been stripped of all its
conquests and its leaders had been punished—whereas a plurality of 43
percent were opposed to treating Germany in this manner. Anti-Japanese
sentiment also dominated the thoughts of most opinion makers. In a September "Town Hall Meeting of the Air," for instance, even those who
tended to adopt a more generous stance toward Japan still deemed it incumbent to push for wide-ranging reforms, from complete demilitarization
to the loss of empire, from strict supervision of imports to the dethroning
of the emperor.[45]

Seen in this light, popular attitudes toward Germany remained remarkably benign. Even now, there were no widespread cries of outrage against the barbaric German "Hun," no strident and unanimous calls to impose a harsh peace on the nation as a whole; it was definitely *not* the case, as some historians have argued, that the masses now had "an ignorant animus against Germany."[46] In fact, as the president started to clarify his own thoughts on the German problem, it was not even certain that radical methods for turning Germany into a third-rate power would be widely supported by mass opinion, especially now that the presidential campaign was starting to heat up.

The Morgenthau Plan and the Election Campaign, September to November 1944

While many Americans remained ambivalent or relatively soft in their attitude toward Germany, in private the president continued to embrace a far harsher position. "I think that both here and in England," he remarked on August 26, "there are two schools of thought—those who would be altruistic in regard to the Germans, hoping by loving kindness to make them Christians again—and those who would adopt a much 'tougher' attitude. Most decidedly," he continued, in a vein that would not have been out of place in a SPWW₃ tract, "I belong to the latter school, for though I am not bloodthirsty, I want the Germans to know that this time at least they have definitely lost the war." "The German people as a whole," he declared to Stimson that same day, "must have it driven home to them that the whole nation has been involved in a lawless conspiracy against the decencies of modern civilization."[47]

To make the Germans realize the error of their ways, Roosevelt advocated denazification, demobilization, and a short-term American occupation, preferably in the northwest so that U.S. troops could, if necessary, be withdrawn easily by sea.[48] For the longer term, FDR consistently inclined toward dismemberment, even in the face of State Department opposition. He also favored international control for the Ruhr and Kiel canal, and had recently hinted at the need for substantial economic control and reorganization to destroy "the economic and social bases of ultra-nationalism and militarism."[49]

Yet in the months since Tehran, the president had done little to translate these preferences into concrete policy directives, largely because he had been distracted by illness, a series of long absences from Washington, and a whole host of other problems, from last-minute preparations for the second front to the shape and structure of the new United Nations organization.[50] Lacking detailed instructions from the White House, other departments had tended to go off in a totally different direction. This, at least, was the conclusion of the treasury secretary, Henry Morgenthau, who trav-

PROPOSAL FOR POST-WAR GERMAN BOUNDARIES

Henry Morgenthau's Proposal for Postwar German Boundaries. Source: *Henry Morgenthau,* Germany Is Our Problem. *Reprinted by permission of HarperCollins Publishers Inc.*

eled to Europe in the first weeks of August. There, he not only had the opportunity to read State Department planning documents but was also able to discuss the German problem with British officials and the top military brass at Allied headquarters.[51]

Morgenthau quickly concluded that most military planners were adopting a dangerously pragmatic stance toward their forthcoming occupation duties: preoccupied with ensuring that the Germans would be orderly and placid subjects, they generally saw the whole problem in terms of "get[ting] things running," "pick[ing] up the pieces," and minimizing "the potential financial chaos and economic disorder that is likely to occur."[52] State Department officials, meanwhile, seemed largely concerned with integrating Germany quickly back into the world economy: believing that a revived Germany would be vital to European reconstruction, they deemed it essential to rebuild and convert rather than demolish and dismantle German factories and plant.[53] In addition, Morgenthau also gained the impression that the three Allied leaders had "decided" on a far harsher program at Tehran than anything envisaged by either the War or State departments. As Anthony Eden revealed in one conversation, at Tehran the president had clearly favored dividing Germany "into three or fifteen parts" and had apparently created the EAC to study this very question.[54]

Arriving back in Washington in the middle of August, Morgenthau hastened to inform Roosevelt that nobody had been "studying how to treat Germany roughly along the lines you wanted." In a meeting on August 19, FDR wholeheartedly agreed. "We have got to be tough with Germany," the president muttered darkly, "and I mean the German people and not just the Nazis. You either have to castrate the German people or you have got to treat them in such a manner so they can't just go on reproducing people who want to continue the way they have in the past." Roosevelt, Morgenthau recorded soon after, "left no doubt whatsoever in my mind that he personally wants to be tough with the Germans. He said, 'They have been tough with us.'"[55]

With the president clearly perturbed by the comparatively soft paths the War and State departments were taking, Morgenthau glimpsed an opportunity to get government policy back on track. In another meeting on August 25, he handed FDR some extracts from a proposed "Handbook of Military Government," which highlighted the benign stance being adopted by the army. After studying this document, the president agreed that it was "pretty bad." He then sent off a stinging memorandum to Stimson, berating the military both for giving the "impression that Germany is to be restored just as much as the Netherlands or Belgium" and for implying that "the people of Germany [will] be brought back as quickly as possible to their pre-estate." Instead, while FDR did "not want to starve them to death," he did favor using army soup kitchens to feed the Germans, for this would impress on them the "fact that they are a defeated nation, collectively and individually."[56]

Driving home the lesson of defeat would be a preliminary method of discouraging the German people from initiating a future war, but it offered no guarantee that this nation would not seek to rearm some time in the future. To deal with this fundamental aspect of the whole problem, Roosevelt turned once more to Morgenthau to flesh out concrete policies consistent with his stern views. The two men met again over the Labor Day weekend. Morgenthau quickly raised the subject of Robert Murphy's recent appointment as Eisenhower's political adviser, pointing out how, "in the minds of the people, it connotes Darlan and everything that goes with him." FDR, who hated to be reminded of this fact, responded with a lengthy defense of how the Darlan deal had saved ten thousand American lives. He also elaborated on his desire to be tough with the Germans. After carefully and slowly reading a memorandum that Morgenthau had prepared on the subject, Roosevelt emphasized that his own inclination was to deprive Germany of all aircraft, to ensure that no Germans were allowed to wear a uniform, and to prevent parades and "marching of any kind." "That's very interesting, Mr. President," Morgenthau replied, "but I don't think it goes nearly far enough." To really prevent another outbreak of German aggression, Morgenthau insisted, would require completely dismantling all the industry in the Ruhr and giving the machinery "to those countries that might need it." FDR was easily convinced. He was hungry for this kind of stuff, Morgenthau noted soon after—so hungry, in fact, that the treasury secretary was encouraged to go away and toughen his proposals. On September 5, Morgenthau then circulated his plan "To Prevent Germany from Starting World War III." This focused on solving the question that had long plagued the president: how to ensure German disarmament?[57]

For Morgenthau, disarmament entailed more than simply demobilizing the German army and dismantling the factories actually producing weapons, because these initiatives failed to address the prospect of future "indirect" rearmament—the possibility that ostensibly "respectable" industries could either be a front for munitions production or be used to produce materials that could easily be turned into arms. Instead, he not only sought to "solve the problem of the itching trigger finger by removing the trigger" but also to ensure that no triggers would ever be produced again.[58] This would be achieved first by truncating Germany in such a way that some of its main industrial regions would be given to neighboring states; thus Poland would get the "southern portion of Silesia," France "the Saar and adjacent territories bounded by the Rhine and Moselle Rivers." Second, the Ruhr area, described as "the heart of German industrial power, the caldron of wars," would "be stripped of all presently existing industries" and so "weakened and controlled that it can not in the foreseeable future become an industrial area"; it would then be designated an "International Zone." Third, "the remaining portion of Germany" would be "divided into two autonomous, independent states, (1) a South German state comprising Bavaria, Wuerttemberg, Baden, and some smaller areas and (2) a North German state comprising a large part of the old state of Prussia, Saxony, Thuringia, and several smaller states." Fourth, as an added insurance, "During a period of at least twenty years after surrender adequate controls, including controls over foreign trade and tight restriction on capital imports, shall be maintained by the UN designed to prevent in the newly-established states the establishment or expansion of key industries basic to the German military potential and to control other key industries."

The Morgenthau plan therefore sought to protect against future Ger-

FDR and Morgenthau, 1944.

man rearmament and aggression by employing a variety of mechanisms: the annexation of Germany's industrial areas by its neighbors, the eradication of industry in the Ruhr, the partition of the remaining portion into two states, and the control of the economies of these two states. In addition, Roosevelt's idea that uniforms, parades, and aircraft should all be denied to Germany was included, as was a proposal to promptly execute all arch-war criminals.[59]

To discuss the German problem, the president convened a special cabinet committee, which met on September 5, 6, and 9. Here, the Treasury's stern approach met with a mixed response. On one side, Stimson was adamantly opposed to pastoralization, for in his considered opinion the urgent need for postwar reconstruction made it unrealistic to suggest that Germany "can be turned into a non-productive 'ghost territory.'[60] Hull and Hopkins were more ambivalent, lacing their comments with anti-German statements but never fully endorsing the Treasury's position. Hopkins, for instance, preferred a compromise solution, which implied the elimination of Germany's dominant economic position in Europe on the one hand, but envisaged converting rather than eradicating its industrial capacity on the other.[61]

Despite the absence of a clear bureaucratic consensus, on September

9 FDR made it clear where he stood. He began by reiterating his support for partition. Then, referring to Morgenthau's contention that it was "a fallacy that Europe needs a strong industrial Germany," the president remarked that "'this is the first time I have seen this stated.' He says that everybody seems to disagree on this point," recorded Morgenthau, "but he said, 'I agree with this idea. . . . Furthermore, I believe in an agricultural Germany."[62] Three days later, Roosevelt then invited Morgenthau to Quebec, where yet another Anglo-American conference was about to begin. Ostensibly, the treasury secretary would be on hand to help in the tricky negotiations over the postwar phase of Lend-Lease. But clearly FDR also wanted Morgenthau to sell his German plan to the British, and on arriving in Quebec the two men again talked at length. After going through the Treasury's briefing book "item by item," FDR then expressed his confidence that the British would accept the Treasury's proposals, commenting that Churchill "is going to be tough too."[63]

At the first Anglo-American discussion on Morgenthau's proposals, at dinner on September 13, Roosevelt's optimism about British toughness seemed misplaced. "I'm all for disarming Germany," was Churchill's initial response, "but we ought not to prevent her living decently. . . . I agree with Burke," he then growled. "You cannot indict a whole nation." In the ensuing argument, FDR was at pains to remind the prime minister that in terms of Big Three politics clinging to this position would doom the British to be in a minority of one. After all, the president recalled, at Tehran it had been Stalin who had pointed out that "the manufacture of metal furniture can be quickly turned into the manufacture of armament." All the Americans were trying to do, he implied, was to devise a method that would reassure the Soviets on this point.[64]

The next day, perhaps persuaded by this argument, perhaps influenced by the more stringent views of his close adviser, Lord Cherwell, or perhaps aware that the postwar Lend-Lease negotiations would proceed more smoothly if he changed course, Churchill, as Morgenthau recorded, "seemed to accept the program designed to weaken the German economy."[65] On September 15, the prime minister was even prepared to dictate a memorandum, which the two leaders then initialed, encapsulating some of Morgenthau's broad goals. This declared that "an essential feature" of postwar planning

> was the future disposition of the Ruhr and the Saar. The ease with which the metallurgical, chemical, and electric industries in Germany can be converted from peace to war has already been impressed on us by bitter experience. . . . The industries referred to in the Ruhr and in the Saar . . . [should] therefore be necessarily put out of action and closed down. It was felt that the two districts should be put under some body under the world organization which would supervise the dismantling of these industries and make sure that they were not started up again by some subterfuge. This program for eliminating the war-making industries in the Ruhr and in the Saar

is looking forward to converting Germany into a country principally agricultural and pastoral in character.[66]

This memorandum was narrower and more ambiguous than the actual Morgenthau plan. In particular, it did not address the question of France annexing the Saar or Poland getting southern Silesia, it was silent on the issue of partition, and it was vague on the extent of the deindustrialization to be undertaken.[67] Yet, even though the details remained somewhat sketchy, the president and prime minister had nevertheless specifically endorsed a program brimming with punitive connotations. Gone was the goal of the Atlantic Charter of equal access to raw materials for victors and vanquished alike; gone was the aim of State Department planners and Henry Stimson of an ultimate reintegration of Germany back into the international economic fold as an engine of growth. In its place was the radical vision of a Germany forbidden any industry, of a pastoralized nation of farmers driven back into a nineteenth-century agrarian state and deprived of the benefits of economic progress lest they use these to menace international peace. At Quebec, such radicalism did not trouble Roosevelt; as he remarked in one meeting, it would not be "an undue hardship to require Germany to revert toward an agricultural status such as she had enjoyed in the latter part of the last century. She had shown that she could not be trusted with all these facilities for making weapons."[68]

In certain respects, the president's motives for endorsing such a radical policy at this particular moment are simple to discern. Over the past few weeks, battlefield fortunes had swung dramatically in the Allies' favor. With the liberation of Paris, the Wehrmacht in apparent disarray, and the Combined Intelligence Committee estimating that "organized resistance under the effective control of German High Command [was] unlikely to continue beyond December 1, 1944, and . . . it may end even sooner," FDR now recognized the need to start making some detailed plans for Germany's future.[69]

The general tenor of the Treasury's approach also dovetailed neatly with the sterner attitude that the president had developed over the past year. Indeed, contrary to the claims of some historians, there was nothing erratic or capricious about Roosevelt's actions at Quebec; nor was it a case of sudden bad judgment brought on by ill-health—an instance of his attitudes hardening at the same rate as his arteries.[70] On the contrary, for more than eighteen months FDR had been convinced that the entire German nation was to blame for the war and had therefore favored stringent measures to protect against future aggression. Now, deindustrialization seemed to offer the perfect way of preventing this nation from ever becoming a menace again.

Pastoralization and partition also seemed to be acceptable to America's two main allies. At Tehran, it had been Stalin who had talked about the desirability of dividing Germany into several states and had first raised the whole problem of preventing indirect rearmament. Now at Quebec, Roosevelt had not only persuaded the ally who had hitherto been the most resistant to harsh terms, but Churchill had even drafted and endorsed a memorandum on the subject. Of course, back in Washington Stimson and the War Department were clearly opposed to the Morgenthau plan, while Hull and Hopkins were far from enthusiastic. But bureaucratic opposition had rarely troubled the president in recent months, when he had consistently favored measures like partition despite State Department disapproval. Now, he simply sidestepped Hull, Hopkins, and Stimson by not taking them with him to Quebec.

Yet all these calculations omitted one crucial variable: domestic opinion.[71] When first informed of the Churchill-Roosevelt memorandum on deindustrialization, a horrified Eden had promptly remarked to his prime minister that "you can't do this. After all, you and I publicly have said quite the opposite."[72] Although none of the president's advisers echoed this sentiment at Quebec, they would have been perfectly justified in reacting in a similar manner. After all, FDR had done little to generate a domestic consensus on specific postwar plans; he had also failed to develop a broad conception of the German enemy that indicted all the people and implied that harsh terms would be applied to the nation as a whole. In fact, pressured into elaborating on the unconditional-surrender formula, he had continued not only to make a distinction between Nazis and Germans but also to reassure the latter that they would not be treated too harshly. As a result, he too had persistently and publicly "said quite the opposite."

Back in Washington, even Treasury officials recognized that the administration's paltry and sometimes misleading publicity efforts were likely to cause problems. As Morgenthau lamented, "the great trouble is that the American people are not prepared for anything."[73] The president was equally pessimistic. "Too many people here," he grumbled in August, ". . . hold to the view that the German people as a whole are not responsible for what has taken place—that only a few Nazi leaders are responsible." "There were certain groups in the United States," he observed at Quebec, ". . . who evinced a kindly attitude toward the Germans. Their theory was that evil could be eradicated from the German make-up and that the nation could be rejuvenated by kindness."[74]

Given these concerns, Roosevelt's actions at Quebec suddenly seem less explicable, particularly now that the presidential campaign was starting to heat up. Four years previously, as Waldo Heinrichs points out, the election had "had a numbing effect on policy."[75] Now, however, far from descending into lethargy and caution lest he frighten off potential voters, FDR had endorsed a radical program for postwar Germany without ever attempting to lay the groundwork for popular acceptance. Why had he behaved in this way?

Several reasons for Roosevelt's action suggest themselves. As we have seen, recent polls had indicated some stiffening of the popular mood, so that 73 percent now wanted to keep Germany as a third-rate power, while 51 percent opposed rebuilding any German industries possessing war potential. More visibly, many of Roosevelt's traditional liberal supporters, those whose opposition to Darlan and Badoglio had so disturbed him back in 1942 and 1943, also seemed to be leaning toward a punitive peace, as exemplified by the creation of SPWW3 and the minor uproar over Robert Murphy's appointment. Perhaps the administration could build on these hardening views in order to establish broader popular support for a truly harsh peace.

Certain elements in the Morgenthau approach were also perfectly in tune with what Roosevelt believed the American public had traditionally been prepared to accept. In the 1920s and 1930s, for instance, reparations had been deeply unpopular, for Americans had come to suspect that they had footed the bill for this act of folly.[76] With current polls indicating that a plurality of 43 percent still opposed reparations, FDR probably felt that the Treasury's emphasis on immediate restitution (a one-off transfer of industrial plant to neighbors), rather than recurrent reparations (which would simply enable Germany to rebuild its economic base in order to pay the Allies back), could well prove popular with the public.[77] Congress and the masses had also been deeply suspicious in the past of prolonged military entanglements on the European continent. The president clearly recalled the overwhelming opposition to an AEF in the months before Pearl Harbor, not to mention the reluctance to fund a large land army even in 1942 and 1943. He was aware, too, that the Dewey campaign was making an intensive effort (in over four hundred radio broadcasts a day) to charge that the administration was "afraid to release men from [the] army after victory" and to claim that the Republicans would bring "the boys back home sooner."[78] In this context, FDR probably felt that pastoralization would appeal to the public, since it was a self-enforcing measure that, as Morgenthau pointed out, would enable "U.S. troops to be withdrawn within a relatively short time."[79]

Such calculations probably played some role in Roosevelt's thinking. He undoubtedly feared the public's reaction both to a long-term occupation of Germany and to reparations. He may also have intended *ultimately* to sell the Morgenthau plan to the public on the basis that it would avoid both. Yet although some aspects of this approach were likely to prove popular, FDR and Morgenthau were both keenly aware that most Americans were unprepared to accept the central elements of the Treasury's truly stern approach. In this context, the only plausible explanation for Roosevelt's decision to sanction pastoralization is that he intended to place the whole project under wraps, at least until after polling day.

Throughout this period, the president was remarkably optimistic about the prospects of keeping explosive foreign-policy issues out of the public eye. Just a few weeks before he had successfully hushed up Stalin's demand that all sixteen Soviet republics be made members of the new United Nations organization, fearing that if this became public knowledge it would ruin any chance of American participation in the future UN.[80] Now, he also wanted to place the Morgenthau plan under lock and key, intending for it to remain a closely guarded secret until an opportune moment came along.

Nor was there any great hurry to go public with the pastoralization program. Roosevelt had long been convinced that when the war ended there would be a period, "lasting perhaps many months," before any peace treaty would be concluded.[81] So even if Germany now collapsed immediately, he thought that implementation of this measure could wait; as he remarked to Morgenthau on September 6, "you can do this economic thing in six months—a year; there is no particular hurry."[82] This, of course, meant that there would be an interim period during which plans for deindustrialization could be finalized, the election could be won, and after that the task of selling the measure could be started—perhaps by emphasizing the benefits of a short occupation and no reparations, perhaps by waiting for external events to stiffen American attitudes still further. But as yet, there was little need to go public with so controversial a measure.

Roosevelt's actions at Quebec certainly confirm such an interpretation. Although Steve Early went up to Canada with the presidential party, his task was largely to fend off questions rather than to educate reporters. As one British official recalled, "everyday there was a press conference in which Steve . . . made anodyne statements about nothing in particular, being reduced to describing in detail the dresses which Mrs. Roosevelt and Mrs. Churchill were wearing, or what Churchill had for breakfast that morning. Denied their natural diet of news, the correspondents became cantankerous and complained about the facilities. It was all very disagreeable."[83] On his return, FDR was scarcely any more informative. At a press conference on September 22, he even had the gall to say that nothing significant had occurred at Quebec, responding to the question "can you give us any idea of what might have been discussed there regarding the future of Germany?" by nonchalantly commenting that "there isn't anything in the way of news yet, except that we talked a lot."[84]

This assurance was disingenuous at best and in the next few weeks an already "cantankerous" press quickly failed to share the president's view of what was newsworthy. But journalists were only given the chance to focus their attention (and their ire) on the Morgenthau plan because Roosevelt's intention to keep the whole episode secret was frustrated by the age-old tactic of a leak. The instigator was probably Hull, piqued at not being invited to Quebec, and like Eden aware of the growing disjunction between the government's public and private positions.[85]

A press conference at Quebec, September 1944 (Churchill, FDR, and McKenzie King).

The story broke on September 22, when Arthur Krock—who had often been a conduit for State Department leaks in the past—wrote an article for the *New York Times* condemning Morgenthau's role at Quebec.[86] Although sketchy on the specific proposals, Krock referred to the Treasury plan, placing it in the wider context of the Darlan deal. "A blast of criticism," he wrote, "which is still blasting in some degree, assailed that policy and fear was expressed that it forecast 'soft' treatment." Morgenthau, who had "never accepted the necessity of General Eisenhower's invasion policy in North Africa," had become a staunch opponent of the State–War Department tendency to be too lenient with defeated enemies, and he now had FDR's support. The next day, the conservative *Wall Street Journal* took up the story, revealing more of the detail. "On the industrial side," it reported, "the Treasury plan would change Germany's economic system, the chief source of livelihood would be agriculture." But, it concluded, this had not yet been agreed by all departments and so remained a set of proposals rather than official policy.[87]

Thus far, the leak had been confined to two New York–based newspapers. But on September 24, the Associated Press (AP) produced an article that was syndicated across the country, thereby bringing the issue to a far wider audience. According to the AP, a harsh peace plan "for destroying Germany as a modern industrial state and converting it into an agricultural country of small farms" had divided the cabinet. The article then went on to enumerate the different elements of Morgenthau's original measure (rather than the memorandum initialed at Quebec), pointing out that it included deindustrialization, the annexation of the Saar and southern Silesia, and the principle of restitution.[88]

Taking this as their starting point, press and radio commentators from across the political spectrum quickly launched a savage attack on Morgenthau's proposals. Most deemed the plan to be unworkable, even counterproductive. As a *Baltimore Sun* editorial declared, because it was doubtful "whether there would actually be room on German farmland for the full employment of Germany's manpower," the "twin consequences of any such policy would most probably be a condition of creeping starvation coupled with an enormous volume of unemployment."[89] The Treasury scheme, the *Washington Post* agreed, was not only "the product of a feverish mind from which all sense of realities had fled," but would also make the German problem permanent, for "a festering sore would be implanted in the heart of Europe, and there would be installed a chaos which would assuredly end in war."[90] Rather than destroying German industry, divisionist organs like the *Washington Evening Star*, together with liberal journals like *PM Daily*, both argued that the Ruhr should be used to reconstruct Europe.[91]

To make matters worse, by September 26 Josef Goebbels's propaganda machinery had also picked up on the Morgenthau plan and, as a *Washington Post* lead story pointed out, was starting to use "it as a threat to spur Germans to greater resistance against the Allies."[92] This was clearly reminiscent of the earlier concern that unconditional surrender had improved the Wehrmacht's fighting zeal. Ominously for the administration, this story also coincided with the stiffening of German resistance after weeks of Allied success. That very same day, Allied headquarters announced a serious setback around Arnhem, where the Germans had halted an ambitious attempt to capture the bridges across the Maas, Waal, and lower Rhine. Although historians now agree that this defeat was basically due to logistical problems, an overoptimistic plan to capture too many bridges with airborne troops, and the chance presence of panzer divisions in some of the key landing zones, journalists at the time reached a very different conclusion.[93] Indeed for most, the fact that news of the Morgenthau plan was now competing with newspaper space next to an important Allied reverse was seen as no coincidence. As the *Washington Herald-Tribune* asked, was it "smart to advertise in advance of victory in this war that the Allies intend to show no mercy to Germany after the Allies win ... [?] We should think nothing could be better calculated to spur the Germans to make a last-ditch fight."[94] The columnist Ernest Lindley agreed. This plan,

*One line of criticism leveled at the Morgenthau plan was that it strengthened
Germany's will to resist.* © *1944,* Chicago Daily Tribune. *Reprinted with permission.*

he argued, was "too severe to win the approval of the American public." It
also "confirmed the worst that Goebbels had been telling the German people in order to make them fight to the very end."[95]

Within days, legislators on Capitol Hill were echoing such sentiments. On September 29, Senator Edwin Johnson attacked Morgenthau's
"poorly conceived plan" for costing the Allied armies a "frightful loss
of life." "Prior to the announcement," he insisted, "the Germans were
surrendering in droves; now they are fighting like demons."[96] Even Senator Kilgore, who had recently chaired an investigation into the need to
eradicate German cartels, seemed to distance himself from the Treasury
scheme. "Any plans to strip Germany of her industry and divide the country into family-sized farms," he asserted, "would not prove workable.
Let Germany keep her industry and simply break up her industrial
monopolies."[97]

The White House mailbag also started to fill with complaints. In one letter, a former official responsible for German reparations in the 1920s told the president that it was "of vital importance to have a prosperous and reasonably contented Germany," because "otherwise she will be a festering sore in Europe and the world, doubtless affecting the prosperity and contentedness of her neighbors and perhaps the U.S." In another, this controversy was placed in an even more pertinent context. Morgenthau's proposals, a correspondent warned, "will not only cost the Allied Nations the lives of half a million boys but will cost you a decisive number of votes in the coming election. It was an affront both to the conscience and the historical intelligence of the American people and only a vigorous disavowal of his views can relieve you of responsibility for them."[98]

As the pressure started to mount, Morgenthau called together his key advisers for a series of frantic discussions about how best to respond. Although some were optimistic that all this media coverage might focus the public's mind on the need for a punitive peace, the general consensus was that the Treasury was losing the publicity battle.[99] Morgenthau was particularly incensed both by charges that he had a "fevered mind" and by suggestions that his plan was resulting in the needless deaths of American GIs. He therefore called key publishers, such as Eugene Meyer of the *Washington Post*, to plead his case.[100] On September 25, his subordinates then began to spread the story that both Britain and the U.S.S.R. supported their approach; they even informally told reporters that since the Soviets had originated the idea, it would be more accurate to label it the "Stalin Plan" than it was to name it after Morgenthau.[101] Three days later, the treasury secretary also wrote to the president, trying to convince him that below the surface of this press criticism the wider public actually favored a harsh peace. Of the ninety letters the department had received, he pointed out, seventy-five were in support and only fifteen were opposed.[102]

While the Treasury tried to react to the savage attacks, Morgenthau's bureaucratic rivals sought to fan the flames of press discontent. Stimson, to be sure, found the "publicity which has been excited over this matter . . . most deplorable" and remained out of the limelight. But Hull and the State Department soon grasped the opportunity to dig the knife in deeper. At a press conference on September 25, Hull first refused to deny that there was a cabinet split on the German question and then implied that pastoralization was not the agreed Allied policy.[103] Meanwhile, in background briefings, State Department officials hastened to inform reporters that the destruction of German industry would complicate the work of reconstruction in the liberated countries. They also cast doubt on the president's support for pastoralization, pointing out that Roosevelt, in a recent public letter, had advocated eradicating German cartels but not German industry in its entirety.[104]

With the election just seven weeks away, the president was greatly angered by all this activity. Just about the last thing he wanted was his Treasury and State departments airing their disagreements in public. Given the

Another line of criticism leveled against the Morgenthau plan was that it exempli-fied the chaotic nature of FDR's administration. © *1944,* The Washington Post. *Reprinted with permission.*

widespread media opposition to the Morgenthau plan, Roosevelt also rec-ognized the enormous mayhem that Dewey could create if he seized on the issue of pastoralization. He therefore decided to intervene, in an at-tempt to defuse the whole situation before it spiraled completely out of control.

On the public front, FDR announced at a press conference on September 29 that he was taking the issue of economic planning for Germany out of the fractious cabinet committee and placing it in the hands of the Foreign Economic Administration (FEA). He then went on the offensive, charging that the press had got its facts wrong on this issue. "Every story that has come out," he indignantly told reporters, "is essentially untrue in the basic facts."[105] In subsequent days, the president also responded to the growing number of protest letters, telling one correspondent that "there is obviously no 'idea of turning [the] German economy upside down and expecting it to work'" and another "not to believe everything you read in the papers." Journalists, he insisted, had "raised up a straw man in which even the straw is synthetic."[106]

But Roosevelt's reassurances were not merely cosmetic attempts to disengage public interest in the lead-up to the election. Acutely aware of the extent and fury of the press criticism, he also privately backed away from pastoralization. On September 29, Morgenthau certainly found a marked change when he visited the White House. Rather than enjoying yet another long discussion about the evils of the German character, he was now "gently but forcibly" led away from the Oval Office by FDR's daughter and curtly informed that "the president said he definitely doesn't want to see you."[107] By stark contrast, Roosevelt now went out of his way to placate Hull, writing him a letter that explained that his main aim at Quebec had simply been "to keep Britain from going into complete bankruptcy at the end of the war." In a remarkable volte-face, the president then denied that his intention was "to make Germany a wholly agricultural nation again, and yet somebody down the line has handed this out to the press." "No one wants complete eradication of German industrial productive capacity in the Ruhr and Saar," he continued; all that was required was "rather complete controls."[108]

It was a similar story a couple of days later, when Roosevelt met with Henry Stimson. The president immediately "grinned and looked naughty and said 'Henry Morgenthau pulled a boner'. . . . He had no intention of turning Germany into an agrarian nation," FDR insisted. And when the redoubtable Stimson then pulled a copy of the Quebec memorandum out of his pocket, Roosevelt refused to own up; he simply pleaded a convenient memory lapse. "He was frankly staggered by this," Stimson recorded, "and said he had no idea how he could have initialed this; that he had evidently done it without much thought."[109]

Roosevelt's decision to abandon the Morgenthau plan was clearly congruent with the media's opposition to the notion of pastoralization. But how much weight should we ascribe to this one variable? One conceivable alternative is that FDR was forced to change course by the dynamics of alliance politics. Here, previous interpretations have fallen into two categories. On the one hand, at the height of the Cold War John L. Snell argued that evidence of Soviet unilateral aggression in September, in Warsaw, Finland, Hungary, Rumania, Bulgaria, and Yugoslavia, encouraged Roosevelt to reassess a measure that would leave a dangerous vacuum in the heart of Europe. "Soviet policy in the autumn of 1944," he writes, "was unquestionably the best ally of those who favored a moderate policy for postwar Germany."[110] This argument seems overdrawn, however. During these months, FDR was relatively unconcerned about Soviet actions. At the end of August, he dismissed Churchill's worried premonition that a weak Germany would leave a dangerous void between the white snows of Russia and the white cliffs of Dover, with the confident comment that he planned to work with the Soviets rather than to balance against them.[111] Throughout the fall, the president also appeared untroubled by the prospect of a Soviet sphere of influence in Eastern Europe, as long as Stalin only sought to establish a protective buffer along his borders and did not attempt to dominate the internal and economic activities of this region.[112]

On the other hand, rather than abandoning the Morgenthau plan because of a new threat from the U.S.S.R., Roosevelt might have retreated because he was aware that his two allies vehemently opposed deindustrialization. The State Department certainly tried to generate the impression that Moscow's desire for reparations and London's preference for economic controls could not be reconciled with the Morgenthau's approach.[113] In a similar vein, some historians have subsequently pointed out that during the autumn the Soviets repeatedly "expressed opposition to the Treasury's scheme."[114] Yet it is doubtful whether Roosevelt shared these perceptions. We have already noted that he saw deindustrialization partly as a way of dampening Stalin's fears that Germany could in the future turn metal factories into munitions plants; at Quebec, Roosevelt also believed that Churchill's opposition to a harsh peace had been overcome. In subsequent weeks, both men again hinted at their support for the Treasury's proposal. On October 9, Churchill flew to Moscow for a conference with the Soviet leader. From there, he wired that the two of them had discussed and agreed on partition. "As to Prussia," he reported, Stalin "wished the Ruhr and the Saar detached and put out of action and probably under international control and a separate state formed in the Rhineland. He would also like the internationalization of the Kiel Canal. I am not opposed to this line of thought," the prime minister concluded.[115]

If FDR's decision to backtrack was not consistent with alliance pressure, then perhaps it was a reaction to bureaucratic opposition: after all, both the War and State departments were hostile to the Treasury scheme.[116] On its own, however, this factor was also insufficient. On numerous occasions in the past eighteen months Roosevelt had been perfectly willing to ignore opposition from within his administration. Indeed, whenever Hull or Stimson had previously expressed their unease about measures such as dismemberment, FDR had either excluded them from key conferences or dissembled in their presence—but not once had he decided meekly to change course. What is more, immediately after Quebec top officials were profoundly pessimistic about their ability to overturn a presidential decision; as Stimson recorded, FDR "dislikes opposition when he has made up his mind."[117] It was not until the very end of September, when this bureaucratic hostility was combined with a popular outcry, that the president did decide to change his mind. In this instance, then, domestic opinion was clearly the crucial variable, for only after the press leak did FDR pay any heed to Stimson and Hull; only after the "incessant flow of stories" on the Morgenthau plan did he deem it necessary to back away from the course decided upon at Quebec.[118]

But while public opinion was vital, the process at work was almost the complete opposite to that suggested by Walter Lippmann or George Kennan in their classic books on American diplomacy. After all, Roosevelt was not ultimately trapped by the overheated and exaggerated rhetoric he had employed to arouse popular interest early in the war. On the contrary, he was trapped by the cautious nature of his initial message—specifically, by his repeated emphasis on Nazi rather than German brutality, with the corollary that most Americans had never been convinced that the nation as a whole would have to be treated harshly to ensure future peace. Far from being a case of a circumspect statesman being forced to act more intemperately by an overzealous mass hysteria, this was in fact an example of an increasingly vehement president being reigned in by a more prudent public.

For Roosevelt, the one bright spot in all this was that his September 29 press conference had at least helped to dampen the outcry. Some journalists, to be sure, took umbrage at the president's claim that their stories had been untrue.[119] But for the most part, as a State Department media survey found, FDR's press statement was "approved, as expressing agreement with the reported program of Secretaries Hull and Stimson for a 'firm,' but not 'Carthaginian,' peace." The New York Herald Tribune, for instance, welcomed news that Morgenthau's project had been scrapped.[120] Likewise, the Washington Post, in an editorial entitled "Back on the Beam," was pleased that the president had "removed a weapon out of the hands of Dr. Goebbels, to whom the Morgenthau plan came as a godsend."[121] And in a CBS broadcast, Quincy Howe, pointing out that a prosperous Europe needed German industry, was relieved that the Treasury plan had been "put in cold storage, and the State Department has been put in charge."[122] Within days, then, opinion makers proved remarkably willing to accept the president's disingenuous press conference remarks at face value.

Yet not everyone was satisfied with Roosevelt's change of course. Even at the height of the popular uproar that greeted the Morgenthau plan leak, there had remained a vocal minority, mostly connected with the SPWW3, who were convinced of the benefits of pastoralization.[123] So it was hardly surprising that when reports started to filter out that FDR was having a change of heart, the SPWW3 chairman, Rex Stout, immediately wrote to the White House imploring Roosevelt to correct the impression that the Morgenthau plan was about to be abandoned.[124] In the next few weeks, Stout and his cohorts—often with the Treasury's support and guidance—then took to the airwaves to argue the case for transforming Germany from an industrial to an agricultural nation.[125]

That the SPWW3 now had a clear opening to advocate a harsh peace highlights the somewhat paradoxical impact that the Morgenthau plan leak was having on the public debate. Although almost all the media reaction remained negative and this had forced the president to back away from pastoralization, at the same time this episode had at least made the German question a central topic for discussion. In the space of just a few weeks in October, the *March of Time* newsreel devoted a whole film to the question of "What to Do with Germany," NBC sponsored a Foreign Policy Association broadcast on ways of effectively disarming Germany, and numerous newspapers and magazines from across the political spectrum editorialized on the subject. Virtually all this comment remained critical of the Morgenthau plan itself, but the deindustrialization proposal had nevertheless set the parameters for the public discussion. So even when attacking pastoralization, most opinion makers still felt obliged to address the underlying problem of how to prevent Germany from launching a new war in the future; and almost all conceded that the minimum of denazification and demobilization would be insufficient.[126]

For Roosevelt, however, the fact that the Morgenthau plan leak had helped to nudge the public debate forward was now a distinctly secondary concern. Far more significant was the mileage that his political opponents were making out of the whole episode. According to some opinion makers, it was even a compelling reason not to reelect the president. As the *Saturday Evening Post* savagely put it, "the fact that Mr. Roosevelt thought well enough of such fantastic nonsense to permit Mr. Morgenthau to loose it on the delegates at the Quebec Conference does not suggest an irreplaceable genius at work."[127]

The Dewey team naturally concurred. Scenting the administration's vulnerability on this issue, on October 18 the Republican candidate decided to launch a vigorous attack on Morgenthau in a nationally broadcast foreign-policy speech. Dewey began by sarcastically pointing out that the treasury secretary's "qualifications as an expert on military and international affairs are still a closely guarded secret." In an attempt to dent the government's reputation for military competence, which had been heightened by the victories since June, he then declared that publication of the Treasury plan had enabled Goebbels "to terrify the Germans into fanatical resistance." "On the basis of the Treasury Department's ill-conceived proposals," he continued, "the German people were told that a program of destruction was in order for them if they surrender. Almost overnight the morale of the German people seemed wholly changed. Now they are fighting with the frenzy of despair. We are paying in blood for our failure to have ready an intelligent program for dealing with invaded Germany."[128]

On other occasions, Dewey sought to link the administration's warnings about complacency with the Morgenthau plan, so that he had a double-edged sword to wield against the White House. Roosevelt, he pointed out, had recently told us that the war has a long way to go. But surely, he averred, this was only because the publication of the Morgenthau plan has been "as good as ten fresh German divisions. It put the fight back into the German army, it stiffened the will of the German nation to resist. Almost overnight the headlong retreat of the Germans stopped." "What does [this] mean," he asked? "It means the blood of our fighting men are paying for this improvised meddling which is so much part and parcel of the whole Roosevelt administration."[129]

As election day loomed, the president became ever more sensitive to such charges. Back at the start of September, one aide had reported that "Roosevelt leads Dewey in the public's estimate of his ability to handle: (1) peace making; (2) winning the war."[130] Now, however, with the furor over the Morgenthau plan and the GOP's exploitation of this issue, the president seemed vulnerable on both scores. Even worse, during October polls started to indicate that the race was tightening, with Roosevelt losing ground in such vital states as New York and Pennsylvania, where there were large German-American populations.[131] As Ickes repeatedly informed the White House, the furor over the Morgenthau plan "was very harmful politically" and the administration "ought to do something about this."[132] In full agreement, FDR decided to make a concerted effort to respond to these charges and definitively defuse the German issue before polling day. A series of presidential speeches would also dispel any rumors that the president's health was failing.

Roosevelt began by distancing himself from the more vehement harsh-peace advocates. At one stage, he had contemplated inviting Stout to the White House to reassure the SPWW3 chairman about his vision for postwar Germany. But on October 16 his appointment secretary called Stout and "suggested [that he] wait [until] after the election when [there would be] more time to talk at length."[133] Five days later, after a drive through a windswept and rainy New York City in an open-top car, Roosevelt made a keynote address to the Foreign Policy Association. He started by reassuring a nationwide radio audience that no Badoglio-style deal would be attempted with the Germans, declaring that "as for Germany, that tragic Nation which has sown the wind and is now reaping the whirlwind—we and our allies are entirely agreed that we shall not bargain with the Nazi conspirators, or leave them a shred of control—open or secret—of the instruments of government. We shall not leave them a single element of military power—or of potential military power." But, he continued, it would also be a mistake to go too far in the other direction. "I should be false to the very foundations of my religious and political convictions," he declared, "if I should ever relinquish the hope—or even the faith—that in all peoples, without exception, there live some instinct for truth, some attraction toward justice, some passion for peace—buried as they may be in the Germany case under a brutal regime." "The German people," he insisted, "are not going to be enslaved. Because the UN do not traffic in human slavery. But it will be necessary for them to earn their way back into the fellowship of peace-loving and law-abiding Nations. And, in their climb up that steep road, we shall certainly see to it that they are not encumbered by having to carry guns. We hope they will be relieved of that burden forever." In an attempt to encourage any wavering German-Americans to vote for the Democratic ticket, the president also asserted that "we bring no charge against the German race, as such, for we cannot believe that God has eternally condemned any race of humanity. We know in our own land, in the United States of America, how many good men and women of German ancestry have proved loyal, freedom-loving, and peace-loving citizens. But," he concluded, "there is going to be stern punishment for all those in Germany directly responsible for this agony of mankind."[134]

Historians have generally viewed this as a soft speech. John Morton Blum, for instance, has characterized it as "carefully moderate," while John Lewis Gaddis has argued that on this occasion FDR "took a noticeably moderate position on the postwar treatment of Germany."[135] In certain respects, this interpretation is correct. Not only did the president eschew his private view that all Germans were inherently militaristic and so only trustworthy when deprived of twentieth-century machinery, but he also sought to reassure German-Americans that his government did not view them as members of an inherently aggressive race. Yet when viewed in the context not of FDR's private views but of his previous public utterances, then this speech was actually a good deal harsher than what had gone before. After all, the president promised not to leave Germany any element of "potential" military power, which could be construed to mean that he envisaged eliminating certain indirect munitions industries. When delivering the speech, Roosevelt's phrases on the German character also dripped with sarcasm; so, for instance, he placed emphasis on the fact that Germany's climb back to respectability would be "steep," or that Germans only had "some" instinct for truth and justice, which in any case was "buried" deep.[136] Seen in this light, Roosevelt's campaign address again exemplifies the somewhat ambivalent impact that the Morgenthau plan was having on the public debate, for while FDR now felt constrained to backtrack from pastoralization, he had also been granted the opportunity to toughen up his public conception of the enemy while at the same time appearing relatively mild. Once more, then, press criticism of deindustrialization not only narrowed options, it also helped to move the debate forward.

In the last weeks of the campaign, the president continued to reassure German-Americans that nothing too tough was in the offing, brushing aside worries of a SPWW3 backlash and even writing to a German-Amer-

ican newspaper, congratulating it on seventy-five years in press and reassuring its readers about administration intentions.[137] Other Democrats followed suit, relieved that FDR's publicly expressed views now seemed
more in tune with the popular mood. Many party leaders were certainly
quick to publicize the president's kind words about German-Americans,
anxious to prevent large numbers of this group from defecting from the
Democratic ticket.[138]

By polling day, all this maneuvering had done little to clarify the government's internal debate on Germany's future. But it had helped to take
the force away from some of Dewey's more extravagant claims. This became clear on the evening of November 7. As Roosevelt settled into his
old election-night routine, sitting at the table in his Hyde Park dining
room to tabulate the returns, it soon became clear that he had been reelected for yet another term of office. The final margin of victory in the
popular vote was 53.5 to 46 percent, which translated into 432 electoral
votes compared to his rival's 99. Although this was the closest presidential
election result since Woodrow Wilson's razor-thin triumph back in 1916, a
clear majority of Americans had nevertheless decided that the president
who had played such a large role in winning the war should now be given
a shot at establishing an enduring peace.

The Lingering Impact of the Morgenthau Plan
Debate, November 1944 to April 1945

On November 12, just five days after the election, Senator Harley Kilgore's
subcommittee finally published its findings on German cartels. Before
polling day, key members of this subcommittee, including the chairman
himself, had sought to distance themselves from the Morgenthau plan.
Now, however, their report was widely seen by journalists as giving a
much-needed public boost to the Treasury's proposals. "Germany's industry," the subcommittee declared, "must be reorganized so as to eliminate its aggressive power. . . . A real disarmament program requires not
only the dismantling of all direct munitions industries but also the dismantling and removal to the devastated areas of Europe of the primary indirect
munitions industries, including the metallurgical and chemical industries."[139] Morgenthau was naturally delighted. "I thought you got out a
swell report," he told Kilgore, who responded that the Treasury had been
"badly misinterpreted. . . . I think your plan and mine fairly well coincide."
The treasury secretary then hastened to the White House, where he found
that FDR seemed to share his reaction. The president, Morgenthau
recorded, "thinks the Kilgore report was so wonderful," and with all the
"publicity they got, his attitude on this whole business is just like lifting a
cloud." In the presence of Morgenthau, Roosevelt even stated that "as far as
he is concerned, what the public thinks now he doesn't care."[140]

This comment is striking, for it suggests that FDR's recent retreat from pastoralization had merely been a short-term campaign maneuver, designed to dampen criticism prior to the election but to be quickly abandoned thereafter. In fact, it raises a larger question: Now that he had emerged triumphant in the only opinion poll that really mattered, would the president continue to pay attention to what the public thought? In the postelection environment, would he start to treat popular opinion with impunity?

The answer, it soon became clear, was a categorical no. Far from suddenly forgetting all about the outcry over the Morgenthau plan, over the winter the president seemed almost obsessed by the leak that had triggered the whole public debate. In a conversation with Stettinius on November 10, he intimated, "in a joking way, of course," that the administration should handle leaks "like the Russians do, mentioning that Krock and Pearson would then be eliminated." Later, with less humor and in a vein that might have appealed to some of his successors, he even recommended putting FBI agents in different departments to act as plumbers—"make a Foreign Service officer out of the agent; let him roam around the place," he suggested.[141]

Despite the bravado in his comment to Morgenthau, Roosevelt also remained an avid aficionado of opinion polls, and was "greatly pleased" when the State Department began sending him a series of short, sharp, snappy memoranda, normally only two or three pages in length, highlighting the public's main foreign policy concerns in any given week.[142] As victory approached, the mood on Capitol Hill also began to loom larger in the president's thoughts than at any time since Pearl Harbor. The Senate, after all, would have to approve by any prospective terms for Germany included in a peace treaty, and the fate of the Versailles Treaty was an apposite reminder that this was no foregone conclusion. As a result, officials now began to devise means of improved liaison with Congress, including more regular briefings, speeches, and bipartisan membership of foreign delegations. Part of this task would be undertaken by the new position of assistant secretary of state for public and cultural relations, which Stettinius created in a reorganization of the State Department in the middle of December. Although ironically something of an initial public-relations disaster, since the Senate refused to confirm the administration's nominee without open hearings, this obstacle was quickly overcome. By December 13, the State Department not only had an enhanced public relations capacity, but this position was now occupied by none other than Archibald MacLeish, former director of the OFF and assistant director of the OWI—a figure, of course, with much experience in devising an information campaign.[143]

Yet an enhanced opinion-persuading capacity was of little use without an agreed policy to sell. During November and December, as the president's mind again turned toward concrete measures for Germany's future, memories of the Morgenthau plan leak continued to exert a profound influence over his policy preferences. For one thing, there was no escaping the stark fact that pastoralization was widely unpopular. As Roosevelt ruefully recalled on December 22, "Morgenthau had made a great mistake in stirring this whole thing up during the campaign, and . . . the agrarian thing was absurd."[144] Given this calculation, the president was now keen to inform his subordinates that "he had no intention of turning Germany into an agrarian state." With respect to Germany, Stettinius confirmed in December, FDR now felt that "we should let her come back industrially to meet her own needs."[145]

As well as backing away from pastoralization, the most controversial and criticized aspect of the Morgenthau plan, Roosevelt also adopted a more pragmatic stance toward partition, favoring some form of dismemberment but preferring not to sanction any concrete proposal until it became clear what the conditions would be like inside Germany.[146] Meanwhile, on other issues his actual policy preferences remained relatively clear but his underlying motives were now suddenly quite murky. On December 4, for instance, the president categorically stated that "we are against reparations." But he failed to state whether this was because his views were softening toward Germany, or because he was still convinced by Morgenthau's argument that reparations would simply enable Germany to rebuild a strong economic base in order to pay the Allies back.[147] Similarly, FDR remained determined to bring U.S. troops back from Europe as soon as possible, which would clearly preclude a long-term and large-scale American occupation of Germany.[148] But again, he was silent on whether he now thought occupation unnecessary or irrelevant—whether Germany could be trusted to behave, or, as the Morgenthau plan envisaged, whether it would be subjected to so many other controls that it would find it impossible to reoffend. Perhaps he was still convinced that the public would never accept either reparations or a long-term occupation.

While Roosevelt therefore continued to distance himself from complete deindustrialization, was reluctant to make detailed plans on many issues, and was hazy on the purpose of particular policies, on one subject his views were clearly more punitive than anything previously envisaged by the State and War departments: initial occupation policies. Significantly, this was the one area that the media had left untouched when lambasting the Morgenthau plan. Moreover, when opinion makers had started to focus on the American occupation of Aachen, the first German city to fall under U.S. control, a majority had actually criticized the army for being too lenient rather than for being too harsh; reporters had certainly been quick to express their indignation when it was revealed that the army had inadvertently appointed numerous Nazis to help it administer the city.[149] Agreeing with the press for once, Roosevelt soon began to talk about the prospect of placing top civilians in control of the U.S. occupation, on the basis that they were likely to have a far tougher point of view than the military.[150]

The postelection weeks were thus a period for taking stock and contemplating what was acceptable in the wake of Morgenthau plan furor. Coming on top of all the rigors of the election campaign, it was also an extremely taxing period for the ailing president, and on November 27 he decided to escape to Warm Springs in Georgia for a three-week rest. Edward Stettinius was left to man the shop in Washington, having just replaced the ill and embittered Cordell Hull as secretary of state.[151] Although dismissed by many as an inexperienced diplomat and an intellectual lightweight, Stettinius was not only acutely sensitive to public opinion, but was also well attuned to the president's complex and somewhat confusing set of policy preferences.

Assisted by John J. McCloy, Stimson's deputy, Stettinius quickly set about the task of forging a new compromise position on Germany. This was achieved by making a sharp distinction between "the period immediately following the cessation of organized resistance" and "long-range objectives and measures."[152] For the short term, the State Department now abandoned its previous talk of restoration, reconstitution, or maintenance.[153] In its place, was a harsher tone that more closely reflected the president's proclivities. "Germany will not be occupied for the purpose of liberation but as a defeated nation," declared JCS 1067, the new draft instructions for the occupation of Germany. "The clear fact of German military defeat must be appreciated by all levels of the German population."[154] However, recognizing that Roosevelt had abandoned pastoralization and was less strident on partition, Stettinius glimpsed the opportunity to proclaim that America's eventual goal remained "the assimilation—on a basis of equality—of a reformed, peaceful and economically non-aggressive Germany into a liberal system of world trade." He also opposed division, but with the caveats that any final decision should await events and that in the interim decentralization should be encouraged.[155]

When Roosevelt returned to Washington in the middle of December he looked frailer than ever. But he remained mentally alert and was largely satisfied that Stettinius's approach was "satisfactory" and "sufficiently tough." Significantly, he also decided to invite Stettinius rather than Morgenthau to the next Big Three meeting, scheduled to be held in the Crimea early in the New Year. Amazingly, this would be the first time a secretary of state would accompany the president to a wartime conference outside the Western Hemisphere.[156] Before this meeting could be convened, however, battlefield fortunes would take one final twist.

At dawn on December 16, in freezing and foggy conditions, a quarter of a million German troops suddenly and unexpectedly slashed through the meager American defensive positions in the Ardennes. Images of May 1940 quickly flashed through minds of Allied leaders, for Hitler's intentions were transparent to all: he aimed to make a last desperate attempt to knock the Allies off balance, reach the sea at Antwerp, and thereby relive his greatest ever military moment.

Preoccupied with mounting a desperate defense, the first instinct at

Allied headquarters was to impose a total news blackout. Journalists back home, having endured repeated lectures on how their optimistic reporting had fueled complacency, reacted with predictable fury. As the *Philadelphia Inquirer* pointed out, now that a real crisis had erupted the administration seemed to be saying "that the American people are temperamentally unfit to stand up under bad news."[157] Worse still, this official silence also seemed to fit into a pattern, already established over peace plans for Germany, whereby the government said little and the press had to rely on leaks. In some quarters there was even the suggestion that perhaps something more sinister was at work—that perhaps this reticence denoted that the government had a lot to hide, that perhaps it might now be preparing to sell out to the Soviets and the British when the time came to make the peace.

In December, such suspicions were greatly heightened by indications that the Soviets were unilaterally imposing their own government in Poland, while the British were taking sides in the Greek civil war. Did this mean, journalists asked, that spheres of influence rather than self-determination would characterize the postwar order? Roosevelt's response did little to allay their fears, for in an off-the-cuff remark at a press conference on December 19 he incautiously suggested that there was no actual copy of the Atlantic Charter, "just some scraps of paper," and that nothing had ever been signed.[158] Of course, government policy toward Germany had long since deviated from the position of postwar equality envisaged in the Atlantic Charter. But now reporters were left with the impression that the provisions for the occupied territories were about to be discarded, too.

By the end of December, this growing frustration with government secrecy and the associated suspicions about what it might denote, started to filter through to mass opinion. The public, Stettinius wrote to the president, interprets the events in Poland and Greece as British and Russian "attempts to create 'spheres of influence' and as desertion of announced peace aims, such as the Atlantic Charter." Largely for this reason, polls indicated that confidence in America's two main allies had "reached the lowest point since the Moscow Conference," with only 60 percent saying they could trust Britain and 44 percent believing they could trust the Soviets. Such attitudes also fed into American responses to an international organization. Although nine out of ten respondents still supported the general proposition that "the U.S. should join . . . in an effort to prevent future wars," 50 percent were now convinced that developments in Europe "would make success more difficult."[159] There was a sharp decline, too, in the number who thought that "this country's interests abroad are being well taken care of by the president," down from a high of 65 percent in June to just over 50 percent in December.[160] Such sentiments, Stettinius informed FDR, "may affect not only the negotiation of the peace, but the successful conduct of the war."[161]

Roosevelt was acutely sensitive to such findings. Ever since Pearl Harbor he had continued to worry about the persistence of divisionism. Now it seemed possible, if not likely, that with the war all but over isolationism might again have an appeal. The president was particularly concerned that these political complications would be a gift to those isolationists who had always wanted to turn their backs on Europe and focus on Asia. Douglas MacArthur was very much of this ilk, and the general now seized the opportunity to reenter the fray, mischievously telling a *New York Herald Tribune* reporter that the administration was persisting in "the same old mistake of interfering in European quarrels which we can't hope to solve because they are insoluble."[162]

Three years after Pearl Harbor, Roosevelt suddenly found himself in a situation strangely reminiscent of the old phony war months. He responded in typical fashion. At one press conference, the president took a swipe at "a certain element, particularly the Hearst press" who were "still yelling about us using the wrong strategy, that we should take the American troops out of Germany and put them in the Pacific."[163] Then, in his annual message to Congress, FDR launched a stinging attack on those "short-sighted people" who "would have had us throw Britain and Russia to the Nazi wolves and concentrate against the Japanese. Such people," he reminded listeners, "urged that we fight a purely defensive war against Japan while allowing the domination of all the rest of the world by Nazism and Fascism."[164] Roosevelt's advisers also lambasted other strands of the isolationist faith, especially Senator Burton K. Wheeler's depiction of unconditional surrender as an "asinine" and "brutal" policy. Turning the tables on Wheeler, Stettinius accused the senator of prolonging the war at the cost of American lives, charging that his statement provided the enemy with hope that a negotiated peace was still possible.[165]

Roosevelt was clearly exasperated by all the eruptions that accompanied Hitler's surprise offensive, but he soon took heart from the rapid response of Eisenhower's armies. Within weeks, they had not only halted the German panzers but had also recovered much of the ground lost in the middle of December. In so doing, Allied forces also uncovered an incident that the president believed he could use to his advantage. On December 17, at the start of the German offensive, SS troops had massacred eighty-six U.S. prisoners of war. News of this outrage filtered up to the White House two weeks later, when Stimson informed the president that 150 GIs had been slaughtered, not only inflating the figure but then embellishing his account with eyewitness reports. FDR's response was suggestive. Rather than recoil in horror or disgust, he merely thought of the practical advantages that might accrue. "Well," he told the secretary of war, "it will only serve to make our troops feel toward the Germans as they already have learned to feel toward the Japs." Perhaps it might also fuel anti-German hatred amongst the wider audience of American opinion, for the very next day FDR decided to allow information on this episode to be released to the press, accompanied by a formal protest from the State Department.[166] At long last, then, it appeared that events might well be intervening to enable the president to heighten the public's hatred of Germany.

Three weeks later, and just two days after his fourth inauguration, Roosevelt set off on the grueling journey to the Crimea. After a long cruise across the Atlantic, he briefly met Churchill at Malta, before embarking on a hazardous and uncomfortable seven-hour flight to the small airstrip at Saki. From there, the president and his advisers were driven ninety miles to the Lividia Palace just outside Yalta.

As their cars ambled slowly along the windy roads, through mountain passes, and eventually to the coast, the American party was staggered "by the widespread war destruction"—the "burned-out freight trains, burned-out tanks and other damaged materiel."[167] Roosevelt took particular note, and the next day, in his first meeting at the conference with Stalin, he began by remarking that "he had been very much struck by the extent of the German destruction in the Crimea." As a consequence, he continued, "he was more bloodthirsty in regard to the Germans than he had been a year ago, and he hoped that Marshal Stalin would again propose a toast to the execution of 50,000 officers of the German army." The Soviet leader responded promptly that "the Germans were savages and seemed to hate with a sadistic hatred the creative work of human beings. The president," his translator recorded, "agreed with this."[168]

As this comment suggests, Roosevelt's vivid firsthand experience of the wreckage wrought on the Eastern Front had done nothing to dampen his hatred toward the Germans.[169] Yet significantly, at Yalta FDR's deep-seated animus toward the enemy no longer translated into unequivocal support for truly stern measures. Indeed, despite all this preliminary talk about the depravity and baseness of the German character, as the conference unfolded it soon became clear that the president was far less "bloodthirsty" than he had been at either Tehran or Quebec. The reason for this was simple: keenly aware of what the American public would accept, he now approached the German problem with a new caution and pragmatism.

For a start, in all the plenary meetings the president clearly eschewed any talk of widespread deindustrialization. This subject was first discussed on February 5, when the Soviets raised the possibility of reducing German heavy industry by 80 percent through the transfer to the U.S.S.R. of "iron and steel, electrical power, and chemical industries," together with "all aviation factories, synthetic oil refineries, etc."[170] No doubt recalling the adverse domestic reaction to such measures when they had leaked in a similar guise the previous September, the president was now distinctly lukewarm to this whole approach. Such transfers, he insisted, should be limited to ensure that the German people enjoyed a basic level of subsistence and economic security. Contrary to his position at Quebec, FDR therefore envisioned "a Germany that is self-sustaining but not starving. . . . In rebuilding," he continued, "we must get all we can but we can't get it all. Leave Germany enough industry and work to keep her from starving."[171]

Although Roosevelt opposed extensive deindustrialization, he was willing to concede that the Soviets, who had obviously suffered tremendously at the hands of the Germans, should receive reparations of some sort. But even this, he recognized, raised a number of prospective public opinion difficulties. One was his recollection of the interwar reparations problem, especially the American public's suspicion that they had been hoodwinked into funding the whole fiasco. "We should not make the financial mistakes that followed the last war," he insisted on February 6.[172] Four days later FDR expanded on this theme, commenting "that he was afraid that if reparations and especially if figures were mentioned that the American people would believe that it involved money." To avoid this potential problem, Roosevelt wanted to resort to a familiar ploy. Just as he had with Lend-Lease four years before, so he now wanted to "get rid of the silly, foolish, old dollar sign." In practice, this meant that he favored reparations "in kind," which would entail the transfer of equipment to eliminate Germany's arms industry, as well as the use of German labor to help Soviet reconstruction.[173]

But it was Churchill, not Roosevelt, who was now the most vehement opponent of a hefty reparations bill. On February 5, the prime minister, also retreating from the stance he had taken at Quebec, insisted that the Germans must be allowed some economic future. "If you wished a horse to pull a wagon," he declared, "you would at least have to give it fodder." "That is right," Stalin sharply rebutted, "but care should be taken to see that the horse did not turn around and kick you." After much wrangling between the two, the Soviets ultimately—and reluctantly—accepted that the whole matter should be referred to the Moscow Reparations Commission. Roosevelt, playing the role of the adjudicator, happily endorsed this compromise, relieved that a formula had been found to paper over a damaging split within the alliance and no doubt well aware that he would now have more time to drum up domestic support for what remained an unpopular measure back home.[174]

The third issue on the agenda was partition, and here too the president backed away from his more strident demands of November 1943 and September 1944. On February 5, to be sure, when Stalin raised this issue and expressed his own support for division, FDR responded that he was still "in favor of [the] dismemberment of Germany," just as he had been at Tehran. He also intimated (presciently) that "the permanent treatment of Germany might grow out of the zones of occupation." But apart from these two comments, Roosevelt generally favored a wait-and-see approach, accepting the idea of partition in principle but postponing the details for another time and place. He also thought it would be "a great mistake to have any public discussion of the dismemberment of Germany," ostensibly because the Big Three would then be inundated with prospective proposals but undoubt-

The big three in discussion at Yalta (to FDR's right are Leahy and Marshall, to his left are Stettinius and King)

edly because he felt the U.S. public might block this measure, too.[175] Partition had, after all, been an integral part of the Morgenthau plan, and, although criticism had largely been reserved for pastoralization, polls had consistently shown that only 30 to 40 percent of the American public favored such a measure. FDR was therefore content with the final protocol, which left the matter to another committee and also watered it down by stating that the Big Three would only seek partition "as they deem requisite for future peace and security." He was also pleased that the public communiqué omitted any mention of this agreement.[176]

This left occupation. When Churchill brought up the question of giving France a zone, Roosevelt responded that this would be acceptable to the American delegation. But then, revealing once again his growing concern about what the American people would accept, FDR declared that the period of occupation in the U.S. zone would be short, remarking that "he did not believe that American troops would stay in Europe much more than two years."[177] This, of course, was a refrain he had repeated on numerous occasions over the past year. It was partly a product of his perception of what Americans had traditionally found acceptable, partly a result of Congress' dislike of funding large armies, and partly due to the Republican party's attempt to turn this into a hot political issue during the previous campaign. But FDR's worries had also been greatly heightened by the recent isolationist minirevival, and especially by his renewed concern that an excessive commitment in Europe would be an ideal weapon for all those divisionist critics who had long wanted to reorientate America's focus away from this continent. For all these reasons, the president made it clear that American's occupation of Germany would be temporary and short.

Yalta, then, marked yet another important point in Roosevelt's thinking about the German problem. Although his own beliefs were harsher than ever before, this no longer translated into firm support for stern measures; unlike at Tehran or Quebec, he was no longer such an adamant proponent of partition or pastoralization. His position here is interesting in a number of respects. To start with, on German policy FDR either opposed or quibbled with Soviet proposals. This was an obvious departure from his actions at Tehran, when he had been willing to side with Stalin on a whole host of subjects pertaining to Germany, from division to controlling the economy. It was also a deviation from his general approach during the past few years, when his basic strategy had been to cooperate with the Soviets, believing this to be the key to a peaceful postwar order. Clearly, Roosevelt's more combative Yalta position on Germany was due to the fact that he had been burnt once by a press leak that linked him to a punitive peace plan and was not about to repeat this mistake. Instead, he thought it better to soften his position on deindustrialization, while delaying the details on vexatious matters like reparations and dismemberment.

Yet this stance also begs an important question: how did FDR now intend to stop the German nation from again becoming a threat? After all, a short-term occupation had only been acceptable under the Morgenthau plan because other tools like deindustrialization, dismemberment, and extensive controls had been envisaged to stop any future trouble. Now there seemed to be little left.

For Roosevelt, the answer to this problem was twofold. In the first place, the UN organization finally agreed on at Yalta would fill any vacuum left by a direct U.S. withdrawal from Germany. In the president's view, American participation in the new international organization might educate the public about the need and desirability of deploying troops in Germany.[178] If not, even after the GIs had departed, the UN led by the four policemen (the United States, Britain, the Soviet Union, and China) would still be on hand to quell any potential resurgence, either through blockade or perhaps the use of air power.

In the second place, Roosevelt had not totally abandoned his harsh approach to the German problem. Throughout March, he continued to reiterate that on partition and reparations "our attitude should be one of study and postponement of final decision," but this did not mean he had not backed away from both measures altogether.[179] When it came to dismemberment, it seems likely that he hoped both to test the waters back home and to see what conditions were found in Germany before fully determining the U.S. position; in the meantime, he supported a Treasury–War Department proposal to encourage decentralization within the area occupied by the United States.[180] When it came to reparations, he probably wanted to give the public a hint of what it could expect before any details were finalized.

Roosevelt was certainly planning to launch a more intensive publicity campaign on his return from Yalta, aided by Stettinius who already had the State Department reorganized and primed to begin the task. With the possible exception of a long-term occupation of Germany, FDR was supremely confident of his ability to garner a domestic consensus behind any of the measures that had been tentatively agreed on at the conference. Perhaps buoyed up by the success of his annual message to Congress, which Stettinius had told him had "won praise from most commentators, including some recent critics," he told Churchill and Stalin on February 5 that "he felt he could obtain support in Congress and throughout the country for any reasonable measures designed to safeguard the future peace."[181]

The long voyage home was a sad and upsetting experience for Roosevelt. Already exhausted and frail after all the arduous traveling, the testing living conditions in the Crimea, and a week of tough negotiations, FDR was deeply angered when Harry Hopkins insisted on remaining at Marrakech to recuperate from his own ailments. Worse news then followed, when the president's long-serving appointments secretary, Edwin "Pa" Watson suddenly collapsed and died.[182]

Although the loss of two close confidants deeply affected Roosevelt, he wasted little time in trying to drum up popular support for the Yalta accords. On the way home, he even held an impromptu press conference aboard ship, in which he dwelt on the destruction he had seen in the Crimea, especially the buildings the Germans had looted and then gutted.[183] Then, almost immediately after returning to Washington, the president went before Congress to explain and elaborate on the various measures agreed at the end of the conference.

Roosevelt began by emphasizing the importance of reaching a domestic consensus on the peace, for unless both legislators and the public actively supported "the general conclusions reached at Yalta" then there was little hope that the meeting would produce lasting results. Germany, he continued, was clearly the number-one problem of "vital political consequence." After calling once again for unconditional surrender, FDR for the first time began to publicly explain what this would entail for the German people. Essentially, the Allies had six major demands: first, temporary control and occupation; second, denazification and the eradication of all Hitler's "barbaric laws and institutions"; third, "the termination of all militaristic influence in the public, private, and cultural life of Germany"; fourth, punishment of war criminals; fifth, "reparations in kind for the damage which has been done to the innocent victims of its aggression; and sixth, "the complete disarmament of Germany."

When it came to these last two measures, Roosevelt was careful to issue a number of qualifications, partly to reassure the Germans that unconditional surrender would not mean slavery and destruction, but also, in the post-Quebec environment, to reassure domestic critics that nothing on the scale of the Morgenthau plan was now envisaged. Thus, he pointed out that reparations would only be in kind, "to avoid the mistake . . . after the last war, the demanding of reparations in the form of money which Germany could not pay." He also insisted that reparations would not be levied at such a level that Germany would starve or "become a burden on the rest of the world." And he implied, too, that disarmament would be restricted so as to include only the dismantling of direct munitions industry and not the wholesale destruction of industrial plant.

The president ended this passage of his speech by offering two justifications for these measures. One was simply to recount his firsthand experience of German destructiveness. "I have read about Warsaw and Lidice and Rotterdam and Coventry," he told the assembled legislators "—but I *saw* Sevastopol and Yalta! And I know that there is not room enough on earth for both German militarism and Christian decency." FDR then elaborated on this, by offering his most expansive public conception of the enemy to date. No longer content, as he had been in 1942 and 1943, just to blame it all on the Nazis and a few other elites, the president now revealed for the first time his belief that the roots of German militarism dated back to the advent of Kaiser Wilhelm II. The Allies' postwar plans, he declared, were designed to protect the German people "from a repetition of the fate which the General Staff and *Kaiserism* imposed on them before, and which Hitlerism is now imposing on them again a hundredfold. It will be removing a cancer from the German body politic which for generations has produced only misery and only pain to the whole world."[184]

In subsequent weeks, State Department officials took to the airwaves in a series of NBC broadcasts to expand on the different elements included in this speech. In a program on March 24, devoted to answering the question "What About the Enemy Countries?" Archibald MacLeish, supported by Robert Murphy and other State Department officials, addressed a whole range of issues. The first was unconditional surrender, which was defended by pointing out the impossibility of compromise with the Nazis. "Germany's choice now," insisted Murphy, "is between unconditional surrender and pulverization, and if they choose pulverization, they will only have themselves to blame for following vicious leadership." The second question was the less controversial one of punishing war criminals. Here, it was pointed out that not only top Nazis but anyone responsible for committing crimes would be subject to trial and punishment, even those Germans who had committed atrocities against other Germans. The third problem was denazification, which Murphy tackled by pointing out that both Nazis and those who adhered to "Pan-German theories" would be removed from responsible positions. Murphy was also pessimistic about the basis for a new representative government within Germany, remarking that he did not expect "the early discovery of many 'democratic' Germans." The fourth issue was thornier. "How long," MacLeish asked his colleagues in a scripted question, "do you think Germany will probably have to be occupied?" Reflecting FDR's concerns about this matter, his colleagues essentially hedged, responding that controls would have to be imposed for quite some time but that these need not entail a large military presence. On dismemberment, too, State officials were circumspect. Decentralization, Murphy argued, should certainly be encouraged, but ultimately the question would have to "be answered in accordance with what seems to us to be our best interests, and the best interests of Europe as a whole." On deindustrialization, meanwhile, the issue that MacLeish pointed out had been the subject of "the biggest storm center" and the object of most press and public criticism, these spokesmen gave Morgenthau's "alleged proposal" short shrift, but they did accept that Germany should be stripped of "all industry she might conceivably use for war purposes."[185]

In another broadcast that same month, State Department officials, while stressing that a long-term occupation was unlikely, were keen to insist that the new UN organization would be on hand to fill this gap. Vitally, it would also have sufficient "teeth" to stop any country from "running amuck," as Germany and Japan did in the 1930s. According to Joseph Grew, now undersecretary of state, the Military Staff Committee of this new organization would "devise a strategy" to tame any aggressors. In his opinion, it was most likely that "the air resources of the pooled UN would be called into play."[186]

These efforts were undoubtedly the government's most detailed and concerted public presentation of its stance to date. In certain respects, they were also far harsher than anything that had come before. After all, Germany was for the first time openly depicted as a nation where militarism was deeply rooted and where the prospect for postwar democratic government was consequently quite slim. The administration also admitted that to keep this threat under control it would be necessary not only to occupy Germany temporarily, denazify it, and destroy its army, but also to levy reparations in kind and to remove all industry that could *conceivably* be used for war; if this all failed, the UN would then be available to bomb the aggressor into submission. Yet, as with Roosevelt's campaign speech the previous October, viewed in the context of his private convictions, these measures were actually relatively mild; they were certainly a far cry from the Morgenthau plan. The president, in particular, had omitted any mention of dismemberment, an issue that was now under active discussion in London. He had also been careful to qualify all these proposals: Germany, he reiterated to the American people, would continue to enjoy a measure of economic security and it certainly would not be enslaved.

As polls and media surveys soon indicated, by retreating from the radical vision that had been ascendant at Quebec, FDR had accurately gauged what the American public would accept. Overall, the press hailed the Yalta Conference as a triumph. "Never have I seen such overwhelming praise for anything as for your achievement at Yalta," his son-in-law, John Boettiger, cabled on February 13. "It has even swept the enemies off their feet, and I mean American enemies as well as the Nazis and Japs."[187] More specifically, most commentators approved of FDR's report on Germany, believing that it struck a reasonable balance of "hard-but-just." Thus, the *Washington Post* and the Scripps-Howard press both endorsed reparations in kind as an "improvement over Versailles," while the *Baltimore Sun* and Raymond Gramm Swing were pleased that the Morgenthau plan had effectively been shelved. Even members of SPWW3 were ready to accept this package, believing that it was at least a distinct improvement over what had seemed likely nine months previously.[188] The only criticism came from a few commentators like Dorothy Thompson and David Lawrence, together with the *New Republic*, who felt the Yalta approach was too stern. But these soft-peace advocates were now in such a small minority that Roosevelt simply dismissed all their complaints out of hand; he even rejected sending Thompson a letter that would have reassured her that all the Allies' plans were quite mild.[189]

The measures the president unveiled in March were also generally acceptable to the mass public. Support for unconditional surrender certainly remained exceedingly high, with 81 percent still approving the formula.[190] In a *Fortune* poll, 86 percent now appeared to favor the principle of reparations, but like their president many had reservations, with only 22 percent believing it would be possible to force Germany to pay large sums. In addition, measures like denazification, demobilization, and temporary occupation were widely endorsed. However, on subjects such as partition and deindustrialization, where the administration had now adopted a more cautious stance, public attitudes, although hardening, had yet to crystallize.

By the spring of 1945, then, there was at last something approaching a consensus between government rhetoric and public opinion on how Germany should be treated. To reach this point, Roosevelt had had to abandon his punitive stance of the previous fall in favor of a series of measures that were seen by most Americans as not too vindictive but firm and fair. Whether in time the president would have sought to go beyond this, to seek once the war had ended an endorsement for stiffer measures like partition, perhaps even more extensive economic control, remains a matter for speculation, because in the weeks following Yalta his health started to deteriorate sharply. He had already been showing signs of physical wear and tear for almost a year, but during this period he had often had good moments and had invariably remained mentally alert. Even in the immediate aftermath of the grueling journey from the Crimea, one close aide recorded that "the president has come home in the pink of condition—

POLL (MARCH 1945)

We have listed a number of things here that might be done with Germany when we are victorious. Do you think the UN should or should not:	March 1945		January 1944	
	Should (%)	Should Not (%)	Should (%)	Should Not (%)
Abolish the Nazi Party	93.0	1.8	87.9	3.2
Completely demobilize the German army and keep them from having an army again	84.7	9.3	77.2	13.0
Govern Germany with an occupation force for several years	85.5	6.3	73.2	11.4
Break up Germany into smaller states	40.5	33.7	29.5	40.5
Prevent the Germans from rebuilding their steel, chemical and automotive industries	43.0	41.0	30.9	52.8
Make German labor rebuild devastated areas in other countries at rate paid to POWs	62.4	21.8	46.1	31.9

Source: OWI, "Current Opinions," No. 8, March 9, 1944, entry 149, box 1719, RG 44, NA.

hasn't looked better in a year. . . . His color is good and his spirits high."
But shortly thereafter, FDR's final demise began. Throughout March he
constantly complained of tiring quickly, and at the end of the month he
again went to Warm Springs to recuperate. By then, the same aide who had
written so optimistically just weeks before, now remarked that "he is slip-
ping away from us and no earthly power can keep him here."[191]

Roosevelt was therefore in a poor condition on April 11, when Henry
Morgenthau came to Warm Springs for dinner. Inevitably, the conversation turned toward Germany. Morgenthau began by saying, "Look, Mr.
president, I am going to fight hard, and this is what I am fighting for. . . .
A weak economy for Germany means that she will be weak politically, and
she won't be able to make another war. . . . I have been strong for winning
the war, and I want to help win the peace." In response Roosevelt, somewhat wearily, remarked: "Henry, I am with you 100 percent."[192] The president may have been expressing a firm conviction; more likely, given his
awareness of what the public would support, it was just an off-the-cuff re-

mark to placate and perhaps silence the vehement Morgenthau. Whatever his intention, it was FDR's last comment on the issue. The very next day he suffered a massive stroke and died.

On many issues Roosevelt left behind a somewhat vague and inchoate position. This was certainly the case with matters like partition and reparations, not to mention details such as whether reparations should take precedence over Germany's basic needs, or whether all Nazis or only "active Nazis" should be purged. More widely, he also bequeathed a series of highly ambiguous Yalta accords—as Leahy famously remarked the agreement on Poland was "so elastic that the Russians can stretch it all the way from Yalta to Washington without ever technically breaking it."[193] FDR also left a successor who was astonishingly ill informed and ill prepared, not only to deal with specific problems like Germany but also to face the broader challenges of the presidency. And, of course, this mixture of inexperience and ambiguous policy positions would exacerbate the friction and misunderstanding between the United States and U.S.S.R. that erupted shortly thereafter.

Yet for all his equivocation and secrecy, FDR had at least adopted a stance on issues like denazification, occupation, demobilization, and short-term economic control that was acceptable to most Americans. In recent weeks, he had also used his "bully pulpit" to explain these measures both to Congress and to the wider public, thereby laying the groundwork for their acceptance by the Senate whenever the peace treaty was finalized. But above all, there could be no escaping the fact that Roosevelt's decisions earlier in the war had helped to ensure that the Allies, despite all their growing disagreements, would soon be in a position to apply these measures to Germany; indeed, on the very day Roosevelt died U.S. troops were only sixty-three miles from Berlin. As a result, the fears that the president had long entertained, first about the Nazi danger, later about liberal criticisms over "Darlanism," had now become quite irrelevant. That morning's *New York Times*, in speculating on whether the Führer had been killed and replaced by Himmler, pointed this out quite succinctly. "What does it matter," it declared, "whether Hitler is alive or dead."[194] Germany's unconditional surrender was now certain.

7

Conclusion and Aftermath

Yes, the decisions of a democracy might be slowly arrived at. But when that decision is made, it is proclaimed not with the voice of one man but with the voice of one hundred and thirty million.

—FDR, March 15, 1941

On April 12, 1945, generals Dwight D. Eisenhower, Omar D. Bradley, and George S. Patton arrived at the Nazi concentration camp at Ohrdruf. This camp had been liberated more than a week earlier, when units of the Fourth Armored Division, racing through the heart of Germany in search of a secret Nazi communication center, had unexpectedly stumbled across it. Ohrdruf was not the first camp to be liberated by the Allies, nor was it an extermination camp on the same order as Auschwitz or Treblinka, designed purely for industrialized mass slaughter. But the conditions there deeply shocked and appalled the three generals. Indeed, nothing they had witnessed in two-and-a-half years of bitter fighting prepared them for the horrific sight of "more than 3,200 naked bodies" lying in "shallow graves, with lice crawling "over the yellow skin of their sharp, bony frames." Patton became physically ill at the sight, while Eisenhower found it difficult to control his anger, incredulous that "such cruelty, bestiality, and savagery could really exist in this world."

"I made this trip deliberately," Eisenhower wrote to Marshall a few days later, "in order to be in a position to give *first-hand* evidence of these things if ever, in the future, there develops a tendency to charge these allegations merely to 'propaganda.'" To make doubly certain that no one back home would question the extent of the savagery, he immediately called for twelve congressional leaders and twelve editors to come and view the camps.

The two delegations, comprising individuals from across the political spectrum, were hastily assembled. Arriving in Europe two weeks later, they were taken around three camps—Buchenwald, Nordhausen, and Dachau—and spared nothing. Not only was the apparatus of torture and execution still in place, but corpses were strewn everywhere and the remaining survivors were emaciated and barely alive. Utterly shocked, the entire delegation hastened back to the United States to awaken the wider public to the full horrors of the Nazis' New Order. Soon, newspapers and magazines were flooded with photographs of the mounds of corpses and starving survivors, all adorned with the caption "Lest We Forget." A one-hour newsreel of the camps shot by the army's signals corps was distributed to cinemas nationwide. And pressure groups like SPWW3 organized rallies for victims of German brutality, which were attended by many of the congressmen recently returned from the Reich.[1]

Americans were appalled by these concentration camp scenes. Within days, a State Department opinion survey noted that press reports of the German atrocities "have led many commentators to speak of 'the German problem' in harsher terms than heretofore. Radio commentators, in particular, have set forth the thesis that the German people must share with the Nazis responsibility for war guilt."[2] A confidential memorandum compiled for the new president found a similar trend. "During April and May," it concluded, "the attitude of the American people toward Germany and the German people has hardened in a number of important respects," with most increasingly coming to "regard the German people as well as the German Government as having been our enemy."

According to this report, one event had precipitated this sudden change.

> Responsibility for cruelties discovered in German concentration camps is . . . assigned to the German people by a large number of Americans. Although 72 percent of a national cross-section consider German officials "chiefly responsible" for these cruelties, one-quarter of the nation (23 percent) places primary blame on the German people, an additional 32 percent say that even though the German people are not chiefly to blame, they should also be held "responsible" (total, 55 percent).[3]

Conclusion: FDR, American Opinion, and Nazi Germany

Franklin Roosevelt would not have been surprised by the public's reaction to the liberation of the concentration camps. He had long been aware of the

POLL (MAY 1945)

In the war with Germany, do you feel that our chief enemy is (has been) the German people as a whole, or the Germany Government?	Feb. 1942 (%)	Jan. 1945 (%)	Mar. 1945 (%)	May 1945 (%)
1. German government	71	60	70	53
2. German people	9	12	10	8
3. People and government	14	25	17	34
4. No opinion	6	3	3	5
Total of 2 and 3	*23*	*37*	*27*	*42*

Source: Grew to Truman, "Latest Opinion Trends in the United States," June 5, 1945, folder 2, PSF 175, HSTL.

close relationship between dramatic external events and fundamental changes in the popular mood—how the fall of France had awakened many Americans to the danger of the Nazi threat, how Pearl Harbor had ended opposition to full and formal involvement in the war, how TORCH had helped to erase the phony war mindset. During 1944 and 1945, he had also periodically contemplated the publication of comprehensible and believable evidence of German atrocities in order to harden the public's attitude toward the German nation as a whole.

Of course, Roosevelt never lived to see the time when Americans started to share his conviction that the German people were to blame for the deeds of their Nazi leaders. But the fact that the decisive incident occurred on the very day he died does serve to underline the belated nature of the public's response to developments in Europe. Throughout the period covered in this study, FDR was invariably one step ahead of public opinion. In the first phase, he clearly recognized the extent of the Nazi threat by the autumn of 1938. Until the fall of France, however, most Americans refused to believe that Hitler posed a real threat to the Western Hemisphere, and even then the administration remained constantly worried that mass opinion was too complacent about the Third Reich's intentions and capabilities. In the second phase, Roosevelt was increasingly convinced that Germany's penchant for aggression and militarism was deeply rooted in the national psyche. Until the liberation of the camps, however, most Americans were content to differentiate between Nazis and Germans, blaming the former for the current conflagration but remaining confident that the latter could be reintegrated quickly back into the international fold.

Roosevelt, it is true, did not face the extent of opposition and discontent that plagued other presidents in other wars—the fear of Lincoln in August 1864 that with Union offensives stalled outside Petersburg and Atlanta he would lose the forthcoming election to a negotiated-peace candidate; the concern of Lyndon Johnson in March 1968 that the Tet Offensive had seriously eroded the public's support for the Vietnam War. In World War II, there were undoubtedly divisionists who hated communism more than nazism, "misguided" individuals who wanted the United States to focus on Asia rather than Europe, liberals who worried that the Allies might conclude a deal with elites in the Reich, and ultimately just "too many people" who held "the view that the German people as a whole are not responsible for what has taken place." But only at the extreme margins of society did anyone ever contemplate an appeasement deal with Hitler and his Nazi cohorts.

An optimist by nature, after Pearl Harbor FDR retained "an inward conviction that the people themselves are with us and that there is none of the tragic disunity that split our country in the [18]60s."[4] But this did not stop him from worrying that opposition to the war effort might suddenly mount at any moment. Incidents, after all, could work both ways, and the defeats in the Pacific in 1942, the stalemate in Italy in the winter of 1943–44, and the sharp and unexpected reverse in the Ardennes in December 1944 all starkly demonstrated how the vagaries of war might fuel the complex and confusing moods of complacency and divisionism. In the end, of course, all these setbacks turned out to be temporary and short, and over time America's battlefield fortunes improved steadily, with successive and successful offensives in North Africa, Italy, and then France. But until a strong second front was established in the summer of 1944, Roosevelt could never be sure that a really devastating defeat was not just around the corner. He therefore had to guard against the possibility that a sudden reverse might swiftly turn the public's intermittent unease, apathy, or defeatism into a more widespread and concerted attack against America's whole participation in the European war.

Roosevelt's perception of previous public opinion problems also greatly sharpened his sensitivity to each and every ebb and flow in the popular mood. The president never forgot the depth of isolationist sentiment in the years before Pearl Harbor, especially the public's dogged and stubborn opposition to a full and formal involvement in the war. Even in 1942, he worried that popular support for a large standing army might be ephemeral —hence his determination to get GIs into combat against the Germans by the end of the year. Even in 1943 and 1944, he fretted that the public would not support a long-term commitment on the European continent—hence his desire for a self-enforcing peace settlement with Germany that would enable "U.S. troops to be withdrawn within a relatively short time."

FDR was also keenly aware that when it came to fundamental reorientations in policy, a wide consensus was essential if the government's bold new course was to endure. Forging such a consensus might well be a difficult, long-term task. It might require backing away from preferred positions, waiting patiently for exactly the right moment to speak or act, periodically attempting to persuade and cajole potential supporters, and constantly having to rebut and refute persistent opponents. But Roosevelt realized that the stakes were extremely high: nothing less than America's full and enthusiastic participation in the struggle against the Axis in the first phase; the country's continued participation in enforcing the peace in the second. Woodrow Wilson's inability to get the Versailles Treaty ratified in 1919 was a stark and disturbing reminder of what waited should he fail. But the prospect of a legitimate and widely supported transformation of America's world role was the prize that waited if he succeeded.

To keep a constant eye on the popular mood, Roosevelt regularly consulted opinion polls, habitually scoured six daily newspapers as well as a variety of media surveys, often paid close attention to the White House mailbag, and eagerly read the gossipy material periodically supplied by the likes of John Carter and Morris Ernst. Of course, FDR did not treat every piece of information equally. He valued Cantril's data more highly than that of Republican-sympathizer George Gallup, while he deemed the views expressed by Walter Lippmann or the *New York Times* to be far more important than those of inveterate "Roosevelt haters" such as the McCormick, Hearst, or Patterson press. Nor did his sources for measuring opinion remain static over time. During 1943, for instance, the OWI's activities became less important, while the following year Cantril's influence waxed in the period prior to polling day. But throughout the war, the president always retained a wide array of channels for measuring what Americans thought about the main foreign-policy issues of the day.

In comparison to current standards, these mechanisms, still in their infancy in the 1940s, now appear somewhat crude. For one thing, Roosevelt received few polls based on research into the attitudes of key focus groups.[5] Although his electoral successes were based on forging a coalition of different interests—from organized labor and city dwellers, to Catholics, Jews, and African-Americans[6]—the polls he obtained were largely issue based, and thus centered on whether or not the general public favored measures like a second front or a negotiated peace, dismemberment or unconditional surrender. This was even true during the 1944 campaign, when Cantril's data tended to emphasize the issues on which the president was popular, rather than the sections of the population from which he was likely to draw support.

Unlike today, when a president facing a crisis is informed almost immediately of the public's latest response to any new development, the compilation and dissemination of polls in this period was also cumbersome and slow. As a result, polling data were only really useful for tabulating responses to the same questions over a long period of time, and then seeing if a trend had emerged—for instance, was the public now more inclined to support "Germany first" or reparations than it had been this time last month or last year?[7] It was all but worthless when it came to gauging reaction during the periodic crises and outbursts of popular opposition. For instance, during the furor over "Darlanism" and the eruption over the Morgenthau plan, Roosevelt was supplied with no up-to-the-minute polls. Instead, he had to rely principally on what could be gleaned from the press, and the views of just a few opinion makers could take on enormous significance.

Constantly concerned about the state of American opinion, FDR also made a number of efforts to educate and shape mass attitudes. His periodic speeches and fireside chats were always carefully crafted, beautifully delivered, and usually reached a huge audience. His press conferences were also well attended, even after his illness and preoccupation with security made them less and less informative. More importantly, what strikes the contemporary observer is the extent to which reporters were often prepared to accept the president's comments at face value. Indeed, for all of FDR's constant complaints that editors, columnists, and journalists were biased hacks with little influence, most were perfectly willing to echo his description of the Darlan deal as a "temporary expedient" or were easily satisfied by his claim that there was no truth in their stories on the Morgenthau plan.

Although behind closed doors the Roosevelt administration was generally an unwieldy amalgam of competing individuals, throughout the war years it was nevertheless able to present a fairly united front to the outside world. The president, it is true, rarely attempted to explicitly control the output of other executive branches and agencies—a shortcoming that has been given great prominence in the works of Allan Winkler, Michael Leigh, and Clayton Laurie.[8] But there remained a degree of tacit coordination in the government's output on Germany, especially during 1942–43 when almost all officials reiterated the simple message that nazism and not the German people were responsible for all the carnage and brutality. The OFF and OWI, for instance, both scoured FDR's speeches for clues on how to pitch their own efforts, and on occasion even used his keynote addresses as an "information blueprint."

Yet when it came to the actual content, the Roosevelt administration's publicity efforts were always highly cautious. The president might well have been consistently worried that the public was slow to recognize the extent of the danger, but he never once tried to rectify this by inciting it to paroxysms of hatred. In fact, anxious not to go out on a limb and express views that were clearly at odds with the prevailing public sentiment, he habitually refused even to name the actual aggressor until December 1940. Thereafter, the administration, worried that the public might not comprehend or believe atrocity stories, generally soft-pedaled the extent of Nazi brutality. Concerned about fueling complacency, officials were also reluctant to talk about the prospects of victory and the postwar world. And forced to respond to charges that unconditional surrender was encouraging the Germans to fight harder, they increasingly insisted that the mass of Germans would be treated with a modicum of fairness after the war.

Ultimately, then, although the Roosevelt administration fought World

War II in order to impose unconditional surrender on a particularly evil foe, the relationship between the government and public opinion was very different from that suggested by Walter Lippmann or George Kennan in their classic books on American diplomacy. Indeed, rather than initially seeking to manipulate and arouse a lethargic public by exaggerating the danger Germany represented, Roosevelt's information campaign was always highly cautious. Rather than the statesman's views remaining static while public sentiment hardened, it was FDR's image of the enemy that changed during 1943, while mass opinion, in the absence of any new cues from the administration, continued to blame the Nazis rather than the Germans. And rather than the statesman being trapped by the public hysteria his own exaggerated rhetoric had whipped up, Roosevelt's options were actually narrowed by the cautious nature of his earlier message, by the fact that he had not laid the basis for the popular acceptance of stringent measures. In short, throughout this period it was *not* a case of the statesman pursuing a restrained and unswerving line, while the public initially vacillated and eventually pushed for total victory. On the contrary, it was the statesman who became increasingly vehement in his demands for the complete destruction of the enemy, while popular attitudes remained generally undeviating and more restrained, consistently dedicated to the view that only nazism was the true enemy and that Germany should be allowed some industrial future.

The contrast with American attitudes toward Japan was particularly striking. Here, a small group of officials who concerned themselves with planning Japan's future maintained a relatively benign view of the enemy throughout the war. The president was not among their number, for he largely abstained from the whole debate about Japan's future. Apart from a few brief exchanges with the Chinese leadership at the Cairo Conference in November 1943, where he agreed that Japan should be stripped of her empire and forced to pay reparations, FDR preferred to focus on ensuring Japan's swift defeat after the culmination of the conflict in Europe, and placed far more emphasis on securing the Red Army's participation in the Pacific war at an acceptable political cost.[9] Almost by default, then, the main postwar policy studies were carried out by a small group of State Department officials, who were able to give free reign to their reintegrationist tendencies. Following the lead of Joseph Grew, in May 1944 one planning committee effectively recommended keeping the Japanese emperor after the war. Three months later, another committee drafted a memorandum on the terms and conditions for Japan's surrender. This insisted that the Allies announce their intention to destroy Japanese militarism but not the Japanese state, so as to "give encouragement to whatever democratic and moderate elements still remain in Japan."[10]

By adopting this line, State Department officials were clearly proceeding against the current of American opinion. They were also proceeding in a relatively even-headed and temperate fashion that was far removed from the expectations that the administration's own overheated rhetoric had helped to whip up. After all, officials from the president down had rarely bothered to distinguish the Japanese people from its militaristic leadership; some had even implied that the United States was fighting a race war against the "yellow peril." Small wonder, then, that by 1944 there was little support for a soft peace for Japan. In one poll published at the end of the year, 13 percent of respondents even suggested that every member of this race should be exterminated.[11] Thus a chasm also emerged between the government and the public over Japan. But whereas on the German problem it was the president who preferred sterner measures and was ultimately reigned in by a more prudent public, on Japan it was the State Department that held the more benign view, while most Americans, fed on a diet of anti-Japanese propaganda, increasingly demanded a punitive peace.

What impact did all this have on actual outcomes? At the most fundamental level, public opinion exerted little influence on FDR's basic image of the German enemy. Admittedly, in the last months of 1941, the public's overwhelming opposition to the deployment of an AEF did encourage FDR to emphasize the optimistic strand of his thinking, at a time when such confidence was increasingly at odds with actual events. Similarly, in 1943 the lingering liberal criticism over "Darlanism" also reinforced his growing tendency to dread rather than hope for an internal implosion. But in both cases public opinion was by no means the decisive factor underpinning the president's beliefs. Far more important were other developments—in the early period, the clear examples of Nazi perfidy and aggression, as well as FDR's conviction about the internal fragility of dictatorships; and in the later years, the dynamics of alliance politics, a whole raft of new evidence, and the transformation of the German problem itself. For the most part, then, Roosevelt was *not* a situational politician in the sense that his belief system fluctuated in line with the public mood; he was *not* merely an unprincipled opportunist—a "chameleon on plaid"—who would do whatever was popular.[12] Rather, he had some general beliefs about the enemy, and although these started to shift in 1943 (as the international environment and nature of the problem changed), these assumptions nevertheless played an important role in determining what policies he preferred, from "Germany first" to the effectiveness of bombing and psychological warfare, from pastoralization to dismemberment and truncation.

Regarding the actual policy choices adopted, there were certain conditions and circumstances when public opinion also had a minimal impact. Whenever mass sentiment appeared ambivalent or far from fervent, FDR certainly felt freer to follow his own personal proclivities, as was the case with the Germany-first strategy in 1942. Nor did FDR have any qualms about ignoring the vehement opposition that frequently came from diehard divisionists and "Roosevelt-haters." In 1942, for instance, he dismissed the importance of negotiated-peace sentiment with the disdainful comment that such attitudes were only held by those who wanted to win the war if Britain, the U.S.S.R., and himself were also defeated. Two years later, he likewise simply ignored the criticisms of extreme groups, such as Peace Now, which were calling for the complete abandonment of unconditional surrender and the conclusion of an armistice with the Third Reich. However, outbursts and eruptions from Roosevelt's political supporters were a very different matter, as FDR's acute sensitivity to the liberal charges of "Darlanism" clearly demonstrates. The president also recognized that he could not pursue a particular course in the face of deep-seated and overwhelming popular opposition from across the political spectrum—especially when it was a highly salient issue, such as planning Germany's defeat and then its future. Until Pearl Harbor, he therefore excluded the possibility of America's full and formal involvement in the war on the grounds that this was just not acceptable to a majority of the public. Three years later, he quickly backed away from pastoralization when faced with the popular outcry over the Morgenthau plan leak.

At the third and final level, the timing and implementation of particular policies, public opinion played a particularly important role, but not always in the way that other historians suggest. It is commonplace in the literature to depict the domestic environment as having a negative, deadening effect on policy, restraining the president and preventing him from undertaking a preferred course of action. Although in many respects this was clearly true during the war years, for FDR was a master at biding his time, waiting for popular opposition to die down before he forged ahead with his desired policy, Roosevelt was also an extremely creative leader. Recognizing that action spoke louder than words, he sometimes sought to expedite certain measures in an attempt to shift popular opinion.[13] In 1942, he pushed to get U.S. troops fighting Germans as soon as possible, partly in the hope that this would eradicate defeatism, place support for "Germany first" on a sounder footing, and fire the public's imagination about the war. Then, in January 1943, one of his reasons for making the dramatic flight to Casablanca was to highlight the shrinking of the globe and the fact that the United States could not ignore the outside world in an age of air power. And once in Africa, he enunciated unconditional surrender, principally because he believed this would defuse the ongoing debate over "Darlanism." In all these cases, it is important to note, FDR was not cynically looking for *any* policy that would distract the public from embarrassing revelations or bolster support for himself and his policies. Rather, he already favored an immediate offensive in Northwest Africa, since this would relieve pressure on the Soviets, while his support for unconditional surrender flowed naturally from his conviction that it would be futile to compromise with the mendacious Nazis. In these instances, then, the actual policy choice was *not* made out of a desire to distract public opinion, but Roosevelt's decision to hasten its implementation clearly was.

Aftermath: The Immediate
Postwar Legacy, 1945–48

In the weeks after FDR's death, the war in Europe came to a swift conclusion. On April 25, American and Soviet troops triumphantly met at Torgau on the river Elbe; five days later, Hitler was also dead, having committed suicide in a bunker beneath the rubble of Berlin. The remnants of the Third Reich struggled on for another week, but finally, on May 7 and 8, the fighting came to an end after German representatives signed the documents of unconditional surrender at two ceremonies in Rheims and Berlin.

At long last, the United States could concentrate all its attention on Japan. Even with the bulk of their resources directed against the Wehrmacht, the army and navy had already made great strides in the Pacific war. During Roosevelt's last weeks, large-scale bombing raids had incinerated vast swathes of Tokyo, MacArthur had recaptured the Philippines, fulfilling his pledge to return, and the marines had landed on Okinawa, sparking a fierce battle to capture an island just 350 miles southwest of Japan. Clearly, the Japanese empire was tottering, but would it be possible to end the war without an invasion of the Japanese home islands? As officials under the new president contemplated this question, the legacy of FDR's publicity efforts cast an important shadow over their deliberations.

By July, Stimson and Grew were convinced that Japan's early capitulation could be achieved by giving the Japanese people "the impression that unconditional surrender may not be as bad a matter as they had first believed." In Stimson's opinion, the Allies should reiterate the familiar old formula that Japan would not be enslaved or destroyed. More controversially, the secretary of war also advocated issuing a public pledge that Japan could retain its emperor as a constitutional monarch.[14]

To a certain extent, Stimson's suggestions were reminiscent of the pressure Roosevelt had faced a year before. Then, as now, the prospect of a costly invasion was prodding presidential advisers to recommend elaborating on unconditional surrender in such a way as to weaken the enemy's will to resist. The main difference was that Stimson was now urging that the United States go one stage further. By promising the Japanese that they could keep their emperor, he was proposing to amend unconditional surrender in a way that might raise all the old charges of "Darlanism." He was also flying in the face of recent polling data, which indicated that a clear majority of Americans wanted a harsh peace in the Pacific, with most favoring the "harsh" treatment of the emperor.[15]

This, at least, was the conclusion reached by James F. Byrnes, the new secretary of state and a "born politician," acutely alert to fluctuations in the popular mood. It was a view shared by Archibald MacLeish, now an assistant secretary of state, but also the liberal former director of the OFF, as well as Cordell Hull, now in retirement, but called on for advice and still smarting at all the attacks he had suffered in 1942 and 1943. Truman was quick to listen to their warnings. Having no desire to arouse the ire of the American public, he issued the Potsdam Declaration on July 26, which proclaimed the need for unconditional surrender and reassured the Japanese they would not be enslaved, but studiously avoided any mention of retaining the emperor. Less than a month later, when the Japanese sued for peace after the atomic explosions at Hiroshima and Nagasaki, the American response again skillfully skirted the question.[16] "Only after Japan had capitulated," John Dower points out, "did the maintenance of the emperor become feasible." In the fury of war, "such moderate ideas were politically unpalatable."[17] Roosevelt's public utterances had helped see to that.

Throughout 1945, moderate occupation policies in Germany were politically unpalatable, too, largely because the memories of the concentration camp horrors continued to weigh heavily on the American mind. In May, the State Department's Office of Public Affairs found that opinion makers now thought the task of occupation was being "made more difficult by the German people, who, according to most commentators, remain 'unrepentant' and unconvinced of their 'guilt' even in defeat."[18] Among the mass public, meanwhile, more than 60 percent felt that Germany was "just waiting for a chance to try it again," while other polls revealed a sharp increase in support for harsh measures. Popular approval of reparations, for instance, shot up from 57 to 74 percent between February and May 1945, while only 52 percent were now willing to continue rationing in order to enable the German people to buy enough food to maintain health—a contrast with the 70 percent who took this position even after D-Day.[19]

Throughout the summer and fall, the media then picked up on signs of an ominous laxity in American occupation policies. In August, a report by Earl G. Harrison, a former U.S. commissioner of immigration, uncovered the disturbing fact that large numbers of displaced persons, including many Jews, were still in concentration camps and asked "whether the German people, seeing this, are not supposing that we are following or at least condoning Nazi policy."[20] A short while later, the *New York Times* ran a story emphasizing the army's "lackadaisical attitude" toward denazification, a claim that appeared more than justified when General Patton, now in charge of the occupation in Bavaria, publicly suggested that 98 percent of Nazis were not true believers—"just camp followers who had come in because they had been coerced." "This Nazi thing," he continued in an even more provocative vein, "is just like a Democratic and Republican election fight. The thing was that these damned Nazis got other people by the scruff of the neck and other Germans just didn't have the guts to go back."[21]

The sense of outrage by a press and public less willing than Patton to blame only a select few for the concentration camp atrocities was palpable. Among journalists, the State Department's Office of Public Affairs recorded at the start of October, there was mounting "dismay at the continued employment of Nazis in responsible positions in the government

POLL (OCTOBER–NOVEMBER 1945)

In general, would you say that the Allied program for the treatment of Germany is too hard, about right, or not hard enough?	Oct. 5, 1945 (%)	Oct. 19, 1945 (%)	Nov. 19, 1945 (%)
Too hard	1	2	2
About right	43	40	37
Not hard enough	49	52	50
No opinion	7	6	11

Sources: State Department, "Fortnightly Survey of American Opinion on International Affairs," Survey Nos. 36, 37, and 39, October 5, October 19, and November 19, 1945, entry 568L, box 11, RG 59, NA.

and business." More broadly, a series of polls conducted during the fall found the American public concerned that the Germans were being treated too leniently.

The usual cast of liberals, though not surprised by these reports, quickly grasped the opportunity to push even harder for a harsh peace. The likes of Harley Kilgore and *PM* magazine, for instance, grumbled at length about the Allies apparent reluctance to dismantle IG Farben, while in October Henry Morgenthau published his polemic, *Germany Is Our Problem*, which made a sustained and vehement plea for Germany to be rapidly and irrevocably pastoralized.[22]

In this vengeful atmosphere, the Truman administration went out of its way to reassure the public that the Germans were receiving suitably stern treatment. At the Potsdam Conference in July, the new administration privately backed away from harsh measures such as partition and extensive deindustrialization, and would only accept a reparations agreement that was a far cry from what had been on the agenda back at Yalta—to the obvious disappointment of the Soviets.[23] In public, however, Truman was anxious to accentuate the punitive aspects of the Potsdam Protocol. "The German people," he insisted on his return, are only "beginning to atone for the crimes of the gangsters whom they placed in power and whom they wholeheartedly approved and obediently followed." To make sure they did not reoffend, he continued, the Allied reparations scheme would "take out of Germany everything with which she can prepare for another war." The remaining German industry would then "be centralized in order to do away with concentration of economic power in cartels and monopolies. Chief emphasis is to be on agriculture and peaceful industry."[24]

In October, the administration also decided to publicize the harsh directive that formed the basis of American occupation policies. Originally drafted in the fall of 1944, when the Treasury's influence was at its height, this was replete with phrases such as "Germany will not be occupied for the purpose of liberation but as a defeated enemy nation" or that the occupiers must take no steps "designed to maintain or strengthen the Germany economy." Morgenthau was quick to praise Truman for this decision, pointing out that it would "give the American public the opportunity to back you up in seeing that the Potsdam agreement is carried out."[25]

The public certainly seemed in the mood to endorse stern measures. Whereas in 1944 the media had lambasted anything that smacked of deindustrialization, now, in the aftermath of the concentration camp revelations, the reaction was very different. As the State Department recorded in the wake of Truman's Potsdam speech, "greatest attention has been given to the Germany settlement which had been approved as a 'harsh' and 'realistic' program for preventing future German aggression and which has been characterized as similar to the Morgenthau plan."[26]

Yet the new president was never really a true believer in the need for a harsh peace. Truman had always opposed the Treasury's pastoralization policy, believing that Germany would require "some industry" after the war. Privately, he also considered Morgenthau to be a "blockhead, nut," and in June and July 1945 he first moved to exclude the Treasury from internal policy debates on Germany, before accepting Morgenthau's resignation on the eve of the Potsdam Conference.[27]

The following year, Truman and his advisers then began to reassess the whole thrust of America's German policy. The reasons for this were manifold. For one thing, conditions within Germany were so bad that in order to prevent disease and starvation the Americans were having to import large amounts of food and material into their zone, at a cost to U.S. taxpayers of roughly $200 million a year. Increasingly, there was also a growing fear that communism might thrive amidst the economic chaos of zones occupied by the western powers. Even during the war, relations between the United States and U.S.S.R. had often been strained. But now, with the Nazi threat gone, the adhesive that bound the two powers together quickly evaporated. Worse still, Stalin suddenly seemed bent on expanding his influence, for he was obviously consolidating Soviet control over eastern Europe, clearly probing in Iran, and apparently sponsoring communist activity in Italy, France, and Greece. Moreover, with memories still fresh of how political extremism had flourished amidst economic chaos in the 1930s, it seemed all too possible that the suffering peoples of Germany and Western Europe might in their desperation turn toward communism. This, at least, was the view of a growing number of officials in the Truman administration. It was also the considered opinion of the British ally, who, more vulnerable to the economic pressures of occupation and also more sensitive at this stage to the looming Soviet threat, worked hard to provoke a reassessment of American policy so that it focused on the containment of Soviet, rather than German, power.[28]

As American priorities started to shift, so did government rhetoric. Whereas in 1945 Truman was at pains to stress that "absolute insurance against German or Japanese aggression—ever again—comes first," two years later the president and his spokesmen were emphasizing that "the restoration of Europe involves the restoration of Germany."[29] Significantly, in seeking to justify this fundamental policy change, Truman and his aides were greatly helped by their predecessors' publicity efforts. For the Roosevelt administration had developed two broad images of the enemy, both of which could be used in the very different circumstances of 1946–47.

On the one hand, FDR's wartime focus on the ideological nature of the Nazi danger now provided his successor with a series of ready-made themes that could easily be transferred and deployed against the new threat. It certainly did not take too much imagination to start pointing out that the Soviet regime was also brutal and totalitarian, that it trampled in the rights of its own people and used concentration camps to inspire terror. Nor was it much of a leap to begin exploring the parallels between the intentions and capabilities of the two—how both seemed bent on controlling Europe, how the loss of this continent would pose a "threat to the very existence of the U.S.," and how the Communists like the Nazis employed fifth-column agents to spread their pernicious ideology. "There isn't any difference in totalitarian states," Truman revealingly told reporters in May 1947. "I don't care what you call them, Nazi, Communist, or Fascist."[30]

Of course, during the war Roosevelt's focus on the ideological nature of the Nazi danger had ultimately worked to his detriment, for his failure to educate the public about his hardening attitudes toward the German nation had left many Americans unprepared to support radical measures like deindustrialization. By 1946 and 1947, however, this "failure" suddenly proved a boon to his successors as they began to contemplate using German industry to balance against the new Soviet threat, for they could draw upon the familiar old phrases that FDR had himself used throughout the war years. Shedding the harsh rhetoric uttered in the immediate aftermath of the liberation of the camps, Truman and his advisers therefore began to point out that "Hitler and his minions" were the only real villains. Care had to be taken to ensure that Germany was thoroughly purged of the Nazi incubus and that safeguards were in place to prevent future rogue leaders from running amok. But once this had been achieved, there was no real reason why Germany could not be revived and rehabilitated. This was the thrust of Byrne's famous speech in Stuttgart in September 1946. "The American people have no desire to enslave the German people," he declared in a phrase reminiscent of FDR's words back in 1943 and 1944. Although the Germans would have to endure short-term hardships brought on by Hitler's deeds, the United States had "no desire to increase those hardships or to deny the German people an opportunity to work their way out of those hardships so long as they respect freedom and follow the paths of peace."[31]

The following year, officials made similar claims when arguing the case for the Marshall Plan. Due consideration was still given to the need to reassure the public that Germany must be adequately monitored, including supranational controls over the Ruhr to ensure the revival of the German economy but not the German threat.[32] But spokesmen for the Marshall plan also contended that Germany could be easily reintegrated into a broader European system, not least because the German people—far from being inherently militaristic or authoritarian—were actually no different from their counterparts across the continent. As Dean Acheson succinctly put it on one radio show: "The sixteen countries we are talking about, *with western Germany*, which we call western Europe for short, are the homes of 270 million people—industrialists, industrious, industrialized highly skilled people."[33]

There was naturally some public opposition to the expression of such benign sentiments, especially among liberals connected with the SPWW3 and former-FDR advisers such as Henry Wallace.[34] Yet increasingly, these voices were pushed to the fringes of the public debate. This was partly because America's hatred of Germany soon paled next to its growing fears about the Communist menace, and this quickly ensured that anyone associated with punitive plans for keeping Germany weak was viewed suspiciously as a pro-Soviet dupe—either a naïve idealist or a communist stooge, whose aim was to create a vacuum in Europe into which the Red Army could march. But it was also due to the fact that, in the absence of a sustained anti-German information campaign, the public's hatred of the Germans soon proved to be ephemeral.

During 1946, many Americans retained a lingering suspicion of the old enemy, which clearly stemmed from the atrocity revelations of a year before. Naturally, there was also widespread support for the twelve death sentences meted out to the Nazi leaders at the Nuremberg trials in October. Yet even in 1946, pollsters who scratched below the surface quickly found reasons to conclude that the American image of Germany was not entirely negative. According to one poll, for instance, a clear majority of the public believed that only a "small part" of the German people was "cruel and brutal." Similarly, GIs who had experienced Europe firsthand revealed that they were more favorably impressed by the German enemy than they were by the French ally; the Germans scored particularly high when it came to virtues such as "cleanliness" or "industry and enterprise."[35] By the start of 1947, as passions began to cool still further, American attitudes became even more benign. According to one poll, 45 percent of Americans felt friendly toward the German people, compared with only 28 percent who felt unfriendly, while another survey revealed that no less than 72 percent of Americans now wanted the United States to help get German peacetime industry going again.[36]

Such attitudes did not force Truman and his advisers into a full-scale policy reassessment. Far from it. As officials set about devising the Marshall plan, which they hoped would revive the European economies, including that of western Germany, their thoughts were focused principally on the chaotic conditions in Europe, the prospect that Communists might capitalize on this, and a growing awareness that it was vital to harness the industry of western Germany to the task of European reconstruction. But officials did believe that the problem of reconstruction could "be met only if the American people are taken into the complete confidence of the administration." They also recognized that they faced a difficult legislative battle to obtain an aid package worth approximately $5 billion from a budget-minded, Republican-dominated Congress. In this context, it clearly helped that the mass of Americans had few qualms about reviving Germany, a country that, with the Nazis removed, they now had little to squabble with.[37]

The Europe that soon emerged after the war was therefore very different from the one that Franklin Roosevelt had worked hard to achieve, for he had come to loathe the Germans and had hoped to continue cooperating with the Soviets. But FDR's cautious crusade had nevertheless played a role—albeit small and inadvertent—in helping to ensure that the American people now supported their government's attempts to deal with this new and uncertain world. Indeed, the images and arguments Roosevelt had used to depict the Nazi menace proved extremely useful to Truman and his aides as they sought to rally the public to meet the new Communist danger. Equally, FDR's failure to whip up anti-German hatred ultimately (if unwittingly) helped to ensure that his successor had greater domestic flexibility to turn yesterday's enemy into today's friend.

So within just two years of his death, the international environment was a far cry from what Roosevelt had envisaged. But at least America was playing its part. Isolationism, the "misguided" creed FDR had long battled against, was finally dead.

NOTES

Abbreviations in Notes

AV/NA	Audio–Visual Division, National Archives
CC	Churchill College, Cambridge
C-R Correspondence	*Churchill and Roosevelt: The Complete Correspondence*
DSB	*Department of State Bulletin*
FDRFA, 1st series	*Franklin D. Roosevelt and Foreign Affairs, 1933–1937*
FDRFA, 2nd series	*Franklin D. Roosevelt and Foreign Affairs, 1937–1939*
FDRL	Franklin D. Roosevelt Library, Hyde Park, New York
FDRPC	Franklin D. Roosevelt's Press Conferences
FDRPL	*FDR: His Personal Letters, 1928–1945*
FO	Foreign Office Files, Public Record Office
FRUS	*Foreign Relations of the United States*
HSTL	Harry S. Truman Library, Independence, Missouri
MR	White House Map Room Files
NA	National Archives, College Park, Maryland
OF	Official File
OFF	Office of Facts and Figures
OGR	Office of Government Reports
OH	Oral History Transcript
OWI	Office of War Information
PPF	President's Personal File
PRO	Public Record Office, Kew Gardens, London
PSF	President's Secretary's Files
RG	Record Group, National Archives
RH	Rhodes House Library, Oxford
RSD/LC	Recorded Sound Division, LC
SoIM	Survey of Intelligence Materials
WHCF	White House Central File

Introduction

1. "President Pleads for Support, Cites Hitler, 'Ethnic Cleansing,'" *Washington Post*, March 24, 1999; "Clinton Address to the Nation on NATO Airstrikes," March 24, 1999, *NATO Security Digests*, No. 57.
2. Polenberg, *War and* Society, pp. 38, 134; Blum, *V Was for Victory*, pp. 7–8; idem, "United Against, p. 5, 8; Terkel, *"The Good War,"* p. 13. See also Perrett, *Days of Sadness, Years of Triumph*, p. 215.

3. Leff, "The Politics of Sacrifice," p. 1296; Reynolds, *Rich Relations*, p. 44.

4. Some of these points have been developed before. See Steele, *The First Offensive*, pp. 81–89; idem, "American Popular Opinion and the War Against Germany, pp. 706–11; Dallek, *Roosevelt and American Foreign Policy*, pp.331–33, p. 358; Levering, *The Public and American Foreign Policy*, pp. 79–80; Thorne, *The Issue of War*, p. 122.

5. On the ignorance of public opinion, see Almond, *The American People and Foreign Policy*, esp. pp. 6–7, 54–65, 69, 81, 231–35; Markel, ed., *Public Opinion and Foreign Policy*, esp. pp. 45, 51, 213–15. On the malleability of public opinion, see Cohen, *The Public's Impact on Foreign Policy*, p. 62; Hildebrand, *Power and the People*, pp.6, 202–4; Hughes, *The Domestic Context of American Foreign Policy*, pp.107, 224; Margolis and Mauser, ed., *Manipulating Public Opinion*, pp.1–5; Zaller, *The Nature and Origins of Mass Opinion*, p. 311.

6. Owen, "How Liberalism Produces Democratic Peace," pp. 128–30. For an outline of the debate see Small, *Democracy and Diplomacy*, pp. xii–xiii; Nincic, *Democracy and Foreign Policy*.

7. Lippmann, *Essays in the Public Philosophy*, pp. 22–27; idem, *Public Opinion and Foreign Policy in the United State*, pp. 15, 27–29. See also, Ceadel, *Thinking about Peace and War*, pp. 56–57, 62–67; Holsti, "Public Opinion and Foreign Policy," pp. 444–45; Howard, *War and the Liberal Conscience*, pp. 81–83; Levy, "Domestic Politics and War," p. 85; Small, *Democracy and Diplomacy*, pp. xii–xiii; Nincic, *Democracy and Foreign Policy*, pp. 1–11.

8. On this point, see Wright, *A Study of War*, p. 265; Levy, "Domestic Politics and War," p. 86; Holsti, *Public Opinion and American Foreign Policy*, pp. 4–5.

9. Kennan, *American Diplomacy*, p. 59.

10. Blum, *V was for Victory*, p. 52; Baldwin, *Great Mistakes of the War*, p. 14.

11. Those works that contend that American public opinion hated Germany by the war's end include, Blum, "United Against," p. 8; Snell, *Wartime Origins of the East–West Dilemma Over Germany*, pp. 12–13; idem, "What to Do with Germany?" p. 38; Eisenberg, *Drawing the Line*, p. 45.

12. Overy, *Why the Allies Won*, p. 295. See also Stoessinger, *Crusaders and Pragmatists*, pp. 5–6, 45–46.

13. Page and Shapiro, "Educating and Manipulating the Public," pp. 307–8.

14. Winkler, *The Politics of Propaganda*, pp.38–51; Leigh, *Mobilizing Consent*, pp. 53–55, 93. For an account of the bureaucratic struggles surrounding America's foreign propaganda efforts, see Laurie, *The Propaganda Warriors*.

15. Schlesinger, *The Coming of the New Deal*, pp. 527–28; George, *Presidential Decisionmaking*, pp. 149–50.

16. Watt, *How War Came*, p. 258.

17. Almond, *American People*, pp. 138–39; Rosenau, *Public Opinion and Foreign Policy*, pp. 35–39.

18. Small, "Public Opinion," p. 175.

19. Cohen, *Public's Impact*, p. 11; Leigh, *Mobilizing Consent*, p. xv; Powlick, "The Sources of Public Opinion for American Foreign Policy Officials," pp. 428–30.

20. Foyle, "The Influence of Public Opinion on American Foreign Policy Decision-Making," pp. 68–9; idem, *Counting the Public In*, pp. 9–14; Powlick, "The Attitudinal Bases for Responsiveness to Public Opinion among American Foreign Policy Officials," pp. 634–35.

21. Zaller, "Strategic Politicians, Public Opinion and the Gulf Crisis," pp. 250–51.

22. Graham, "Public Opinion and U.S. Foreign Policy Decision Making," pp. 195–97.

23. Although Foyle, Graham, and Holsti all emphasize this point, my analysis in this section has a somewhat different emphasis. See, Foyle, "The Influence of Public Opinion," pp. 43–44; Graham, "Public Opinion," p. 197; Holsti, *Public Opinion*, pp. 197–98.

24. Mencken cited in Leuchtenberg, *The FDR Years*, p. 2; Burns, *Roosevelt*, p. 262; idem, *Soldier of Freedom*, pp. 133, 152, 607. See also Gaddis, *We Now Know*, p. 21.

25. On the structure of belief systems see, Holsti, "The Belief System and National Images," p. 246; idem, "Cognitive Dynamics and Images of the Enemy," p. 19. The emphasis here, of course, is on beliefs that have changed because of new information about public opinion.

26. Marks, *Wind Over Sand*, esp. pp. 166–67, 266–61, 279–80; Dallek, *Roosevelt and Foreign Policy*, esp. pp. 12, 529; Craig, "The Political Leader as Strategist," pp. 504–8. Graham, "Public Opinion," p. 198 argues that FDR was one of the presidents most sensitive to public opinion.

27. Graham, "Public Opinion," p. 201. Emphasis added.

28. George, "The Causal Nexus between Cognitive Beliefs and Decision–Making Behaviour," pp. 113–19.

29. Holsti, *Public Opinion*, p. 58; Small, *Nixon, Johnson, and the Doves*, p. 4.

30. Cited in Dower, *War without Mercy*, p. 138.

31. George, "Causal Nexus," pp. 105–13.

32. Ibid., p. 109.

33. See, for example, Gellman, *Secret Affairs*; Kolko, *The Politics of War*, pp. 348–50; Lowenthal, "Roosevelt and the Coming of War," p. 413; Utley, *Going to War With Japan*.

34. Edmonds, *The Big Three*; Feis, *Churchill, Roosevelt, Stalin*; Weiss, *Allies in Conflict*.

Chapter 1

1. FDR, *Public Papers*, 1:11–16.

2. *FDRFA*, 1st series, 3:37.

3. Neustadt, *Presidential Power and the Modern Presidents*, p. 136; Hofstadter, *The American Political Tradition and the Men Who Made It*, p. 311.

4. *FDRFA*, 1st series, 2:186–87, 12; *FDRPL*, 1:379–80.

5. Ibid., 2nd series, 8:1565

6. Ibid., 1st series, 3:102–3.

7. FDR qualified this statement with, "eventually, of course, they will have to pay for it." Ibid., 1st series, 3:251. In 1938 Roosevelt again remarked that Germany had solved the problem of unemployment; "not that he wanted to follow in Germany's footsteps," he went on "but that the unemployment problem was the problem which was facing America and frankly he didn't know what the answer was." See Henry Morgenthau, Jr. presidential diary, January 16, 1938, FDRL.

8. For FDR's concerns about the implications of rearmament, see *FDRPL*, 1: 463, 555, 680–81; *FRUS, 1933*, 1:210

9. *FDRFA*, 1st series, 1:485; 2:451. *FDRPL*, 1:370.

10. *The Secret Diary of Harold Ickes*, 2:213, 275. See also Blum, *From the Morgenthau Diaries*, 1:501.

11. *FDRFA*, 1st series, 1:51; Ninkovitch, *The Wilsonian Century*, p. 108.

12. FDR to Early, October 19, 1939, PSF (Subject): Executive Office of the President: Early, FDRL; *FDRPL*, 1:379–80; 2:949. Offner, "Misperception and Reality," p. 611.

13. *FDRPL*, 1:715. That FDR was more willing to accept reports that emphasized that all was not well below the surface, see *FDRFA*, 2nd series, 7:1151.

14. Dodd and Dodd, ed., *Ambassador Dodd's Diary*, p. 447; Martha Dodd, *Through Embassy Eyes*, p. 12.

15. *FDRFA*, 1st series, 1:425; 3:122–23. *FDRFA*, 2nd series, 3:433; *Ickes Diary*, 1:494.

16. *FDRFA*, 2nd series, 3:585. See, for instance, Adolf A. Berle diary, March 26, 1937 and October 13, 1937, Adolf A. Berle Papers, FDRL (and, interestingly, edited out of the published version, Berle and Jacobs, ed., *Navigating the Rapids*). See also, *FDRFA*, 2nd series, 1:29a; 9:1771a, 1781; MacDonald, *The United States*, pp. 14–15.

17. *FDRFA*, 1st series, 3:102–3; 2:501. *FDRPL*, 1:543. *FDRFA*, 2nd series, 1:86.

18. Schlesinger, *Coming of the New Deal*, pp. 9–11; Leuchtenberg, *Franklin D. Roosevelt and the New Deal*, pp. 45, 246–47.

19. FDR to Berle, June 26, 1941, PSF (Departmental): State, FDRL. See also *FDRPL*, 1:555, 680–81.

20. *FDRFA*, 1st series, 3:102–3, 251.

21. *FDRPL*, 2:876. In other words, FDR was anticipating the "structuralist" interpretation of Nazi diplomacy, see Kershaw, *The Nazi Dictatorship*.

22. *Ickes Diary*, 2:315. See also, *FDRFA*, 2nd series, 1:11; Berle diary, August 30, 1939.

23. Barnes and Barnes, *Hitler's Mein Kampf in Britain and America*, p. 49.

24. *Ickes Diary*, 2:291. See also, *FDRFA*, 1st series, 3:251.

25. On public appeals, see *FDRPL*, 1:625–26; Berle diary, April 11, 1939, April 19, 1939; *Ickes Diary*, 2:619; FDR, *Public Papers*, 8:213. On a blockade, see Offner, *American Appeasement*, p. 105; *FDRPL*, 1:472–73. See also FDR, *Public Papers*, 6:409; *FDRFA*, 2nd series, 1:206; *Ickes Diary*, 2:474; Henry A. Wallace to FDR, September 11, 1939, PSF (Departmental): Commerce: Wallace, FDRL. For an early development of this notion, see *FRUS, 1934*, 1:70.

26. *FDRFA*, 2nd series, 5:904; 7:898. Dallek, *Roosevelt and Foreign Policy*, pp. 124, 138–39.

27. Ronald I. Lindsay to Lord Halifax, September 20, 1938, copy in PSF (Diplomatic): Britain, FDRL; Berle diary, September 30, 1938; *FDRFA*, 2nd series, 7:1341; MacDonald, "Deterrent Diplomacy," pp. 300–1;

28. William C. Bullitt to FDR, March 12, 1939, PSF (Diplomatic): Bullitt, FDRL; *Ickes Diary*, 2:609, 568; *FDRFA*, 2nd series, 8:1565.

29. Murray, *At Close Quarters*, p. 95; Berle diary, March 16, 1939; Langer and Gleason, *Challenge to Isolation*, p. 76; Farnham, *Roosevelt and Munich*, pp. 114–15, 146, 164–65.

30. *Ickes Diary*, 2:483, 707.

31. *FDRFA*, 2nd series, 10:1860, 401–2, 437–38, 8:1565.

32. *Ickes Diary*, 2:568, 353; *FDRFA*, 2nd series, 7:1413a; 8:1482. See also Dallek, *Roosevelt Foreign Policy*, p. 175; Farnham, *Roosevelt and Munich*, p. 159; Reynolds, *Creation*, pp. 40–41.

33. FDR to Frank Knox, December 29, 1939, PSF (Departmental): Navy: Knox, FDRL; Farnham, *Roosevelt and Munich*, p. 120.

34. *Ickes Diary*, 2:474; Sherwood, *Roosevelt and Hopkins*, pp. 100–1; *Morgenthau Diaries*, 2:47–50; *FDRFA*, 2nd series, 8:1453. See also, ibid., 9: 1826; 10:1919. Sherry, *The Rise of American Air Power*, pp. 176–86.

35. *Ickes Diary*, 2:469, 474, and 3:37, 9.

36. Reynolds, "1940: The Fulcrum of the Twentieth Century?" pp. 325–50; Zahniser, "Rethinking the Significance of Disaster," pp. 252–76.

37. *Ickes Diary*, 3:210. See also Bullitt to FDR, May 16, 1940 and May 31, 1940, PSF (Safe): Bullitt, FDRL; *FRUS, 1940*, 2:452.

38. FDR to cabinet officers, September 27, 1940, OF 87, FDRL. See also, Harold Stark to FDR, June 2, 1940, attached to FDR to Sumner Welles, June 3, 1940, PSF (Departmental): State: Welles, FDRL; Knox to FDR, January 27, 1941, PSF (Departmental): Navy, FDRL; Dallek, *Roosevelt and Foreign Policy*, p. 233.

39. Bland, ed., *The Papers of Marshall*, 1:178–80; Henry L. Stimson diary, August 12–13, 1941, microfilm copy, RH; Reynolds, *Creation*, p. 41. Waldo Heinrichs refers to the "Aura of German Power" in Washington in March 1941. Heinrichs, *Threshold of War*, pp. 13–31.

40. Berle diary, May 26, 1941.

41. At the end of April 1940, Britain's impending disaster in Norway prompted FDR to remark that "if things kept going the way they were going, the English were going to get licked"; see Morgenthau presidential diary, April 29, 1940. Both in the summer of 1940 and the spring of 1941 there were again signs that FDR's confidence was waning, see Reynolds, *Creation*, pp. 108–20, 197; Heinrichs, *Threshold of War*, pp. 81–82; *C-R Correspondence*, R-38x, 1:178–80.

42. FDR to William D. Leahy, June 26, 1941, PSF (Diplomatic): France, FDRL; Kimball, *Juggler*, pp. 21–41; Heinrichs, *Threshold of War*, p. 102.

43. Berle diary, September 22, 1939. Similar expressions can be found in *FDRFA*, 2nd series, 1:207; Berle diary, March 16, 1939.

44. See, for example, Cordell Hull to FDR, March 5, 1941, PSF (Safe): Germany, FDRL; John Franklin Carter to FDR, March 6, 1941, March 31, 1941, PSF (Subject): Carter, FDRL.

45. *C-R Correspondence*, R-21x, 1:129. For a similar conclusion, see Harry E. Carlson to Leland Morris, April 22, 1941, PSF (Confidential): Dispatches: Austria, FDRL.

46. See, for example, Carter to FDR, June 25, 1941, PSF (Subject): Carter, FDRL; Hull to FDR, August 7, 1941, PSF (Safe): Atlantic Charter (2), FDRL; Welles to FDR, August 20, 1941, PSF (Departmental): State: Welles, FDRL; J.R. Beardall to FDR, September 26, 1941, PSF (Safe): Navy, 1934–42, FDRL; William J. Donovan to FDR, October 1, 1941, and memorandum, "The German Military and Economic Position: Summary and Conclusion," December 12, 1941, both in PSF (Safe): Germany, FDRL; Donovan to FDR, memorandum, "Report on Germany—Spring and Autumn—1941," November 17, 1941, PSF (Subject): Coordinator of Information, FDRL. See also Breckenridge Long diary, December 18, 1941, Breckenridge Long Papers, LC.

47. *FDRPL*, 2:1093–95.

48. *Ickes Diary*, 3:203; Cole, "American Appeasement," p. 12.

49. *FDRPL*, 1:342–43, 732–33; 2:1093–95.

50. FDR, "Shall We Trust Japan?" *Asia*, 23 (1923):476; *Ickes Diary*, 2:277; *FDRPL*, 1:752; *FRUS: Japan*, 2:528, 530; Heinrichs, *Diplomacy and Force*, p. 141; Graebner, "Hoover, Roosevelt, and the Japanese," pp. 46, 41–42.

51. Minutes, 2nd Pacific Council Meeting, April 10, 1942, MR 168, FDRL. See also *Morgenthau Diaries*, 3:380–81; Morgenthau presidential diary, June 16, 1942; FDR to King, July 15, 1942, PSF (Safe): King, FDRL

52. FDR to Welles, memorandum, undated, Welles Mission, 1940, box 155, Sumner Welles Papers, FDRL; Dallek, *Roosevelt and Foreign Policy*, pp.206–7. For a contrary view see Offner, "Appeasement Revisited," p. 385.

53. FDR to Leahy, November 1, 1941, PSF (Diplomatic): France, FDRL. Similar sentiments are also contained FDR to Murray, September 11, 1939, PSF (Diplo-

matic): Britain: Murray, FDRL; Berle and Albert Gore, June 6, 1941, box 65, Berle Papers; "Joint Board Estimate of U.S. Over-all Production Requirements," September 11, 1941, PSF (Safe): American-British JCS, FDRL; *FRUS: Conference at Washington, 1941–1942*, p. 120.

54. *Ickes Diary*, 3:200; FDR to King George VI, November 22, 1940, PSF (Diplomatic): Britain; *FDRPL*, 2:1093–95. Reynolds, *Creation*, pp. 108–20.

55. *C-R Correspondence*, R-38x, 1:178–80.

56. *FDRPL*, 2:1204–5. See also FDR to Fulton Oursler, June 23, 1941, PPF 2993, FDRL; FDR to Myron C. Taylor, September 1, 1941, PSF (Diplomatic): Italy, FDRL. On FDR's attempts to hasten delivery, see Harry L. Hopkins to FDR, August 1, 1941, PSF (Safe): Russia, FDRL; *FDRPL*, 2:1179; FDR to Wayne Coy, August 2, 1941, PSF (Diplomatic): Russia, FDRL; *Ickes Diary*, 3:592; FDR to Stimson, August 30, 1941, PSF (Departmental): War: Stimson, FDRL. See also Kimball, *Juggler*, pp. 21–41.

57. Stimson diary, October 21, 1941; Hopkins to Hall, November 12, 1941, box 308, Harry L. Hopkins Papers: Sherwood Collection, FDRL.

58. Berle diary, September 21 and 22, 1939.

59. Morgenthau presidential diary, May 16, 1940; Reynolds, *Creation*, p. 111.

60. Heinrichs, *Threshold of War*, pp. 78, 159.

61. See, for example, *Ickes Diary*, 3:466, 523; Stimson diary, May 23, 1941. For a full list of these references, see Reynolds, *Creation*, footnote 38, p. 347. See also Langer and Gleason, *The Undeclared War*, pp. 457–58.

62. Watson, *Chief of Staff*, pp. 366–77; Matloff and Snell, *Strategic Planning for Coalition Warfare*, p. 46. See also, *Marshall Papers*, 2:391–92.

63. Steele, *First Offensive*, pp. 17–18; Heinrichs, *Threshold of War*, pp. 82, 110–11.

64. *FRUS: Conference at Washington, 1941–42*, p. 64.

65. This analysis differs somewhat from that in Reynolds, *Creation*, pp. 212, 218, and Carr, *Poland to Pearl Harbor*, pp. 143–44. It is closer to that in Langer and Gleason, *Undeclared War*, pp. 734–35, Dallek, *Roosevelt and Foreign Policy*, pp. 263–67, 285–94, and implied in Heinrichs, *Threshold of War*, pp. 151, 159–61.

66. As he would in 1942, when the domestic environment changed. See chapter 3 below.

67. Anthony Eden to Winston S. Churchill, March 14, 1943, Lord Avon Papers, FO 954/US/43/24, PRO.

68. *FDRPL*, 1:466–67; 2:1298, 1300. *Ickes Diary*, 3:428.

69. *FDRFA*, 2nd series 5:1030; *FDRPL*, 2:1216.

70. Bell, *John Bull and the Bear*, p. 18–19.

71. *FDRPL*, 1:610; Winfield, *FDR and the News Media*, pp. 21–22, 179.

72. *FDRFA*, 1st series, 2:387; 3:119. Berle diary, September 15, 1937; *FDRPL*, 2:1037–38; FDR to Archibald MacLeish, August 12, 1940, PSF (Subject): MacLeish, FDRL.

73. FDR, *Public Papers*, 7:283–84.

74. *FDRPL*, 1:626–27; 2:785–6. Winfield, *FDR and the Media*, pp. 127–28.

75. Sherwood, *Roosevelt and Hopkins*, p. 206; Schlesinger, *Coming of the New Deal*, pp. 511–12.

76. These reports can be found in PSF (Subject): Lend–Lease, FDRL, for March 14 to 29, 1941; and PSF (Departmental): Treasury: Morgenthau: Editorial Opinion, FDRL, for April 25, 1941 to February 27, 1942.

77. FDR's request to Lowell Mellett, July 18, 1941, OF 857, FDRL. First editions of the "Weekly Summary" in PSF (Subject): Mellett; and OF 1413. For reports from March 6 to July 10, 1942 see OF 788; for reports from July 24 to October

30, 1942, see OF 5015; all in FDRL. See also Winfield, *FDR and the Media*, pp. 80–81; Steele, "The Pulse of the People," pp. 196–99.

78. John Franklin Carter, Oral History Interview, February 9, 1966, FDRL. Carter's reports in PSF (Subject): Carter, FDRL. Ernst's "Tidbits" in PSF (Subject): Ernst. For background on Carter's operation see Berle to Welles, January 20, 1941, State Department Subject File, 1938–45: J. F. Carter, Berle Papers; Smith to FDR, October 16, 1941, OF 4514, FDRL. See also, Steele, "Pulse of the People," pp. 200–1; Andrew, *For the President's Eyes Only*, pp. 132–33; Block, ed., *Current Biography*, pp. 308–9; Casey, "Roosevelt and the 'S-Project,'" pp. 341–42.

79. Dickinson, *Bitter Harvest*, pp. 80–81; Schlesinger, *Coming of the New Deal*, pp. 545–46; Herbst, *Reading Public Opinion*, pp. 142–43; Lincoln, "My Public Opinion Baths," pp. 284–85.

80. FDR to "Mac," September 6, 1941, PSF (Subject): McIntyre, FDRL. See also, Kearns, *No Ordinary Time*, pp. 27–29; Langer and Gleason, *Challenge to Isolation*, p. 5.

81. Schlesinger, *Coming of the New Deal*, p. 526. Letters in response to FDR's speeches are in PPF 200B, FDRL.

82. Steele, "Pulse of the People," p. 205.

83. Gallup, *Gallup Poll*, p. 39.

84. "The President's Map Audience Speech," March 30, 1942, OF 4619, FDRL. See also Bell, *John Bull and the Bear*, p. 9.

85. *Fortune* polls are in OF 3618; and OF 857, FDRL. Eugene Meyer to FDR, May 30, 1940; Edwin M. Watson to Meyer, January 25, 1941; both in OF 857, FDRL. Stephen T. Early to FDR, August 16, 1940, box 24, Stephen T. Early Papers, FDRL.

86. James Rowe to FDR, October 3, 1940, PSF (Subject): Rowe, FDRL; Robert J.C. Butow, "The FDR Tapes," pp. 18–19. For another indication that FDR was distrustful of the Gallup poll, see Wallace to FDR, October 15, 1940, PPF 1820, FDRL. This matter was followed up by Edward C. Eicher, memorandum to FDR, October 9, 1940, PSF (Subject): Opinion Polls, FDRL. Even in 1944, the White House considered that Gallup was a Republican partisan, and attempted to monitor what advice he was giving to Thomas E. Dewey. See Hadley Cantril to David K. Niles, July 9, 1944, box 6, Philleo Nash Papers, HSTL.

87. *Ickes, Diary*, 3:324.

88. Mellett to FDR, August 7, 1940, PPF 4721, FDRL; Rowe to FDR, August 12, 1940, PSF (Departmental): Justice, FDRL.

89. FDR to Mellett, August 12, 1940, PPF 4721, FDRL; Mellett to FDR, September 4 and 30, 1940, PPF 4721.

90. For FDR's desire to consult Cantril's polls, see Rowe to FDR, August 9, 1940, OF 463–C, FDRL; Niles to Grace Tully, November 11, 1942; FDR to Cantril, November 12, 1942; both in PPF 8229, FDRL. See also, Cantril, *The Human Dimension*, p. 35–43; Winfield, *FDR and the Media*, pp. 215–21; Steele, "Pulse of the People," pp. 205–13. Two years later, an FDR aide was still stressing that "the Princeton poll is much more sensible and accurate than Gallup or Roper"; see Rowe to Tully, October 8, 1942, PSF (Subject): EOP: Rowe, FDRL.

91. Steele, "Preparing the Public for War," p. 1651.

92. For the techniques used in compiling these reports see OFF, "SoIM" No.23, May 13, 1942, PSF (Subject): OWI, FDRL; and Barth, "The Bureau of Intelligence," pp. 66–76.

93. FDR to Tully, January 13, 1942, OF 4619, FDRL; MacLeish to Tully, February 3, 1942, PSF (Subject): OFF, FDRL. "SoIM" can be found in PSF (Subject):

OFF, for December 15, 1941 to February 23, 1942; PSF (Subject): OWI, for February 23, 1942 to February 26, 1943; and OF5015, for March 5 to 12, 1943; all in FDRL. From July 29, 1942 it was renamed "Intelligence Report."

94. *FRUS, 1933*, 1:296.
95. Offner, *American Appeasement*, pp. 63, 234; Berger, *The Story of the New York Times*, p. 396; Shirer, *Berlin Diary*.
96. Schneider, *Should America Go To War?* pp. 12, 43. Even Hearst, who became notorious for his pro–Nazi sympathies, allowed indictments of Nazi brutality to appear in his newspapers in 1933 and 1934. See Nasaw, *The Chief*, pp. 474–77, 488–99, 552–55
97. *Gallup Poll*, pp. 121, 125, 128.
98. *Fortune* (October 1939), copy in PPF 1820, FDRL.
99. *Fortune* (December 1939), pp. 118–20, attached to Yorke to Early, November 21, 1939, OF 3618, FDRL.
100. Vaughn, *Holding Fast the Inner Lines*, pp. 71–73, 81; Rochester, *American Liberal Disillusionment in the Wake of World War I*, p. 54.
101. Nagler, "From Culture to Kultur," pp. 133, 137–38, 150–52.
102. On the negative strand in the American image, see Jonas, *The United States and Germany*, p. 64.
103. Hofstadter, *The Progressive Historians*, pp. 15, 25; Croly, *The Promise of American Life*, pp. 250–51; Forcey, *The Crossroads of Liberalism*, p. 60; Thompson, *Reformers and War*, pp. 105–8; Gatzke, *Germany and the United States*, pp. 88, 94–95; Strout, *The American Image of the Old World*, pp. 141, 206–7.
104. White, *FDR and the Press*, p. 29; Steel, *Lippmann and the American Century*, pp. 330–31.
105. Shirer, *This Is Berlin*, pp. 25, 28–29, 74. Walter Winchell to FDR, September 2, 1939, OF 463–C, FDRL; McKelway, *Walter Winchell*, p. 128.
106. Barth, "The Aftermath of the Conference," August 22, 1941, p. 5, PSF (Departmental): Treasury: Morgenthau: Editorial Opinion, FDRL.
107. *Fortune* [undated], p. 171, attached to Early to Marguerite "Missy" LeHand, October 26, 1939, OF 3618, FDRL.
108. *Fortune*, undated, p. 90, received by the White House, December 28, 1939, OF 857, FDRL.
109. For the core convictions underpinning isolationism in this period, see Jonas, *Isolationism in America*, esp. pp. 273–74.
110. *Fortune*, undated, received by the White House, December 28, 1939, OF 857, FDRL
111. Jonas, *Isolationism*, p. 1; *FDRPL*, 1:716–17.
112. Divine, *The Illusion of Neutrality*, p. 79; *Fortune* (December 1939) attached to Yorke to Early, November 21, 1939, OF 3618, FDRL.
113. *FDRPL*, 2:968; FDR to Knox, December 29, 1939, PSF (Departmental): Navy, FDRL. See also, FDR to Sir Alan Lascalles, November 13, 1939, PSF (Diplomatic): GB: King and Queen, FDRL; *FDRPL*, 2:950;
114. Cantril to James W. Young, "America Faces the War—The Reaction of Public Opinion," undated [January 1941?], Chart 4, OF 857, FDRL.
115. Polls attached to Mellett to FDR, August 7, 1940, and September 30, 1940; both in PPF 4721.
116. Dallek, *Roosevelt and Foreign Policy*, p. 223.
117. Polls attached to Meyer to Early, May 30, 1940, OF 857, FDRL; Mellett to FDR August 7, 1940, PPF 4721.
118. *Fortune* (August 1940), OF 3618, FDRL.

119. See, for example, Bullitt to FDR, April 1, 1940, PSF (Diplomatic): Bullitt, FDRL; Welles to FDR, April 12, 1940, folder 12, box 150, Welles Papers; memorandum, "Hamilton Fish," undated [1941], PSF (Subject): Congress, FDRL; Carter, "Memorandum on the Chicago Situation and the 'America First' Set–Up," July 22, 1941, PSF (Subject): Carter, FDRL; FDR to William D. Hassett, September 1, 1941, and attached clippings, OF 463–C, FDRL.

120. FDR to Stimson, May 21, 1940, PSF (Departmental): War: Stimson, FDRL. See also, Dorothy Thompson, "What Lindbergh Really Wants," clipping in OF 92, FDRL.

121. Rowe to FDR, January 15, 1941 and October 13, 1941, both in PSF (Subject): Rowe, FDRL. See also, Cole, *America First*, pp. 81–85, 99–100, 156; Doenecke, "Power, Markets, and Ideology,"pp. 136–40, 147–49.

122. "Hamilton Fish," undated, PSF (Subject): Congress, FDRL. See also, Doenecke, "Germany in Isolationist Ideology,"pp. 215–22; Cole, *Roosevelt and the Isolationists*, pp. 343–45.

123. See, for instance, Early to FDR, January 3, 1941, box 24, Early Papers; Early to FDR, May 22, 1941, PSF (Subject): Executive Office of the President: Early, FDRL. Also, FDR to Watson, January 7, 1941; "Mac" to FDR, October 29, 1941; Mellett to FDR, October 30, 1941; all in OF 4320, FDRL

124. See, for instance, CDAAA, "Official Statement of Policy," March 17, 1941, referred to FDR, March 25, 1941, OF 4230, FDRL; Joseph C. Harsch, "The 'Unbelievable' Nazi Blueprint," *New York Times Magazine*, May 25, 1941, clipping in PSF (Diplomatic): Germany, FDRL; Thompson, "The World Germanica," *Reader's Digest*, 37 (July 1940): 115–18, clipping in PPF 1820, FDRL; Walter Lippmann, "The Economic Consequences of a German Victory," *Life*, July 22, 1940, pp. 64–69; Doenecke, "Power, Markets and Ideology," p. 133–34.

125. CDAAA, "Official Statement."

126. William Allen White, "The Yanks are Not Coming," *Washington Daily News*, December 23, 1940, clipping in PPF 1820, FDRL; White to FDR, December 28, 1940, OF 4230, FDRL. See also Chadwin, *The Hawks of World War II*, pp. 254, 261–62; Cole, *America First*, p. 8; Schneider, *Should America Go To War?* pp. 79–81.

127. Early to FDR, August 16, 1940, box 24, Early Papers; poll attached to Mellet to FDR, September 4, 1940, PPF 4721, FDRL.

128. Leuchtenberg, *Roosevelt and the New Deal*, pp. 313–14.

129. For a summary of Willkie's key speeches see Hull to FDR, November 1, 1940, PSF (Departmental): State: Hull, FDRL.

130. Willkie, speech, August 17, 1940, reprinted in *New York Times*, August 18, 1940, copy in PPF 1820, FDRL.

131. Willkie, speech, October 23, 1940, reprinted in *New York Times*, October 24, 1940; Divine, *Foreign Policy and U.S. Presidential Elections*, pp. 65–68.

132. *Fortune*, (August 1940), OF 3618, FDRL.

133. For an analysis of the vote, see Mellett to FDR, February, 8 1941, PSF (Subject): Mellett, FDRL.

134. Cantril, "Latest returns on Princeton Ballot," July 19, 1941, PSF (Subject): Opinion Polls, FDRL.

135. Cantril to Anna Rosenberg, July 3, 1941, PSF (Subject): Opinion Polls, FDRL. See also Barth, "The Fourth Climacteric: Eyes on the Target," June 27, 1941, PSF (Departmental): Treasury: Morgenthau: Editorial Opinion, FDRL; Cole, *Roosevelt and the Isolationists*, pp. 434–35.

136. Tupper and McReynolds, *Japan in American Public Opinion*, pp. 319–26, 421–24.

This survey points out that media opinion became "almost completely hostile to Japan" at the start of 1932, after a Sino–Japanese clash in Shanghai. Poll attached to Rowe to FDR, October 14, 1940, PSF (Subject): Opinion Polls, FDRL; Cantril to Rosenberg, June 3, 1941, PPF 1820, FDRL. See also, *Gallup Poll*, pp. 159, 168, 177, 208, 246, 296.

137. *Gallup poll*, p. 131. See also Borg, *The United States and the Far Eastern Crisis of 1933–1938*, pp. 88–92.

138. Barth, "East and West," July 18, 1941, PSF (Departmental): Treasury: Morgenthau: Editorial Opinion, FDRL; "America Faces the War: Clusters and Determinants of Opinion," January 28, 1941, Table 9, OF 857, FDRL. See also Schneider, *Should America Go To War?*, pp. 133, 150.

139. Cantril, "Princeton Public Opinion Research Project," January 28, 1941, OF 857. Cantril, "For Trend Charts," April 25, 1941; and Cantril, "Summary of American Public Opinion Concerning the War," June 3, 1941; both in PPF 1820, FDRL.

140. Halifax to Churchill, October 11, 1941, Lord Halifax Papers, document 4.11, microfilm, CC.

141. *FDRPL*, 2:757.

142. Steele, *Propaganda in an Open Society*, pp. 8–13, 112; Winfield, *FDR and the Media*, pp. 29–30; Schlesinger, *Coming of the New Deal*, pp. 650–63; Kernell, *Going Public*, p. 66.

143. White, *FDR and the Press*, pp. 10–15.

144. Steele, *Propaganda*, pp. 11–13.

145. FDR to Kennedy, July 22, 1939, PSF (Subject): K, FDRL; Steele, *Propaganda*, pp. 43–44; White, *FDR and the Press*, pp. 16–17,60–1.

146. Rosenman, *Working with Roosevelt*, p. 511.

147. Steele, *Propaganda*, p. 22.

148. Rosenman, *Working with Roosevelt*, pp. 1–12, 228–29, 233; Sherwood, *Roosevelt and Hopkins*, pp. 212–13. See also Langer and Gleason, *Challenge to Isolation*, p. 6.

149. Schlesinger, *Coming of the New Deal*, pp. 559–60; Winfield, *FDR and the Media*, p. 105; Ryan, *Roosevelt's Rhetorical Presidency*, pp. 19–24.

150. Cantril, September 17, 1941, PSF (Subject): Opinion Polls, FDRL; MacLeish to FDR, April 8, 1942, OF 4619, FDRL; Winfield, *FDR and the Media*, pp. 104–105.

151. Steele, *Propaganda*, pp. 14, 34–35; White, *FDR and the Press*, pp. 33–34. See also, *C-R Correspondence*, R-373, 2:491.

152. *FDRPL*, 2:1298.

153. FDR to King George VI, May 1, 1940, PSF (Diplomatic): Britain: King and Queen, FDRL.

154. FDR, *Public Papers*, 10:386–90. On the genesis of the *Greer* speech, see Sherwood, *Roosevelt and Hopkins*, p. 370. The administration was highly sensitive to press charges that it had "deliberately distorted the truth" on this incident; see Knox to Patterson, undated, [November 1941?] PSF (Departmental): Navy: Knox, FDRL.

155. FDR, *Public Papers*, 6:409; 7:2, 70; 8:1. *FDRPL*, 1:221.

156. See, for example, FDR, *Public Papers*, 7:2.

157. FDR, *Public Papers*, 6:409, 423–25.

158. *FDRFA*, 2nd series, 8:1562; Farnham, *Roosevelt and Munich*, pp. 188–94.

159. FDR, *Public Papers*, 8:513, 518. See also ibid., 9:4, 7; and Berle diary, September 4, 1939; Divine, *Illusion of Neutrality*, p. 297; Rosenman, *Working with Roosevelt*, p. 191.

160. "Conference of the President with Democratic and Republican Leaders," September 20, 1939, PPF1–P, FDRL.

161. *Ickes Diary*, 2:532–33; Schlesinger, *Coming of the New Deal*, pp. 243–44; Dallek, *Roosevelt and Foreign Policy*, pp. 201–3.

162. *FDRPL*, 2:967–68, 810–11, 933.

163. For such connections during the neutrality revision debate in the fall of 1939 see, Early to FDR, September 14, 1939, OF 1561, FDRL; Berle diary, September 30, 1939; *Ickes Diary*, 3:8; FDR to Archbishop Francis J. Spellman, October 2, 1939, PSF (Subject): Neutrality, FDRL; Dallek, *Roosevelt and Foreign Policy*, p. 201.

164. FDR, *Public Papers*, 9:198–200, 231, 261.

165. FDR, *Public Papers*, 9:198, 238–39, 415, 507. On FDR's assault on isolationism, see Cole, *Roosevelt and the Isolationists*, pp. 410–12

166. On FDR's elation after the Charlottesville speech, attacking Mussolini, see Berle diary, 10 June 1940; Sherwood, *Roosevelt and Hopkins*, p. 226.

167. FDR, *Public Papers*, 9:517; Divine, *Presidential Elections*, pp. 80–81; Rosenman, *Working with Roosevelt*, pp. 241–42.

168. FDR, *Public Papers*, 9:638–39; 10:368–69.

169. Laurie, *Propaganda Warriors*, pp. 37–39, 46; Steele, *Propaganda*, pp. 79, 142–44; *DSB*, 3:331–37; 4:85–89, 491–5, 307–8.

170. FDR, *Public Papers*, 10:62.

171. Ibid., 9:260–62, 520, 638–40

172. Ibid., 10:186, 68.

173. Ibid., 10:443, 410.

174. As Steele argues in "American Popular Opinion," p. 710.

175. Kinsella, for example, argues that by 1941 FDR had long "foreseen with certainty the inevitability of the American war commitment" but was constrained by an isolationist public. Kinsella, Jr., *Leadership in Isolation*, esp. pp. 209–14

176. Greenfield, *American Strategy in World War II*, p. 52.

177. Heinrichs, *Threshold of War*, pp. 17–19; Dickinson, *Bitter Harvest*, pp. 167–8, 172–82; McJimsey, *Harry Hopkins*, pp. 156, 171, 222; Gullan, "Expectations of Infamy," pp. 510–20.

178. Stark to Knox, November 12, 1940, PSF (Safe): Navy: "Plan Dog," FDRL; "Joint Board Estimate," p. 4; Kirkpatrick, *An Unknown Future and a Doubtful Present*, pp. 41, 81.

179. *C-R Correspondence*, C-114x, 1:238; Reynolds, *Creation*, pp. 98–100, 182, 214–25; Heinrichs, *Threshold of War*, pp. 19, 171, 213.

180. Sherwood, *Roosevelt and Hopkins*, p. 311; FDR, *Public Papers*, 10:463.

181. Morgenthau presidential diary, August 4, 1941; Wilson, *The First Summit*, p. 118; Sherry, *Rise of American Air Power*, pp. 97–98.

182. FDR to Early, December 1, 1940, PPF 75, FDRL; *FDRPL*, 2:1176. FDR to Welles, June 23, 1941; Welles to FDR, August 20, 1941; both in PSF (Departmental): State: Welles, FDRL.

183. Pogue, *Marshall: Ordeal and Hope*, pp. 77–79; Watson, *Chief of Staff*, pp. 362–66.

184. Stimson diary, September 25, 1941.

185. Kirkpatrick, *Unknown Future*, p. 73; Heinrichs, *Threshold of War*, pp. 149, 56,

186. Reynolds, *Creation*, p. 42; *Marshall Papers*, 2:53; Watson, *Chief of Staff*, p. 157. That FDR believed an AEF would only be politically acceptable after a direct attack is demonstrated by his desire to change the instructions for the ABC Meeting so that they read "should the U.S. be compelled to resort to war," rather than "should the U.S. desire to resort to war." See Watson, *Chief of Staff*, pp. 372–73.

187. *Marshall Papers*, 2:601–2; Pogue, *Marshall: Ordeal and Hope*, p. 105.

188. On the narrowness of the selective service vote, see Early to FDR, telegram, "Black Serial 13," [undated, August 1941] PSF (Safe): Atlantic Charter (1), FDRL.

189. Watson, *Chief of Staff*, pp. 366–77; Matloff and Snell, *Strategic Planning*, pp. 40–46.

190. Halifax to Churchill, October 11, 1941, Halifax Papers, document 4.11; Dallek, *Roosevelt and Foreign Policy*, p. 267.

Chapter 2

1. Sherwood, *Roosevelt and Hopkins*, pp. 430–34; Perkins, *The Roosevelt I Knew*, pp. 303–5; Dallek, *Roosevelt and Foreign Policy*, p. 311; Goodwin, *No Ordinary Time*, pp. 288–90; Kennedy, *Freedom from Fear*, pp. 520–22.

2. Cited in Kennett, *For the Duration*, p. 15.

3. Lindbergh, *The Wartime Journals*, pp. 560–61; Cole, *Roosevelt and the Isolationists*, pp. 13, 509–10, 530–31.

4. Barth to Kuhn, "Editorial Opinion on Foreign Affairs: The Nation Rallies," December 12, 1941, PSF (Departmental): Treasury: Morgenthau: Editorial Opinion, FDRL. For a similar analysis see Long diary, 14 December 1941, Long Papers.

5. On the "Maginot mentality" see Barth to MacLeish, "Editorial Opinion on the War: The Basic Cleavage," February 20, 1942.

6. FDR to Tully, January 13, 1942, OF 4619, FDRL; MacLeish to Tully, February 3, 1942, PSF (Subject): OFF, FDRL; Harold F. Goswell, "Office of Facts and Figures," November 15, 1943, p. 36, entry 6E, box 12, RG 208, NA.

7. "SoIM," No.5, January 10, 1942; Barth to MacLeish, "Editorial Opinion on the War: The Best Defense," February 6, 1942. See also FDR to Knox, December 23, 1941, and attached memorandum, Lewis B. Hershey to FDR, December, 20 1941, PSF (Departmental): Navy, FDRL.

8. Cantril, "Opinion Concerning Offensive and Defensive Strategy," April 10, 1942, entry 171, box 1853, RG 44, NA; "SoIM," No.28, April 17, 1942.

9. Agenda, Committee of War Information Meeting, December 29, 1941, entry 6E, box 11, RG 208, NA.

10. FDR, *Public Papers*, 11:39. See also Buhite and Levy, ed., *FDR's Fireside Chats*, pp. 208–9.

11. Spector, *Eagle Against the Sun*, pp. 100–39; Thorne, *Allies of a Kind*, pp 154–67; Weinberg, *A World at Arms*, pp. 310–27.

12. Barth to Kuhn, "Editorial Opinion on Foreign Affairs: The Nation Rallies," December 12, 1941; Barth to MacLeish, "Editorial Opinion on the War: The Indivisible War," January 23, 1942; Barth to MacLeish, "Editorial Opinion and the War: Response to Candor," January 30, 1942. See also, *Chicago Daily Tribune*, January 14, 1942.

13. "SoIM" No.21, April 29, 1942, pp. 10–12; and No.23, May 13. See also OFF, "The Nature of the Enemy and the Fighting Job," No.17, April 8, 1942; idem, "Public Attitudes Toward War Strategy and Tactics," No.20, April 22, 1942; both in entry 164, box 1797, RG 44, NA. And also OFF, "American Public Opinion in the First Five Months of War," May 5, 1942, entry 162, box 1785, RG 44, NA.

14. "SoIM" No.19, April 15, 1942; Lubin to FDR, March 16, 1942, PPF 1820, FDRL.

15. "SoIM" No.19, April 15, 1942.

16. Dallek, *Roosevelt and Foreign Policy*, pp. 324–27; Thorne, *Allies of a Kind*, pp. 146–47. In April, 386 editorials viewed events in India with distaste. See "Weekly Analysis of Press Reaction," April 23, 1942.

17. "SoIM" No.12, March 2, 1942, p. 5; Barth to MacLeish, "Editorial Opinion on the War: The Basic Cleavage," February 20, 1942.

18. "SoIM" No.12, March 2, 1942; and No.19, April 15, 1942. Emphasis added.

19. *FDRPL*, 2:1298,1285, 1321–22. See also FDRPC, No.806, February 17, 1942, 19:148–49; *C-R Correspondence*, R-123/1, 1:421.

20. Barth to MacLeish, "Editorial Opinion on the War: The War Grows Real," February 13, 1942.

21. Ibid.

22. "SoIM" No.23, May 13, 1942. On this mood see also "SoIM" No.11, February 23, 1942; and Long diary, February 15, 1942, Long Papers.

23. Barth to MacLeish, "Editorial Opinion on the War: Preparing to Fight," January 16, 1942.

24. FDRPC, No.804, February 10, 1942, 19:129–30.

25. FDR, *Public Papers*, 11:78.

26. MacLeish to FDR, January 21, 1942; FDR to MacLeish, January 27, 1942; both in OF 4619, FDRL. See also Donaldson, *Archibald MacLeish*, p. 350; Laurie, *Propaganda Warriors*, pp. 64–65.

27. Captain Kintner to MacLeish, minutes, CWI meeting, January 21, 1942, entry 6E, box 11, RG 208, NA; "Our Current Information Objectives," undated, entry 6E, box 12, RG 208, NA. There is also a copy attached to MacLeish to Tully, April 9, 1942, OF 4619, FDRL. See also "SoIM" No.16, March 25, 1942.

28. Goswell, "Office of Facts and Figures"; Steele, "Preparing the Public for War," pp. 1652–53; Leigh, *Mobilizing Consent*, pp. 66–67.

29. Hawkins and Pettee, "OWI—Organization and Problems," p. 17; Winnick, ed., *Letters of Archibald MacLeish*, pp. 306, 320; Drabeck and Ellis, ed., *Archibald MacLeish*, pp. 146–50.

30. "SoIM" No.16, March 25, 1942.

31. OFF, "Media Trend Report," No.1, March 31, 1942, entry 171, box 1844, RG 44, NA; idem, "Weekly Media Report," No.20, June 20, 1942, entry 151, box 1720, RG 44, NA.

32. OFF, "Media Trend Report," No.1, March 31, 1942; OFF, "Analysis of Newsreels," Special Intelligence Reports No.37, No.51, No.63, April, May, June 1942, entry 171, box 1845, RG 44, NA.

33. OFF, "Weekly Media Report," No.20, June 20, 1942, and No.29, August 22, 1942; Barth to Media Division, "Nature of the Enemy in American Media," August 29, 1942, entry 171, box 1846, RG 44, NA.

34. OWI, "Analysis of June 1942 Newsreels," Special Intelligence Report No.63, August 10, 1942, entry 171, box 1845, RG 44, NA.

35. OFF, "Plan for 12 Network Radio Series," June 1, 1942, entry 98, box 638, RG 208, NA.

36. OWI, "Intelligence Report: American Estimates of the Enemy," September 2, 1942, PSF (Subject): OWI, FDRL; Dallek, *Roosevelt and Foreign Policy*, p. 358.

37. "SoIM" No.17, April 1, 1942; and No.26, June 3, 1942.

38. FDR to MacLeish, February 12, 1942, box 19, Archibald MacLeish Papers, LC.

39. Ickes diary, 15 February 1942, p. 6354, Harold L. Ickes Papers, LC. See also Stimson diary, 16 March 1942.

40. "SoIM" No.16, 25 March 1942; and No.23, May 13.

41. NBC, *America's Town Hall Meeting of the Air*, January 15, 1942, Ref.: LWO 15731 42B1–4, NBC Archive, Recorded Sound Division, LC; Paul Lyness to George Pettee, "Who Is the Enemy? Peoples? Or Regimes?" August 11, 1942, entry 171, box 1849, RG 44, NA.

42. Ickes diary, April 11, 1942, p. 6537. According to the OFF, both the British and the Soviets were starting to indict the Germans as a well as the Nazis, see "SoIM" No. 24, May 20, 1942, PSF (Subject): OWI, FDRL

43. Ickes diary, April 11, 1942, p. 6537.

44. *FDR's Fireside Chats*, p. 221; FDR, *Public Papers*, 11:288, 349.

45. Watson to Emil Ludwig, February 19, 1942; Watson to MacLeish, March 12, 1942; both in PPF 3884, FDRL. On FDR's relationship with Ludwig in the 1930s, see LeHand to Ludwig, November 3, 1937; Early, memorandum for the president, November 22, 1937; both in PPF 3884, FDRL; Lash, *Eleanor and Franklin*, p. 509. FDR's lukewarm attitude to Ludwig at this stage is significant, because some authors have argued that their friendship was indicative of FDR's long–standing Germanophobia. See Hönicke, "Know Your Enemy," p. 244.

46. *FDRPL*, 2:1317.

47. FDR to Lehman, June 3, 1942, PPF 133, FDRL. See also FDR to Stimson, May 5, 1942, OF 4619, FDRL; Stimson diary, May 15, 1942. On the number of German aliens compared to Japanese, see Cranston to MacLeish, "For CWI Members," May 19, 1942, entry 6E, box 11, RG 208, NA. See also Burns, *Soldier of Freedom*, pp. 217, 268; Polenberg, *War and Society*, p. 61.

48. "Weekly Analysis of Press Reaction," July 24, 1942; OFF, "Weekly Media Report," No.19, June 13, 1942.

49. "Minutes, Joint Committee on Information Policy, Sixth Meeting," September 17, 1942, OWI: Records of the Director, entry 1, box 5, RG 208, NA.

50. Adolph Held, "Report on the Visit to the President," December 8, 1942, Lebowitz and Malmgreen, ed., *Archives of the Holocaust*, vol. 14, document 148. See also Carter, OH, p. 12.

51. Berle diary, May 2, 1942; Berle to FDR, May 9, 1942, box 67, Berle Papers. The CWI agreed with the president on this issue see, minutes CWI Meeting, March 9, 1942, entry 6E, box 11, RG 208, NA.

52. Casey, "Roosevelt and the 'S–Project,'" pp. 339–59.

53. Discussions on this matter can be found in minutes CWI Meeting, September 2, 1942, entry 1, box 2, RG 208, NA; minutes of the Joint Committee on Information Meeting, September 10 and 17, 1942, entry 1, box 5, RG 208, NA. This argument differs from that of Hönicke, who contends that FDR was a consistent Germanophobe throughout the war and asserts that the president "did not bother" to translate this attitude "into basic guidelines that would have helped the information officials in their definition of the nature of the enemy." Hönicke, "American Wartime Images," p. 253.

54. Elmer Davis, "Report to the President on the OWI, June 13, 1942 to September 15, 1945," undated, box 10, Davis Papers. See also Robert Huse to MacLeish, "Suggested Minutes, CWI Meeting—June 1, 1942," June 2, 1942, entry 6E, box 11, RG 208, NA

55. FDR, *Public Papers*, 11:111, 303. See also Steele, *Propaganda*, pp. 107–8, 118, 125; Winfield, *FDR and the Media*, pp. 202–3.

56. Hassett, *Off the Record with FDR*; Rosenman, *Working with Roosevelt*, pp. 349–55; Burns, *Soldier of Freedom*, pp. 199–200.

57. *Time*, February 2, 1942; Dallek, *Roosevelt and Foreign Policy*, pp. 360–61; Burns, *Soldier of Freedom*, pp. 276–80.

58. MacLeish to Hopkins, February 20, 1942; and MacLeish to FDR, February 25, 1942; both in box 52, MacLeish Papers. Stimson diary, April 11, 1942.

59. FDR, *Public Papers*, 11:275; Winkler, *Politics of Propaganda*, pp. 22–31. FDR kept a close eye on the OWI's output, see Tully to Milton Eisenhower, November 16, 1842, OF 5015, FDRL.

60. OFF, minutes of Board Meeting, March 10, 1942, box 52, MacLeish Papers.

61. Minutes CWI Meeting, May 12, 1942, and attached memorandum, "Pros and Cons on Hate Atrocities," entry 6E, box 11, RG 208, NA

62. Lyness to Pettee, "Who Is the Enemy? Peoples? Or Regimes?" August 11, 1942.

63. Huse to George Barnes, July 24, 1942, entry 1, box 4, RG 208, NA. See also, minutes, CWI Meeting, September 2, 1942, entry 1, box 2, RG 208, NA.

64. OWI, "Radio Background Material, Our Enemies: The Nazis," January 12, 1943, entry 43, box 3, RG 208, NA.

65. See, in particular, OWI Scripts, "You Can't Do Business With Hitler," Episode 24, "They Sleep for Hitler," entry 146, box 765, RG 208, NA; OWI, "You Can't Do Business With Hitler," Episode 26, "Hitler is My Conscience," RG 208–026A, Audiovisual Division, NA.

66. Lyness to Pettee, "Who Is the Enemy? Peoples? Or Regimes?" August 11, 1942.

67. OWI Scripts, "This Is Our Enemy," Episode 10. See also Episodes 4, 6, and 12. All in entry 146, boxes 761–762, RG 208, NA.

68. *The Price of Victory* (War Production Board–Paramount Films, 1942), Dir. William H. Pine, RG 179.011, Audiovisual Division, NA.

69. Davies, *Mission to Moscow*, pp. 34, 511, 551–52; Koppes and Black, *Hollywood Goes to War*, pp. 185–208; Friedrich, *City of Nets*, p. 154.

70. FDR, *Public Papers*, 11:3. For FDR's draft copy see PSF (Safe): Atlantic Charter (1), FDRL. See also Gaddis, *The United States and the Origins of the Cold War*, pp. 36–37; Levering, *American Opinion and the Russian Alliance*, chap. 4; Dallek, *Roosevelt and Foreign Policy*, p. 298.

71. OWI Scripts, "You Can't Do Business With Hitler," Episode 11, "Swastikas Over the Equator," entry 146, box 765, RG 208, NA; OWI, "Information Guide: The Enemy," Sheet 1, April 1943, entry 149, box 1713, RG 44, NA.

72. OWI, "Information Guide: The Enemy," Sheet 1, April 1943.

73. Ducas to Bell, June 30, 1942, entry 1, box 8, RG 208, NA; MacLeish to FDR, "Definition of Our Cause and Statement of Our Aims," March 17, 1942, OF4619, FDRL. Cantril, "Propaganda for Victory," *New Republic*, 106 (23 February 1942):262. See also *FDR's Fireside Chats*, p. 208.

74. See, for example, *DSB*, 4:715; FDR, *Public Papers*, 11:36, 228; memorandum for General W.B. Smith, May 25, 1942, PSF (Safe): War Department, FDRL. See also MacDonnell, *Insidious Foes*, p. 139

75. OFF, *Divide and Conquer*, pp. 11, 14; OWI, *Unconquered People*, p. 1. Both in OF 5015, FDRL

76. Hassett to Early, March 21, 1942, OF 1661–B, FDRL; MacLeish "Freedom House Address," March 19, 1942, box 19, MacLeish Papers; FDR, *Public Papers*, 11:161–62.

77. OFF, minutes, [Board] Meeting, April 30, 1942, box 52, MacLeish Papers.

78. OWI, "Information Guide: The Enemy," Sheet 6, April 1943.

79. MacLeish, "Address to Annual Meeting of the American Booksellers Association," May 6, 1942, box 19, MacLeish Papers. This was reprinted in a slightly different form in *Publishers Weekly*, May 16, 1942, and *The Saturday Review*, May 23, 1942.

80. MacLeish to All Radio Stations, June 23, 1942, entry 98, box 637, RG 208, NA. Ellipses in original. On using Lidice as a "symbol" of Nazi brutality, see Huse to MacLeish and Bingham, July 2, 1942, entry 6E, box 12, RG 208, NA. That FDR shared this concern over Lidice's fate, see FDR to Wladyslaw Sikorski, 3 July, 1942, PSF (Diplomatic): Poland, FDRL.

81. OWI, press release, No.84, June 19, 1942, OF 5015, FDRL; Knox, speech, June 14, 1942, entry 1, box 9, RG 208, NA; McAleer, *Rex Stout*, pp. 314–15.

82. Phillip Knightley, *The First Casualty*, pp. 83–84.

83. Minutes, CWI Meeting, May 12, 1942 and attached memorandum, "Pros and Cons on Hate Atrocities," entry 6E, box 11, RG 208, NA; *FRUS, 1942*, 1:48–49; Gardner Cowles, "Interpretation of Enemy Atrocities," February 18, 1943, box 11, Nash Papers.

84. OWI Scripts, "You Can't Do Business With Hitler"; WJZ–Blue Network, "The Nature of the Enemy," May 17, 1943, entry 43, box 3, RG 208, NA.

85. OWI "Information Guide: The Enemy," Sheet 6, April 1943.

86. Wyman, *The Abandonment of the Jews*, pp. 27–29; Bowyer, *Blind Eye to Murder*, pp. 35–53.

87. OWI, *Unconquered People*, p. 10.

88. MacLeish to all radio stations, June 23, 1942, entry 98, box 637, RG 208, NA; OWI, press release, No.425, August 28, 1942, entry 1, box 8, RG 208, NA.

89. *FRUS, 1942*, 1:56–57.

90. FDRPC, No.842, August 21, 1942, 20:52–55; FDR, *Public Papers*, 11:410; *FRUS, 1942*, 1:58–59; Welles to FDR, October 6, 1942, PSF (Diplomatic): GB: Winant, FDRL.

91. FDR, *Public Papers*, 11:155, 288, 348.

92. Minutes, CWI Meeting, September 2, 1942, entry 1, box 2, RG 208, NA.

93. Heinrichs, *American Ambassador*, pp. 362–65.

94. Dower, "Race, Language, and War in Two Cultures,"pp. 169–70; Thorne, *Issue of War*, p. 60.

95. Dower, *War without Mercy*, pp. 36–37, 78–79.

96. MacLeish to branch directors, bureau chiefs, and administrative assistants, "General Position as Regards the Concept of Japan and the Japanese people," December 21, 1942, box 3, Nash Papers.

97. Lyness to Pettee, "Who Is the Enemy? Peoples? Or Regimes?" August 11, 1942.

98. Koppes and Black, *Hollywood Goes to War*, pp. 60–61, 248–54; Dower, *War without Mercy*, p. 81.

99. Blum, *V Was for Victory*, pp. 157–67; Polenberg, *War and Society*, pp. 61–72.

100. "SoIM" No.17, April 1, 1942; "American Estimates of the Enemy," September 2, 1942.

101. Significantly, Grew's efforts did not appear to have this effect. According to OWI research, the ambassador's speeches, "though occasionally serving as the basis for newspaper comment picturing Japan as our main enemy, have not been extensively used for that purpose," even by leading isolationist papers. Herbert Brucker to Leo Rosten, "Isolationist Use of Ambassador Grew's Speeches," January 8, 1943, entry 171, box 1846, RG 44, NA.

102. See schedules for "This Is Our Enemy," undated, entry 146, box 761, RG 208, NA; "You Can't Do Business with Hitler," undated, entry 146, box 768, RG 208, NA.

103. *FDR's Fireside Chats*, p. 204; FDR, *Public Papers*, 11:32–33. See also MacLeish to Hopkins, December 31, 1941, box 312, Hopkins Papers: Sherwood Collection.

104. FDR, *Public Papers*, 11:111.

105. Knox, "Speech at Boston Gardens," June 14, 1942, entry 1, box 9, RG 208, NA.

106. OFF, "The President's 'Map' Speech Audience," March 30, 1942; OFF, BoI, "The President's Speech of February 23: Complete Report," Special Intelligence Report, No.20, March 31, 1942; both in OF 4619, FDRL. Carter, February 25, 1942, PSF (Subject): Carter, FDRL.

107. "Weekly Analysis of Editorial Opinion," May 7 and 14, 1942, OF 788, FDRL.

108. Hamburger to Douglas, "Divide and Conquer," May 8, 1942, entry 1, box 8, RG 208, NA; OFF, minutes Board Meeting, April 7, 1942, box 52, MacLeish Papers.

109. OWI, "Weekly Media Report," No.24, July 18, 1942 and No.25, July 25, 1942.

110. "Weekly Analysis of Press Reaction," July 24, 1942.

111. "American Estimates of the Enemy," September 2, 1942. Gallup reached an almost identical conclusion in June, finding that 79 percent blamed the German government and only 6 percent the German people, see *New York Times*, June 13, 1942.

112. OWI, "Weekly Media Report," No.31, September 5, 1942.

113. "Weekly Analysis of Editorial Opinion," June 18, 1942; "American Estimates of the Enemy," September 2, 1942. See also, OFF, "Weekly Media Report," No.20, June 20, 1942.

114. *New York Herald Tribune*, June 20, 1942; OFF, "Weekly Media Report," No.21, June 27, 1942; OFF, BoI, Division of Information Channels, "Lidice," Special Intelligence Report, No.50, July 1, 1942, entry 171, box 1845, RG 44, NA.

115. "American Estimates of the Enemy," September 2, 1942. See, for example, Barnet Nover, "Lidice: The Mark of the Beast," *Washington Post*, June 15, 1942.

116. "American Estimates of the Enemy," September 2, 1942.

117. Ibid.

118. In 1942, the Jewish lobby (noted for its influence over policy makers in the Cold War period) was relatively weak, and unable even to persuade the media to give prominence to evidence that suggested a wholesale slaughter was occurring in Europe. See Wyman, *Abandonment*, pp. 24–27.

119. "American Estimates of the Enemy," September 2, 1942. Like a number of reports that reached the president, this omitted the actual polling figures. These were that 71 percent thought the Nazis were treating the Poles badly, 57 percent thought the same for the French. See OPOR, "The Nature of the Enemy," August 13, 1942, entry 171, box 1853, RG 44, NA.

120. Ibid.

121. OWI, "Intelligence Report," No.51, November 27, 1942, PSF (Subject): OWI, FDRL.

122. "Weekly Analysis of Press Reaction," April 9 and 23, 1942.

123. Barth to MacLeish, "Editorial Opinion on Foreign Affairs: Testament of Faith," January 2, 1942.

124. "American Estimates of the Enemy," September 2, 1942. Again, this report omitted the actual polling figures, which were that 46 percent wanted to kill Nazi leaders, while 35 percent were inclined toward friendly treatment of the German people. See OPOR, "The Nature of the Enemy," August 13, 1942, entry 171, box 1853, RG 44, NA.

125. *FDR's Fireside Chats*, pp. 207–17.

126. FDRPC, No.827, 22 May 1942, 19:345.

127. "SoIM" No.20, July 1, 1942.

128. Erickson, *The Road to Stalingrad*, vol. 1, *Stalin's War With Germany*, pp. 376–82; Glantz and House, *When Titans Clashed*, pp. 117–25.

129. Hassett, *Off the Record With FDR*, pp. 103–4.
130. FDRPC, No.795, December 30, 1941, 18:398; FDRPC, No.807, February 24 1942, 19:157. John J. McCloy had made the same point earlier, see minutes, CWI Meeting, January 21, 1942, entry 6E, box 11, RG 208, NA.
131. MacLeish to FDR, "Our Current Information Objectives," April 8, 1942, OF 4619, FDRL.
132. FDRPC, No.816, April 3, 1942, 19:252; FDR, *Public Papers*, 11:193; Rosenman to FDR, April 24, 1942, OF 4619, FDRL.
133. King cited in Winkler, *Politics of Propaganda*, p. 49. See also Leigh, *Mobilizing Consent*, p. 53; Blum, *V Was for Victory*, pp. 33–34.
134. "SoIM" No.23, May 13, 1942; Reston, *Prelude to Victory*, p. 73; Leigh, *Mobilizing Consent*, pp. 68–71. For press accusations see also, FDRPC, No.827, May 22, 1942, 19:345.
135. "SoIM" No.17, April 1, 1942. See also OWI, "Review of the Findings of the Surveys Division, May 6, 1942 to September 7, 1942," entry 162, box 1784, RG 44, NA
136. OWI, "Intelligence Report: Trends in American Public Opinion Since Pearl Harbor," September 11, 1942, PSF (Subject): OWI, FDRL.
137. Cantril to FDR, September 14, 1942, OF 857, FDRL; "Editorial Reaction," April 30, 1942 OF 788, FDRL; Darilek, *A Loyal Opposition in a Time of War*, pp. 52–53.
138. Cantril to FDR, September 14, 1942, OF 857, FDRL. See also Steele, "American Popular Opinion," pp. 711, 722
139. "SoIM" No.27, June 10, 1942.
140. FDR to Gallup, October 2, 1942, PPF 4721, FDRL. See also, Hassett, *Off the Record With FDR*, p. 130. Hull was also convinced that isolationism persisted, see Blum, ed., *The Price of Vision*, p. 129.
141. State Department, "Summary of Opinions and Ideas on International Post-War Problems," Nos.1–2, July 15 and 29, 1942, folder 1, box 190, Welles Papers, FDRL.
142. Cole, *Roosevelt and the Isolationists*, p. 539; Darilek, *Loyal Opposition*, pp. 54–55.
143. OWI, "Intelligence Report," No.49, November 13, 1942.

Chapter 3

1. Churchill, *Second World War*, 3:537–39; Harriman and Abel, *Special Envoy to Churchill and Stalin*, pp. 111–12.
2. Kimball, *Forged in War*, pp. 18–21; Sainsbury, *Churchill and Roosevelt at War*, pp. 7–8.
3. On Churchill's determination to have everything in writing, see Churchill, *Second World War*, 2:17. On FDR's aversion to written notes, see FDR to Hull, September 16, 1943, PSF (Departmental): State: Hull, FDRL; minutes, 1st Pacific Council Meeting, April 1, 1942, MR box 168, FDRL; *Marshall Papers*, 3:276; Stoler, *The Politics of the Second Front*, p. 56.
4. Kearns, *No Ordinary Time*, pp. 301–3, 310–11.
5. Pogue, *Marshall*, p. 306; Stimson diary, May 27, 1942. See also Thorne, *Allies of a Kind*, pp. 114–115.
6. Emerson, "FDR", p. 158–60; Burns, *Soldier of Freedom*, pp. 493–94; Larrabee, *Commander in Chief*, pp. 20–21, 24–25.
7. *FRUS: Conference at Washington, 1941–1942*, pp. 214–17. For FDR's continued

determination to pursue a "Germany–first" strategy, see minutes, 2nd Pacific Council Meeting, April 10, 1942, MR box 168, FDRL; FDR to Stimson, Marshall, Arnold, Knox, King, and Hopkins, May 6, 1942, PSF (Departmental): War: Marshall, FDRL; Morgenthau, presidential diary, June 16, 1942, microfiche, FDRL; FDR to King, July 15, 1942, PSF (Safe): King, FDRL; FDR to Stalin, "Draft Telegram," August 18, 1942, PSF (Safe): Russia, 1942–1945, FDRL.

8. Conference at the White House, December 26 and 28, 1941, box 312, Hopkins Papers: Sherwood Collection; Matloff and Snell, *Strategic Planning*, pp. 117–18, 139, 265, 358; Spector, *Eagle Against the Sun*, pp. 144, 147.

9. Stoler, "The 'Pacific First' Alternative," pp. 436–42; Pogue, *Marshall*, p. 260; King, memorandum to JCS, undated [May 1942], Bolero File, box 133, Hopkins Papers; William D. Leahy diary, September 20, 1942, box 5, William D. Leahy Papers, LC.

10. JCS, Minutes of Meeting, July 10, 1942, entry 1, box 194, RG 218, NA. Matloff and Snell, *Strategic Planning*, pp. 215, 268.

11. *Marshall Papers*, 3:276.

12. FDR, memorandum to go with memorandum from Stimson, July 29, 1942, PSF (Safe): Marshall, 1942–1944, FDRL.

13. Minutes, 11th Pacific Council Meeting, June 17, 1942, MR box 168, FDRL; FDR to Stimson, Marshall, Arnold, Knox, King, and Hopkins, May 6, 1942, PSF (Departmental): War: Marshall, FDRL.

14. Stoler *Politics of the Second Front*, pp. 25, 28–29, 36. See also Kimball, *Forged in War*, p. 153; Ross, *American War*, p. 25; Steele, "American Popular Opinion," p. 709; Thorne, *Allies of a Kind*, pp. 156, 714.

15. This was a point Hopkins made to the British, see War Cabinet, minutes of Meeting, April 14, 1942, copy in box 308, Hopkins Papers: Sherwood Collection.

16. Barth to MacLeish, "Editorial Opinion and the War: Call to Arms," February 27, 1942, PSF (Departmental): Treasury: Morgenthau: Editorial Opinion, FDRL.

17. Sherwood, *Roosevelt and Hopkins*, p. 557.

18. Berle diary, May 2, 1942; minutes, 13th Pacific Council Meeting, July 13, 1942, MR box 168, FDRL. On FDR's continued hopes in 1942, see also Stimson diary, October 19, 1942.

19. Minutes, 9th Pacific Council Meeting, May 28, 1942, MR box 168, FDRL.

20. FDR to Thayer Lindsley, November 3, 1942, OF198A, FDRL.

21. Stimson to FDR, January 8, 1942; and FDR to Stimson, January 13, 1942; both in PSF (Safe): War Department, FDRL. FDR to Smith, June 12, 1942; FDR to Stimson and Marshall, August 11, 1942; both in PSF (Departmental): War, FDRL. During the summer, FDR still expressed some doubts about the need for a large army, see Harold D. Smith, conferences with the president, June 13, 1942, box 3, Harold D. Smith Papers, FDRL.

22. See, for instance, "Germany: Morale," undated [December 1941], PSF (Subject): OSS Reports, FDRL; memorandum attached to Biddle to FDR, January 30, 1942, PSF (Diplomatic): Biddle, FDRL; Donovan to FDR, 9 May 1942, PSF (Subject): OSS Reports, FDRL. See also Ickes diary, December 21, 1941, p. 6147.

23. *C-R Correspondence*, R-129, 1:437.

24. FDR to Marshall, King, and Hopkins, "Instructions for London Conference — July 1942," July, 15, 1942, PSF (Safe): King, FDRL; FDR to Stimson, Marshall, Arnold, Knox, King, and Hopkins, May 6, 1942, PSF (Depart-

mental): War: Marshall, FDRL. See also *C-R correspondence*, R-152, 1:503; *FDRPL*, 3:1338.

25. FDR to Stimson, Marshall, Arnold, Knox, King, and Hopkins, May 6, 1942, PSF (Departmental): War: Marshall, FDRL. See also *C-R Correspondence*, R-131/1, 1:441; *FDRPL*, 3:1305. Glantz and House, *When Titans Clashed*, p. 117.

26. Sherwood, *Roosevelt and Hopkins*, pp. 574–75; Kimball, *Forged in War*, p. 144.

27. Sainsbury, *The North African Landings*, pp. 20–21, 111; Churchill, *Second World War*, 4:346–50.

28. Stoler *Politics of the Second Front*, p. 36; Ross, *American War Plans*, p. 32; Sainsbury, *North African Landings*, p. 107.

29. "Editorial Reaction," April 9, 1942; June 25, 1942; July 16, 1942; all in OF 788, FDRL.

30. For the *New York Times'* hardening view on this issue see, editorial, "Russia: Thirteen Months," *New York Times*, July 22, 1942; editorial, "Second Front," *New York Times*, August 2, 1942. See also "Toward the Volga," *Washington Post*, July 14, 1942; OFF, "Weekly Media Report," No.22, July 3, 1942.

31. OWI, "Intelligence Report," No.29, July 29, 1942, p. 6. See also OWI, "Weekly Media Report," No.26, August 1, 1942.

32. *FRUS: Conference at Washington, 1941–1942*, p. 64. FDR made a similar point in November, when he gave journalists a review of the decision-making process. See FDRPC, No. 859, November 10, 1942, 20: 223-24.

33. Howard, *History of the Second World War*, 4:xviii–xix; Stoler, *Politics of the Second Front*, p. 53; Sainsbury, *North African Landings*, pp. 106–8, 110. While the decision to act in 1942 was made on June 21, the choice of invading North Africa was not taken for another month.

34. Minutes, 15th Pacific Council Meeting, July 22, 1942, MR 168, FDRL.

35. OWI, Media Division, "Leading Editorial and Column Topics, September 30 to October 5," October 6, 1942, entry 171, box 1847, RG 44, NA. In September, 222 editorials applauded the Dieppe raid, see "Editorial Reaction," September 4, 1942, OF 788, FDRL. On the second-front issue, see also Levering, *American Opinion and the Russian Alliance*, pp. 84-89. On FDR's dismissive attitude toward the *Nation's* second-front campaign in September, see FDR to Wallace, September 9, 1942, PPF 5107, FDRL.

36. *C-R Correspondence*, R-170, R-175, R-180, 1:544, 555-56, 584. See also Stoler, *Politics of the Second Front*, p. 63.

37. Bland, ed., *Marshall Papers*, p. 593. See also *C-R Correspondence*, R-182, 1:588. And also Howe, *U.S. Army in World War II*, pp. 25–26.

38. Minutes, 10th Pacific Council Meeting, June 10, 1942, MR box 168, FDRL.

39. *FRUS: Conference at Washington, 1941–1942*, p. 72; Pogue, *Marshall: Ordeal and Hope*, p. 330. See also Matloff and Snell, *Strategic Planning*, p. 272; Steele, *First Offensive*, pp. 81–92.

40. "Editorial Reaction," 9 July 1942, OF 788, FDRL.

41. Churchill, *Second World War*, 4:342–33; Sainsbury, *North African Landings*, pp. 18–19, 85.

42. *FRUS: Conference at Washington, 1942*, p. 430. For Marshall's strategic views see *Marshall Papers*, 3:27; Matloff and Snell, *Strategic Planning*, pp. 104, 188; Pogue, *Marshall: Ordeal and Hope*, p. 304. For Stimson's views see *FRUS: Conference at Washington*, p. 459; Stimson diary, July 23, 1942.

43. Minutes, 3rd Pacific Council Meeting, April 19, 1942, MR box 168, FDRL; Stoler, *Politics of the Second Front*, pp. 32–33.

44. FDR to Marshall, April 28, 1942, PSF (Safe): Marshall, 1942–1944, FDRL;

FDR to Marshall, King, and Hopkins, "Instructions for London Conference—July 1942," July 15, 1942, PSF (Safe): King, FDRL.

45. For the best brief summary, see Howard, *The Mediterranean Strategy in the Second World War*, pp. 14–18, 31–32; Sainsbury, *Churchill and Roosevelt at War*, pp. 20–29.

46. *FRUS: Conference at Washington, 1941–1942*, p. 430.

47. FDR to Hopkins, Marshall, and King, undated [but in response to message of July 22 1942], PSF (Safe): Hopkins, FDRL. Minutes, 8th Pacific Council Meeting, May 23, 1942; minutes, 14th Pacific Council Meeting, July 16, 1942; both in MR box 168, FDRL. Steele, *First Offensive*, p. 35.

48. *C-R Correspondence*, R-170, 1:543.

49. Howard, *Grand Strategy*, 4:112; Howe, *The U.S. Army in World War II*, pp. 89–179; "North African Campaign," in Dear and Foot, ed., *The Oxford Companion to the Second World War*, pp. 813–18; Burns, *Soldier of Freedom*, p. 292.

50. Carter to FDR, "Report on Change in Political Sentiment in New York," November 12, 1942, PSF (Subject File): Carter, FDRL.

51. See daily reports in *Chicago Daily Tribune*, *New York Times*, and *Washington Post*. OWI, "Intelligence Report," No. 53, December 4, 1942,. See also, Levering, *American Opinion and the Russian Alliance*, p. 89.

52. *Christian Science Monitor*, November 21, 1942.

53. OWI, "Intelligence Report," No.53, December 11, 1942.

54. Ibid., No.51, November 27, 1942.

55. Ibid., No.49, November 13, 1942; No. 52, December 4. See also OWI, "Military Information," November 17, 1942, entry 171, box 1843, RG 44, NA.

56. OWI, "Intelligence Report," No.53, December 11, 1942.

57. Carter to FDR, "Change in Political Sentiment," November 12, 1942, PSF (Subject File): Carter, FDRL.

58. FDRPC, No.857, November 6, 1942, 20:196–97.

59. OWI, "Intelligence Report," No.51, November 27, 1942, p. 5; OWI, "Special Intelligence Report: America and the Postwar World," December 16, 1942.

60. Eden to Churchill, No.1244, March 15, 1943, PREM 3/476/9/396, PRO. See also Eden to Moscow, April 22, 1943, FO 800/404/1–E/281, PRO.

61. OWI, "Intelligence Report," No.52, December 4, 1942, p. 7; *FDRPL*, 2:1372.

62. "Madame Chiang Asks for Defeat of Japan, and House Cheers," *New York Times*, February 19, 1943.

63. William C. Bullitt to FDR, May 12, 1943, PSF (Diplomatic): Bullitt, FDRL. Bullitt later wrote an "Asia–first" speech for Senator Chandler that received national coverage; see Isaiah Berlin, "Minute on Senator Chandler's 'Pacific first' speech," May 17, 1943, FO 371/34181/A5569, PRO.

64. FDR to Hull, April 8, 1943, PSF (Departmental): State, FDRL; Long diary, April 21, 1943, Long Papers; FDR, *Public Papers*, 12:179.

65. Swing cited in Halifax to Eden, April 23, 1943, FO 371/34181/A3886, PRO.

66. OWI, "Intelligence Report," No.64, February 26, 1942. See also, OWI, "Leading Topics and Comment," February 22, 1943, entry 171, box 1847, RG 44, NA; Costello, February 9, 1943, *Congressional Record*, 78th Cong., 1st sess., 89, pt. 1:758–59.

67. "Japanese Execute Our Airmen; US Will Punish All Responsible," *New York Times*, April 22, 1943; editorial, "On the Uses of Anger," *New York Times*, April 24, 1943. For some of the most prominent of these speeches, see *New York Times*, May 19, 1943; Halifax to Eden, April 23, 1943, FO 371/34181/A3886, PRO. See also Darilek, *Loyal Opposition*, p. 72.

68. Carter to FDR, "Report on Willkie–Republican Strategy for 1944 Campaign," March 11, 1943, PSF (Subject): Carter, FDRL.

69. Cantril, March 29, 1943, PSF (Subject): Public Opinion Polls, FDRL.

70. "Tunisian Losses Blamed on Plan for Huge Army," *Chicago Daily Tribune*, February 21, 1943. Matloff, *Strategic Planning for Coalition Warfare*, p. 117

71. Editorial, "Congress and the Army," *Chicago Daily Tribune*, February 2, 1943; editorial, "The Army at Home and the AEF," *Chicago Daily Tribune*, February 16, 1942; "Tunisian Losses Blamed on Plan for Huge Army," *Chicago Daily Tribune*, February 21, 1942. See also OWI, "Weekly Media Report," No.40, November 11, 1942; ibid., No.53, February 6, 1943. OWI, "Leading Editorial and Column Topics, December 15–21, 1942," December 22, 1942, entry 171, box 1847, RG 44, NA. FDRPC, No.881, February 19, 1943, 21:169.

72. FDRPC, No.879, February 12, 1943, 21:141; FDR, *Public Papers*, 12:77, 79; FDRPC, No.881, February 19, 1943, 21:164. For the public's reaction, see OWI, "Intelligence Report," No.63, February 19, 1943, OF 5015, FDRL.

73. Matloff, *Strategic Planning*, pp. 117–20. Stimson's speech reprinted in *Congressional Record*, 78th Cong. 1st sess. 89, pt. 2:1791–92. For the background, see Stimson diary, February 26, 1943.

74. Pogue, *Marshall: Organizer of Victory*, p. 169.

75. On Churchill's speech see *New York Times*, May 20, 1943.

76. Halifax to Eden, No.770, February 16, 1942, FO 800/404/1E, PRO; Blum, *Morgenthau Diaries*, 3:102–6.

77. *FRUS: Conference at Washington, 1943*, p. 30; Leahy diary, May 12, 1943.

78. OWI, "Intelligence Report," No.64, February 26, 1943.

79. Editorial, "Lady from China," *New York Times*, February 19, 1943. See also, editorial, "One World," *New York Times*, May 23, 1943.

80. The only polls on this subject are located in OWI files. See OWI, "Enemy Conditions and Propaganda," Report No.12, April 8, 1943, p. 19–20, entry 149, box 1717, RG 44, NA; OWI, "Public Attitudes Toward a Negotiated Peace and Current Military Strategy," Special Memorandum No.81, August 18, 1943, p. 4, entry 164, box 1802, RG 44, NA. That the White House took note of the lack of mass support for "Asia first" is evident in Hopkins to Eden, April 23, 1943, box 329 Hopkins Papers: Sherwood Collection.

81. Matloff, *Strategic Planning*, pp. 117–20. On the impact of Stimson's speech see, OWI, "Weekly Media Report," No.59, March 20, 1943; War Department, "Radio Digest," No. 536, March 11, 1943, entry 497, box 2, RG 165, NA.

82. Howard, *Grand Strategy*, 4:xxiii–xiv.

83. Ibid., 4:449; Thorne, *Allies of a Kind*, pp. 295, 402.

84. "Log of the Trip to the Casablanca Conference," 9–31 January 1943, MR box 24, FDRL; *C-R Correspondence*, R-224, 2:55.

85. *FRUS: Conference at Casablanca*, pp. 714–15, 774–75.

86. Minutes, 19th Pacific Council Meeting, September 2, 1942, MR box 168, FDRL.

87. *FRUS: Conference at Casablanca*, p. 781. See also Hastings, *Bomber Command*, pp. 184–88; Overy, *The Air War*, pp. 73–74, 204–5.

88. Optel No.244, July 25, 1943, MR 203(5), British Ops Telegrams ("Optels"), MR box 154, FDRL; Army–Navy Daily Intelligence Report, July 26, 1943, Daily G–2 Reports—Enemy Situation and Operations, Enemy Capabilities, MR box 68, FDRL. More generally, see Arnold, memorandum for the president, March 26 1943, box 313 Hopkins Papers: Sherwood Collection. On FDR's Map Room, see Goodwin, *No Ordinary Time*, pp. 310–11.

89. Minutes, 34th Pacific Council Meeting, August 11, 1943, MR box 168, FDRL; *C-R Correspondence*, R-270, 2:186.

90. For similar views expressed at this time see, *FRUS: Conference at Washington, 1943*, p. 154.

91. *FRUS: 1939*, 1:542.

92. OGR, "Weekly Analysis of Press Reaction," May 8, 1942, p. 7, OF 788; "Weekly Analysis of Press Reaction," August 7, 1942, p. 1, OF 5015. See also Sherry, *Rise of American Air Power*, pp. 138–39.

93. OWI, "Intelligence Report," No.66, March 12, 1943.

94. FDR to Sikorski, July 3, 1942, PSF (Diplomatic): Poland, FDRL. A similar concern was expressed inside the OWI a year later, see Leo C. Rosten to Elmer Davis, June 4, 1943, OWI: Administration, Leo Rosten Files, box 1, Nash Papers.

95. *FDR: Public Papers, 1943*, 12: 392. Similar views expressed in FDR to Sterrett, February 22, 1944, OF 4675, FDRL.

96. Schaffer, "American Military Ethics in World War II," p. 321; idem, *Wings of Judgment*, p. 61; Crane, *Bombs, Cities, Civilians*, pp. 28, 33; Sherry, *Rise of American Air Power*, p. 144; Roeder, *Censored War*, p. 84.

97. OWI Scripts, "This Is Official," July 11, 1943, entry 146, box 765, RG 208, NA. A similar message was contained in an OWI drama broadcast at the same time, entitled "The Enemy—The Bombing of Axis Cities." See OWI, "Estimated Audiences for Scheduled Campaigns," week beginning July 5, 1943, entry 99, box 639, RG 208, NA.

98. Hopkins to Eden, April 23, 1943, box 329, Hopkins Papers: Sherwood Collection.

99. Ewing to FDR, June 16, 1943, OF 857, FDRL. Very similar results were contained in Niles to Tully, April 8, 1943, ibid. For examples of radio commentators' optimistic reaction to the North African victory, see Winegar to Hatton, May 21, 1943, OF 5015, FDRL.

100. FDR to Hopkins, Marshall, and King, undated [but in response to two messages dated July 22, 1942], box 308, Hopkins Papers: Sherwood Collection, FDRL.

101. See, for instance, editorial, "Germany Faces War on Two Fronts," February 25, 1943; editorial, "On the Uses of Anger," *New York Times*, April 24, 1943; Lippmann, *Washington Post*, July 24, 1943.

102. OWI, "Trends and Attitudes Toward the Progress of the War," Special Memorandum No.75, August 2, 1943, entry 164, RG 44, NA.

103. FDR's comment was scrawled on JCS, memorandum for the president, May 8, 1943, MR A/16: General Correspondence, MR box 164, FDRL.

104. *FRUS: Conference at Washington, 1943*, p. 25; Pogue, *Marshall: Organizer of Victory*, p. 243; Matloff, *Strategic Planning*, pp. 157–60.

105. Stoler, *Politics of the Second Front*, p. 104;

106. Dear and Foot, *Oxford Companion*, p. 1183.

107. Minutes of Meeting between FDR and JCS, August 10, 1943, Central Decimal File, entry 1, box 196, RG 218, NA; Matloff, *Strategic Planning*, p. 125; Greenfield, *American Strategy*, p. 74.

108. *FRUS: Conference at Washington, 1943*, p. 30; CCS Minutes, August 15, 1943, entry 1, box 170, RG 218, FDRL; Matloff, *Strategic Planning*, p. 163; Stoler, *Politics of the Second Front*, pp. 91, 101, 112–15; Weiss, *Allies in Conflict*, pp. 83–88.

109. Sainsbury, *The Turning Point*, pp. 134, 144.

110. *FRUS: Conference at Tehran*, pp. 488–89; Sainsbury, *Turning Point*, p. 256.

111. Arnold, journal, trip to Sextant, December 6–7, 1943, box 3, Henry H. Arnold Papers, LC.

Chapter 4

1. "Log of the Trip to the Casablanca Conference," January 9–31, 1943, MR box 24, FDRL; FDRPC, No.875, January 24, 1943, 21:87–89. See also *FRUS: Conference at Casablanca*, pp. 635, footnote 6; 835–37.
2. Churchill, *Second World War*, 4:613–18.
3. Those works that posit a link with the Darlan Deal include, Sherwood, *Roosevelt and Hopkins*, pp. 696–97; O'Connor, *Diplomacy for Victory*, p. 49; Balfour, "The Origin of the Formula, 'Unconditional Surrender' in World War II," p. 287; Campbell, "Franklin Roosevelt and Unconditional Surrender,"pp. 226–27; Dallek, *Roosevelt and Foreign Policy*, p. 366.
4. Those works that minimize the role of domestic factors include, Armstrong, *Unconditional Surrender*, p. 39; Feis, "Some Notes on Historical Record–keeping," pp. 109–13; Gellman, *Secret Affairs*, pp. 295–96; Kimball, *Forged in War*, pp. 188–90; Stoler, *Politics of the Second Front*, p. 77.
5. John Chase is one writer who looks at other public–opinion explanations, arguing that FDR saw unconditional surrender as a way of countering "domestic indifference" to the war, see Chase, "Unconditional Surrender Reconsidered," pp. 358–60
6. Minutes P–6 Meeting, April 11, 1942, box 192, Welles Papers; "Passages in the Minutes of Advisory Committee and Its Subcommittee Reflecting Consultation with President," May 20, 1942, Post–World War II Foreign Policy Planning: Records of Harley A. Notter, 1939–1945, file 548–1; U.S. Department of State, *Postwar Foreign Policy Preparation*, pp. 124–27. On December 15, FDR also told the Canadian Prime Minister that he favored unconditional surrender; see Pickersgill, *The MacKenzie King Record*, 1:433.
7. FDR, *Public Papers*, 10:528; 11:35.
8. FDR, *Public Papers*, 11:112, 352, 234. This content analysis is derived from ibid., vols. 9–11.
9. Berle diary, May 2, 1942; Rosenman, *Working with Roosevelt*, p. 362.
10. Minutes, CWI Meeting, January 21, 1942, entry 6E, box 11, RG208, NA.
11. FDRPC, No. 864 December 1, 1942, 20:221; FDR, *Public Papers*, 11:485.
12. *FDRPL*, 2:1382; FDR, *Public Papers*, 11:469; 12:25.
13. *FDRPL*, 2:1371; Halifax to Eden, memorandum of conversation with FDR, October 30, 1942, FO 954/US/41/225, Avon Papers, PRO.
14. *FDRPL*, 2:1366–67; FDR, *Public Papers*, 12:3.
15. On the background to the Darlan deal see *FRUS: 1942*, 2:392–93; 393–96; Leahy diary, October 17, 1942, Leahy Papers; Funk, "Negotiating the 'Deal' with Darlan," pp. 164–71.
16. "North African Campaign," in Dear and Foot, eds., *Oxford Companion*, pp. 14–15.
17. Bullitt to FDR, November 29, 1942, PSF (Confidential): War Department, FDRL; Bell, *John Bull and the Bear*, p. 191, footnote 3.
18. "Intelligence Report," No. 50, November 20, 1942, p. 2; "Text of Swing's Comments," November 16, 1942, OF 5015, FDRL.
19. Minutes, 24th Pacific Council Meeting, November 18, 1942, MR box 168, FDRL.
20. Bliss, ed., *In Search of Light*, p. 53.
21. Blum, ed., *Public Philosopher*, pp. 427–28.
22. Morgenthau diary, November 16, 1942, book 584, pp. 170E–G, and 17 November 1942, book 585, Morgenthau Papers.
23. Stimson diary, November 16, 1942.

24. Minutes, 24th Pacific Council Meeting, November 18, 1942, MR box 168, FDRL. See also *C-R Correspondence*, R-213, 2:8.

25. FDR to Eisenhower, November 16, 1942, MR box 167, FDRL.

26. *Marshall Interviews*, p. 487; London to AGWAR, No.5306, November 28, 1942, MR.000.7, Press and Publicity, MR box 46, FDRL.

27. Stimson diary, November 16, 1942.

28. Morgenthau presidential diary, November 17, 1942. For FDR's similar comments before the cabinet and the Pacific War Council, see Ickes diary, November 22, 1942, pp. 724–25; Minutes, 24th Pacific Council Meeting, November 18, 1942, MR box 168, FDRL.

29. Davis to FDR, November 16, 1942, PSF (Subject File): OWI, FDRL; Berle to Hull, November 16, 1942, Berle diary; FDRPC, No. 861, November 17, 1942, 20:245–47. The OWI took care to espouse the same line, see MacLeish to deputies and bureau chiefs, November 18, 1942, box 3, Nash Papers.

30. Editorial, "Common Sense in North Africa," *New York Times*, November 18, 1942; editorial, "Clearing the Air," *Washington Post*, November 18, 1942. See also OWI, "Intelligence Report," No.50, November 20, 1942.

31. Lippmann, "America and France," *Washington Post*, November 19, 1942. A similar view was expressed the day before by Lindley, "Depends on Politics and Diplomacy," *Washington Post*, November 18, 1942.

32. OWI, "Intelligence Report," No. 56, January 1, 1942; and No.59, January 22, 1943. See also, Vandenberg and Morris, ed., *Private Papers of Vandenberg*, p. 33; *Congressional Record*, 78th Cong., 1st sess., 89, pt.1:344.

33. OWI, "Intelligence Report," No. 52, December 4, 1942.

34. Editorial, "Temporary Expedient?" *Washington Post*, December 4, 1942; Berle diary, November 25, 1942; "Who Shall Make the Peace?" *New Republic*, 107 (December 14, 1942):780.

35. Krock, "Stating, but Not Solving, the French Puzzle," *New York Times*, November 17, 1942. See also, Freda Kirchwey, "America's First Quisling," *Nation*, 155 (November 21, 1942):530.

36. Editorial, "Darlan Policy," *Washington Post*, December 11, 1942; "U.S. at War: QED," *Time*, November 30, 1942. See also OWI, BoI, Media Division to Davis, "North Africa," February 12, 1943, entry 171, box 1846, RG 44, NA.

37. OWI, "Intelligence Report," No.59, January 22, 1943; Lippmann, "Plain Words about North Africa," *Washington Post*, January 19, 1943; idem, "Super-Duper Realism," *Washington Post*, January 21, 1943; Kingsbury Smith, "Our Government's Case for Expediency," *The American Mercury*, 56 (February 1943):135–43.

38. BoI, "Weekly Media Report," No.52, January 23, 1943, entry 151, box 1721, RG 44, NA; Brucker to William D. Whitney, "North Africa," February 8, 1943, entry 171, box 1846, RG 44, NA. See also Murphy, *Diplomat Among Warriors*, pp. 198–203.

39. For the letters of protest see OF 203-A, FDRL. See also Brucker to Whitney, "North Africa," Special Memorandum No.36, February 8, 1943; OWI, "North Africa," Special Memorandum No.37, February 12, 1943; both in entry 171, box 1846, RG 44, NA. And also, "The Role of the State Department in the North African Economic and Political Program from its Inception to the Invasion," undated, box 65, Cordell Hull Papers, LC.

40. Correspondence Panels Section to Barth, "North Africa Mess—People Feel Ashamed," February 16, 1943, entry 149, box 1710, RG 44, NA. This research was incorporated in OWI, "Intelligence Report," No.63, February 19, 1943, pp. 7–8.

41. Berle diary, November 28, 1942. See also Hull, *Memoirs*, 2:1194, 1199; Hull, press conference, December 16, 1942, January 19 and 20, 1943, box 141, Hull Papers.

42. Rosenman, *Working with Roosevelt*, p. 335. See also Burns, *Soldier of Freedom*, p. 298.

43. *Wallace Diary*, pp. 135–36.

44. *C-R Correspondence*, R–234–1, 2:73–74.

45. Casey, "Roosevelt and the 'S-Project,'" pp. 339–59.

46. FDR, press release, December 16, 1942, OF 203, FDRL.

47. FDR, *Public Papers*, 12:30–33.

48. Hull to FDR, "Daily Summary," No.3, January 14, 1943, MR box 15, FDRL.

49. "Utah 34," January 14, 1943, MR box 15, FDRL. See also Algiers to AGWAR USFO, January 23, 1943, annex to minutes CCS meeting, February 12, 1943, entry 1, box 170, RG 218, NA; Algiers to War, No. 6965, January 24, 1942, MR.000.7, Press and Publicity, MR box 46, FDRL.

50. FDR to Hull, January 16, 1943, MR box 15, FDRL. See also *FRUS: Conference at Casablanca*, pp. 606–7. A similar conclusion was reached back in Washington by Breckenridge Long, see Long diary, January 24, 1943.

51. FDRPC, No. 875, January 24, 1943, 21:87–89. Hopkins, "Notes for FDR," undated, box 330, Hopkins Papers: Sherwood Collection, FDRL. See also "Log of the Trip to the Casablanca Conference," January 9–31, 1943, MR box 24, FDRL; and *FRUS: Conference at Casablanca*, p. 635, footnote 6; pp. 835–37.

52. OWI, "Intelligence Report," No.60, January 29, 1943, p. 1; No.61, February 5, 1943, p. 1; OWI, "Leading Editorial and Column Topics in the Media Division's Advance Newspaper Sample," February 2, 1943, entry 171, box 1847, RG 44, NA.

53. *Time*, February 1, 1943, pp. 11–12; "The British–American Conference," *U.S. News*, 14 (February 5, 1943):22. See also OWI, "Regional Roundups," No.16–3, January 26, 1943 and No.16–4, February 2, 1943, entry 171, box 1838, RG 44, NA.

54. *Wallace Diary*, p. 178. On FDR's illness, see *C-R Correspondence*, 2:149–50.

55. FDRPC, No.876, February 2, 1942, 121:101–4. FDR to Early, February 5, 1943, PPF 6646, FDRL, also demonstrates FDR's continued concern about press comment on Peyrouton.

56. Totten to FDR, February 11, 1943, PPF 1820, FDRL. See also Hull, *Memoirs*, 2:1207–8.

57. Hopkins, "Memorandum for the files," February 11 and 19, 1943, box 24, Samuel I. Rosenman Papers, FDRL.

58. Berle to FDR, February 12, 1943, OF 20, FDRL. This action appears to contradict Hull's later claim that he had always opposed the enunciation of unconditional surrender. See Hull, *Memoirs*, 2:1570–71. See also Early, memorandum for the president, February 12, 1943, Early Papers, box 24.

59. FDRPC, No.879, February 12, 1943, 21:138.

60. FDR, *Public Papers*, 12:72, 78, 80.

61. The term *liberal* is used here and in subsequent pages because this was how FDR described his critics on February 12. It is accurate in the sense that many of these writers inclined toward the liberal end of the political spectrum. But there were also important exceptions—most notably, of course, Walter Lippmann, who had not only broken with the New Deal in 1935 but was also to become a proponent of realism.

62. Nicholas, ed., *Washington Despatches*, pp. 123, 126–27.

63. On different decision contexts, see Foyle, *Counting the Public In*, pp. 14–16.

64. *Postwar Foreign Policy Preparation*, p. 127. Marshall also "played little part," see Pogue, *Marshall: Organizer of Victory*, p. 32.

65. *C-R Correspondence*, C-193, 2:7.

66. Gilbert, *Road to Victory*, pp. 309-10; Dallek, *Roosevelt and Foreign Policy*, pp. 374-75.

67. FDR to Stalin, December 8, 1942; Stalin to FDR, December 14, 1942; both in MR box 8, FDRL. See also, Kimball, *Forged in War*, p. 190; Pogue, *Marshall: Organizer of Victory*, pp. 32-33.

68. Leahy, *I Was There*, p. 147. See also Hinsley et al., *British Intelligence in the Second World War*, 2:615.

69. Minutes of FDR-JCS meeting, January 7, 1943, MR 29, FDRL.

70. *Stalin's Correspondence with Roosevelt and Churchill*, pp. 51-52. See also Campbell, "Unconditional Surrender," p. 226.

71. Lippmann, "Casablanca," *Washington Post*, January 28, 1943; Freda Kirchwey, "The President's Pledge," *Nation*, 155 (February 20, 1943):257.

72. Willkie, *One World*, pp. 89, 14.

73. Dear and Foot, *Oxford Companion*, pp. 100-1, 588-89.

74. OWI, "Summary of Press and Radio Comment on OWI Broadcasts on Mussolini Resignation," August 6 and 18, 1943, entry 107, box 1026, RG 44, NA; Lippmann, "Italy After Mussolini," *Washington Post*, July 27, 1943.

75. Berle diary, September 18, 1943; Ickes diary, September 29, 1943, p. 8111. Gellman, *Secret Affairs*, chap. 14.

76. State Department, "Public Attitudes on Foreign Policy," No.3, November 1, 1943, Schuyler Foster Files, entry 568J, box 1, RG 59, NA.

77. Ickes diary, March 6, 1943, p. 7521. See also Berle diary, February 24, 1943.

78. *C-R Correspondence*, R-334, 2:359; FDR to Von Windigger, 1 September 1943, PPF 7213, FDRL. See also FDR to Carter, June 10, 1943, and attached memorandum, "Report on 'PM' and Foreign Policy, June 8, 1943, PSF (Subject): Carter, FDRL; *FRUS: Conference at Quebec, 1943*, pp. 600-1.

79. Stettinius to Tully, November 10, 1943; and attached memoranda by FDR, November 8, 1943; Donovan, October 29, 1943; Sherwood, October 26, 1943; and Morde, October 5-6, 1943; all in PSF (Subject): OSS: Donovan Reports, FDRL. Stettinius to Hull, "discussion with the president, November 10-11, 1943," November 12, 1943, folder 376, box 87, Hull Papers.

80. *FRUS: Conference at Quebec 1943*, pp. 1014-15, 942.

81. *FDR's Fireside Chats*, pp. 258-59; FDRPC, No.912, July 30, 1943, 22:49-50; *C-R Correspondence*, R-331, 2:360-62.

82. FDRPC, No.898, May 21, 1943, 21:335; minutes, CCS Meeting, May 22, 1943, entry 1, box 170, RG 218, NA.

83. Sherwood, *Roosevelt and Hopkins*, p. 791.

84. Holborn, ed., *War and Peace Aims of the United Nations*, 2:227, 231-32; FDR, *Public Papers*, 12:368. See also OWI, "Information Guide: The Enemy," Sheet 7, April 1943.

85. FDR, *Public Papers*, 12:391.

86. Davis, "Flow of War Information," September 23, 1943, copy in entry 197, box 1038, RG 208, NA.

87. *FRUS: Conference at Tehran*, p. 154; Feis, *Churchill, Roosevelt, Stalin*, pp. 350-54; Mastny, *Russia's Road to the Cold War*, pp. 145-46.

88. Hull to FDR, January 14, 1944, PSF (Departmental): State: Hull, FDRL. See also *FRUS, 1944*, 1:484-85; Hull to FDR, April 4, 1944, PSF (Departmental): State, FDRL.

89. Hull to FDR, March 25, 1944, PSF (Departmental): State, FDRL. See also Hull, *Memoirs*, 2:1572.

90. Hull to FDR, April 4, 1944, PSF (Departmental): State, FDRL. See also *FRUS, 1944*, 1:501.

91. Leahy to FDR, March 25, 1944, MR370 (2), sec.1 (Surrender of Germany), MR box 110, FDRL; Stettinius to Hull, "S–50325," April 13, 1944, MR370, sec.1, MR box 110, FDRL.

92. FDR to Hull, January 17, 1944, PSF (Departmental): State: Hull, FDRL; FDR to Hull, April 5, 1944, PSF (Departmental): State, FDRL. Emphasis added.

93. Armstrong, *Unconditional Surrender*, p. 39; Chase, "Unconditional Surrender Reconsidered," p. 357; Gaddis, *The U.S. and the Origins of the Cold War*, p. 10; O'Connor, *Diplomacy for Victory*, p. 101.

94. Bullock, *Hitler*, pp. 743–50.

95. Berle diary, June 10, 1944.

96. Ickes diary, June 11, 1944, p. 8994. Taylor to FDR and Hull, June 21, 1944; Taylor, "Notes for use in Second Audience," June 27, 1944; both in "Report by Taylor, Personal Representative of the President to Pope Pius XII, 1944–1945," box 2, Taylor Papers, LC. FDR to Taylor, undated, "Documentation of the Mission of President Roosevelt to Pope Pius XII by Taylor," box 5A, Taylor Papers.

97. Rosenman, *Working with Roosevelt*, p. 407; *FDRPL*, 2:1525

98. Heideking and Mauch, ed., *American Intelligence and the German Resistance to Hitler*, p. 386; FDRPC, No.962, July 29, 1944, 24:31–32.

99. Campbell, "Roosevelt and Unconditional Surrender," p. 235.

Chapter 5

1. *FRUS: Conference at Tehran*, p. 602.

2. FDR to Stimson, August 28, 1944, PSF (Departmental): War, FDRL; Morgenthau presidential diary, August 19, 1944.

3. *FDRPL*, 2:1372; Halifax to Eden, October 30, 1942, FO 954/US/41/225, Avon Papers, PRO. See also *FRUS: Conference at Washington 1942*, p. 444.

4. *FDRPL*, 2:1366–67.

5. Halifax, "Talks with President," April 6, 1941, FO 115/3465/1799/1, PRO; Welles, memorandum of FDR–Churchill Meeting, August 11, 1941, box 62, Hull Papers.

6. *FRUS, 1941*, 1:367–69. Emphasis added. Berle diary, November 9, 1942.

7. Works that stress that FDR had hated Germany and the Germans since the 1890s include Gaddis, *U.S. and the Origins of the Cold War*, pp. 99–100; Herzstein, *Roosevelt and Hitler*, esp. pp. 46–7, 62–63; Kinsella, *Leadership in Isolation*, pp. 8–26; idem, "The Prescience of a Statesman," pp. 74–82; Range, *Franklin Roosevelt's World Order*, p. 80; Sainsbury, *Churchill and Roosevelt at War*, pp. 134–35; Everen, "Franklin D. Roosevelt and the Problem of Nazi Germany," pp. 137–39.

8. FDRPC, No.992, February 23, 1945, 13:136; Hassett, *Off the Record with FDR*, pp. 199–200; *FRUS: Conference at Quebec, 1944*, pp. 144–45. Wilson and McKenzie, "The Masks of Power," p. 166. FDR had made some comments in a similar vein in earlier years, but not as frequently. See, for instance, FDR to Murray, March 4, 1940, PSF (Diplomatic): Britain: Murray, FDRL; minutes, 13th Pacific Council Meeting, July 8, 1942, MR 168, FDRL.

9. Hönicke, "Roosevelt's View of Germany before 1933," pp. 16–19. On FDR's

tendency to "simply alter the past to suit the present" and his "creative memory," see Ward, *A First–Class Temperament*, pp.92 footnotes 5, 66; 332 footnote 28; 484 footnote 33.

10. Long diary, August 10, 1943.

11. Minutes, 32nd Pacific Council Meeting, June 9, 1943, MR box 168, FDRL. See also Hopkins, "Eden Conferences," March 22, 1943, box 329, Hopkins Papers: Sherwood Collection.

12. Arnold to FDR, January 27, 1944, and attached memorandum, "Germany's War Potential," December 1943, MR (Naval Aides File: Axis War Potential), MR box 164, FDRL.

13. Marshall to Hopkins, September 29, 1943, Selected Correspondence: Hopkins File, box 71, microfilm reel 19, George C. Marshall Papers, LC.

14. FDR to Marshall, February 22, 1944, and attached memorandum, Hoover to Watson, February 19, 1944, PSF (Departmental): Justice: Hoover, FDRL. A similar conclusion was contained in Donovan to FDR, March 20, 1944, PSF (Safe): OSS, March 1944, FDRL.

15. Donovan to FDR, "Interrogation of German Prisoners of War," October 11, 1943, PSF (Subject): OSS: Donovan Reports, FDRL. In July 1943 there was also a discussion in cabinet on the troublesome nature of German POWs, especially their tendency to escape. See Ickes diary, July 25, 1943, p. 8019.

16. *FRUS, 1943*, 3:15; 1:631; *FRUS: Conference at Tehran*, p. 154.

17. On this aspect of FDR's thinking see Gaddis, *Strategies of Containment*, p. 9–10; Kimball, *Swords or Ploughshares?* p. 12.

18. In other words, it was one of the conditions that would have made Operation SLEDGEHAMMER—an emergency cross–Channel attack—feasible. For FDR's comments in this context see, for instance, *C–R: Correspondence*, R–222, 2:41; *FRUS: Conference at Casablanca*, p. 629.

19. *FRUS, 1944*, 1:502.

20. Held, "Report on the Visit to the President," *Archives of the Holocaust*, document 148; Stephen Wise to FDR, December 2, 1942, box 85, Welles Papers. For reports reaching FDR that confirmed the extent of the Nazi atrocities, see Taylor, "Memorandum for the President and the Secretary of State," October 20, 1942, box 84, Welles Papers; Carter, "Reports on Poland and Lithuania," December 30, 1942, PSF (Subject): Carter, FDRL. See also Wyman, *Abandonment*, pp. 51–53.

21. *MacKenzie King Record*, 1:431.

22. Sherwood, *Roosevelt and Hopkins*, p. 708; Kimball, *Juggler*, pp. 102, 182, 198.

23. White House usher diaries, March 24, 1943, microfiche, FDRL. Hassett to Tully, March 23, 1943, and FDR to Hull, May 31, 1943, and enclosure of Ludwig's testimony before Foreign Affairs Committee, House of Representatives, March 26, 1943, PPF 3884, FDRL.

24. Yergin, *Shattered Peace* p. 42. Kimball, *Forged in War*, pp. 200–6.

25. *FRUS, 1943*, 3:15. That FDR now firmly distrusted the Prussians can be inferred from Taylor to FDR, April 8, 1943, and attached memorandum, Amery to Taylor, February 12, 1943, PSF (Diplomatic): Taylor, FDRL. A few weeks earlier FDR had also stressed that "East Prussia should go to Poland," Notter Records, February 22, 1943, File 548–1.

26. See, for example, Sainsbury, *Churchill and Roosevelt at War*, p. 135; Kuklick, *American Policy and the Division of Germany*, p. 26; Backer, *The Decision to Divide Germany*, p. 15; Eisenberg, *Drawing the Line*, p. 20.

27. *FRUS, 1943*, 3:15; Eden to Churchill, March 29, 1943, FO 800/404/1E/1470, PRO; minutes, FDR–JCS Meeting, November 19, 1943, MR box 29, FDRL.

28. Gellman, *Secret Affairs*, pp. 15-16, 20, 88, 164, 326-28. Dallek, *Roosevelt and Foreign Policy*, p. 421.

29. Dallek, *Roosevelt and Foreign Policy*, p. 419.

30. *FRUS, 1943*, 1:542; Leahy diary, October 5, 1943. See also Notter Records, February 11, 1944, file 548-1.

31. Hull to FDR, September 1, 1943, box 52, Hull Papers; *FRUS, 1943*, 1:720-23 *FRUS: Conference at Quebec, 1943*, pp. 761-62, 927-28. See also Stephen J. Schwark, "The State Department Plans for Peace," pp. 219-23.

32. Sherwood, *Roosevelt and Hopkins*, p. 768; *FDRPL*, 2:1469.

33. Goodwin, *No Ordinary Time*, p. 475; *FRUS: Conference at Tehran*, p. 483

34. *FRUS: Conference at Tehran*, pp. 510, 513.

35. Ibid., pp. 532-33. See also Bohlen, *Witness to History*, pp. 143-53. For FDR's views on the length of occupation see also, "Minutes, FDR-JCS Meeting," November 19, 1943, MR box 29, FDRL; Kimball, *Juggler*, pp. 99, 245-46.

36. *FRUS: Conference at Tehran*, pp. 600-3. See also Sainsbury, *Turning Point*, pp. 233-34, 277-79

37. *FRUS: Conference at Tehran*, p. 511. The difference between "direct and indirect rearmament" is developed by Overy, *War and Economy in the Third Reich*, pp. 20-21.

38. *C-R Correspondence*, R-483/1, 2:766. See also minutes, 30th Pacific Council Meeting, March 31, 1943, MR 168, FDRL.

39. *FRUS: Conference at Tehran*, pp. 603-04.

40. Ickes diary, December 19, 1943, pp. 8473-74; *Wallace Diary*, pp. 280-85.

41. OWI, "Current Surveys," No.48, March 29, 1944, entry 149, box 1715, RG 44, NA.

42. Hassett to FDR, May 8, 1943, and attached *Fortune* Survey, undated [but scheduled for release on 30 May 1943], PSF (Subject): Opinion Polls, FDRL.

43. State Department, "Public Attitudes on Foreign Policy: Treatment of Germany," No.18, April 13, 1944. See also OWI, "Current Surveys," No.28, November 3, 1943; Gallup, "Four Nations Favor Control, Not Destruction, of Germany," *Washington Post*, January 9, 1944.

44. Gallup to FDR, September 23, 1942, and attached report, "An Analysis of American Opinion Regarding the War," PPF 4721, FDRL.

45. See, for example, OWI, *This Is Our Enemy*, episode 27, entry 146, box 762, RG208, NA; McAleer, *Stout*, pp. 314-20.

46. Stout, "We Shall Hate, or We Shall Fail," *New York Times Magazine*, January 17, 1943. See also Stout's letter, *New York Times*, February 4, 1943.

47. Don Whitehead, "Split Up Reich, Gerard Proposes," June 17, 1943, *Chicago Times*, clipping in PPF 977, FDRL.

48. U.S. House, Committee on Foreign Affairs, *The German People: Testimony of Mr. Emil Ludwig, March 26, 1943*, 78th Cong. 1st sess. See also OWI, "Weekly Media Report," No.60, March 27, 1943, entry 151, box 1721, RG 44, NA. Ludwig also lobbied the OWI to change its propaganda emphasis. He even sent Elmer Davis a copy of his testimony to the House Committee on Foreign Affairs, but Davis simply read it and then "threw it away." See Rosten to Davis, March 29, 1943; Ludwig to Davis, June 2, 1943, box 1, Nash Papers.

49. Bowie, "Hate Is Moral Poison," *New York Times Magazine*, January 31, 1943. See also letters, *New York Times*, February 4, 1943; John Haynes Homes, *If We Hate, We Shall Fail!* (New York: Community Church Pamphlet, 1943).

50. "Topic of the Times," *New York Times*, February 2, 1943; Editorial, "The Peace as it Looks Today," *Chicago Daily Tribune*, March 2, 1943.

51. Long to Early, October 10, 1943, and attached memorandum, Oscar Ewing to FDR, October 6, 1943, PSF (Subject): Post War Plans, FDRL.

52. Lippmann, "The Problem of Germany," *Washington Post*, April 20, 1943; idem, "The Disarmament of Germany," *Washington Post*, April 22, 1943; idem, "The Reorientation of Germany," *Washington Post*, April 24, 1943. See also idem, "The Preparation of the Western Front," Washington Post, July 16, 1942; "Shall We Govern Germany?" *Washington Post*, October 5, 1943; "Concerning the German Settlement," *New York Herald Tribune*, March 30, 1944.

53. Forrest Davis, "Roosevelt's World Blueprint," *Saturday Evening Post*, 215 (April 10, 1943):110. On FDR's close interest in the framing of this article, see Welles to Early, February 10, 1943, and attached memoranda, OF 4287, FDRL.

54. FDRPC, No.929, December 28, 1943 and October 29, 1943, 22:251, 185.

55. FDR, *Public Papers*, 12:333.

56. *FRUS: Conference at Tehran*, pp. 638–640; John Boettiger, wartime diary, December 1, 1943, John Boettiger Papers, FDRL.

57. Early to Hopkins, "White 107," December 7, 1943, MR box 17, FDRL.

58. OWI, "Cairo and Tehran Conferences," December 7, 1943, p. 7, entry 108, box 1027, RG 44, NA; *PM Daily*, December 12, 1943.

59. "Lack of Details on War Parley Vexes Capital," *Chicago Daily Tribune*, December 7, 1943; *PM Daily*, December 12, 1943; OWI, "Cairo and Tehran Conferences," December 7, 1943, p. 6, entry 108, box 1027, RG 44, NA; OWI, "Tehran Declaration," December 10, 1943, entry 149, box 1712, RG 44, NA. See also Divine, *Second Chance*, pp. 193–93.

60. Divine, *Second Chance*, pp. 83–84, 184–85, 205–8; Hoopes and Brinkley, *FDR and the Creation of the UN*, p. 78; Burns, *Soldier of Freedom*, pp. 427–28.

61. State Department, "Public Attitudes on Foreign Policy," Report No.3, November 1, 1943.

62. *FDR's Fireside Chats*, pp. 250–51.

63. Ibid., pp. 278–79.

64. "First Draft of December 24, 1943 Speech," undated, box 24, Rosenman Papers FDRL. FDR also considered announcing that "the Germans are not so much a people as they are a state of mind." But this passage never appeared in any of his speeches. FDR, "S.I.R. for speech material," January 24, 1944, ibid., box 19.

65. *FDR's Fireside Chats*, p. 277.

66. FDR, *Public Papers*, 13:31.

67. Ibid., 13:104–05; FDRPC, No.944, March 24, 1944, 23:114. At the same time, FDR clearly blamed the atrocities in the Pacific on the entire Japanese nation.

68. Hopkins, "What Victory Will Bring Us," *American Magazine*, 137 (January 1944): 87.

69. FDR to Marshall, January 10, 1944, PSF (Departmental): War: Marshall, FDRL.

70. Officials, including the president, still felt that the public was unlikely to comprehend or believe news of the Holocaust and so remained reluctant to publicize news about it. See Wyman, *Abandonment*, p. 315; Roeder, *Censored War*, p. 127.

71. OWI, "Intelligence Report," No.63, February 19, 1943, pp. 10–12. See also Bailey to Byrnes, forwarded to Tully, February 10, 1943, PSF (Subject): Executive Office of the President: Byrnes, FDRL

72. Noyes to Barnes, July 20, 1943, PPF 1820, FDRL. See also Barnes to FDR, September 24, 1943, OF 857, FDRL.

73. Cantril to Niles, March 23, 1943, box 6, Nash Papers, HSTL; Leigh, *Mobilizing Consent*, pp. 81–82.

74. FDR *Public Papers*, 12:113; Hopkins, "We Can Win in 1945," *American Magazine*, 137 (October 1943): 22. See also FDRPC, No.903, June 11, 1943 and December 17, 1943, 21:385, 224.

75. FDRPC, No.908, July 13, 1943, 22:11. See also, FDRPC, No.888, March 30, 1943, 21:248; Early, memorandum for the president, January 18, 1944, OF 5015, FDRL; and Hull, press conference, No.26, March 22, 1943, box 141, Hull Papers.

76. Churchill, *Second World War*, 5:383-84, 410-23.

77. State Department, "Public Attitudes on Foreign Policy," No.7, January 7, 1944. Peace Now material can be found in House of Representatives, Special Committee on Un-American Activities, *Investigation of Un-American Propaganda Activities in the U.S.: Report on the Peace Now Movement*, 78th Cong. 2nd sess., esp. pp. 7-9.

78. OWI, "European Theater of War," January 31, 1944, p. 7, entry 107, box 1026, RG 44, NA; editorial, "Peace Now," *Washington Post*, January 28, 1944; Shirer, "'Peace Now' Chatter is Similar to Nazi Propagandists' Line," *Washington Post*, February 4, 1944.

79. *Report on Peace Now*, p. 9.

80. Early to FDR, December 6, 1943, "Cairo and Tehran Conferences," December 4, 1943, p. 3, OF 5015, FDRL. There were some rumors that the Big Three were about to send an ultimatum to Berlin; see, for instance, Horace M. Coats, "Surrender Ultimatum Reported Sent to Nazi Army by 'Big 3,'" *Washington Post*, November 30, 1943.

81. OWI, "Cairo and Tehran Conferences," December 7, 1943, p. 7, entry 108, box 1027, RG 44, NA; State Department, "Public Attitudes on Foreign Policy: Increasing Demand for a More Positive Statement on Foreign Policy," No.16, March 20, 1944. See also, editorial, "Looking to the End," *Washington Post*, February 10, 1944.

82. Dr Clarence Poe to FDR, telegram, December 23, 1943, PPF 1820, FDRL.

83. FDR to Hull, January 17, 1944, PSF (Departmental): State: Hull, FDRL; FDR to Hull, April 5, 1944, PSF (Departmental): State, FDRL; *C-R Correspondence*, R-431, 2:652.

84. Holborn, ed., *War and Peace Aims of the United Nations*, 2:232.

85. Armstrong, *Unconditional Surrender*, pp. 19-20, 34; Baldwin, *Great Mistakes*, pp. 24-25; Daugherty, "Unconditional Surrender," p. 274; Kimball, *Swords or Ploughshares?*, pp. 18-19; idem, *The Juggler*, pp. 76, 99, 199; Snell, *Wartime Origins*, p. 31; Van Everen, "Roosevelt and the Problem of Germany," pp. 139-41.

86. Ferrell, *The Dying President*, pp. 27-46; Jim Bishop, *FDR's Last Year*, pp. 3-12; Dallek, *Roosevelt and Foreign Policy*, p. 442; Kimball, *Forged in War*, esp. pp. 339-41.

87. This was soon noted by the media. See, for instance, editorial, "President and the Press," February 2, 1944. In April, FDR also refused to break-off his recuperation in South Carolina to meet with the nation's editors. See FDR to Early, April 15, 1944, box 24 Early Papers.

88. The material on this "Nature of the Enemy" exhibit is in entry 43, box 3, RG 208, NA.

89. Koppes and Black, *Hollywood Goes to War*, p. 134; Weinberg, "What to Tell America," pp. 82-89.

90. Almond to Rosten, "A Suggested Release on the Characteristics of the German Army Leadership," May 12, 1943, entry 149, box 1717, RG 44, NA; OWI Scripts, *This is Our Enemy*, Episode 30, "The German Army," entry 146, box 762, RG 208, NA.

91. OWI, "Information Guide: The Enemy," Sheet 7, April 1943; OWI, Magazine Bureau, "The German Junkers," undated, box 11, Nash Papers.

92. Winkler, *Politics of Propaganda*, pp. 56, 67, 70–71; "Vote to Abolish OWI Domestic Branch," *New York Times*, June 19, 1943.

93. Davis, "Report to the President,"; Milton S. Eisenhower, "Legal Restrictions on Distribution of Publications," July 19, 1943, OWI: Administration, Office Memoranda, box 2, Nash Papers.

94. These campaigns were: The Second War Loan Drive, April 12–May 2, 1943; The Third War Loan Drive, September 6–October 3, 1943; War Bonds for Christmas, November 8–December 24, 1943; The Fourth War Loan Drive, January 17–February 15, 1944; and the Fifth War Loan Drive, June 12–July 8, 1944.

95. OWI, "Summary of Radio Campaign for the Treasury Department's Second War Loan," undated, entry 120, box 710, RG 208, NA.

96. Colegrove, "The Role of Congress and Public Opinion in Formulating Foreign Policy,"pp. 956-69; Leigh, *Mobilizing Consent*, pp. 103–06.

97. Kingsbury Smith, "Our Government's Plan for Postwar Germany," *American Mercury*, 56 (April 1943):391–92.

98. Berle, "The Jewish Massacres and German Responsibility," May 2, 1943, *DSB*, 8:395. Berle was unable to deliver this speech in person, see his note, undated, box 146, Berle Papers.

99. *DSB*, 8:23, 121; idem, "Ten Tragic Years," *Los Angeles Times*, January 24, 1943; State Department, "Speech Clearance, January 1, 1943 to February 23, 1944," entry 1587, box 128, RG 59, NA. See also State Department, *National Socialism: Basic Principles, Their Application by the Nazi Party's Foreign Organization, and the Use of Germans Abroad for Nazi Aims* (Washington DC: GPO, 1943). By March 1944, when Berle drafted a speech for Hull, his views had mellowed considerably and were more in line with the prevailing State Department line. See Berle, "Memorandum: The Secretary's Forthcoming Speech," March 13, 1944, box 58, Berle Papers.

100. OWI, "Special '2nd War Loan' Announcement," Week of April 26, 1943, attached to "Summary of Radio Campaign for the Treasury Department's Second War Loan," undated, entry 120, box 710, RG 208, NA; OWI, "Information Program on Third War Loan Drive," undated, p. 3, entry 149, box 1715, RG 44, NA. Emphasis added. Morgenthau, "Address," September 6, 1943, entry 405N, box 1, RG 56, NA.

101. Hönicke, "'Know Your Enemy,'" pp. 268–69.

102. Bland, ed., *Marshall Papers*, 4:27.

103. On OWI's role in the distribution of the film, and especially a wrangle with Lowell Mellett over its release, see Culbert, ed., *Film and Propaganda in America*, 3:164–90, documents 50–57.

104. *Why We Fight. Part One: Prelude to War* (Signal Corps, 1942), RG 111/OF1, AV/NA. On the background to this film see Steele, "'The Greatest Gangster Movie Ever Filmed," pp. 221–35; Culbert, "'Why We Fight,'" pp. 173–91.

105. "Bases of the Foreign Policy of the United States," Press Release No.88, March 21, 1944, box 144, Hull Papers. On the background to this, see Halifax to Eden, March 24, 1944, FO 461–3/36027, PRO. See also *DSB*, 9:176–78.

106. In 1943, Berle was an exception. See Strang, "Minute of Conversation with Berle," March 24, 1943, FO 371/34205/A3109, PRO. For other stern views, especially by the secretary of the navy, Frank Knox, see *Wallace Diary*, p. 123; Stimson diary, April 4, 1944.

107. Stimson diary, December 18, 1943, April 4, 1944. See also Stimson and Bundy, *On Active Service in Peace and War*, pp. 566–67.

108. Eisenberg, *Drawing the Line*, p. 25; Burns, *Soldier of Freedom*, p. 453; Schwark, "State Department Plans for Peace," p. 259.
109. Smith, "The Rise and Fall of the Morgenthau Plan," p. 33.
110. OWI, "Information Roundup," No.8, May 30, 1944, pp. 19–21, entry 149, box 1712, RG 44, NA; State Department, "Public Attitudes on Foreign Policy: Treatment of Germany," No.18, April 13, 1944.
111. See, for instance, FDR to Stimson, August 26, 1944, PSF (Departmental): War, FDRL; FDR to Kenneth McKellar, August 21, 1944, PPF 3715, FDRL; *FRUS: Conference at Quebec*, p. 318. The OWI was aware, too, see "Information Roundup," No.8, May 30, 1944.

Chapter 6

1. FDR, *Public Papers*, 13:152.
2. Ambrose, *D–Day*, p. 495; Dear and Foot, *Oxford Companion*, pp. 805–12; Overy, *Why the Allies Won*, pp. 135–79.
3. State Department, "Public Attitudes on Foreign Policy: The Republican and Democratic Platform on Foreign Policy," Special Report No.31, August 15, 1944.
4. Divine, *Foreign Policy*, pp. 98, 121, 130–31.
5. *C-R Correspondence*, R-435, 2:649–50. This distinction was publicized just before D–Day, see FDRPC, No.951, May 26, 1944, 23:183; OWI, "OWI and Government Information Policy," May 31, 1944, entry 106, box 1025, RG 44, NA.
6. FDRPC, No.962, July 29, 1944, 24:30–32.
7. FDRPC, No.963, August 15, 1944, 24:49–50; Hassett, *Off the Record with FDR*, p. 264.
8. U.S. Senate, Committee on Military Affairs, Subcommittee on Military Affairs, *Scientific and Technical Mobilization, Hearings*, 78th Congress, 1st sess., pt. 16, pp. 1944, 1966; Maddox, *The Senatorial Career of Harley Martin Kilgore*, pp. 176–77.
9. OWI, "OWI and Government Information Policy," August 3 and 4, 1944, entry 106, box 1025, RG 44, NA; *New York Times*, August 4, 1944.
10. Rosenman to FDR, August 17, 1944; FDR to Hull, September 6, 1944; both in PSF (Departmental): State: Hull, FDRL.
11. Ernst to FDR, "Tidbits," June 29, 1944, PSF (Subject): Ernst, FDRL.
12. *Stettinius Diary*, p. 97.
13. FDR, *Public Papers*, 13:168, 226.
14. State Department, "Fortnightly Survey of American Opinion on International Affairs," No.11, September 19, 1944, entry 568L, box 11, RG 59, NA.
15. Early to Porter, September 1, 1944, box 24, Early Papers.
16. Davis to FDR, June 26, 1944, OF 5015, FDRL; Marshall, King, Arnold, "White House Press Release," June 29, 1944, MR (A/16: General Correspondence), MR box 164, FDRL; Hassett, *Off the Record with FDR*, p. 256. See also War Department, "Radio Digest," July 26, 1944, entry 497, box 4, RG 165, NA.
17. FDR to Beaverbrook, July 20, 1944, PSF (Diplomatic): Britain, FDRL. See also *C-R Correspondence*, R-564, 3:194.
18. Ickes diary, September 24, 1944, p. 9243.
19. Rosenman, *Working with Roosevelt*, p. 461–62; Ferrell, *Dying President*, pp. 80–83.
20. Long to FDR, July 12, 1944, box 189, Long Papers. See also Divine, *Second Chance*, pp. 178, 182; Gellman, *Secret Affairs*, pp. 351–52; *Stettinius Diary*, p. 101.

21. Welles, *The Time for Decision*, pp. 259–79. FDR did pass some highly critical State Department comments to Welles, but without endorsement or comment; see FDR to Welles, June 19, 1944, PSF (Departmental): State: Welles, FDRL. Welles was by now also a prominent columnist, see, for instance, Welles, "Disintegration Within Germany," *Washington Post*, August 16, 1944.

22. SPWW3, "Statement of Policy," *Prevent World War III*, 1 (June–July 1944): i.

23. Stout, "Sense or Sentiment," *Prevent World War III*, 1 (May 1944): 3.

24. Sigrid Arne, "Battle Looms Over Rival Peace Plans," *Washington Post*, April 2, 1944. See also Sir Ronald I. Campbell to Eden, August 8, 1944, FO 461–3/36027/C11016/712/18, PRO.

25. Creel, "The 'Good German' Myth"; Brown, "These are German Crimes"; both in *Prevent World War III*, 1 (September 1944):21, 18.

26. Louis Nizer, "The Return of the Trojan Horse," *Prevent World War III*, 1 (June–July 1944):5; F. W. Foerster, "Don't Let Us be Fooled Again!" *Prevent World War III*, 1 (May 1944):12.

27. Gerard, "There is Only One Germany," *Prevent World War III*, 1 (May 1944):10.

28. Ludwig, "Fourteen Rules for the American Occupation Officer in Germany," *Prevent World War III*, 1 (September 1944):15–16. Ludwig had already sent a copy of this to FDR, see FDR to Ludwig, January 26, 1944, PPF 3884.

29. Stout to Edgar Ansel Mowrer, August 30, 1944, box 26, Edgar Ansel Mowrer Papers, LC.

30. "It Is High Time to Call a Spade a Spade," *New York Times*, April 22, 1944.

31. Tetens, *Know Your Enemy*, p. 109. Arne, "Battle Looms Over Rival Peace Plans," *Washington Post*, April 2, 1944, explains how this book was circulated.

32. OWI, "WJZ and Blue Network, War Effort Reports," June 1944, entry 120, box 715, RG208, NA. For a summary of SPWW3 activities see *Prevent World War III*, 1 (November 1944):21.

33. McAleer, *Stout*, p. 328. See also Stout to FDR, September 29, 1944, OF 2527; FDR to Stout, and accompanying notations, October 2, 1944, OF 5160, FDRL; FDR to John Boettiger, January 16, 1945, and attached memoranda, PSF (Diplomatic): Germany, FDRL.

34. Stout to Betty Wilson, May 9, 1944, Miscellaneous, 1932–48: WWB folder, Democratic National Committee Papers, FDRL.

35. FDRPC, No.963, August 15, 1944, 24:49–50.

36. Editorial, "The Shame of American Writers," *Common Sense*, 13 (May 1944):187. For background on the WWB, see Palmer Hoyt, "War Writers' Board," October 11, 1943, box 2, Nash Papers, HSTL; O'Neill, *A Democracy at War*, p. 141; Kennett, *For the Duration*, p. 66

37. Davis, "Letter," *Common Sense*, 13 (June 1944):206.

38. State Department, "Public Attitudes on Foreign Policy: Treatment of Germany, August 1944," No.33, September 9, 1944.

39. Lippmann, "The Flying Bombs Over London," *New York Herald Tribune*, July 8, 1944.

40. War Department, "Radio Digest," July 25, 1944.

41. Mowrer, "No Way Out for the German Army," *New York Post*, July 24, 1944. Mowrer also broadcast this article, see Edgar Marrar [sic], "Talk on Evil of German Army and Attempted Assassination of Hitler by Army Officers," July 22, 1944, RG208–504A, NA/AV.

42. Cantril to Tully, August 9, 1944, OF 857, FDRL.

43. War Department, "Radio Digests," July 20, 1944.

44. Welles, *Time for Decision*, pp. 270–71; State Department, "Public Attitudes on

Foreign Policy: Treatment of Germany, August 1944," No.33, September 9, 1944. On the debate between Welles and Lippmann over collective security, see Divine, *Second Chance*, pp. 180–81.

45. State Department, "Public Attitudes on Foreign Policy: Postwar Treatment of Japan," Special Report No.47, December 7, 1944.

46. Snell, "What to Do with Germany?" p. 38; idem, *Wartime Origins*, p. 13. Other historians who argue that American opinion was now definitely anti–German include Eisenberg, *Drawing the Line*, p. 45; Ninkovitch, *Germany and the United States*, pp. 21, 26.

47. *FDRPL*, 2:1535; FDR to Stimson, August 26, 1944, PSF (Departmental): War, FDRL.

48. *FRUS 1944*, 1:184; *FRUS: Conference at Quebec, 1944*, pp. 145–58.

49. Taylor, "Notes for use in Second Audience," June 27, 1944, box 2, Taylor Papers. FDR to Taylor, undated, "Documentation of the Mission of President Roosevelt to Pope Pius XII by Taylor," box 5A, ibid.

50. Eisenberg, *Drawing the Line*, p. 25; Hoopes and Brinkley, *FDR and the UN*, pp. 127, 137; Schwark, "State Department Plans for Peace," p. 259.

51. On background to Morgenthau's participation in the German problem, see Henry Morgenthau, Jr., "Our Policy Toward Germany," *New York Post*, November 24, 1947; Chase, "The Development of the Morgenthau Plan," pp. 329–34. For an assessment of the historical literature on Morgenthau's views, see Hönicke, "Prevent World War III," pp. 155–72.

52. Morgenthau to FDR, undated, but attached to FDR to Stimson, August 26, 1944, PSF (Departmental): War, FDRL.

53. *FRUS, 1944*, 1:284.

54. Morgenthau diary, August 18, 1944, 763:202–5, Morgenthau Papers. Morgenthau had, of course, gained the wrong impression. As Hopkins reassured the British, while FDR and Stalin had inclined toward partition at Tehran, nothing had been definitively "decided." See Halifax to Eden, "memorandum of conversation with Hopkins," August 28, 1944, FO 954/US/44/203, PRO.

55. Morgenthau presidential diary, August 19, 1944, pp. 1387–88.

56. Morgenthau presidential diary, August 25, 1944, pp. 1389–90; FDR to Stimson, August 26, 1944, and attached Morgenthau to FDR, undated, PSF (Departmental): War, FDRL.

57. Morgenthau presidential diary, September 2, 1944, pp. 1422–25; Morgenthau diary, September 4, 1944, 768:125, Morgenthau Papers. The original draft of September 1 differs from that given to FDR on September 5 in that section 3, on "The Ruhr Area," is far more explicit about how deindustrialization is to proceed. See *FRUS: Conference at Quebec 1944*, p. 86; "Suggested Post–Surrender Program for Germany" undated [September 5, 1944], PSF (Diplomatic): Germany, FDRL.

58. Morgenthau, "Our Policy Towards Germany," *New York Post*, November 24, 1947.

59. Morgenthau to FDR, "Suggested Post–Surrender Program for Germany" undated [September 5, 1944], PSF (Diplomatic): Germany, FDRL.

60. Stimson to Hull, September 5, 1944, PSF (Diplomatic): Germany, FDRL.

61. Morgenthau diary, September 5, 1944, 769:11–12, Morgenthau Papers; Morgenthau presidential diary, September 9, 1944, pp. 1431–32. On Hopkins' attitudes, see also Halifax to Eden, "Memorandum of Conversation with Hopkins," August 28, 1944, FO 954/US/44/203, PRO; Hopkins to Hull, September 5, 1944, PSF (Diplomatic): Germany, FDRL; McJimsey, *Hopkins*, pp. 345–46. For the compromise see *FRUS: Conference at Quebec 1944*, pp. 96–97.

62. Morgenthau, presidential diary, September 9, 1944, pp. 1431–32.

63. *FRUS: Conference at Quebec 1944*, pp. 323–24.

64. Ibid., pp. 325, 327.

65. Morgenthau presidential diary, September 15, 1944, pp. 1444–45; *FRUS: Conference at Quebec 1944*, p. 343. On Churchill's change of heart, see Churchill, *Second World War*, 6:138; Kimball, *Swords or Ploughshares?*, p. 39.

66. FDR to Hull, "MR*IN-157," September 15, 1944, MR box 20, FDRL

67. *Morgenthau Diaries*, 3:375; Kimball, *Swords or Ploughshares*, p. 4; Mausbach, *Zwischen Morgenthau und Marshall*, pp. 55–66.

68. *FRUS: Conference at Quebec 1944*, p. 344.

69. Ibid., p. 238.

70. Those who argue that FDR's behavior was erratic or the product of ill health include, Tugwell, *The Democratic Roosevelt*, p. 657; Buhite, *Decisions and Yalta*, p. 23; Marks, *Wind Over Sand*, p. 284; Campbell, "Roosevelt and Unconditional Surrender," pp. 236–37; Ferrell, *The Dying President*, p. 149.

71. The following analysis differs from Kimball, who maintains that FDR believed the plan could command general support among the American public. See Kimball, *Swords or Ploughshares?*, p. 42.

72. *FRUS: Conference at Quebec 1944*, p. 362; Stimson diary, September 20, 1944.

73. Morgenthau diary, August 23, 1944, 765:41, Morgenthau Papers. Some of Morgenthau's subordinates shared this concern, see Morgenthau diary, September 4, 1944, 768:112, 121, Morgenthau Papers.

74. FDR to Stimson, August 26, 1944, PSF (Departmental): War, FDRL; FDR to Kenneth McKellar, August 21, 1944, PPF 3715, FDRL; *FRUS: Conference at Quebec*, p. 318.

75. Heinrichs, *Threshold of War*, p. 11

76. On this point see John Backer, *Decision to Divide Germany*, chap. 4.

77. *FRUS: Conference at Quebec 1944*, pp. 128–40.

78. FDR to Rosenman, October 24, 1944, and attached memorandum from Paul Porter, PPF 1820, FDRL; Thomas E. Dewey, "New Deal Afraid to Release Men from Army after Victory," September 7, 1944, *Republican Party Pamphlets, 1944*, LC.

79. Morgenthau to FDR, "Suggested Post-Surrender Program for Germany" undated [September 5, 1944], PSF (Diplomatic): Germany, FDRL.

80. Hoopes and Brinkley, *FDR and the Creation of the UN*, p. 147.

81. FDR to George Norris, February 17, 1944, OF 292, FDRL. See also *FRUS, 1943*, 3:34.

82. Morgenthau diary, September 6, 1944, 769:118, Morgenthau Papers.

83. Marett, *Through the Back Door*, pp. 110–11. See also Morgenthau diary, September 19, 1944, 772:155, Morgenthau Papers.

84. FDRPC, No.969, September 22, 1944, 24:129.

85. Long diary, September 26, 1944. For Hull's views see also *FRUS: Conference at Yalta*, pp. 134–35. On the leak, see also British Embassy, "Weekly Political Summary," October 1, 1944, FO 461–3/36027/AN3708/20/45, PRO.

86. In September 1943, at the time of Welles's resignation, Krock had stood by Hull. See Gellman, *Secret Affairs*, p. 320; Divine, *Second Chance*, p. 138; Kimball, *Forged in War*, p. 355, footnote 20.

87. Krock, "Why Secretary Morgenthau Went to Quebec," *New York Times*, September 22, 1944; Alfred F. Flynn, "Post-War Germany," *Wall Street Journal*, September 23, 1944. Clippings of both articles in PSF (Departmental): Treasury: Morgenthau, FDRL.

88. The AP article was a page–one lead story on September 24 in a number of pa-

pers, including *Baltimore Sun, Chicago Tribune, New York Herald Tribune,* and *Washington Evening Star.*

89. Editorial, "Mr. Morgenthau's Scheme for Deindustrializing Germany," *Baltimore Sun,* September 26, 1944.

90. Editorial, "Samson In the Temple," *Washington Post,* September 26, 1944.

91. Editorial, "The Morgenthau Plan," *Washington Evening Star,* September 27, 1944; Lerner, "The German Industrial Machine," *PM Daily,* September 27, 1944.

92. AP, "Germans Are Aroused by Morgenthau Proposal," *Washington Post,* September 26, 1944.

93. See, for instance, Calvocoressi, Wint, and Pritchard, *Total War,* 1:547–49; Ryan, *A Bridge Too Far.*

94. Editorial, "Morgenthau's Plans for Germany," *Washington Times–Herald,* September 26, 1944.

95. Lindley, "Future of Germany: Reaction to Morgenthau Plan," *Washington Post,* September 29 1944.

96. Cited in Ted Lewis, "Morgenthau Plan Blamed for Stiffening of Nazis," *Washington Times–Herald,* September 30, 1944.

97. "Kilgore Asks Labor Own Reich Industry," *New York Times,* October 2, 1944.

98. Pierre Jay to FDR, September 26, 1944; Albert E. Barnett to FDR, October 9, 1944. Both in OF 198A, FDRL.

99. Morgenthau diary, September 25, 1944, 774:123–32, Morgenthau Papers.

100. Morgenthau diary, September 26, 1944, 775:31–3; September 29, 1944, 777:1–18, Morgenthau Papers.

101. Which is ironic in light of the later Cold War charge that the Morgenthau plan was devised by those who were soft on communism. It also highlights the fact that at this stage the Soviet dimension was largely absent from the domestic debate.

102. Morgenthau to FDR, September 28, 1944, OF 198A, FDRL.

103. Hull, press conference, No.102, September 25, 1944, box 141, Hull Papers.

104. Paul W. Ward, "Nazis Berate Hard Peace," *Baltimore Sun,* September 26, 1944.

105. Hopkins to FDR, September 28, 1944, OF 198, together with press release, marked "not given out," September 26, 1944, PSF (Diplomatic): Germany, FDRL; FDR, *Public Papers,* 13:297–98; FDRPC, No.970, September 29, 1944, 24:133–34.

106. FDR to Jay, October 9, 1944, OF 198A, FDRL; FDR to Wade Chance, October 2, 1944, OF 5258, FDRL; FDR to Stout, October 2, 1944, OF 5160, FDRL.

107. Morgenthau diary, September 29, 1944, 777:21, Morgenthau Papers.

108. FDR to Hull, September 29, 1944, PSF (Departmental): State: Hull, FDRL; *FRUS: Conference at Yalta,* p. 142.

109. Stimson diary, October 3, 1944.

110. Snell, *Dilemma Over Germany,* pp. 94–96.

111. Morgenthau presidential diary, August 25, 1944, p. 1392.

112. *C-R Correspondence,* R-632, R-635, 3:366, 371; Mark, "Bohlen and the Acceptable Limits of Soviet Hegemony," pp. 201–13; Kimball, *Juggler,* pp. 164, 168–69.

113. Hammond, "Directives for the Occupation," p. 397; *FRUS: Conference at Yalta,* pp. 165–69.

114. Gaddis, *U.S. and the Origins of the Cold War,* p. 128.

115. *C-R Correspondence,* C-801, 3:364–65; *Stalin's Correspondence,* p. 165. The Soviet ambassador in Washington, Andrei A. Gromyko, had also given the Treasury Department the impression that the U.S.S.R. would support the Morgenthau plan; see Morgenthau diary, October 5, 1944, 779:281–82, Morgenthau Papers.

116. Kimball, *Swords or Ploughshares?*, p. 44; Van Everen, "Roosevelt and the Problem of Germany," pp. 137-57; Hull, *Memoirs*, 2:1621-22.

117. Stimson diary, September 16, 1944.

118. For a summary of the incessant flow of stories, see Morgenthau, memorandum for the president, Morgenthau diary, October 5, 1944, 779:304, Morgenthau Papers.

119. See, for instance, Lerner, "The Story Behind Our Plans for Germany," *PM Daily*, October 1, 1944.

120. State Department, "Public Attitudes of Foreign Policy: 'Morgenthau Plan' for the Economic Treatment of Germany," Special Report No. 39, October 18, 1944, entry 568J, box 1, RG 59, NA.

121. Editorial, "Back on the Beam," *Washington Post*, September 30, 1944.

122. War Department, "Radio Digest," September 30, 1944.

123. See, for instance, Major George Fielding Eliot, "German Industry's Destruction Called Only Way to Clinch Peace," *New York Herald Tribune*, September 25, 1944. War Department, "Radio Digest," September 28 and 29, 1944.

124. Stout to FDR, September 29, 1944, OF 2527, FDRL.

125. "On the Air from Coast to Coast," *Prevent World War III*, 1 (November 1944): 21; Mowrer, "Economic Plans for Germany," *Prevent World War III*, pp. 35-36. On links between the Treasury and SPWW3 members, see Morgenthau diary, September 28, 1944, 776:187-95; September 30, 1944, 777:177, Morgenthau Papers.

126. "What to Do With Germany?" *March of Time*, vol.11, no.2 (October 1944), RG 200 MT 11.2, AV/NA; "Effective Disarmament of Germany and Japan," Foreign Policy Association Broadcast, October 7, 1944, Ref. RWA 6308 A4-B1, NBC Archive, RSD/LC.

127. Editorial, "Is It Foreign Policy or Guesswork?" *Saturday Evening Post*, 217 (October 28, 1944):112.

128. Dewey, "This Must be the Last War," October 18, 1944, *Republican Party Pamphlets*.

129. "Text of Dewey's Address," *New York Times*, November 5, 1944.

130. Niles to Tully, September 8, 1944, PSF (Subject): Opinion Polls, FDRL.

131. See maps dated September 24 and October 27, 1944, PSF (Subject): Opinion Polls, FDRL. See also Grace Robinson to Early, October 20, 1944, OF 857, FDRL, which reported to the White House that there was "anti-Roosevelt sentiment" amongst German-Americans.

132. Ickes diary, September 24, 1944, pp. 9245-46, October 6, 1944, p. 9256.

133. Tully to Watson, October 6, 1944; Watson to Stout, October 10, 1944; Stout to Watson October 11, 1944, and accompanying notations; all in OF 5160, FDRL.

134. FDR, *Public Papers*, 13:352-53.

135. Gaddis, *U.S. and the Origins of the Cold War*, p. 121; *Morgenthau Diaries*, 3:382.

136. A recording of FDR's October 21, 1944 radio address is in RG-118, AV/NA.

137. Haws to FDR, 2 October 1944; FDR to Haws 2 November 1944; and attached memoranda; PPF 8942, FDRL.

138. See, for instance, Thomas T. Connally, "Address at Duke University," October 6, 1944, box 561, Thomas T. Connally Papers, LC.

139. U.S. Senate, Committee on Military Affairs, Subcommittee on War Mobilization, *Cartels and National Security*, 78th Congress, 2nd sess., 1944, S. Res. 107, pp. 8-9. FDR received a summary of this report, see Stettinius, "Comparison of the Recommendations of the Kilgore subcommittee with those of the Department on the Economic Treatment of Germany," December 30, 1944, PSF (Diplomatic): Germany, FDRL.

140. *Morgenthau Diaries*, 3:391.

141. *Stettinius Diary*, pp. 168, 171.

142. Ibid., p. 208. The reports are in PSF (Departmental): State: Stettinius, FDRL

143. Leigh, *Mobilizing Consent*, pp. 105–09.

144. *Stettinius Diary*, p. 203.

145. FDR to Hull, September 29, 1944, PSF (Departmental): State: Hull, FDRL; Stimson diary, October 3, 1944; *FRUS, 1944*, 1:414, 423. *FRUS, 1944*, 3:79; *Stettinius Diary*, p. 179.

146. FDR to Hull, October 20, 1944, PSF (Diplomatic): Germany, FDRL; *FRUS, 1944*, 1:409–10.

147. *FRUS, 1944*, 1:414. That FDR's opposition to reparations could be a "tough" policy, in line with Morgenthau's recommendations, is ignored by some historians. See, for instance, Snell, "What to Do with Germany," p. 47.

148. FDR to Leahy, "MR–OUT–468," October 9, 1944, MR box 20, FDRL; *C-R Correspondence*, R-649, 3:394.

149. Eisenberg, *Drawing the Line*, pp. 127–28.

150. *FRUS, 1944*, 1:409–10.

151. Ferrell, *The Dying President*, pp. 94–97.

152. Hammond, "Directives for the Occupation," p. 409.

153. See, in particular, *FRUS, 1944*, 1:281, 284.

154. *FRUS: Conference at Yalta*, pp. 143, 149, 153, 171, 190–92; *FRUS, 1944*, 1:412.

155. *FRUS, 1944*, 1:412; *FRUS: Conference at Yalta*, pp. 185, 187.

156. That FDR remained "mentally alert and fully capable of dealing with each situation as it arose," see Stettinius, *Roosevelt and the Russians*, p. 73. See also Dallek, *Roosevelt and Foreign Policy*, p. 519; Kimball, *Forged in War*, p. 341; Park, *The Impact of Illness on World Leaders*, pp. 222, 272–73. On FDR's closer connections with the State Department see Bohlen, *Witness to History*, pp. 166, 172. For FDR's attitude toward Stettinius' work, see *FRUS: Conference at Yalta*, pp. 171–72; *Stettinius Diary*, pp. 215, 202.

157. Byron Price, memorandum, undated, box 25 Early Papers; OWI, "OWI and Government Information Policy," December 21, 1944, entry 106, RG 44, NA

158. FDRPC, No.984, December 19, 1944, 24:266–67. See also Dallek, *Roosevelt and Foreign Policy*, pp. 503–06.

159. Stettinius to FDR, "American Opinion on Recent European Developments," December 30, 1944, PSF (Departmental): State: Stettinius, FDRL; idem, "American Opinion on Selected Questions," January 16, 1945, PSF (Departmental): State, FDRL.

160. Niles to Tully, January 11, 1945, and attached memorandum, Cantril, "Recent Trends of Opinion Concerning Foreign Affairs," January 11, 1945, OF 857, FDRL.

161. Stettinius to FDR, "Statement on Foreign Policy Aspect of State of Union Message," December 28, 1944, PSF (Departmental): State, FDRL; *Stettinius Diary*, pp. 207–8; Dallek, *Roosevelt and Foreign Policy*, pp. 502–6.

162. Millis, ed., *The Forrestal Diaries*, p. 36.

163. FDRPC, No.992, February 23, 1945, 25:67.

164. FDR, *Public Papers*, 13:483–85, 497.

165. *DSB*, 12 (7 January 1945): 43.

166. Stimson diary, December 31, 1944; *New York Times*, January 1, 1945, January 14, 1945. Officials also released photographs showing the Americans troops the Germans had killed after their surrender. See Roeder, "Censoring Disorder," p. 51.

167. Stettinius, *Roosevelt and the Russians*, p. 81; *FRUS: Conference at Yalta*, p. 560; Bishop, *FDR's Last Year*, pp. 302–3; Bohlen, *Witness to History*, p. 173. This is the one exception to John Keegan's comment that FDR "saw nothing of the war at first hand, no bombed cities, no troops at the front, no prisoners, no after-effects of battle, and probably did not choose to." See John Keegan, *The Second World War*, p. 458.

168. *FRUS: Conference at Yalta*, p. 571.

169. That "vivid information" that "is emotionally involving, concrete, and based on personal experience or first-hand knowledge" is likely to change a decision maker's attitude, see Deborah Welch Larson, *Origins of Containment*, pp. 38–40.

170. *FRUS: Conference at Yalta*, p. 620.

171. Ibid., pp. 632, 622.

172. Leahy diary, February 6, 1945.

173. *FRUS: Conference at Yalta*, pp. 901–2.

174. Ibid., p. 979.

175. Ibid., pp. 612, 614; Bohlen, *Witness to History*, p. 183.

176. *FRUS: Conference at Yalta*, p. 978.

177. Ibid., p. 617.

178. De Senarclens, *Yalta*, p. 57.

179. Leahy diary, February 11, 1945.

180. *FRUS, 1945*, 3:204–5, 221, 471.

181. *FRUS: Conference at Yalta*, p. 617.

182. Sherwood, *Roosevelt and Hopkins*, pp. 873–74.

183. FDRPC, No.991, February 19, 1945, 25:48–49.

184. FDR, *Public Papers*, 13:570–77. Emphasis added.

185. *DSB*, 12 (March 25, 1945):480–86.

186. Ibid., 12 (March 4, 1945):357. As Michael Howard points out, in practice this Military Staff Committee "rapidly became a non-entity." See Howard, "The Historical Development of the UN's Role in International Security," pp. 65–66.

187. Boettiger to FDR, February 13, 1945, MR box 21, FDRL.

188. State Department, "Fortnightly Survey of American Opinion on International Affairs," No.21, February 20, 1945, entry 568L, RG 59, NA; editorial, "For Victory and Peace," *New York Times*, February 13, 1945; AP, "Peace Program Wins Applause from both Parties," *Chicago Daily Tribune*, February 13, 1945. See also Theoharis, *The Yalta Myths*, pp. 18–23.

189. FDR to Thompson, March 8, 1945, and attached draft letter, not used, OF 198A, FDRL.

190. State Department, "Public Attitudes on Foreign Policy: 'Unconditional Surrender' from Casablanca to Yalta," Special Report No.56, March 9, 1945.

191. Hassett, *Off the Record with FDR*, pp. 318, 327; Ferrell, *The Dying President*, pp. 110–19; Ward, ed., *Closest Companion*, pp. 398ff; Kimball, *Forged in War*, p. 341

192. Morgenthau presidential diary, April 11, 1945, p. 1503.

193. Leahy, *I Was There*, pp. 315–16.

194. Editorial, "Hitler to Himmler," *New York Times*, April 12, 1945.

Chapter 7

1. Ambrose *The Supreme Commander*, p. 659; Abzug, *Inside the Vicious Heart*, pp. 30, 128–39; U.S. Congress, Joint Committee on Conditions in Concentration

Camps in Germany, *Atrocities and Other Conditions in Concentration Camps in Germany*, 79th Cong., 1st sess, 1945. On the public demand to see the Signals Corps newsreel, see Mayor Aloys P. Kaufmann to Stimson, May 12, 1945, OF 325, HSTL.

2. State Department, Office of Public Affairs, "Fortnightly Survey of American Opinion on International Affairs," Survey Nos. 25 and 26, April 24 and May 9, 1945, entry 568L, box 11, RG 59, NA.

3. Grew to Truman, "Latest Opinion Trends in the U.S.," June 5, 1945, folder 2, PSF 175, HSTL.

4. FDR to Hon. John F. Carew, March 10, 1943, PPF 2940, FDRL.

5. Polls conducted within the OWI did attempt to distinguish between the attitudes of different geographic, ethnic, or age groups, but many of these did not filter up to the White House.

6. Badger, *The New Deal*, pp. 247–60; Schlesinger, *The Politics of Upheaval*, pp. 434–40.

7. Cantril later testified that "of all our material sent [to] President Roosevelt during World War II, nothing interested him more than the trend charts, which repeated the same questions from time to time to reflect the movement of opinion as circumstances changed." Cantril, *The Human Dimension*, p. 43.

8. Winkler, *Politics of Propaganda*, pp. 38–51; Leigh, *Mobilizing Consent*, pp. 53–55, 93; Laurie, *Propaganda Warriors*.

9. *FRUS: Conference at Tehran*, pp. 323–24.

10. Iriye, *Power and Culture*, pp. 226–27; Heinrichs, *American Ambassador*, pp. 369–70; Thorne, *Issue of War*, pp. 135–36.

11. Thorne, *Allies of a Kind*, pp. 492–93.

12. A point also made by Harper, *American Visions of Europe*, pp. 2–13. The characterization of FDR as a "chameleon on plaid" was by Herbert Hoover, see Leuchtenberg, *FDR Years*, p. 2.

13. Dallek, *Roosevelt and Foreign Policy*, p. 530.

14. Stimson and Bundy, *On Active Service*, pp. 376–78.

15. State Department, "Fortnightly Survey of American Opinion on International Affairs," Survey No.30, July 4, 1945, entry 568L, box 11, RG 59, NA

16. Iriye, *Power and Culture*, pp. 254–56; Messer, *The End of an Alliance*, pp. 8–9, 118.

17. Dower, *War Without Mercy*, p. 139.

18. State Department, "Fortnightly Survey," Survey No.27, May 23, 1945.

19. Ibid., No.28, June 9, 1945.

20. "Report of Earl G. Harrison," August 1945; Truman to Eisenhower, August 31, 1945; both in OF 127, HSTL.

21. Eisenberg, *Drawing the Line*, pp. 132–34.

22. State Department, "Fortnightly Survey," Nos.36 and 37, October 5 and 19, 1945; SPWW3 to Truman, October 13, 1945, OF 190, HSTL. Morgenthau, *Germany Is Our Problem*.

23. *FRUS: Conference at Potsdam*, 2:296–97, 428–31; Leffler, *A Preponderance of Power*, p. 67.

24. Truman, *Public Papers*, 1:203, 207. This speech was drafted by Rosenman; see "Draft of Speech by President Truman on Berlin Conference," August 9, 1945, box 4, Samuel I. Rosenman Papers, HSTL. For similar expressions by the new president, see Truman to General Evangeline Booth, May 25, 1945, OF 325, HSTL; Truman to Senator Milton R. Young, December 6, 1945, OF 198, HSTL; Truman to Senator Albert W. Hawkes, December 21, 1945, ibid.

25. Informal Policy Committee on Germany, "Directive to Commander–in–Chief

of Occupation regarding the Military Government of Germany," IPCOG 1/4, May 11, 1945, WHCF: Confidential File, State Department Correspondence, 1945, folder 1, Truman Papers, HSTL; Morgenthau to Truman, October 18, 1945, OF198, HSTL.

26. State Department, "Fortnightly Survey," Survey No.33, August 21, 1945.

27. Hamby, *Man of the People*, p. 306; Gaddis, *U.S. and the Origins of the Cold War*, p. 238.

28. Ziemke, "The Formulation and Initial Implementation of U.S. Occupation Policy in Germany," p. 33; Gaddis, *The Long Peace*, pp. 40–43; Eisenberg, *Drawing the Line*, pp. 132–34, 266–67; Deighton, *The Impossible Peace*.

29. Statement by the president, May 15, 1945, OF 198, HSTL; *DSB*, 17 (November 30, 1947): 1027.

30. Truman, *Public Papers*, 3:238; Lynch and Southard to Snyder, "Hearings on ERP by Senate Foreign Relations Committee and House Foreign Affairs Committee—January 15, 1948," January 16, 1948, box 11, John W. Snyder Papers, HSTL; Adler and Paterson, "Red Fascism," pp. 1046–64; Hogan, *A Cross of Iron*, pp. 165–66, 426–27

31. *DSB*, 15 (September 15, 1946):496–501; Messer, *End of an Alliance*, pp. 202–5.

32. Hogan, *The Marshall Plan*, pp. 90–91. See also, James P. Warburg, "The U.S. and the World Crisis," October 20, 1947, box 4, Dean Acheson Papers, HSTL; William P. Bundy to Mr. Stein, January 6, 1948, box 3, ibid.

33. "What Should We Do for Europe Now?" Town Meeting, October 14, 1947, copy in box 4, Acheson Papers. Emphasis added.

34. See, for instance, George G. Sadowski, "Rebuilding Germany for World War III?" July 15, 1947; S.Z. Dushkes to Truman, September 22, 1947; both in OF 198, HSTL. "Testimony by Henry A. Wallace before the House Committee on Foreign Affairs," February 24, 1948, copy in box 11, Snyder Papers. For a summary of the SPWW3's testimony on the Marshall Plan, see Lynch and Southard to Snyder, "Congressional Activities on ERP—January 29, 1948," January 30, 1948, ibid. There was also some opposition from within the administration to reviving a "German colossus." See Hogan, *Marshall Plan*, pp. 34–35.

35. *Fortune Survey*, 32 (December 1945):305; *Fortune Survey*, 34 (December 1946):6.

36. State Department, "Fortnightly Survey," Survey No.67, January 22, 1947; *Gallup Poll*, 1:625; Leffler, *Preponderance of Power*, p. 151.

37. William L. Clayton "The European Crisis," May 31, 1947, box 60, William L. Clayton Papers, HSTL; Trachtenberg, *A Constructed Peace*, p. 56; Wala, "Selling the Marshall Plan at Home," pp. 247–65.

BIBLIOGRAPHY

Primary Sources

Manuscripts and Archives

CHURCHILL COLLEGE, UNIVERSITY OF CAMBRIDGE.

Halifax, Lord. Papers. Microfilm copy.

LIBRARY OF CONGRESS, MANUSCRIPTS DIVISION, WASHINGTON D.C.

Arnold, Henry H. Papers.
Connally, Thomas T. Papers.
Davis, Elmer. Papers.
Hull, Cordell. Papers.
Ickes, Harold L. Diary.
Leahy, William D. Diary.
Long, Breckenridge. Papers.

MacLeish, Archibald. Papers.
Marshall, George C. Papers.
    Microfilm copy.
Mowrer, Edgar A. Papers.
NBC Radio Broadcasts, 1941–45.
Taylor, Myron C. Papers.

NATIONAL ARCHIVES, COLLEGE PARK, MARYLAND.

Record Group 44. Office of Government Reports.
Record Group 56. Department of the Treasury.
Record Group 59. Department of State. General Records.
Record Group 107. Office of the Secretary of War.
Record Group 111. Office of Chief Signal Officer.
Record Group 165. Department of War. General and Special Staffs.
Record Group 179. War Production Board.
Record Group 200.MT. Gift Collection. *March of Time* Newsreel.
Record Group 208. Office of War Information.
Record Group 216. Office of Censorship.
Record Group 218. Joint Chiefs of Staff.

PUBLIC RECORDS OFFICE, KEW GARDENS, LONDON.

Cabinet Office Files.
  CAB 99.
  CAB 120.
Foreign Office Files.
  FO 115.
  FO 371.

FO 461.
FO 800.
FO 954. Lord Avon. Papers.
Prime Minister's Office Files.
PREM 3.
PREM 4.

RHODES HOUSE LIBRARY, UNIVERSITY OF OXFORD.

Roosevelt, Franklin D. Press Conferences (FDRPC). Microfilm copy.
Stimson, Henry L. Diary. Microfilm copy.

FRANKLIN D. ROOSEVELT LIBRARY, HYDE PARK, NEW YORK.

Berle, Jr., Adolf A. Papers.
Boettiger, John. Papers
Cox, Oscar. Papers.
Early, Stephen T. Papers.
Field, Henry. Papers.
Hopkins, Harry L. Papers.
Lubin, Isador. Papers.
Mellett, Lowell. Papers.
Morgenthau, Jr., Henry.
  Papers.
  Presidential Diary.
Roosevelt, Franklin D.
  Collection of Speeches, 1910–45.

Papers as President of the United
  States, 1933–45.
  Map Room File (MR).
  Official File (OF).
  President's Personal File (PPF).
  President's Secretary's File (PSF).
  White House Usher Diaries.
Rosenman, Samuel I. Papers.
Rowe, James H. Papers.
Smith, Harold D. Papers.
Wallace, Henry A. Diary.
Welles, Sumner. Papers.

HARRY S. TRUMAN LIBRARY, INDEPENDENCE, MISSOURI.

Acheson, Dean. Papers.
Clayton, William L. Papers.
Committee for the Marshall Plan. Papers.
Jones, Joseph M. Papers.
Nash, Philleo Papers.
Niles, David K. Papers.
Rosenman, Samuel I. Papers.
Snyder, John W. Papers.

Truman, Harry S. Papers.
  White House Central File (WHCF).
  Official File (OF).
  President's Personal File (PPF).
  President's Secretary's File (PSF).

Oral History Transcripts

Carter, John Franklin. Oral History Transcript. Copy in Small Collections, FDRL.
Harriman, W. Averell. Transcript. Eleanor Roosevelt Oral History Project. Copy in
  FDRL.
MacLeish, Archibald. *Archibald MacLeish: Reflections*. Bernard A. Drabeck and Helen
  E. Ellis, ed. Amherst: University of Massachusetts Press, 1986.
Marshall, George C. *George C. Marshall: Interviews and Reminiscences for Forrest
  Pogue*. Revised ed. Larry I. Bland, ed. Lexington, Va.: Marshall Foundation,
  1991.
Rosenman, Samuel I. Columbia Oral History Transcript. Copy in FDRL.

Published U.S. Government Documents

Notter, Harley A. *Post–World War II Foreign Policy Planning: Records of Harley A. Notter, 1939–1945.* Microfiche. Bethesda, Md.: Congressional Information Service, 1987.

Roosevelt, Franklin D. *The Public Papers and Addresses of Franklin D. Roosevelt.* Samuel I. Rosenman, ed. 13 vols. New York: Russell and Russell, 1941–1950.

————. *Franklin D. Roosevelt and Foreign Affairs, January 1933–January 1937.* Edgar B. Nixon, ed. First Series, 3 vols. Cambridge, Mass.: Belknap Press, 1969.

————. *Franklin D. Roosevelt and Foreign Affairs, January 1937–August 1939.* Donald B. Schewe, ed. Second Series, 10 vols. New York: Garland Press, 1979.

Stalin, Joseph. *Stalin's Correspondence with Roosevelt and Truman, 1941–1945.* New York: Capricorn Books, 1965.

Truman, Harry S. *Public Papers of the Presidents of the United States: Harry S. Truman.* 8 vols. Washington D.C.: U.S. Government Printing Office, 1961.

U.S. Congress. *Congressional Record: Proceedings and Debates of the 77th–79th Congress.* Washington, D.C.: U.S. Government Printing Office, 1942–1945.

————. House of Representatives, Committee on Foreign Affairs. *Rescue of the Jewish and Other Peoples in Nazi-Occupied Territory. Extracts from Hearings on H. Res. 350 and H. Res. 352.* 8th Congress, 1st Session. Washington D.C.: U.S. Government Printing Office, 1943.

————. House of Representatives, Committee on Un-American Activities. *Investigation of Un-American Propaganda Activities in the United States: Report on the Peace Now Movement. H. Res.282.* 78th Congress, 2nd Session. Washington D.C.: U.S. Government Printing Office, 1944.

————. Joint Committee on Conditions in the Concentration Camps in Germany. *Atrocities and Other Conditions in Concentration Camps in Germany.* Washington D.C.: U.S. Government Printing Office, 1945.

————. Senate, Subcommittee on War Mobilization, Committee on Military Affairs. *Cartels and National Security. S. Res. 107.* 78th Congress, 2nd Session. Washington D.C.: U.S. Government Printing Office, 1944.

U.S. Department of State. *The Department of State Bulletin, 1941–1948.* Vols. 5–18. Washington D.C.: U.S. Government Printing Office, 1941–48.

————. *Foreign Relations of the United States. Japan: 1931–1941.* 2 vols. Washington D.C.: U.S. Government Printing Office, 1943.

————. *National Socialism: Basic Principles, Their Application by the Nazi Party's Foreign Organization, and the Use of Germans Abroad for Nazi Aims.* Washington D.C.: U.S. Government Printing Office, 1943.

————. *Postwar Foreign Policy Preparation, 1939–1945.* Washington D.C.: U.S. Government Printing Office, 1949.

————. *Foreign Relations of the United States, 1933–1945.* Washington D.C.: U.S. Government Printing Office, 1950–1968.

————. *Foreign Relations of the United States: The Conference of Berlin (The Potsdam Conference), 1945.* 2 vols. Washington D.C.: U.S. Government Printing Office, 1960.

————. *Foreign Relations of the United States: The Conferences at Cairo and Tehran, 1943.* Washington D.C.: U.S. Government Printing Office, 1961.

————. *Foreign Relations of the United States: The Conferences at Washington, 1941–1942, and Casablanca, 1943.* Washington D.C.: U.S. Government Printing Office, 1968.

————. *Foreign Relations of the United States: The Conferences at Washington and Quebec, 1943.* Washington D.C.: U.S. Government Printing Office, 1970.

————. *Foreign Relations of the United States: The Conference at Quebec, 1944.* Washington D.C.: U.S. Government Printing Office, 1972.

Published Documents, Diaries, & Collections of Correspondence

Berle, Beatrice, and Travis Beal Jacobs, ed. *Navigating the Rapids, 1918–1971: The Papers of Adolf A. Berle.* New York: Harcourt Brace Jovanovich, 1973.

Berlin, Isaiah. *Washington Despatches: Weekly Political Reports from the British Embassy.* H. G. Nicholas, ed. London: Weidenfeld and Nicolson, 1981.

Culbert, David, ed. *Film and Propaganda in America: A Documentary History. World War II.* 2 Parts. New York: Greenwood Press, 1990.

Dodd, Martha. *Through Embassy Eyes.* New York: Harcourt Brace, 1939.

Dodd, William E., and Martha Dodd, ed. *Ambassador Dodd's Diary, 1933–1938.* New York: Harcourt Brace, 1941.

Drury, Allen. *A Senate Journal, 1943–1945.* New York: McGraw-Hill, 1963.

Forrestal, James V. *The Forrestal Diaries: The Inner History of the Cold War.* Walter Millis, ed. London: Cassell, 1952.

Freedman, Max, ed. *Roosevelt and Frankfurter: Their Correspondence, 1928–1945.* Boston: Little, Brown, 1967.

Hassett, William D. *Off the Record with FDR, 1942–1945.* New Brunswick, N.J.: Rutgers University Press, 1958.

Heideking, Jürgen and Christof Mauch, ed. *American Intelligence and the German Resistance to Hitler: A Documentary History.* Boulder, Colo.: Westview Press, 1996.

Holborn, Louise, ed. *War and Peace Aims of the United Nations: From Casablanca to Tokio Bay.* 2 vols. Boston: World Peace Foundation, 1948.

Ickes, Harold L. *The Secret Diary of Harold L. Ickes, 1933–1941.* 3 vols. London: Weidenfeld and Nicolson, 1955.

Kimball, Warren F., ed. *Churchill and Roosevelt: The Complete Correspondence.* 3 vols. London: Collins, 1984.

Lebowitz, Arieh, and Gail Malmgreen, ed. *Archives of the Holocaust: The Papers of the Jewish Labor Committee.* New York: Garland, 1993.

Lindbergh, Charles A. *The Wartime Journals of Charles A. Lindbergh.* New York: Harcourt Brace, 1970.

Lippmann, Walter. *Public Philosopher: Selected Letters of Walter Lippmann.* John Morton Blum, ed. New York: Tickner and Fields, 1985.

Long, Breckenridge. *The War Diary of Breckenridge Long: Selections from the Years 1939–1944.* Fred L. Israel, ed. Lincoln: University of Nebraska, 1966.

Lowenheim, Francis L., Harold D. Langley, and Manfred Jonas, ed. *Roosevelt and Churchill: Their Secret Wartime Correspondence.* New York: Da Capo, 1990.

MacLeish, Archibald. *Letters of Archibald MacLeish, 1907–1928.* R. H. Winnick, ed. Boston: Houghton Mifflin, 1983.

Marshall, George C. *The Papers of George Catlett Marshall. Volumes 2–4: 1939–1944.* 4 vols. Larry I. Bland, ed. Baltimore: Johns Hopkins Press, 1986–1996.

Moffat, Jay Pierrepoint. *The Moffat Papers: Selections from the Diplomatic Journals of Jay Pierrepoint Moffat, 1919–1943.* Nancy Harvison Hooker, ed. Cambridge, Mass.: Harvard University Press, 1956.

Murrow, Edward R. *In Search of Light: The Broadcasts of Edward R. Murrow, 1938–1961.* Edward Bliss, Jr., ed. London: Macmillan, 1968.

Perkins, Francis. *The Roosevelt I Knew.* London: Hammond and Hammond, 1964.

Pickersgill, J. W., ed. *The Mackenzie King Record. Volume 1, 1939–1944.* 4 vols. Chicago: University of Chicago Press, 1960.

Roosevelt, Elliott. *As He Saw It.* New York: Duell, Sloan, and Pearce, 1946.

Roosevelt, Franklin D. "Shall We Trust Japan?" *Asia* 23 (1923):476

——. *FDR: His Personal Letters.* 2 vols. Elliott Roosevelt, ed. New York: Duell, Sloan, and Pearce, 1950.

Stettinius, Edward R. *The Diaries of Edward R. Stettinius, Jr., 1943–1946.* Thomas M. Campbell and George C. Herring, ed. New York: New Viewpoints, 1975.

Vandenberg, Arthur H. *The Private Papers of Senator Vandenberg.* Arthur H. Vandenberg, Jr. and Joe Alex Morris, ed. London: Victor Gollancz, 1952.

Wallace, Henry A. *The Price of Vision: The Diary of Henry A. Wallace, 1942–1946.* John Morton Blum, ed. Boston: Houghton Mifflin, 1973.

Ward, Geoffrey C., ed. *Closest Companion: The Unknown Story of the Intimate Friendship Between Franklin Roosevelt and Margaret Suckley.* Boston: Houghton Mifflin, 1995.

Newspapers, Magazines, Journals, & Pamphlets

DAILY NEWSPAPERS.

Baltimore Sun.

Chicago Daily Tribune.

New York Herald-Tribune.

New York Times.

PM Daily.

Washington Evening Star.

Washington Post.

Washington Times-Herald.

WEEKLY MAGAZINES.

Collier's.

Nation.

New Republic.

Saturday Evening Post.

Time.

United States News.

MONTHLY MAGAZINES, JOURNALS, AND PAMPHLETS.

America Faces the War.

American Magazine.

American Mercury.

Common Sense.

Life.

New Yorker.

Prevent World War III.

Public Opinion Quarterly.

Reader's Digest.

Republican Presidential Campaign of 1944 Pamphlets. Library of Congress Collection.

Memoirs

Bohlen, Charles. *Witness to History, 1929–1969.* London: Weidenfeld and Nicolson, 1973.

Cantril, Hadley. *The Human Dimension: Experiences in Policy Research.* New Brunswick, N.J.: Rutgers University Press, 1967.

Carroll, Wallace. *Persuade or Perish.* Boston: Houghton Mifflin, 1948.

Churchill, Winston S. *The Second World War.* 6 vols. Ed. London: Penguin, 1948–1953.

Harriman, Averell, and Ellie Abel. *Special Envoy to Churchill and Stalin, 1941–1946.* New York: Random House, 1975.

Hull, Cordell. *The Memoirs of Cordell Hull.* 2 vols. New York: Macmillan, 1948.

Kennan, George F. *Memoirs, 1925–1950.* New York: Pantheon Books, 1967.

King, Ernest J., and Walter Muir Whitehill. *Fleet Admiral King: A Naval Record*. London: Eyre and Spottiswoode, 1953.

Leahy, William D. *I Was There*. London: Victor Gollancz, 1950.

Marett, Robert. *Through the Back Door: An Inside View of Britain's Overseas Information Services*. Oxford: Pergamon Press, 1968.

Mowrer, Edgar Ansel. *Triumph and Turmoil: A Personal History of Our Time*. London: George Allen and Unwin, 1968.

Murphy, Robert. *Diplomat Among Warriors*. London: Collins, 1964.

Rosenman, Samuel I. *Working with Roosevelt*. London: Hart-Davis, 1952.

Sherwood, Robert E. *Roosevelt and Hopkins: An Intimate History*. Rev. ed. New York: Harper and Row, 1950.

Stettinius, Jr., Edward R. *Roosevelt and the Russians: The Yalta Conference*. New York: Doubleday, 1949.

Stimson, Henry L. and McGeorge Bundy. *On Active Service in Peace and War*. New York: Harper and Brothers, 1947.

Secondary Sources

Books

Abzug, Robert H. *Inside the Vicious Heart: Americans and the Liberation of the Nazi Concentration Camps*. Oxford: Oxford University Press, 1985.

Adams, David K., and Cornelis A. Van Minnen, ed. *Aspects of War in American History*. Keele, U.K.: Keele University Press, 1997.

Adler, Selig. *The Isolationist Impulse: Its Twentieth Century Reaction*. Westport, Conn.: Greenwood Press, 1957.

Almond, Gabriel A. *The American People and Foreign Policy*. 2nd ed. Westport, Conn.: Greenwood Press, 1960.

Ambrose, Stephen E. *Eisenhower. Volume 1: Soldier, General of the Army, President-Elect, 1890–1952*. 2 vols. London: George Allen and Unwin, 1983.

———. *D-Day: The Climactic Battle of World War II*. New York: Simon and Schuster, 1994.

Andrew, Christopher. *For the President's Eyes Only: Secret Intelligence and the American Presidency from Washington to Bush*. London: Harper Collins, 1995.

Armstrong, Anne. *Unconditional Surrender: The Impact of the Casablanca Policy upon World War II*. New Brunswick, N.J.: Rutgers University Press, 1961.

Backer, John H. *The Decision to Divide Germany: American Foreign Policy in Transition*. Durham, N.C.: Duke University Press, 1978.

Badger, Anthony. *New Deal: The Depression Years, 1933–1940*. London: Macmillan, 1989.

Baldwin, Hanson W. *Great Mistakes of the War*. New York: Harper and Brothers, 1949.

Balfour, Michael. *Propaganda in War, 1939–1945: Organizations, Policies, and Publics in Britain and Germany*. London: Routledge and Kegan Paul, 1979.

Barclay, David E., and Elisabeth Glaser-Schmidt, ed. *Transatlantic Images and Perceptions: Germany and American since 1776*. Washington D.C.: Cambridge University Press, 1997

Barnes, James J., and Patience P. Barnes. *Hitler's Mein Kampf in Britain and America: A Publishing History, 1930–1939*. Cambridge: Cambridge University Press, 1980.

Barnet, Richard J. *The Rockets' Red Glare. When America Goes to War: The Presidents and the People*. New York: Simon and Schuster, 1990.

Bell, P. M. H. *John Bull and the Bear: British Public Opinion, Foreign Policy, and the Soviet Union, 1941–1945*. London: Edward Arnold, 1990.

Bennett, W. Lance, and David L. Paletz, ed. *Taken by Storm: The Media, Public Opinion, and U.S. Foreign Policy in the Gulf War*. Chicago: University of Chicago Press, 1994.

Berger, Meyer. *The Story of the New York Times, 1851–1951*. New York: Simon and Schuster, 1951.

Bishop, Jim. *FDR's Last Year: April 1944–April 1945*. New York, William Morrow, 1974.

Blake, Robert, and Wm. Roger Louis, ed. *Churchill*. Oxford: Oxford University Press, 1994.

Block, Maxine ed. *Current Biography: Who's News and Why, 1941*. New York: H.W. Wilson 1941.

Blum, John Morton. *From the Morgenthau Diaries*. 3 vols. Boston: Houghton Mifflin, 1959–1967.

———. *'V' Was for Victory: Politics and American Culture During World War II*. New York: Harcourt Brace, 1976.

Borg, Dorothy, and Shumpei Okamoto, ed. *Pearl Harbor As History: Japanese-American Relations, 1931–1941*. New York: Columbia University Press, 1973.

Bowyer. Tom. *Blind Eye to Murder: Britain, America, and the Purging of Nazi Germany—A Pledge Betrayed*. New ed. London: Warner, 1995.

Boyce, Robert, and Esmonde M. Robertson, ed. *Paths to War: New Essays on the Origins of the Second World War*. Basingstoke: Macmillan, 1989.

Braverman, Jordan. *To Hasten the Homecoming: How Americans Fought World War II Through the Media*. Lanham, Md.: Madison Books, 1996.

Brewer, Susan A. *To Win the Peace: British Propaganda in the United States During World War II*. Ithaca, N.Y.: Cornell University Press, 1997.

Brickner, Richard M. *Is Germany Incurable?* Philadelphia: J. B. Lippincott Co., 1943.

Bridgman, Jon. *The End of the Holocaust: The Liberation of the Camps*. London: B. T. Batsford, 1990.

Brinkley, David. *Washington Goes to War*. New York: Ballantine Books, 1988.

Buhite, Russell D. *Decisions at Yalta: An Appraisal of Summit Diplomacy*. Wilmington, Del.: Scholarly Resources, 1986.

Burns, James MacGregor. *Roosevelt: The Lion and the Fox*. New York: Harcourt Brace, 1956.

———. *Roosevelt: The Soldier of Freedom*. New York: Harcourt Brace, 1970.

Butler, J. R. M. *The History of the Second World War. Grand Strategy: Volume 3, Part II, June 1941–August 1942*. London: HMSO, 1964.

Calvocoressi, Peter, Guy Wint, and John Pritchard. *Total War: The Causes and Course of the Second World War*. 2nd ed. Harmondsworth: Penguin, 1989.

Carr, William. *Poland to Pearl Harbor: The Making of the Second World War*. London: Edward Arnold, 1985.

Ceadel, Martin. *Thinking About Peace and War*. Oxford: Oxford University Press, 1987.

Chadwin, Mark Lincoln. *The Hawks of World War II*. Chapel Hill: University of North Carolina Press, 1968.

Clemens, Diane Shaver. *Yalta*. New York: Oxford University Press, 1970.

Cohen, Bernard C. *The Public's Impact on Foreign Policy*. Lanham, Md.: University of America Press, 1983.

Cole, Wayne S. *America First: The Battle Against Intervention, 1940–1941*. New York: Octagon Books, 1971.

————. *Roosevelt and the Isolationists, 1932–45*. Lincoln: University of Nebraska Press, 1983.

————. *Determinism and American Foreign Relations During the Franklin D. Roosevelt Era*. Lanham, Md.: University Press of America, 1995.

Compton, James V. *The Swastika and the Eagle: Hitler, the United States, and the Origins of the Second World War*. London: Bodley Head, 1968.

Crane, Conrad C. *Bombs, Cities, Civilians: American Airpower Strategy in World War II*. Lawrence: University Press of Kansas, 1993.

Croly, Herbert. *The Promise of American Life*. New York: Macmillan, 1909.

Cull, Nicholas John. *Selling War: The British Propaganda Campaign Against American 'Neutrality' in World War II*. New York: Oxford University Press, 1995.

Dallek, Robert. *Franklin D. Roosevelt and American Foreign Policy, 1932–1945*. Oxford: Oxford University Press, 1979.

————. *Franklin D. Roosevelt as World Leader: An Inaugural Lecture delivered before the University of Oxford on 16 May 1995*. Oxford: Clarendon Press, 1995.

Darilek, Richard E. *A Loyal Opposition in a Time of War: The Republican Party and the Politics of Foreign Policy from Pearl Harbor to Yalta*. Westport, Conn.: Greenwood Press, 1976.

Daugherty, William E., and Morris Janowitz, ed. *A Psychological Warfare Casebook*. Baltimore: Johns Hopkins Press, 1958.

Davies, Joseph E. *Mission to Moscow*. London: Victor Gollancz, 1942.

Davis, Kenneth S. *FDR: Into the Storm, 1937–1940*. New York: Random House, 1993.

Dear, I. C. B., and M. R. D. Foot, ed. *The Oxford Companion to the Second World War*. Oxford: Oxford University Press, 1995.

Deese, David A. ed. *The New Politics of American Foreign Policy*. New York: St. Martin's Press, 1994.

Deighton, Anne. *The Impossible Peace: Britain, the Division of Germany, and the Origins of the Cold War*. Oxford: Clarendon Press, 1993.

Dickinson, Mathew J. *Bitter Harvest: F.D.R, Presidential Power, and the Growth of the Presidential Branch*. Cambridge: Cambridge University Press, 1996.

Divine, Robert A. *The Illusion of Neutrality*. Chicago: University of Chicago Press, 1962.

————. *Second Chance: The Triumph of Internationalism in America During the Second World War*. New York: Athenaeum, 1967.

————. *Roosevelt and World War II*. Baltimore: Johns Hopkins Press, 1969.

————. *The Reluctant Belligerent: American Entry into World War II*. 2nd ed. New York: McGraw-Hill, 1979.

Donaldson, Scott. *Archibald MacLeish: An American Life*. Boston: Houghton Mifflin, 1992.

Dower, John W. *War Without Mercy: Race and Power in the Pacific War*. London: Faber and Faber, 1986.

Edmonds, Robin. *The Big Three: Churchill, Roosevelt and Stalin in Peace and War*. New York: W. W. Norton, 1991.

Eisenberg, Carolyn Woods. *Drawing the Line: The American Decision to Divide Germany, 1944–1949*. Cambridge: Cambridge University Press, 1996.

Erenberg, Lewis A., and Susan E. Hirsch, ed. *The War in American Culture: Society and Consciousness During World War II*. Chicago: University of Chicago Press, 1996.

Erickson, John. *The Road to Stalingrad: Stalin's War with Germany: Volume 1*. 1975. Reprint. London: Weidenfeld, 1993.

————. *The Road to Berlin: Stalin's War with Germany: Volume 2.* 1983. Reprint. London: Phoenix Giants, 1996.

Farnham, Barbara Rearden. *Roosevelt and the Munich Crisis: A Study of Political Decision-Making.* Princeton, N.J.: Princeton University Press, 1997.

Feis, Herbert. *Churchill, Roosevelt, Stalin: The War They Waged and the Peace They Sought.* London: Oxford University Press, 1957.

Ferrell, Robert H. *The Dying President: Franklin D. Roosevelt, 1944–1945.* Columbia: University of Missouri Press, 1998.

Fiebig-von Hase, Ragnhild, and Ursula Lehmkuhl, ed. *Enemy Images in American History.* Providence, R.I.: Berghahn Books, 1997.

Forcey, Charles. *The Crossroads of Liberalism: Croly, Weyl, Lippmann, and the Progressive Era.* Oxford, Oxford University Press, 1961.

Foyle, Douglas C., *Counting the Public In: Presidents, Public Opinion, and Foreign Policy.* New York: Columbia University Press, 1999.

Friedel, Frank. *Franklin D. Roosevelt: The Apprenticeship.* Boston: Little, Brown, 1952.

————. *Franklin D. Roosevelt: The Ordeal.* Boston: Little, Brown, 1954.

————. *Franklin D. Roosevelt: A Rendezvous with Destiny.* Boston: Little, Brown, 1990.

Friedrich, Otto. *City of Nets: A Portrait of Hollywood in the 1940s.* Berkeley: University of California Press, 1997

Funk, Arthur L. *The Politics of TORCH: The Allied Landings and the Algiers Putsch, 1942.* Lawrence: University Press of Kansas, 1974.

Fussell, Paul. *Wartime: Understanding and Behaviour in the Second World War.* New York: Oxford University Press, 1989.

Gaddis, John Lewis. *The United States and the Origins of the Cold War, 1941–1947.* New York: Columbia University Press, 1972.

————. *Strategies of Containment: A Critical Appraisal of Postwar American National Security Policy.* Oxford: Oxford University Press, 1982.

————. *The Long Peace: Inquiries into the History of the Cold War.* New York: Oxford University Press, 1987.

————. *We Now Know: Rethinking Cold War History.* Oxford: Clarendon Press, 1997.

Gallup, George H. *The Gallup Poll: Public Opinion, 1935–1971.* 3 vols. New York: Random House, 1972.

Gardner, Lloyd C. *Spheres of Influence: The Great Powers Partition Europe, from Munich to Yalta.* Chicago: Ivan R. Dee, 1993.

Gat, Azar. *Fascist and Liberal Visions of War: Fuller, Liddell Hart, Douhet, and Other Modernists.* Oxford: Clarendon Press, 1998.

Gatzke, Hans W. *Germany and the United States: A "Special Relationship?"* London: Harvard University Press, 1980.

Gellman, Irwin F. *Secret Affairs: Franklin Roosevelt, Cordell Hull, and Sumner Welles.* Baltimore: Johns Hopkins Press, 1995.

George, Alexander L. *Presidential Decision-making: The Effective Use of Information and Advice.* Boulder, Colo.: Westview Press, 1980.

Gilbert, Martin. *Road to Victory: Winston S. Churchill, 1941–1945.* London: Minerva, 1986.

————. *Second World War.* Rev. ed. Glasgow: Collins, 1989.

Gimbel, John. *The American Occupation of Germany: Politics and the Military, 1945–1949.* Stanford, Calif.: Stanford University Press, 1968.

————. *The Origins of the Marshall Plan.* Stanford, Calif.: Stanford University Press, 1976.

Glantz, David M., and Jonathan M. House. *When Titans Clashed: How the Red Army Stopped Hitler*. Lawrence: University of Kansas Press, 1995.

Goodwin, Dorothy Kearns. *No Ordinary Time. Franklin and Eleanor Roosevelt: The Home Front in World War II*. New York: Simon and Schuster, 1994.

Graber, Doris A. *Public Opinion, the President, and Foreign Policy: Four Case Studies from the Formative Years*. New York: Holt, Rinehart and Winston, 1968.

Greenfield, Kent Roberts. *American Strategy in World War II: A Reconsideration*. Baltimore: Johns Hopkins Press, 1963.

Hamby, Alonzo L. *Man of the People: A Life of Harry S. Truman*. New York: Oxford University Press, 1995.

Harper, John Lamberton. *American Visions of Europe: Franklin D. Roosevelt, George F. Kennan, and Dean G. Acheson*. New York: Cambridge University Press, 1994.

Hastings, Max. *Bomber Command: The Myths and Realities of the Strategic Bombing Offensive, 1939–1945*. London: Pan Books, 1979.

Hathaway, Robert M. *Ambiguous Partnership: Britain and America, 1944–1947*. New York: Columbia University Press, 1981.

Heinrichs, Waldo H. *American Ambassador: Joseph C. Grew and the Development of the United States Diplomatic Tradition*. New York: Oxford University Press, 1966.

————. *Threshold of War: Franklin D. Roosevelt and the American Entry into World War II*. New York: Oxford University Press, 1988.

————. *Diplomacy and Force: America's Road to War, 1931–1941*. Marc Gallicchio and Jonathan Utley, ed. Chicago: Imprint Publications, 1996.

Herbst, Susan. *Reading Public Opinion: How Political Actors View the Democratic Process*. Chicago: University of Chicago Press, 1998.

Herzstein, Robert E. *Roosevelt and Hitler: Prelude to War*. New York: John Wiley and Sons, 1989.

Hildebrand, Robert C. *Power and the People: Executive Management of Public Opinion in Foreign Affairs, 1897–1921*. Chapel Hill: University of North Carolina Press, 1984.

Hinsley, F. H., E. E. Thomas, C. F. G. Ransom, and R. C. Knight. *British Intelligence in the Second World War: Its Influence on Strategy and Operations*. Vols. 2–3. London: HMSO, 1981.

Hofstadter, Richard. *The American Political Tradition, And the Men Who Made It*. London: Jonathan Cape, 1962.

————. *The Progressive Historians: Turner, Beard, Parrington*. New York: Vintage Books, 1968.

Hogan, Michael J. *The Marshall Plan: America, Britain, and the Reconstruction of Western Europe, 1947–1952*. Cambridge: Cambridge University Press, 1987.

————. *A Cross of Iron: Harry S. Truman and the Origins of the National Security State, 1945–1954*. Cambridge: Cambridge University Press, 1998.

Holsti, Ole R. *Public Opinion and American Foreign Policy*. Ann Arbor: University of Michigan Press, 1996.

Hoopes, Townsend, and Douglas Brinkley, *FDR and the Creation of the UN*. New Haven: Yale University Press, 1997.

Hoover, Herbert, and Hugh Gibson. *The Problems of Lasting Peace*. New York: Doubleday, Doran and Co., 1942.

Howard, Michael. *The Mediterranean Strategy in the Second World War*. London: Weidenfeld and Nicolson, 1968.

————. *The History of the Second World War. Grand Strategy: Volume 4, August 1942–September 1943*. London: HMSO, 1972.

————. *War and the Liberal Conscience*. London: Temple Smith, 1978.

Howe, George F. *The United States Army in World War II. The Mediterranean Theater of Operations. Northwest Africa: Seizing the Initiative in the West*. Washington D.C.: Office of Chief of Military History, Department of the Army, 1957.

Hughes, Barry B. *The Domestic Context of American Foreign Policy*. San Francisco: W. H. Freeman, 1978.

Hunt, Michael H. *Ideology and U.S. Foreign Policy*. New Haven: Yale University Press, 1987.

Ikenberry, G. John, ed. *American Foreign Policy: Theoretical Essays*. New York: Harper Collins, 1989.

Iriye, Akira. *Power and Culture: The Japanese-American War, 1941–1945*. Cambridge, Mass.: Harvard University Press, 1981.

————. *The Cambridge History of American Foreign Relations: Volume 3. The Globalizing of America, 1913–1945*. 4 vols. Cambridge: Cambridge University Press, 1993.

Jonas, Manfred. *Isolationism in America, 1935–1941*. Ithaca, N.Y.: Cornell University Press, 1966.

————. *The United States and Germany: A Diplomatic History*. Ithaca, N.Y.: Cornell University Press, 1984.

Jowett, Garth S. *Propaganda and Persuasion*. 2nd ed. London: Sage, 1992.

Keegan, John. *The Second World War*. 1989. Reprint. London: Pimlico, 1997.

Kennan, George F. *American Diplomacy, 1900–1950*. 1951. Reprint. New York: Mentor Books, 1963.

Kennedy, David M. *Freedom from Fear: The American People in Depression and War, 1929–1945*. New York: Oxford University Press, 1999.

Kennedy, Paul M. *The Rise of the Anglo-German Antagonism, 1860–1914*. London: The Ashfield Press, 1980.

Kennett, Lee. *For the Duration . . . The United States Goes to War, Pearl Harbor—1942*. New York: Charles Scribner, 1985.

Kernell, Samuel. *Going Public: New Strategies of Presidential Leadership*. Washington D.C.: Congressional Quarterly, 1986.

Kimball, Warren F. *Swords or Ploughshares? The Morgenthau Plan for Defeated Nazi Germany, 1943–1946*. Philadelphia: J.B. Lippincott Co., 1976.

————. *The Juggler: Franklin Roosevelt as Wartime Statesman*. Princeton, N.J.: Princeton University Press, 1991.

————. *Forged in War: Churchill, Roosevelt and the Second World War*. London: Harper Collins, 1997.

Kinsella, Jr., William E. *Leadership in Isolation: FDR and the Origins of the Second World War*. Cambridge, Mass.: Schenkman, 1978.

Kirkpatrick, Charles E. *An Unknown Future and a Doubtful Present: Writing the Victory Plan of 1941*. Washington D.C.: U.S. Army Center of Military History, 1990.

Knightley, Phillip. *The First Casualty. From the Crimea to the Falklands: The War Correspondent as Hero, Propagandist and Myth Maker*. Rev. ed. London: Pan Books, 1989.

Kolko, Gabriel. *The Politics of War: The World and United States Foreign Policy, 1943–1945*. 2nd ed. New York: Pantheon Books, 1990.

Koppes, Clayton R., and Gregory D. Black. *Hollywood Goes to War: How Politics, Profits, and Propaganda Shaped World War II Movies*. Berkeley: University of California Press, 1990.

Kuklick, Bruce. *American Policy and the Division of Germany: The Clash with Russia over Reparations*. Ithaca, N.Y.: Cornell University Press, 1972.

Langer, William L., and S. Everett Gleason. *The Challenge to Isolation, 1937–1940.* London: RIIA, 1952.

———. *The Undeclared War, 1940–1941.* New York: Harper and Brothers, 1953.

Langhorne, Richard ed. *Diplomacy and Intelligence during the Second World War: Essays in Honor of F. H. Hinsley.* Cambridge: Cambridge University Press, 1985.

Larrabee, Eric. *Commander in Chief: Franklin Delano Roosevelt, His Lieutenants, and Their War.* New York: Harper and Row, 1987.

Larson, Deborah Welch. *Origins of Containment: A Psychological Explanation.* Princeton, N.J.: Princeton University Press, 1985.

Lash, Joseph P. *Eleanor and Franklin.* New York: Smithmark, 1971.

Laurie. Clayton D. *The Propaganda Warriors: America's Crusade Against Nazi Germany.* Lawrence: University Press of Kansas, 1996.

Leffler, Melvyn P. *A Preponderance of Power: National Security, the Truman Administration, and the Cold War.* Stanford, Calif.: Stanford University Press, 1992.

Leigh, Michael. *Mobilizing Consent: Public Opinion and American Foreign Policy, 1937–1947.* Westport, Conn.: Greenwood Press, 1976.

Lester, Deegee. *Roosevelt Research: Collections for the Study of Theodore, Franklin, and Eleanor.* Westport, Conn.: Greenwood Press, 1992.

Leuchtenberg, William E. *Franklin D. Roosevelt and the New Deal, 1932–1940.* New York: Harper and Row, 1963.

———. *The FDR Years: On Roosevelt and His Legacy.* New York: Columbia University Press, 1995.

Levering, Ralph B. *American Opinion and the Russian Alliance, 1939–1945.* Chapel Hill: University of North Carolina Press, 1976.

———. *The Public and American Foreign Policy, 1918–1978.* New York: William Morris, 1978.

Lifka, Thomas, E. *The Concept of "Totalitarianism" and American Foreign Policy, 1933–1949.* New York: Garland Publishing, 1988.

Liggio, Leonard P., and James J. Martin, ed. *Watershed and Empire: Essays on New Deal Foreign Policy.* Colorado Springs: Ralph Myers, 1976.

Lippmann, Walter. *Public Opinion.* New York: Macmillan, 1922.

———. *U.S. Foreign Policy: Shield of the Republic.* London: Hamish Hamilton, 1943.

———. *Public Opinion and Foreign Policy in the United States.* London: George Allen and Unwin, 1952.

———. *Essays in the Public Philosophy.* London: Mentor Books, 1955.

Lowenthal, Mark M. *Leadership and Indecision: American War Planning and Policy Process, 1937–1942.* New York: Garland Publishing, 1988.

Ludwig, Emil. *How to Treat the Germans.* New York: Willard, 1944.

McAleer, John. *Rex Stout: A Biography.* Boston: Little, Brown, 1977.

MacDonald, Callum A. *The United States, Britain, and Appeasement, 1936–1939.* Hong Kong: Macmillan, 1981.

MacDonnell, Francis. *Insidious Foes: The Axis Fifth Column and the American Home Front.* New York: Oxford University Press, 1995.

McJimsey, George. *Harry Hopkins: Ally of the Poor and Defender of Democracy.* Cambridge, Mass.: Harvard University Press, 1987.

McKelway, St. Clair, *Walter Winchell.* London: Chapman and Hall, 1941.

Maddox, Robert Franklin. *The Senatorial Career of Harley Martin Kilgore.* New York: Cummings and Hathaway, 1997.

Maney, Patrick J. *The Roosevelt Presence: The Life and Legacy of FDR.* Berkeley: University of California Press, 1992.

Margolis, Michael, and Gary A. Mauser, ed. *Manipulating Public Opinion: Essays on Public Opinion as a Dependent Variable*. Pacific Grove, Calif.: Brooks Cole Publishing, 1989.

Markel, Lester, ed. *Public Opinion and Foreign Policy*. New York: Harper for Council on Foreign Relations, 1949.

Marks, Frederick W., III. *Wind Over Sand: The Diplomacy of Franklin Roosevelt*. Athens, Ga.: University of Georgia Press, 1988.

Mastny, Vojtech. *Russia's Road to the Cold War: Diplomacy, Warfare, and the Politics of Communism, 1941–1945*. New York: Columbia University Press, 1979.

Matloff, Maurice. *Strategic Planning for Coalition Warfare, 1943–1944*. 1959. Reprint. Washington, D.C.: U.S. Army Center of Military History, 1994.

————. *Mr Roosevelt's Three Wars: FDR as War Leader. The Harmon Memorial Lectures in Military History, Number 6*. Colorado Springs, Colo.: United States Air Force Academy, 1964.

Matloff, Maurice, and Edwin M. Snell. *Strategic Planning for Coalition Warfare, 1941–1942*. Washington D.C.: U.S. Army Office of the Chief of Military History, 1953.

Mausbach, Wilfried. *Zwischen Morgenthau und Marshall: Das wirtschaftspolitische Deutschlandkonzept der U.S.A., 1944–47*. Düsseldorf: Droste, 1996.

May, Ernest R., ed. *The Ultimate Decision: The President as Commander in Chief*. New York: George Braziller, 1960

————. *'Lessons' of the Past: The Use and Misuse of History in American Foreign Policy*. New York: Oxford University Press, 1973.

Messer, Robert L. *The End of an Alliance: James F. Byrnes, Roosevelt, Truman, and the Origins of the Cold War*. Chapel Hill: The University of North Carolina Press, 1982

Morgan, Ted. *FDR: A Biography*. London: Grafton, 1986.

Morgenthau, Hans J. *In Defense of the National Interest: A Critical Examination of American Foreign Policy*. New York: Alfred A. Knopf, 1951.

————. *Politics Among Nations: The Struggle for Power and Peace*. 6th ed. New York: Alfred A. Knopf, 1985.

Morgenthau, Jr., Henry. *Germany Is Our Problem*. New York: Harper, 1945.

Moulton, Harold G., and Louis Marlio. *The Control of Germany and Japan*. Washington D.C.: Brookings Institution, 1944.

Mueller, John E. *Wars, Presidents, and Public Opinion*. New York: Wiley, 1973.

Nasaw, David. *The Chief: The Life of William Randolph Hearst*. Boston: Houghton Mifflin, 2000.

Neustadt, Richard E. *Presidential Power and the Modern Presidents: The Politics of Leadership from Roosevelt to Reagan*. 1960. Rev. ed. New York: The Free Press, 1990.

Nincic, Miroslav. *Democracy and Foreign Policy: The Fallacy of Political Realism*. New York: Columbia University Press, 1992.

Ninkovitch, Frank. *Germany and the United States: The Transformation of the German Question since 1945*. Rev. ed. New York: Twayne, 1995.

————. *The Wilsonian Century: U.S. Foreign Policy since 1900*. Chicago: University of Chicago Press, 1999.

O'Connor, Raymond G. *Diplomacy for Victory: FDR and Unconditional Surrender*. New York: W. W. Norton, 1971.

Offner, Arnold A. *American Appeasement: United States Foreign Policy and Germany, 1933–1938*. Cambridge, Mass.: Belknap Press, 1969.

————. *The Origins of the Second World War: American Foreign Policy and World Politics, 1917–1941*. New York: Holt, Rinehart and Wilson, 1975.

O'Neill, William L. *A Democracy at War: America's Fight at Home and Abroad in World War II*. Cambridge, Mass.: Harvard University Press, 1993.

Overy, Richard. *The Air War, 1939–1945*. London: Europa Publications, 1980.

———. *War and Economy in the Third Reich*. Oxford: Clarendon Press, 1994.

———. *Why the Allies Won*. London: Jonathan Cape, 1995.

Paret, Peter, ed. *Makers of Modern Strategy from Machiavelli to the Nuclear Age*. Princeton, N.J.: Princeton University Press, 1986.

Park, Bert Edward. *The Impact of Illness on World Leaders*. Philadelphia: University of Pennsylvania Press, 1986.

Parrish, Thomas. *Roosevelt and Marshall: Partners in Politics and War*. New York: William Morrow and Co., 1989.

Perrett, Geoffrey. *Days of Sadness, Years of Triumph: The American People, 1939–1945*. Madison: University of Wisconsin Press, 1985.

Pogue, Forrest C. *George C. Marshall: Ordeal and Hope, 1939–1942*. London: MacGibbon and Kee, 1965.

———. *George C. Marshall: Organizer of Victory, 1943–1945*. New York: Viking Press, 1973.

Polenberg, Richard. *War and Society: The United States, 1941–1945*. Westport, Conn.: Greenwood Press, 1972.

Range, Willard. *Franklin D. Roosevelt's World Order*. Athens, Ga.: University of Georgia Press, 1959.

Reston, James. *Prelude to Victory*. London: William Heinemann, 1942.

Reynolds, David. *The Creation of the Anglo-American Alliance, 1937–1941: A Study in Competitive Co-operation*. London: Europa Publications, 1981.

———. *Rich Relations: The American Occupation of Britain, 1942–1945*. London: Harper Collins, 1995.

Reynolds, David, Warren F. Kimball, and A. O. Chubarian, ed. *Allies at War: The Soviet, American, and British Experience, 1939–1945*. Basingstoke: Macmillan, 1994.

Rochester, Stuart I. *American Liberal Disillusionment in the Wake of World War I*. London: Pennsylvania State University Press, 1977.

Roeder, George H. *The Censored War: American Visual Experience During World War II*. New Haven: Yale University Press, 1993.

Rosenau, James N. *Public Opinion and Foreign Policy: An Operational Formulation*. New York: Random House, 1961.

Rosenbaum, Herbert D., and Elizabeth Bartelme, ed. *Franklin D. Roosevelt: The Man, the Myth, the Era, 1882–1945*. New York: Greenwood Press, 1987.

Rosencrance, Richard, and Arthur A. Stein, ed. *The Domestic Bases of Grand Strategy*. Ithaca, N.Y.: Cornell University Press, 1993.

Ross, Steven T. *American War Plans, 1941–1945: The Test of Battle*. London: Frank Cass, 1997.

Rossini, Daniela, ed. *From Theodore Roosevelt to FDR: Internationalism and Isolationism in American Foreign Policy*. Keele, U.K.: Keele University Press, 1995.

Russett, Bruce M. *No Clear and Present Danger: A Skeptical View of the United States Entry into World War II*. 1972. Reprint. Boulder, Colo.: Westview Press, 1997.

Ryan, Cornelius. *A Bridge Too Far*. 2nd ed. New York: Touchstone, 1974.

Ryan, Halford R. *Franklin D. Roosevelt's Rhetorical Presidency*. New York: Greenwood Press, 1988.

Sainsbury, Keith. *The North African Landings, 1942: A Strategic Decision*. London: Davis-Poynter, 1976.

———. *The Turning Point: Roosevelt, Stalin, Churchill, and Chiang-Kai-shek, 1943. The Moscow, Cairo, and Teheran Conferences*. Oxford: Oxford University Press, 1986.

————. *Churchill and Roosevelt at War: The War They Fought and the Peace They Hoped to Make*. Basingstoke: Macmillan, 1994.

Schaffer, Ronald. *Wings of Judgment: American Bombing in World War II*. New York: Oxford University Press, 1985.

Schlesinger, Jr., Arthur M. *The Coming of the New Deal*. Boston: Houghton Mifflin, 1959.

————. *The Politics of Upheaval*. Boston: Houghton Mifflin, 1960.

————. *The Imperial Presidency*. Boston: Houghton Mifflin, 1973.

Schmitz, David F., and Richard D. Challener, ed. *Appeasement in Europe: A Reassessment of U.S. Policies*. New York: Greenwood Press, 1990.

Schneider, James C. *Should America Go To War? The Debate over Foreign Policy in Chicago, 1939–1941*. Chapel Hill: University of North Carolina Press, 1989.

Schultz, Sigrid. *Germany Will Try It Again*. New York: Reynal and Hitchcock, 1944.

Schwarz, Jordan A. *Liberal: Adolf A. Berle and the Vision of an American Era*. New York: Free Press, 1987.

Sharp, Tony. *The Wartime Alliance and the Zonal Division of Germany*. Oxford: Clarendon Press, 1975.

Sherry, Michael S. *The Rise of American Air Power: The Creation of Armageddon*. New Haven: Yale University Press, 1987.

Shirer, William L. *Berlin Diary: The Journal of a Foreign Correspondent, 1934–1941*. 1941. Reprint. New York: Galahad Books, 1995.

————. *This is Berlin: Reporting from Nazi Germany, 1938–1940*. London: Hutchinson, 1999.

Short, K. R. M., ed. *Film and Radio Propaganda in World War II*. Knoxville: University of Tennessee Press, 1983.

Small, Melvin. *Johnson, Nixon, and the Doves*. New Brunswick, N.J.: Rutgers University Press, 1988.

————. *Democracy and Diplomacy: The Impact of Domestic Politics on U.S. Foreign Policy, 1789–1994*. Baltimore: Johns Hopkins University Press, 1996.

Snell, John L., ed. *The Meaning of Yalta: Big Three Diplomacy and the New Balance of Power*. Baton Rouge: Louisiana State University Press, 1956.

————. *Wartime Origins of the East-West Dilemma Over Germany*. New Orleans: The Hauser Press, 1959.

Steel, Ronald. *Walter Lippmann and the American Century*. New York: Vintage Books, 1981.

Steele, Richard W. *The First Offensive 1942: Roosevelt, Marshall, and the Making of American Strategy*. Bloomington: Indiana University Press, 1973.

————. *Propaganda in an Open Society: The Roosevelt Administration and the Media, 1933–1941*. Westport, Conn: Greenwood Press, 1985.

Stoessinger, John G. *Crusaders and Pragmatists: Movers of Modern American Foreign Policy*. 2nd ed. New York: W. W. Norton, 1985.

Stoler, Mark A. *The Politics of the Second Front: American Military Planning and Diplomacy in Coalition Warfare, 1941–1943*. Westport, Conn.: Greenwood Press, 1977.

Strout, Cushing. *The American Image of the Old World*. New York: Harper and Row, 1963.

Terkel, Studs. *The Good War: An Oral History of the Second World War*. New York: Ballantine Books, 1984.

Tetens, T. H. *Know Your Enemy*. New York: Society for the Prevention of World War III, 1944.

Theoharis, Athan G. *The Yalta Myths: An Issue in American Politics, 1945–1955*. Columbia: University of Missouri Press, 1970.

Thompson, John A. *Reformers and War: American Progressive Publicists and the First World War*. Cambridge: Cambridge University Press, 1987.

Thorne, Christopher. *Allies of a Kind: The United States, Britain, and the War Against Japan, 1941–1945*. Oxford: Oxford University Press, 1978.

————. *The Issue of War: States, Societies, and the Far Eastern Conflict of 1941–1945*. London: Hamish Hamilton, 1985.

Titus, James, ed. *The Home Front and War in the Twentieth Century: The American Experience in Comparative Perspective*. USAAF: Proceedings of the Tenth Military History Symposium, 1982.

Trachtenberg, Marc. *A Constructed Peace: The Making of the European Settlement, 1945–1963*. Princeton, N.J.: Princeton University Press, 1999.

Trefousse, Hans L., ed. *Germany and America: Essays on Problems of International Relations and Immigration*. New York: Brooklyn College Press, 1980.

Trommler, Frank, and Joseph McVeigh, ed. *America and the Germans: An Assessment of a Three-Hundred Year History*. 2 vols. Philadelphia: University of Pennsylvania Press, 1985.

Tugwell, Rexford G. *The Democratic Roosevelt: A Biography of Franklin Roosevelt*. New York: Doubleday, 1957.

Tupper, Eleanor, and George E. McReynolds. *Japan in American Public Opinion*. New York: The Macmillan Company, 1937.

Utley, Jonathan G. *Going to War with Japan, 1937–1941*. Knoxville: University of Tennessee Press, 1985.

Vaughn, Stephen. *Holding Fast the Inner Lines: Democracy, Nationalism, and the Committee on Public Information*. Chapel: University of North Carolina Press, 1980.

Von Klemperer, Klemens. *German Resistance Against Hitler: The Search for Allies Abroad, 1938–1945*. Oxford: Clarendon Press, 1992.

Ward, Geoffrey C. *A First-Class Temperament: The Emergence of Franklin Roosevelt*. New York: Harper and Row, 1989.

Watson, Mark Skinner. *Chief of Staff: Prewar Plans and Preparations. U.S. Army in World War II: The War Department*. Washington D.C.: U.S. Army Historical Division, 1950.

Watt, Donald Cameron. *Britain Looks to Germany: British Opinion and Policy Towards Germany Since 1945*. London: Oswald Wolff, 1965.

————. *Too Serious a Business: European Armed Forces and the Approach of the Second World War*. London: Temple Smith, 1975.

————. *How War Came: The Immediate Origins of the Second World War, 1938–1939*. London: Mandarin, 1989.

Weigley, Russell F. *The American Way of War: A History of United States Military Strategy and Policy*. Bloomington: University of Indiana Press, 1973.

Weinberg, Gerhard L. *A World at Arms: A Global History of World War II*. Cambridge: Cambridge University Press, 1994.

Weiss, Steve. *Allies in Conflict: Anglo-American Strategic Negotiations, 1938–44*. Basingstoke: Macmillan, 1996.

Welles, Sumner. *Time for Decision*. London: Hamish Hamilton, 1944.

White, Graham J. *FDR and the Press*. Chicago: University of Chicago Press, 1979.

Willkie, Wendell. *One World*. London: Cassell, 1943.

Wilson, Theodore A. *The First Summit: Roosevelt and Churchill at Placentia Bay, 1941*. Rev. ed. Lawrence: University Press of Kansas, 1991.

Winfield, Betty Houchin. *FDR and the News Media*. New York: Columbia University Press, 1994.

Winkler, Allan M. *The Politics of Propaganda: The Office of War Information*. New Haven, Conn.: Yale University Press, 1978.

Wright, Quincy. *A Study of War*. 2nd ed. Chicago: University of Chicago Press, 1965.

Wyman, David S. *The Abandonment of the Jews: America and the Holocaust, 1941–1945*. New York: Pantheon Books, 1985.

Yergin, Daniel. *Shattered Peace: The Origins of the Cold War and the National Security State*. Harmondsworth: Penguin, 1978.

Zaller, John R. *The Nature and Origins of Mass Opinion*. Cambridge: Cambridge University Press, 1992.

Zink, Harold. *American Military Government in Germany*. New York: Macmillan, 1947.

Articles

Adler, Les K., and Thomas G. Paterson. "Red Fascism: The Merger of Nazi Germany and Soviet Russia in the American Image of Totalitarianism, 1930s–1950s." *American Historical Review* 75 (1970): 1046–64.

Balfour, Michael. "The Origin of the Formula: 'Unconditional Surrender' in World War II." *Armed Forces and Society* 5 (1979): 281–301.

Barth, Alan. "The Bureau of Intelligence." *Public Opinion Quarterly* 7 (1943): 66–76.

Blum, John Morton. "United Against: American Culture and Society During World War II." James Titus, ed. *The Home Front and War in the Twentieth Century: The American Experience in Comparative Perspective*. USAAF: Proceedings of the Tenth Military History Symposium, 1982, pp. 5–15.

Bruner, Jerome S. "OWI and the American Public." *Public Opinion Quarterly* 7 (1943): 125–33.

Butow, Robert J. C. "The FDR Tapes." *American Heritage* 33 (1982): 9–24.

Campbell, A. E. "Franklin Roosevelt and Unconditional Surrender." Richard Langhorne, ed. *Diplomacy and Intelligence during the Second World War: Essays in Honor of F.H. Hinsley*. Cambridge: Cambridge University Press, 1985, pp. 219–41.

Cantril, Hadley. "The Issues—As Seen by the American People." *Public Opinion Quarterly* 8 (1944): 331–47.

Casey, Steven. "Franklin D. Roosevelt, Ernst 'Putzi' Hanfstaengl, and the 'S-Project,' June 1942–June 1944." *Journal of Contemporary History* 35 (2000): 339–59.

Chase, John L. "The Development of the Morgenthau Plan through the Quebec Conference." *Journal of Politics* 16 (1954): 324–59.

———. "Unconditional Surrender Reconsidered." Sidney Fine, ed. *Recent America: Conflicting Interpretations of the Great Issues*. New York: Macmillan, 1962, pp. 355–65.

Clifford, J. Garry. "Both Ends of the Telescope: New Perspectives on FDR and American Entry into World War II." *Diplomatic History* 13 (1989): 213–30.

———. "Juggling Balls of Dynamite." *Diplomatic History* 17 (1993): 633–36.

Colegrove, Kenneth. "The Role of Congress and Public Opinion in Formulating Foreign Policy." *American Political Science Review* 38 (1944): 956–69.

Craig, Gordon A. "Roosevelt and Hitler: The Problem of Perception." Klaus Hildebrand and Reiner Pommerin, ed. *Deutsche Frage und europäisches Gleichgewicht: Festschrift für Andreas Hillgruber zum 60. Geburtstag*. Cologne: Böhlau, 1985, pp.169–94.

———. "The Political Leader as Strategist." Peter Paret, ed. *Makers of Modern Strategy from Machiavelli to the Nuclear Age*. Princeton, N.J.: Princeton University Press, 1986, pp.481–509.

———. "Churchill and Germany." Robert Blake and Wm. Roger Louis, ed. *Churchill*. Oxford: Oxford University Press, 1994, pp. 21–40.

Culbert, David. "'Why We Fight': Social Engineering for a Democratic Society at War." K. R. M. Short, ed. *Film and Radio Propaganda in World War II*. Knoxville: University of Tennessee Press, 1983, pp.173–91.

Danchev, Alex. "Being Friends: The Combined Chiefs of Staff and the Making of Allied Strategy in the Second World War." Lawrence Freedman, Paul Hayes, and Robert O'Neill, ed. *War, Strategy, and International Relations: Essays in Honour of Sir Michael Howard*. Oxford: Clarendon Press, 1992, pp.195–210.

Daugherty, William E. "U.S. Psychological Warfare Organizations in World War II." William E. Daugherty and Morris Janowitz, ed. *A Psychological Warfare Casebook*. Baltimore: Johns Hopkins Press, 1958, pp.126–35.

———. "'Unconditional Surrender.'" William E. Daugherty and Morris Janowitz, ed. *A Psychological Warfare Casebook*. Baltimore: Johns Hopkins Press, 1958, pp.273–79.

Davis, Elmer. "OWI Has a Job." *Public Opinion Quarterly* 7 (1943): 5–13.

Doenecke, Justus D. "Power, Markets, and Ideology: The Isolationist Response to Roosevelt Policy, 1940–1941." Leonard P. Liggio and James J. Martin, ed. *Watershed and Empire: Essays on New Deal Foreign Policy*. Colorado Springs: Ralph Myers, 1976, pp. 132–161.

———. "U.S. Policy and the European War, 1939–1941." *Diplomatic History* 19 (1995): 669–98.

Emerson, William R. "FDR." Ernest R. May, ed. *The Ultimate Decision: The President as Commander in Chief*. New York: George Braziller, 1960, pp. 135–77.

Feis, Herbert. "Some Notes on Historical Record-keeping, the Role of Historians, and the Influence of Historical Memories During the Era of the Second World War." Francis L. Loewenheim, ed. *The Historian and Diplomat: The Role of History and Historians in American Foreign Policy*. New York: Harper and Row, 1967, pp.91–121.

Feller, A. H. "OWI on the Home Front." *Public Opinion Quarterly* 7 (1943): 55–65.

Funk, Arthur L. "Negotiating the 'Deal with Darlan.'" *Journal of Contemporary History* 8 (1973): 92–117.

Gardner, Lloyd C. "Isolation and Appeasement: An American View of Taylor's *Origins*." Gordon Martel, ed. *"The Origins of the Second World War" Reconsidered: The A. J. P. Taylor Debate After Twenty–Five Years*. London: Unwin Hyman, 1986.

George, Alexander L. "The Causal Nexus between Cognitive Beliefs and Decision–Making Behaviour: The 'Operational Code' Belief System." Lawrence Falkowski, ed. *Psychological Models in International Politics*. Boulder, Colo.: Westview Press, 1979, pp.95–124.

———. "Domestic Constraints on Regime Change in U.S. Foreign Policy: The Need for Policy Legitimacy." G. John Ikenberry, ed. *American Foreign Policy: Theoretical Essays*. New York: Harper Collins, 1989, pp.583–608.

Gleason, P. "Americans All: World War II and the Shaping of American Identity." *Review of Politics* 43 (1981): 483–518.

Goldman, Aaron. "Germans and Nazis: The Controversy Over 'Vansittartism' in Britain during the Second World War." *Journal of Contemporary History* 14 (1979): 155–91.

Gooch, John. "'Hidden in the Rock': American Military Perceptions of Great Britain, 1919–1940." Lawrence Freedman, Paul Hayes, and Robert O'Neill, ed. *War, Strategy, and International Relations: Essays in Honor of Sir Michael Howard*. Oxford: Clarendon Press, 1992, pp.155–74.

Graham, Thomas W. "Public Opinion and U.S. Foreign Policy Decision Making."

David A. Deese, ed. *The New Politics of American Foreign Policy*. New York: St. Martin's Press, 1994, pp.190–215.

Gullan, Harold I. "Expectations of Infamy: Roosevelt and Marshall Prepare for War, 1938–1941." *Presidential Studies Quarterly* 28 (1998): 510–22.

Hammond, Paul Y. "Directives for the Occupation of Germany: The Washington Controversy." Harold Stein, ed. *American Civil-Military Decisions: A Book of Case Studies*. Birmingham: University of Alabama Press, 1963, pp. 314–460.

Hawkins, Jr., Lester G., and George S. Pettee. "OWI Organization and Problems." *Public Opinion Quarterly* 7 (1943): 15–33.

Heinrichs, Waldo. "President Franklin D. Roosevelt's Intervention in the Battle of the Atlantic, 1941." *Diplomatic History* 10 (1986): 311–32.

Hilton, Stanley E. "The Welles Mission to Europe, February–March 1940: Illusion or Realism?" *The Journal of American History* 58 (1971–72): 93–120.

Holsti, Ole R. "The Belief System and National Images: A Case Study." *Journal of Conflict Resolution* 6 (1962): 244–51.

———. "Cognitive Dynamics and Images of the Enemy." John C. Farrell and Asa P. Smith, ed. *Image and Reality in World Politics*. New York: Columbia University Press, 1968.

———. "Foreign Policy Formation Viewed Cognitively." Robert Axelrod, ed. *Structure of Decision: The Cognitive Maps of Political Elites*. Princeton, N.J.: Princeton University Press, 1976, pp.18–54.

———. "Public Opinion and Foreign Policy: Challenges to the Almond-Lippmann Consensus." *International Studies Quarterly* 36 (1992): 439–66.

Hönicke, Michaela. "'Know Your Enemy': American Wartime Images of Germany, 1942–1943." Ragnhild Fiebig-von Hase and Ursula Lehmkuhl, ed. *Enemy Images in American History*. Providence, R.I.: Berghahn Books, 1997, pp.231–80.

———. "Prevent World War III: An Historiographical Appraisal of Morgenthau's Programme for Germany." Robert A. Garson and Stuart S. Kidd, ed. *The Roosevelt Years: New Perspectives on American History, 1933–1945*. Edinburgh: Edinburgh University Press, 1999, pp.155–72

Howard, Michael. "The Historical Development of the UN's Role in International Security." Adam Roberts and Benedict Kingsbury, ed. *United Nations, Divided World*. 2nd ed. Oxford: Clarendon Press, 1993, pp.63–80.

Hurwitz, John. "Presidential Leadership and Public Followership." Michael Margolis and Gary A. Mauser, ed. *Manipulating Public Opinion: Essays on Public Opinion as a Dependent Variable*. Pacific Grove, Calif.: Brooks Cole, 1989, pp.222–49.

Jacobs, Lawrence R., and Robert Y. Shapiro. "The Rise of Presidential Polling: The Nixon White House in Historical Perspective." *Public Opinion Quarterly* 59 (1995): 163–95.

Janowitz, Morris, and William E. Daugherty. "The Darlan Story." William E. Daugherty and Morris Janowitz, ed. *A Psychological Warfare Casebook*. Baltimore: Johns Hopkins Press, 1958, pp.291–300.

Jeansome, Glen. "America's Home Front." *History Today* 45 (May 1995): 20–26.

———. "An Antiwar Movement that was Not a Peace Movement: The Mothers' Crusade Against World War II." *Peace and Change* 24 (1999): 29–46.

Jones, Alfred Haworth. "The Making of an Interventionist on the Air: Elmer Davis and CBS News, 1939–1941." *Pacific Historical Review* 42 (1973): 74–93.

Kaufmann, William W. "Two American Ambassadors: Bullitt and Kennedy." Gordon A. Craig and Felix Gilbert, ed. *The Diplomats, 1919–1939*. Princeton, N.J.: Princeton University Press, pp.649–681.

Kennedy, David M. "Rallying Americans for War, 1917–1918." James Titus, ed. *The*

Home Front and War in the Twentieth Century: The American Experience in Comparative Perspective. USAAF: Proceedings of the Tenth Military History Symposium, 1982, pp. 5–15.

Kimball, Warren F. "U.S. Economic Strategy in World War II: Wartime Goals, Peacetime Plans." Warren F. Kimball, ed. *America Unbound: World War II the Making of a Superpower.* New York: St. Martin's Press, 1992, pp.139–57.

Kinsella, Jr., William E. "The Prescience of a Statesman: FDR's Assessment of Adolf Hitler before the World War, 1933–1941." Herbert D. Rosenbaum and Elizabeth Bartelme, ed. *Franklin D. Roosevelt: The Man, the Myth, the Era, 1882–1945.* New York: Greenwood Press, 1987, pp. 73–84.

Koppes, Clayton R. "What to Show the World: The Office of War Information and Hollywood, 1942–1945." *Journal of American History* 64 (1977–79): 87–105.

LaFeber, Walter. "American Policy-Makers, Public Opinion, and the Outbreak of the Cold War, 1945–50." Yonosuke Nagai and Akira Iriye, ed. *The Origins of the Cold War in Asia.* Tokyo: University of Tokyo Press, 1977, pp. 43–65.

Landry, Robert J. "The Impact of OWI on Broadcasting." *Public Opinion Quarterly* 7 (1943): 111–15.

Lees, Lorraine M. "National Security and Ethnicity: Contrasting Views During World War II." *Diplomatic History* 11 (1987): 113–125.

Levering, Ralph B. "Public Opinion, Foreign Policy, and American Politics since the 1960s." *Diplomatic History* 13 (1989): 383–93.

Levy, Jack S. "Domestic Politics and War." Robert I. Rotberg and Theodore K. Rabb, ed. *The Origin and Prevention of Major Wars.* Cambridge: Cambridge University Press, 1989, pp. 79–101.

Lincoln, Abraham. "My Public Opinion Baths." Mario Cuomo and Harold Holzer, ed. *Lincoln on Democracy* New York: Harper Collins, 1990 pp.284–85.

Lippmann, Walter. "The Economic Consequences of a German Victory." *Life* (July 22, 1940):64-69.

Lowenthal, Mark M. "Roosevelt and the Coming of War: The Search for United States Policy, 1937–42." *Journal of Contemporary History* 16 (1981): 413–40.

MacDonald, Callum A. "Deterrent Diplomacy: Roosevelt and the Containment of Germany, 1938–1940." Robert Boyce and Esmonde M. Robertson, ed. *Paths to War: New Essays on the Origins of the Second World War.* Basingstoke: Macmillan, 1989, pp.297–329.

Mader, Joseph H. "Government Press Bureaus and Reporting Public Affairs." *Journalism Quarterly* 10 (1942): 194–95

Marks, Frederick W. "Six Between Roosevelt and Hitler: America's Role in the Appeasement of Nazi Germany." *The Historical Journal* 28 (1985): 969–82.

Matloff, Maurice. "Allied Strategy in Europe, 1939–1945." Peter Paret, ed. *Makers of Modern Strategy from Machiavelli to the Nuclear Age.* Princeton, N.J.: Princeton University Press, 1986, pp.677–702.

Miscamble, Wilson D. "Catholics and American Foreign Policy from McKinley to McCarthy: A Historiographical Survey." *Diplomatic History* 4 (1980): 223–40.

Morgenthau, Henry J., Jr. "Our Policy Toward Germany." *New York Post* (24–29 November 1947).

Mosely, Philip E. "Dismemberment of Germany: The Allied Negotiations from Yalta to Potsdam." *Foreign Affairs* 28 (1949–1950): 487–98.

———. "The Occupation of Germany: New Light on How the Zones Were Drawn." *Foreign Affairs* 28 (1949–1950): 580–604.

Mowrer, Paul Scott. "Bungling the News." *Public Opinion Quarterly* 7 (1943): 116–24.

Mueller, John E. "Presidential Popularity from Truman to Johnson." *American Political Science Review* 64 (1970): 18–34.

Nagler, Jörg. "From Culture to Kultur: Changing American Perceptions of Imperial Germany, 1870–1914." David E. Barclay and Elisabeth Glaser-Schmidt, ed. *Transatlantic Images and Perceptions: Germany and American since 1776*. Washington D.C.: Cambridge University Press, 1997, pp.131–54.

Neumann, William L. "Roosevelt's Options and Evasions in Foreign Policy Decisions, 1940–1945." Leonard P. Liggio and James J. Martin, ed. *Watershed and Empire: Essays on New Deal Foreign Policy*. Colorado Springs: Ralph Myers, 1976, pp. 162–81.

Neuringer, Sheldon. "Franklin D. Roosevelt and the Refuge for Victims of Nazism, 1933–1941." Herbert D. Rosenbaum and Elizabeth Bartelme, ed. *Franklin D. Roosevelt: The Man, the Myth, the Era, 1882–1945*. New York: Greenwood Press, 1987, pp 85–99.

Offner, Arnold A. "Appeasement Revisited: The United States, Great Britain, and Germany, 1933–1940." *The Journal of American History* 64 (1977–78): 373–93.

———. "The United States and National Socialist Germany." Wolfgang J. Mommsen and Lothar Kettenacker, ed. *The Fascist Challenge and the Policy of Appeasement*. London: George Allen and Unwin, 1983, pp. 413–27.

———. "Misperception and Reality: Roosevelt, Hitler, and the Search for a New Order in Europe." *Diplomatic History* 15 (1991): 607–19.

Page, Benjamin I. "Democratic Responsiveness? Untangling the Links Between Public Opinion and Policy." *PS: Political Science and Politics* 27 (March 1994): 25–29.

Page, Benjamin I., and Robert Y. Shapiro. "Effects of Public Opinion on Policy." *American Political Science Review* 77 (1983): 175–90.

———. "Educating and Manipulating the Public." Michael Margolis and Gary A. Mauser, ed. *Manipulating Public Opinion: Essays on Public Opinion as a Dependent Variable*. Pacific Grove, Calif.: Brooks Cole, 1989, pp.294–320.

Paterson, Thomas G. "Presidential Foreign Policy, Public Opinion, and Congress: The Truman Years." *Diplomatic History* 3 (1979): 1–18.

Patterson, James T. "Robert A. Taft and American Foreign Policy, 1939–1945." Leonard P. Liggio and James J. Martin, ed. *Watershed and Empire: Essays on New Deal Foreign Policy*. Colorado Springs: Ralph Myers, 1976, pp. 183–207.

Perkins, Dexter. "The State Department and American Public Opinion." Gordon A. Craig and Felix Gilbert, ed. *The Diplomats, 1919–1939*. Princeton, N.J.: Princeton University Press, pp.282–310.

Powlick, Philip J. "The Attitudinal Bases for Responsiveness to Public Opinion among American Foreign Policy Officials." *Journal of Conflict Resolution*, 35 (1991): 634–35.

———. "The Sources of Public Opinion for American Foreign Policy Officials." *International Studies Quarterly* 39 (1995): 427–51.

Reynolds, David. "1940: Fulcrum of the Twentieth Century?" *International Affairs* 66 (1990): 325–50.

Roeder, George H. Jr. "Censoring Disorder: American Visual Imagery of World War II." Lewis A. Erenberg and Susan E. Hirsch, ed. *The War in American Culture: Society and Consciousness During World War II*. Chicago: University of Chicago Press, 1996, p. 46–70.

Ruggie, John Gerard. "The Past as Prologue: Interests, Identity, and American Foreign Policy." Michael E. Brown, Owen R. Coté, Jr., Sean M. Lynn-Jones, and Steven E. Miller, ed. *America's Strategic Choices*. Cambridge, Mass.: The MIT Press, 1997, pp.163–99.

Russett, Bruce M., and Thomas W. Graham. "Public Opinion and National Security Policy: Relationships and Impacts." Manus I. Midlarsky, ed. *Handbook of War Studies*. London: Unwin Hyman, 1989, pp.239–57.

Schaffer, Ronald. "American Military Ethics in World War II: The Bombing of German Civilians." *Journal of American History* 67 (1980): 318–34.

Shapiro, Robert Y., and Benjamin I. Page. "Foreign Policy and Public Opinion." David A. Deese, ed. *The New Politics of American Foreign Policy*. New York: St. Martin's Press, 1994, pp.216–35.

Small, Melvyn. "Public Opinion." Michael J. Hogan and Thomas G. Paterson, ed. *Explaining the History of American Foreign Relations*. Cambridge: Cambridge University Press, 1991, pp.165–76.

Smith, Fred. "The Rise and Fall of the Morgenthau Plan." *United Nations World* 1 (March 1947): 32–37.

Smith, Geoffrey S. "Isolationism, the Devil, and the Advent of the Second World War: Variations on a Theme." *The International History Review* 4 (1982): 55–89.

Smith, Steve. "Belief Systems and International Relations." Richard Little and Steve Smith, ed. *Belief Systems and International Relations*. Oxford: Blackwell, 1988, pp.11–36

Steele, Richard W. "Preparing the Public for War: Efforts to Establish a National Propaganda Agency, 1940–41." *American Historical Review* 75 (1970): 1640–53.

———. "The Pulse of the People: Franklin D. Roosevelt and the Gauging of American Public Opinion." *Journal of Contemporary History* 9 (1974): 195–216.

———. "American Popular Opinion and the War Against Germany: The Issue of a Negotiated Peace, 1942." *Journal of American History* 65 (1978): 704–23.

———. "'The Greatest Gangster Movie Ever Filmed': *Prelude to War*." *Prologue* 11 (1979): 221–35.

———. "News of the 'Good War': World War II News Management." *Journalism Quarterly* 62 (1985): 707–16.

Stein, Arthur A. "Domestic Constraints, Extended Deterrence, and the Incoherence of Grand Strategy: The United States, 1938–1950." Richard Rosencrance and Arthur A. Stein, ed. *The Domestic Bases of Grand Strategy*. Ithaca, N.Y.: Cornell University Press, 1993, pp.96–123.

Stoler, Mark A. "The 'Pacific-First' Alternative in American World War II Strategy." *The International History Review* 2 (1980): 432–52.

———. "From Continentalism to Globalism: General Stanley D. Embick, the Joint Strategic Survey Committee, and the Military View of American National Policy during the Second World War." *Diplomatic History* 6 (1982): 303–21.

———. "A Half Century of Conflict: Interpretations of U.S. World War II Diplomacy." *Diplomatic History* 18 (1994): 375–403.

Thompson, John A. "Another Look at the Downfall of 'Fortress America.'" *Journal of American Studies* 26 (1992): 393–408.

Thorne, Christopher. "Racial Aspects of the Far Eastern War of 1941–1945." *Proceedings of the British Academy* 66 (1980): 329–77.

———. "En Route to Estrangement: American Society and World War Two in the Global Setting." *Border Crossings: Studies in International History*. Oxford: Blackwell, 1988, pp. 275–306.

Tuttle, Jr., William M. "Aid-to-the-Allies Short-of-War versus American Intervention, 1940: A Reappraisal of William Allen White's Leadership." *Journal of American History* 56 (1969–70): 840–58.

Van Everen, Brooks. "Franklin D. Roosevelt and the Problem of Nazi Germany." Clifford L. Egan and Alexander W. Knott, ed. *Essays in Twentieth Century American Diplomatic History Dedicated to Professor Daniel M. Smith*. Washington D.C.: University Press of America, 1982, pp. 137–57.

Villa, Brian L. "The U.S. Army, Unconditional Surrender, and the Potsdam Proclamation." *Journal of American History* 63 (1976–77): 66–92.

Wala, Michael. "Selling the Marshall Plan at Home: The Committee for the Marshall Plan to Aid European Recovery." *Diplomatic History* 10 (1986): 247–65.

Wall, Wendy L. "'Our Enemies Within': Nazism, National Unity, and America's Wartime Discourse on Tolerance." Ragnhild Fiebig-von Hase and Ursula Lehmkuhl, ed. *Enemy Images in American History*. Providence, R.I.: Berghahn Books, 1997, pp.209–30.

Wanger, Walter. "OWI and Motion Pictures." *Public Opinion Quarterly* 7 (1943): 100–10.

Warburg, James P. "The 'Moronic Little King' Incident." William E. Daugherty and Morris Janowitz, ed. *A Psychological Warfare Casebook*. Baltimore: Johns Hopkins Press, 1958, pp.300–3.

Washburn, Patrick S. "FDR Versus His Own Attorney General: The Struggle over Sedition, 1941–42." *Journalism Quarterly* 62 (1985): 717–24.

Weigley, Russell F. "To the Crossing of the Rhine: American Strategic Thought to World War II." *Armed Forces and Society* 5 (1979): 302–19.

Weinberg, Sydney. "What to Tell America: The Writer's Quarrel in the Office of War Information." *Journal of American History* 55 (1968): 73–89.

Wilson, Theodore A., and Richard D. McKenzie. "The Masks of Power: FDR and the Conduct of America Diplomacy." Frank J. Merli and Theodore A. Wilson, ed. *Makers of American Diplomacy*. New York: Scribner, 1974.

Zahniser, Marvin R. "Rethinking the Significance of Disaster: The United States and the Fall of France in 1940." *The International History Review* 14 (1992): 252–76.

Zaller, John. "Elite Leadership of Mass Opinion." W. Lance Bennett and David L. Paletz, ed. *Taken by Storm: The Media, Public Opinion, and U.S. Foreign Policy in the Gulf War*. Chicago: University of Chicago Press, 1994, pp.186–209.

Ziemke, Earl F. "The Formulation and Initial Implementation of U.S. Occupation Policy in Germany." Hans A. Schmitt, ed. *U.S. Occupation in Europe After World War II*. Lawrence: Regents Press of Kansas, 1978, pp.27–44.

Unpublished Works and Theses

Cochran, Jr., Alexander S. "Specter of Defeat: Anglo-American Planning for the Invasion of Italy in 1943." University of Kansas: Ph.D. Thesis, 1983.

Foyle, Douglas Charles. "The Influence of Public Opinion on American Foreign Policy Decision-Making: Context, Beliefs, and Process." Duke University: Ph.D. Thesis, 1996.

Gramer, Regina Ursula. "Reconstructing Germany, 1938–1949: United States Foreign Policy and the Cartel Question." Rutgers University: Ph.D. Thesis, 1997.

Hönicke, Michaela. "Franklin D. Roosevelt's View of Germany before 1933: Formative Experiences for a Future President." University of North Carolina: MA Thesis, 1989.

Schwark, Stephen John. "The State Department Plans for Peace, 1941–1945." Harvard University: Ph.D. Thesis, 1985.

INDEX